EUTHANASIA AND LAW IN THE NETHERLANDS

EUTHANASIA AND LAW IN THE NETHERLANDS

John Griffiths
Alex Bood
Heleen Weyers

Amsterdam University Press

Cover design: In Petto / Stephanie de Witte, Amsterdam
Typesetting: MAGENTA, Amsterdam

ISBN 90 5356 275 3

Contents

Extended Table of Contents

List of Figures and Tables

Acknowledgements

We have written this book as a collective project, but nevertheless some of us are more responsible for some chapters than for others. Griffiths bears primary responsibility for chapters 1, 3, 5, 6, 7 and the appendices, Bood for chapter 4, and Weyers for the Prologue, the Intermezzo, and chapter 2. Griffiths' work on the book is the culmination of a project that began about 10 years ago and has resulted in a number of publications, several of which form the basis of various chapters of this book.[1] Bood and Weyers are both engaged in dissertation research, Bood on the legal-philosophical foundations of the Dutch euthanasia debate, Weyers on the process of legal change concerning euthanasia and other medical practices that shorten life.

A book such as this could not have been written without the help and criticism we have received from a large number of people and organizations. We are in particular grateful for the continuous collegial support we have enjoyed from members of the Department of Legal Theory and, more generally, of the Faculty of Law of the University of Groningen, throughout the entire history of this project. In the final stages of preparation of the manuscript we enjoyed the stimulating support of the CHAZERAS Society.

Specific thanks are due to a number of Dutch colleagues who helped us improve the accuracy of our presentation and interpretation of data derived from their research: Dr. J. Blad (lecturer in criminal law, Erasmus University Rotterdam), Dr. J.M. Cuperus-Bosma (research associate, Free University of Amsterdam), Dr. A. van der Heide (research associate, Erasmus University Rotterdam), Dr. L. Pijnenborg (former research associate, Erasmus University Rotterdam), Dr. M. Trappenburg (lecturer in political science, Leiden University), Prof. G. van der Wal (former Medical Inspector, now professor of social medicine, Free University of Amsterdam).

For reading and commenting on (parts of) the manuscript and saving us from greater and lesser errors of law, fact and interpretation, we would particularly like to thank: A.N.A. Josephus Jitta (former chief prosecutor, Alkmaar), Prof. H.J.J. Leenen (emeritus

---

1   In particular, Griffiths 1987, 1994, 1995a, 1995b and 1995c. The insistence of Dr. A. Klijn (Center for Research and Documentation, Ministry of Justice) that the argument of these articles be presented in a systematic way in book form was the initial inspiration for undertaking the enterprise of writing this book.

professor of social medicine and medical law, University of Amsterdam), Prof. L.C.M. Meijers (former Advocate-General of the Supreme Court), Prof. J. Remmelink (former Procurator-General of the Supreme Court), and Dr. M. Trappenburg (see above). We also received valuable criticisms of (parts of) the manuscript from: W. Davids (member of the Supreme Court of the Netherlands), F. Janssens (former lecturer in criminal law, University of Groningen), Prof. J. Legemaate (professor of medical law, Erasmus University Rotterdam, and staff lawyer of the Royal Dutch Medical Association), F. le Poole (vice-president of the District Court, Assen, and member of the First Chamber of Parliament), Prof. A. Soeteman (professor of philosophy of law, Free University of Amsterdam), and Dr. A.J. Tholen (chef de clinique, psychiatry, University Hospital Groningen, and chairman of the Committee on Assistance with Suicide of the Dutch Association for Psychiatry).

Prof. G. Griffiths (emeritus professor of history, University of Washington) read the manuscript thoroughly and saved us from countless errors of style and obscurity; Prof. J. Dombrink (professor of criminology, University of California, Irvine) helped us track down sources and gave us the benefit of his critical reaction to the manuscript; J. Weiss (Center for the Legal Rights of the Elderly, New York) reacted in his usual challenging way to what we wrote.

Obviously, while all of those mentioned contributed to whatever merits the book may have, none of them is responsible for the flaws that remain.

Finally, we acknowledge the support of the Netherlands Organization for Scientific Research (NWO) and of the Ministry of Justice, for earlier stages of the project of which this book is one fruit. Weyers' research is currently supported by a grant from the Foundation for Law and Government (Reob), which is part of NWO.

Groningen, October 1997

John Griffiths
Alex Bood
Heleen Weyers

Glossary

ABSTINEREN [ABSTAINING FROM TREATMENT, ABSTINENCE]
  refers both to ending (life-sustaining) treatment that has already been undertaken and to refraining from beginning such treatment.
ACTIEVE EUTHANASIE [ACTIVE EUTHANASIA]
  formerly contrasted with passive euthanasia but now referred to simply as 'euthanasia'.
ADVOCAAT-GENERAAL (AG) [ADVOCATE-GENERAL]
  a lawyer (of whom there are several) attached to the Supreme Court who submits a brief to the Court setting out his views as to how a case should be decided; this brief is published together with the decision and generally gives a more extensive account than the Court's decision itself of the legal considerations involved in the case. (Also the title of a prosecutor at the level of the Courts of Appeals.)
ARRONDISSEMENTSRECHTBANK [DISTRICT COURT]
  the base-line court of general jurisdiction (in civil and criminal cases); there are 19 judicial districts in the Netherlands; serious or difficult criminal cases are heard by a panel of three judges.
BEHANDELENDE ARTS [DOCTOR RESPONSIBLE FOR TREATMENT – ATTENDING PHYSICIAN]
  the doctor(s) regarded as having a doctor-patient relationship with the patient and responsible for his care.
COMMISSIE AANVAARDBAARHEID LEVENSBEËINDIGEND HANDELEN (CAL) [COMMISSION ON THE ACCEPTABILITY OF TREATMENT THAT TERMINATES LIFE]
  a commission appointed by the Royal Dutch Medical Association, author of four reports on severely deformed newborn babies, long-term coma patients, the demented elderly, and psychiatric patients.
CDA – CHRISTEN DEMOCRATISCH APPEL [CHRISTIAN DEMOCRATIC APPEAL]
  the Christian Democratic Party.
CONSULTATIE [CONSULTATION]
  formal request by a doctor for a second opinion from another doctor.
D66 – DEMOCRATEN 66 [DEMOCRATS 66]
  the left-of-center liberal party.
DIRECTE EUTHANASIE [DIRECT EUTHANASIA]
  formerly contrasted with indirect euthanasia (i.e., death due to pain relief) but now referred to simply as 'euthanasia'.

EUTHANASIE [EUTHANASIA]
> killing another person at his request – prohibited by article 293 of the Criminal Code but when performed by a doctor under specific conditions taken to be justified; the term 'euthanasia' is often used more generally in public discussion and in this book to include assistance with suicide.

GEZONDHEIDSRAAD [HEALTH COUNCIL]
> official advisory body of the Dutch Government on health matters.

GERECHTSHOF [COURT OF APPEALS]
> intermediate appellate court in civil and criminal cases; conducts a trial *de novo*; hears criminal cases in a panel of 3 judges; there are 5 Courts of Appeals in the Netherlands.

HOGE RAAD DER NEDERLANDEN [SUPREME COURT]
> the highest court in the Netherlands in civil, criminal and tax cases; considers in *cassation* only legal questions; hears criminal cases in a panel of 5 judges.

HUISARTS [GENERAL PRACTITIONER (GP)]
> a family doctor, usually in solo private practice; generally speaking, all Dutch residents have a semi-permanent relationship with a GP, who provides general medical care and referrals for the rest of the health-care system (see the *Intermezzo*).

HULP BIJ ZELFDODING [ASSISTANCE WITH SUICIDE]
> prohibited by section 294 of the Criminal Code but when rendered by a doctor under specific conditions taken to be justified; for most purposes having to do with its legality not distinguished from killing a person at his request (euthanasia).

HULPVERLENER [PERSON WHO RENDERS PROFESSIONAL ASSISTANCE]
> general term in Dutch for all kinds of institutionalized/professional assistance (legal, medical, social, etc.); art. 7:446 of the Civil Code (added by the Law on Contracts for Medical Treatment (see chapter 3 note 12)) refers to a *hulpverlener* as a natural or legal person engaged in a medical profession or business; art. 7:453 imposes as the general duty of care that care characteristic of a 'good *hulpverlener*' and in conformity with the 'professional standard'.

INDIRECTE EUTHANASIE [INDIRECT EUTHANASIA]
> term formerly used to refer to causing death as a result of the use of pain killers (usually morphine) in doses known to be likely to shorten life; no longer referred to as a form of euthanasia.

INSPECTIE VOOR DE GEZONDHEIDSZORG – MEDISCHE INSPECTEUR [MEDICAL INSPECTORATE – MEDICAL INSPECTOR]
> semi-independent agency charged, among other things, with enforcement of legal provisions relating to medical care; empowered to bring disciplinary proceedings against medical professionals.

KANSLOOS MEDISCH HANDELEN [MEDICAL TREATMENT THAT HAS NO CHANCE OF SUCCESS]
> medical treatment whose chance of success is insufficient to legitimize it; proposed by NVK 1992 as one of two elements in an alternative approach to the standard term

medisch zinloos handelen, distinguished from *zinloos medisch handelen* in that the latter concept refers to the possible benefit to the patient.

KONINKLIJKE NEDERLANDSE MAATSCHAPPIJ TER BEVORDERING DER GENEESKUNST (KNMG) [ROYAL DUTCH MEDICAL ASSOCIATION]

    professional association of Dutch doctors, author of a number of position papers on euthanasia and assistance with suicide (see chapters 2 and 3).

KONINKLIJKE NEDERLANDSE MAATSCHAPPIJ TER BEVORDERING DER PHARMACIE (KNMP) [ROYAL DUTCH ASSOCIATION FOR PHARMACY]

    professional association of Dutch pharmacists, author of a position paper on the 'requirements of careful practice' for pharmacists asked to supply euthanatica (see chapter 3.1.3).

LEEFBAAR LEVEN [LIFE WORTH LIVING]

    overall term introduced by NVK 1992 for the criteria by which 'quality-of-life' considerations are assessed in connection with decision-making concerning termination of life in the case of newborn babies.

LEVENSBEËINDIGING ZONDER UITDRUKKELIJK VERZOEK [TERMINATION OF LIFE WITHOUT AN EXPLICIT REQUEST]

    intentional, active, direct, non-voluntary termination of life (including coma patients, newborn babies, 'help in dying').

MBSL – MEDICAL BEHAVIOR THAT SHORTENS LIFE; ALSO REFERRED TO AS *MEDISCHE BESLISSINGEN ROND HET LEVENSEINDE* (MBL) [MEDICAL DECISIONS CONCERNING THE END OF LIFE (MDEL)]

    the general category that includes euthanasia and other acts or omissions by doctors that intentionally shorten life.

MEDISCHE EXCEPTIE [MEDICAL EXCEPTION]

    the (proposed or implied) exclusion of doctors, acting as such, from the coverage of provisions of the criminal code dealing with offences against the person.

MEDISCH ZINLOOS HANDELEN [MEDICALLY FUTILE TREATMENT]

    technical term for treatment that a doctor need (and even may) not initiate or continue, with or without the consent of the patient, because to do so is in conflict with the medical-profesional standard governing the authority to practice medicine; NVK 1992 proposes to divide the concept of medical futility into two categories: *kansloos medisch handelen* and *zinloos medisch handelen*.

NAASTEN [FAMILY AND INTIMATE FRIENDS]

    those who, in the context of MBSL, are thought of as potential surrogate decision-makers (the Law on Contracts for Medical Treatment, art. 7:465(3) of the Civil Code, refers to spouses or partners, parents, children and siblings).

NATUURLIJKE DOOD [NATURAL DEATH]

    death resulting from 'internal causes'; if the responsible doctor considers the death of a patient a natural one, he can file a certificate of natural death, which permits burial or cremation without further legal control.

NEDERLANDSE VERENIGING VOOR KINDERGENEESKUNDE (NVK) [DUTCH
ASSOCIATION FOR PEDIATRICS]
> author of a report on MBSL in the case of severely defective newborn babies (see
> chapter 3.3).

NEDERLANDSE VERENIGING VOOR OBSTETRIE EN GYNAECOLOGIE (NVOG) [DUTCH
ASSOCIATION FOR OBSTETRICS AND GYNECOLOGY]
> author of a report on late-term abortion (see chapter 3.3.2).

NEDERLANDSE VERENIGING VOOR PSYCHIATRIE (NVP) [DUTCH ASSOCIATION FOR
PSYCHIATRY]
> author of a report on assistance with suicide in the case of psychiatric patients (see
> chapter 3.5.1).

NEDERLANDSE VERENIGING VOOR VRIJWILLIGE EUTHANASIE (NVVE) [DUTCH
ASSOCIATION FOR VOLUNTARY EUTHANASIA]
> the most important Dutch organization committed to legalization of euthanasia
> and to giving practical support to those seeking it.

NOODTOESTAND [SITUATION OF NECESSITY]
> a defence (justification) to a criminal charge, provided for in article 40 of the Dutch
> Criminal Code (see appendix II-1), as interpreted by the courts.

NORMAAL MEDISCH HANDELEN [NORMAL MEDICAL PRACTICE]
> behavior that falls within the legal authorization to practice medicine and is regulat-
> ed by medical ethics and medical disciplinary law.

ONDRAAGLIJK LIJDEN [UNBEARABLE SUFFERING]
> term used in conjunction with *uitzichtloos* (hopeless) to indicate one of the condi-
> tions of the legality of euthanasia and assistance with suicide; includes but is not
> limited to pain and can be somatic or non-somatic in origin.

ONTLUISTERING [MENTAL AND PHYSICAL DETERIORATION INVOLVING LOSS OF
HUMAN DIGNITY]
> one of the forms of (anticipated) suffering that can support a request for euthanasia.

ONVRIJWILLIGE EUTHANASIE [NON-VOLUNTARY EUTHANASIA]
> termination of life without an explicit request, no longer referred to as euthanasia.

OPENBAAR MINISTERIE (OM)
> collective term for the prosecutorial authorities; members of the OM are associated
> with the various courts and are responsible to the Minister of Justice.

OVERMACHT [LITERALLY: 'SUPERIOR FORCE']
> the defence of *overmacht* in art. 40 of the Dutch Criminal Code (see appendix I-A) has
> been interpreted to include both an excuse (duress) and a justification (necessity).

PASSIEVE EUTHANASIE [PASSIVE EUTHANASIA]
> term formerly used to refer to death caused by abstaining from life-sustaining treat-
> ment; no longer referred to as a form of euthanasia.

PVDA – PARTIJ VAN DE ARBEID [LABOR PARTY]
> the Dutch social-democratic party.

PROCUREUR-GENERAAL (PG) [PROCURATOR-GENERAL]

the highest prosecutorial authority at the level of the Courts of Appeal; the five PGs formed until 1996 the national Committee of Procurators-General that, subject to instructions from the Minister of Justice, makes all final decisions whether or not to prosecute cases of euthanasia and termination of life without an explicit request; since 1996 the Committee consists of 3 PGs. (Also the title of the most senior of the Advocates-General attached to the Supreme Court.)

SPECIALIST [MEDICAL SPECIALIST]

usually attached to and practising within a hospital (see the *Intermezzo*).

STERVENSBEGELEIDING [SUPPORT IN THE DYING PROCESS]

general support of a dying person and his family and intimates; sometimes more loosely used as synonymous with *stervenshulp*.

STERVENSHULP [HELP IN DYING]

administration of lethal drugs to facilitate the final stages of the dying process, in particular in the situation in which the decision has already been taken to allow the patient to die by abstaining from (further) life-prolonging treatment.

TUCHTRECHT (MEDISCH) [MEDICAL DISCIPLINARY LAW]

a set of legal standards, procedures and tribunals applicable to the behavior of medical professionals; can be invoked by interested private persons (usually patients), by the governing body of the institution in which the person concerned works, or by the Medical Inspector.

UITZICHTLOOS LIJDEN [HOPELESS SUFFERING]

term used in conjunction with *ondraaglijk* (unbearable) to indicate one of the conditions of the justifiability of euthanasia and assistance with suicide; it usually carries the specific additional meaning of irreversibility – lacking any prospect of improvement – but it is also sometimes used in the more general sense of 'without hope' as in: 'abandon hope, all ye who enter here'.

UITZICHTLOZE NOODSITUATIE [SITUATION OF HOPELESS NECESSITY]

term sometimes used to characterize the patient's situation when euthanasia is considered justifiable (see e.g. proposed legislation of the State Commission and of Wessel-Tuinstra, appendix I-C-1, 2).

VERPLEEGHUISARTS [NURSING-HOME DOCTOR]

doctor specialized in the care of nursing-home patients (see the *Intermezzo*).

VERSTERVING [LETTING ONESELF DIE]

self-willed death, particularly of the very old, brought about by ceasing to eat (and to drink), possibly accompanied by palliative care.

VERZUILING [PILLARIZATION]

characteristic feature of Dutch political culture during the greater part of the twentieth century, in which many different sorts of social institutions (politics, health, education, etc.) are organized along the lines of the fundamental religious divisions (see the *Prologue*).

VVD – VOLKSPARTIJ VOOR VRIJHEID EN DEMOCRATIE [PEOPLE'S PARTY FOR
FREEDOM AND DEMOCRACY]
> the right-of-center liberal party.

WELOVERWOGEN [WELL-CONSIDERED]
> requirement (in addition to voluntariness) of a valid request for euthanasia or assistance with suicide.

WILSBEKWAAMHEID [COMPETENCE]
> prerequisite of a voluntary and well-considered request and hence of a valid request for euthanasia or assistance with suicide and for a valid refusal of treatment.

WILSBESCHIKKING (SCHRIFTELIJKE) [ADVANCE DIRECTIVE]
> (written) request for euthanasia and/or for abstinence under specified circumstances, should the person concerned be unconscious or incompetent.

ZINLOOS MEDISCH HANDELEN [MEDICAL TREATMENT THAT CANNOT
SIGNIFICANTLY BENEFIT THE PATIENT]
> medical treatment whose possible benefit to the patient is insufficient to legitimize it, in particular because, if successful, it would condemn the patient to an *onleefbaar leven* (unacceptably poor quality of life); proposed by NVK 1992 as one of two elements in an alternative approach to the standard term *medisch zinloos handelen;* distinguished from *kansloos medisch handelen* in that it refers not to the technical chance of success but to the possible benefit to the patient.

ZORGVULDIGHEIDSEISEN [REQUIREMENTS OF CAREFUL PRACTICE]
> in particular those applicable to euthanasia – distinguishable into substantive requirements (conditions of legal euthanasia) and procedural requirements (*zorgvuldigheidseisen* sometimes refers more narrowly to these latter requirements). Since absence of *zorgvuldigheid* is the basis of liability for a negligent tort and thus equivalent to the Common Law idea of lack of 'due care', one might translate the Dutch term as 'requirements of due care'. However, this would wrongly suggest a connection with tort liability, which is the reason we have preferred to translate the term as 'requirements of careful practice'.

Prologue: the Netherlands and the Dutch

This book is about euthanasia and other medical practices that shorten life, and about their legal regulation. The Netherlands is the setting, but it is not the subject. Nevertheless, in interpreting the information and arguments to be presented in the coming chapters, it is necessary to know something about the local context. We try to provide a thumbnail sketch here that goes beyond the relaxed Dutch approach to sex and drugs, or the story of the little boy who put his finger in the dike. We make no pretention to thoroughness or depth.

The Netherlands is a small, flat country of some 16 million inhabitants, one of the most densely populated in the world. It emerged as an independent country in the seventeenth century after a struggle of some 80 years against the authority of the Spanish crown, and with brief interludes in the Napoleonic period and the Second World War, it has been independent ever since. The independence struggle began as one to preserve traditional privileges, especially that of freedom from additional taxation. The opposition gained force when joined by that part of the population (led by Calvinists) which sought reform of the Church. In 1648 the Spaniards finally accepted the independence of the Netherlands, which for a century and a half thereafter was a Republic.

Despite the intermittent warfare, it was in the seventeenth century that the rebellious provinces enjoyed their economic and cultural 'Golden Age'. The Republic was the financial, trading and transport center of the world. Conquests in Asia, Africa and America made of the Netherlands one of the major colonial powers. Men such as Rembrandt van Rijn, Frans Hals, Baruch de Spinoza, Hugo de Groot (Grotius) and Constantijn Huygens made the Republic preeminent in the arts and sciences. Foreign visitors such as Descartes and Locke were attracted to the Netherlands by the abundance of libraries and of publishers, and the intellectual and religious freedom of Dutch life.

During its 'Golden Age' the Dutch Republic attracted a great deal of foreign interest. Jonathan Israel[1] characterizes the contemporary reaction as follows:

> Numerous features of Dutch society ... seemed aberrant or abhorrent to outsiders. Until the late seventeenth century many were appalled by the diversity of churches which the authorities permitted and the relative freedom with which religious and

---

1   Israel 1995: 1-4.

intellectual issues were discussed. Others disapproved of the excessive liberty, as it seemed to them, accorded to specific groups, expecially women, servants, and Jews… [The Netherlands] were widely perceived in Europe as a seedbed of theological, intellectual, and social promiscuity which subverted the usual, and proper, relations between men and women, Christians and non-Christians, masters and servants, nobles and non-nobles, soldiers and civilians.…

During the seventeenth and eighteenth centuries, outsiders thought of the Republic as giving its citizens, and foreign residents, greater 'freedom' than other European societies of the time.… This celebrated 'freedom' of the Dutch Republic was based on freedom of conscience. But as the English ambassador Sir William Temple wrote, around 1672, it extended much further, creating a 'general liberty and ease, not only in point of conscience, but all others that serve to the commodiousness and quiet of life, every man following his own way, minding his own business, and little enquiring into other men's.'

After the seventeenth century, the Republic of the Netherlands entered a doldrums of economic and cultural stagnation from which it did not really emerge until the end of the nineteenth century. After the wars of the Napoleonic period the Netherlands became a kingdom. In 1848 a constitution was adopted that reflected the emergence of liberal political ideals of representative government, separation of powers and the rule of law. It was not until 1919, however, that the democratic promise was realized with universal suffrage for men and women. In the latter part of the nineteenth century, the contours of the modern parliamentary system emerged, in which the government is responsible to the Lower House (Second Chamber) of Parliament and requires the support of a majority of the members of that house.

Dutch elections are on the basis of proportional representation, so that a party's share of the national vote determines its share of the seats in Parliament. From the time universal suffrage was achieved, voters have been able to choose from a large number of parties: a Catholic party, several Protestant parties, and some secular parties of which the most important are liberal or socialist. The three largest religious parties, since 1980 united in the Christian Democratic Appeal (CDA), dominate the political center. There are two liberal parties, one to the left of the political center (D66, founded in 1966) and the other to the right (VVD), and one social-democratic party (PvdA). None of these parties has ever received a majority of the seats in the Lower House of Parliament. The Dutch government is therefore always based on a coalition, and until the present coalition of the two liberal parties and the PvdA, the Christian parties had always been pivotal members of any coalition.

During the nineteenth and early twentieth centuries, the Netherlands had remained a largely agrarian country, economically backward and socially somnolent. According to the American anthropologist Ruth Benedict, who wrote a report for the Office of War Information during the Second World War, the 'typical Dutchman' of the time was

> a moralizing, individualistic, freedom-loving, tolerant, self-assured, proud, ironic, puritanical, proper, careful, thrifty, conservative, domestic, serious and somewhat melancholic person, highly conscious of social station.[2]

Dutch political culture at the beginning of the twentieth century and until well after the Second World War can best be characterized with the term '*verzuiling*', which literally means 'pillarization', that is, the organization of many social institutions in terms of the 'pillars' of society, defined in essentially religious terms.[3] There was a deep social segregation in which people of different religious persuasion lived in considerable isolation from each other. Each 'pillar' had its own ideology and its own trade unions, schools, employers' organizations, newspapers, radio and TV stations, hospitals, etc. Social contacts over the boundaries of the 'pillar' to which one belonged were – except at the level of the leaders – rare.

Another important feature of Dutch socio-economic organization is 'corporatism', based on the originally Catholic social philosophy that rejects both the socialist idea of class struggle and the bourgeois-capitalist idea of competitive individualism in favor of an ideology of common responsibility for the common good, subject to general supervision by the state. In its Dutch version, 'corporatism' traditionally emphasized the primary responsibility of middle-level social organization, in which, for example, trade union leaders and representatives of employers' organizations (both of them organized in terms of 'pillars') are included, for the regulation of the economic life of a given branch of the economy.[4]

Despite its pluriform and segregated character, the Netherlands was – as it still is – a stable democracy.[5] The reason for this must be sought in the specific political style adopted by the Dutch elite. Pacification of the differences between the 'pillars' was accomplished because the elites, who practised a pragmatic toleration, were businesslike in their dealings with each other and tended to solve differences concerning the distribution of scarce goods on the basis of proportionality. Once the decision was taken to support a particu-

---

2   Van Ginkel 1997: 102.

3   Lijphart distinguishes three 'pillars': Catholic, Calvinist and secular (Lijphart 1968: 17). The latter 'pillar' consists of a socialist and a liberal bloc.

4   See Andeweg & Irwin 1993: 170-171.

5   See generally Lijphart 1968. The idea among some political theorists that strong divisions at the base of society lead to instability at the top seems to be falsified by the case of the Netherlands. Lijphart shows that it is the cooperation between the leaders of the different 'pillars' and the passivity of their followers that accounts for Dutch political stability.

lar activity – radio, schools, hospitals – this was done in proportion to the number of listeners, students, patients, etc.

When an issue could not be solved by applying the principle of proportionality – for example, in the case of ideological yes-or-no questions like decolonization or abortion – avoidance of a definitive resolution was the solution generally sought. Such avoidance took three forms: by postponing consideration of the issue (for example by referring the issue to a prestigious committee, preferably constituted according to the principle of proportionality), by redefining it in such a way that the government was no longer responsible for dealing with it, or by 'depoliticizing' it.[6] 'Depoliticizing' involved making the issue appear a 'procedural' or a 'technical' one and therefore politically neutral. In the case of abortion, all three forms of avoidance were used before abortion legislation was finally passed, which came long after abortion had become *de facto* legal and ceased to be any kind of social problem. First, the issue was defined as 'medical' and left to doctors. Then the Government appointed an expert committee to study the issue. And when legislation came to seem inevitable, it was long postponed by endless debates on procedural questions.[7]

In order to pacify political issues in these various ways, the elites had to be able to negotiate with each other without the greater public getting involved in what was going on. Political passivity was an important characteristic of Dutch political life until the 1960s.

After the Second World War, the Netherlands (thanks partly to the Marshall Plan) quickly became a reasonably modern industrialized society with an advanced social security system rooted in the strong Dutch tradition of social solidarity. 'Pillarization' and 'corporatism' continued, however, to influence political affairs. In the post-War years, for example, governments were able to carry out an anti-inflationary incomes policy with little disturbance from strikes and the like at least in part because the leaders of both trade unions and employers' organizations regularly encountered each other in the various institutions of their respective 'pillars' and were prepared to cooperate on behalf of what was seen as the common good. Such cooperation takes place to this day in more or less formal consultations between the Government and the leaders of relevant social organizations. In the case of euthanasia, for example, there have since the 1980s been regular consultations on policy between officials of the criminal justice system and representatives of the Medical Association.

The 1960s and 1970s were a crucial watershed for Dutch society. From a conservative, tradition-bound country the Netherlands were transformed into one that once again, as in the seventeenth century, was a hotbed of social and cultural experimentation. The

---

6   See Andeweg & Irwin 1993: 38.
7   See Outshoorn 1986: 296.

Netherlands took a prominent place in the sexual revolution, the legalization of abortion, the acceptance of drugs, the democratization of educational institutions, the questioning of religious authority (in particular that of the Catholic Church), and so forth. Societal relationships changed, too, in this period, becoming far more 'democratic' (as the Dutch would say): the social distance between ordinary people and those in positions of authority declined, and ordinary Dutchmen (workers, students, those affected by public projects, etc.) now generally expect to have their views listened to on issues that affect them. In public discussions of important social questions, among them euthanasia, politicians no longer command the respect they used to.

These changes sent shockwaves through the once so quiescent Dutch political landscape. In particular the process of secularization that started in the 1960s gradually undermined the position of the traditional 'pillars' and their institutions. Nevertheless, even such dramatic changes did not lead to political or social instability. To some extent this can be explained in terms of the position that the political elite adopted in response to calls for change. On the whole, after some initial resistance, they did not form a bloc opposed to change; in many cases they supported the new ideas and were even spokesmen for them.[8] The political culture of conflict-avoidance, the traditional conviction that it is better to guide social developments than to try to stop them, was of great importance in keeping the social turmoil of these years within limits the society could cope with.

In 1996 the Dutchman Van der Horst attempted to explain the Netherlands and the Dutch to people in other countries. He characterizes them as egalitarian, tolerant, freedom-loving, believers in social solidarity, practical, conscientious, careful, moralistic, paternalistic, inclined to respect authority, conformist, punctual, calm, and very attached to their privacy.[9]

This, then, is the social and cultural context within which the medical practices and legal developments to be discussed in this book must be understood.

---

8   See Kennedy 1995: 14.
9   Van der Horst 1996.

1 Introduction

1.1 What this book is about and for whom it is intended

The Netherlands is presently the only country in the world in which euthanasia, under specific circumstances, is legally permissible.[1] Considerable attention has been paid over a number of years to the problem of regulating it. And information has been systematically collected concerning actual practice. The Dutch experience is therefore of considerable interest both to the Dutch themselves and also to people elsewhere who are considering whether or not to make similar practices legal and, if this is done, how they might most effectively be regulated.

The central focus of the book is on Dutch law pertaining to euthanasia and a number of closely related sorts of medical behavior. We will deal with the legal norms and procedures currently in place, with how these have come to be what they are, and with the direction in which they seem to be moving (chapters 2 and 3). But the book is not confined to the law itself: we will also critically consider the arguments that play a role in the Dutch debate (chapter 4), the available evidence bearing on actual practice and on the effectiveness of current law as an instrument of control (chapter 5), and possible alternative forms of legal control (chapter 6). The book ends (chapter 7) with brief reflections on two questions often asked in connection with the Dutch experience: does that experience confirm or refute the fear of a 'slippery slope' from legalization of euthanasia to social practices that are abhorrent? and is the Dutch experience in some sense 'exportable' to other countries?

We have written this book with a reader in mind who is unfamiliar with the Dutch situation and has no specific technical knowledge of law, and certainly not of Dutch law. We do assume that our reader is interested enough in the problems of public policy surrounding euthanasia to want an account of the Dutch situation that goes beyond generalizations and superficialities and includes as much as possible of the legal and factual information that is important for an informed assessment of Dutch practice and its relevance for other countries. We also assume that our reader has an open mind and does not expect us to tell a tendentious story whose moral is preconceived from the start.

---

1   There are a handful of partial exceptions to this generalization, all of them as far as we are aware concerning assistance with suicide. The most important is Switzerland, where assistance with suicide (by non-doctors) is not illegal and is an institutionalized practice.

On the whole, the descriptions of Dutch law and practice concerning euthanasia available in English are either so uncritically apologetic,[2] or so obviously and even maliciously biassed,[3] that the reader who is looking not for an advocate's brief or an exercise in axe-grinding but just a straightforward presentation of the evidence is left not knowing what to believe.[4] Our ambition has therefore been to present the interested reader with reliable information and serious, balanced assessments. It would be wise for him, however, to respond to such a promise by holding onto his intellectual wallet with both hands. The most biassed writers on Dutch euthanasia law and practice proclaim their lack of preconception most vigorously. We will therefore state our own personal convictions here at the outset and try to keep them out of the rest of the book as much as possible. The reader is in any case forewarned about what they are and can keep an eye out for unintended distortion. In general terms, we believe:

–   that the law should allow ample room for people to decide for themselves the moment and the manner of their death;
–   that effective legal control is absolutely essential to prevent abuse of the power unavoidably involved in medical care in connection with death (but not *more* necessary for euthanasia than it is in the case of a number of related sorts of medical behavior that shortens life).

The subject is so controversial that with the best will in the world even the attempt simply to state the facts and the law proves to be susceptible to vigorous disagreement, as we discovered when we submitted the text of this book to a large number of experts for their reaction.[5] Thus, for example, the question what exactly the 'requirements of careful practice' include (see chapter 3), is a matter on which it is possible for informed persons to disagree.

In chapter 6 we develop an argument about the limitations of current legal regulation and alternative possibilities. Here, by contrast with the rest of the book, we drop all pretense of being neutrally descriptive, although the argument is firmly rooted in the legal

---

2   See for example J. Zaritsky, *An Appointment with Death* (Corporation for Public Broadcasting, 1993), a film which accurately conveys the way the Dutch look at the question of euthanasia and provides interesting information about several cases, but which explores none of the problematic aspects of Dutch practice.

3   See section 1.4 below for some examples.

4   Battin (1994) is a rather lonely exception to this generalization. While she is not always completely reliable on matters of legal detail (for example, she wrongly describes Dutch euthanasia law as falling under the concept of *gedogen*, or systematic toleration of violations of the law), her account of the Dutch situation is, as far as the essentials are concerned, objective and critical.

5   See the Acknowledgements for some of the persons whose advice and criticism we sought.

and empirical material presented earlier in the book. The position we take is not widely shared – most Dutch participants in the euthanasia debate reject, for example, the idea that euthanasia could be considered 'normal medical practice' subject to the 'medical exception' (see chapter 6.3.1). But we hope that the clarity of the analysis will appeal even to people who quite disagree with us about the legal acceptability of the medical behavior involved and how society should deal with it.

Finally, a note on sources. Where possible, we have referred to sources in English and have relied as little as possible on secondary sources in Dutch. The Dutch literature is extensive, but it seems pointless to try to do justice to it in a book intended in the first place for non-readers of Dutch.

1.2   The definition of 'euthanasia' and of other 'medical behavior that shortens life' (MBSL)

'Euthanasia' in the strict – and in the Dutch context the only proper – sense refers to the situation in which a doctor[6] kills a person who is suffering 'unbearably' and 'hopelessly' at the latter's explicit request (usually by administering a lethal injection). When a distinction is made, then 'euthanasia' is in the Netherlands reserved for killing on request as opposed to assistance with suicide, but generally the two are treated together. We will follow this practice and will often loosely use the single term 'euthanasia' to cover both where the distinction is not relevant.

As we will see in chapters 4 and 5, euthanasia in the limited Dutch sense is only separated by rather problematic boundaries from related phenomena, such as pain relief in doses known to be likely to cause the death of the patient, or the termination or non-initiation of life-prolonging treatment that is either medically futile or is rejected by the patient. Nevertheless, these other practices are generally considered legitimate in the Netherlands and elsewhere even by many vigorous opponents of euthanasia;[7] they are referred to in Dutch medical law as 'normal medical practice' and regarded as quite different from euthanasia.

---

6   Euthanasia by persons not acting in a medical capacity plays essentially no role in the current Dutch political debate and is outside the scope of this book. The difficult position of medical professionals other than doctors – in particular, nurses – will be dealt with in chapter 3.1.3.

7   See e.g. Callahan 1993. Fenigsen (1989) is a notable exception: most of his fulmination against 'euthanasia' in the Netherlands in fact concerns other medical practices. Battin (1994: 136) makes the interesting observation that much of the domestic opposition to Dutch practice seems to concern "passive nonvoluntary euthanasia [abstinence], a practice much more accepted in the United States than in the Netherlands". (It might be safer to have said: at least as accepted in the United States.)

There is another category of behavior which is also closely related to euthanasia but which is more controversial: the administration of lethal drugs to shorten the life of persons who cannot or do not explicitly request this (severely defective newborn babies, persons in long-term coma, persons in the final stages of dying, persons no longer competent who at some earlier time indicated a general wish for euthanasia if the time should come). Also controversial is assistance with suicide in the case of psychiatric patients and others whose suffering is not somatic in origin, and of elderly persons who are not currently suffering at all but who do not wish to continue living.

Together with euthanasia proper, all of the behavior described above, when engaged in by doctors, is part of a complex of 'medical behavior that shortens life' (MBSL). Although there are, of course, important distinctions between different sorts of MBSL, and some may well be morally and legally more problematic than others, we will see that for purposes of philosophical analysis (chapter 4), empirical description (chapter 5), and effective regulation (chapter 6), the whole complex must be considered together.

A terminological note: We use the expression 'shortening of life' when referring generally to behavior that the doctor knows is likely to cause the patient to die earlier than he otherwise would have done and in fact leads to the patient's death. We use the expression 'termination of life' (sometimes with the qualifier 'active' when this emphasis is needed in the context) to refer to euthanasia (and assistance with suicide) together with what is referred to in the Dutch discussion as 'termination of life without an explicit request'. In other words, 'termination of life' involves 'active' and 'direct' shortening of life (to use expressions now obsolete in the Dutch discussion), to the exclusion of death due to abstinence and pain relief. Were it not for the fact that drugs like morphine and insulin, and occasionally means like the 'plastic bag method', can be used to terminate life, the category 'termination of life' could be defined in terms of the administration of euthanatica.

1.3   A sketch of the current legal situation

Euthanasia is explicitly and apparently absolutely prohibited by two articles of the Dutch Criminal Code. Article 293 prohibits killing a person at his request (the offence is a 'qualified' variety of homicide, in the sense that the homicide would otherwise be murder). Article 294 prohibits assisting a suicide (suicide itself is not a crime in Dutch law).

Despite the apparently forbidding text of these provisions, the courts have held that article 40 of the Criminal Code makes a defence of justification available to a doctor charged under articles 293 or 294. The first acquittal took place in 1983 and this was upheld by the Dutch Supreme Court in the *Schoonheim* case in 1984. The Supreme Court held that a doctor could invoke the defence of justification due to necessity if, confronted by a conflict between a duty to his patient whose suffering is 'unbearable and hopeless,' and the requirements of the Criminal Code, and exercising the care required of a medical profes-sional, his choice was "objectively justified". The decision in *Schoonheim* led to a series of judicial decisions in which the conditions and limitations of the defence were gradually worked out.

The opening created by the courts came in the course of the 1980s to be reflected in pros-ecution policy, which now offers the doctor who keeps within the accepted limits a high degree of safety from prosecution. In this sense, euthanasia in the Netherlands is no longer illegal. Contrary to the impression in much of the foreign press, legislation recent-ly enacted by the Dutch parliament (see chapter 3.2) does not affect the legality of euthanasia but only the procedure for reporting it.

As far as the legal norms concerning euthanasia are concerned, the process of legaliza-tion is largely complete, and there is little controversy over the results reached. Legal developments concerning euthanasia itself will in the coming years deal essentially with fine-tuning of the existing system (the requirement of consultation with a second doc-tor, for example, while itself completely non-controversial, leads to complications in some cases). There are, of course, some exceptions to this generalization. An important example is the status of written euthanasia requests made by persons who later become incompetent (especially due to senile dementia); other remaining problems include such things as how to deal with persons of diminished competence and with minors. But the most important legal developments to be expected in the near future concern not the applicable norms but the system of legal control; in particular, the question whether this could not be better accomplished outside of the criminal law is being asked with increas-ing insistence.

What has been said of euthanasia proper does not apply to situations in which a doctor administers lethal drugs without the patient having made an explicit request, although here, too, the general contours of the emerging legal norms are becoming clear. In the case of coma patients, severely defective newborn babies, and patients in the final stages of the dying process, recent legal developments seem, as we will see in chapter 3.3, to point the way to a generally acceptable outcome, but these matters remain far more con-troversial than euthanasia proper.

By contrast with the various forms of 'active termination of life' dealt with so far, pain relief and abstention account for the lion's share of all MBSL (almost 10 times as many deaths as those due to the use of lethal drugs). They have nevertheless received relatively little attention as problems of regulation of medical behavior. Death due to the adminis-tration of pain relief in doses known to be likely to shorten life is regarded, legally as well as in medical ethics, as subject to the 'doctrine of double effect': so long as the doctor's 'primary intent' is to relieve suffering, the fact that the earlier death of the patient is also a foreseen and even welcome consequence does not, according to this doctrine, entail that the doctor 'intended' that death. The case is regarded as one of 'normal medical practice' not subject to any special regulation, rather than one of euthanasia (if there is a request) or murder (if there is not). Apart from the general rules applying to medical practice, there are no substantive or procedural protections surrounding pain relief so long as it falls within the scope of the 'doctrine of double effect'.

Much the same applies to abstinence, often in practice done with the express purpose of causing the death of the patient, but regarded for purposes of legal analysis as an 'omission' and therefore not covered by the prohibitions of euthanasia (in the case of request) or murder (in other cases). Abstinence is considered 'normal medical practice' not subject to any special regulation. In the last few years there has been a growing appreciation of the importance of timely decisions to abstain from life-prolonging treatment (including artificial means of administering food and drink). The increasing legitimacy afforded to abstinence has come to be seen both as providing an alternative in many cases to the use of lethal drugs (euthanasia and termination of life without an explicit request) and as affording a justification for the use of such drugs in other cases, in which the patient's death from abstinence threatens to be an inhumane one. Procedural protections surrounding abstinence decisions are still extremely primitive, but there are signs of growing concern about this situation, and this is an area in which legal development is surely to be expected.

1.4   Criticisms from abroad and the Dutch reaction

As we have seen in the *Prologue*, Dutch society has over the centuries attracted considerable foreign attention. Admiration for Dutch achievements in commerce, social organisation, science, the arts, and engineering (especially water control and land reclamation) has been mixed with scepticism, disapproval, and shock. But foreign characterizations of Dutch society, favorable or unfavorable, often tell us more about the situation in the observer's own country than they do about the Netherlands.[8] The German traveller in the seventeenth century who is shocked at the fact that "servant girls in Holland behaved and dressed so much like their mistresses that it was hard to tell which was which,"[9] tells us more about how dramatic social differences were expected to be in contemporary Germany than he does about whether such differences were readily visible in Holland.

Of no current subject is this more true than it is of euthanasia. Although the Dutch experience with euthanasia has attracted a great deal of comment, little of this goes beyond expressions of moral outrage to consider what is actually happening in the Nether-

---

8   Compare Van Ginkel 1997: 15-42.
9   Israel 1995: 2.

lands.[10] The Dutch experience is seen primarily as a source of ammunition to be used for domestic purposes.[11] Dutch practice, about which a great deal is known, is used to condemn not so much the Dutch but, via them, proposals for liberalization elsewhere where very little is known about actual practice.

Those who are inclined to react to Dutch developments in this way are invited in the succeeding chapters of this book to consider the complexities of the legal, moral and empirical questions involved: on careful reflection, none of these seem to lend themselves to simple, absolute answers. And those who are seriously interested in keeping medical behavior that shortens life under legal control must consider the substantial evidence of various sorts to the effect that simply papering-over behavior of a sort that occurs in all modern medical systems with a moral taboo is not likely to be an effective way of subjecting it to public control.

The general tenor of the criticisms made of Dutch euthanasia practice can be summarized under three headings:[12] (1) there are terrible things happening in the Netherlands and these are the result of the Dutch acceptance of euthanasia; (2) requests for euthanasia cannot in the nature of things be 'really' voluntary, so that euthanasia in the Dutch sense is impossible; (3) legal control in the Netherlands is inadequate and adequate control would be impossible to achieve, so that legalizing euthanasia necessarily leads – as it already has in the Netherlands – to forms of 'involuntary euthanasia'.

---

10 See for example the resolution of the European Parliament of 8 April 1997, urging member states to prohibit "euthanasia" [sic] of the handicapped, those in long-term coma, defective babies and the elderly. Dutch practice is explicitly referred to in the debates. The proposed text of the resolution referred to "active euthanasia" but the word 'active' was deleted during the debates, making the ultimate meaning quite obscure. The change would seem to imply that the resolution is intended to cover 'passive euthanasia', that is, abstention. However, there is no indication in the debates that the members of the EP wanted to forbid abstention, which is of course generally considered normal and proper medical practice.

11 This is particularly true of Gomez 1991 and Hendin 1997, both written essentially as contributions to the American discussion. See also New York State Task Force 1994; British Medical Association 1988.

12 Another possibly important criticism sometimes made by doctors from other countries is that there is too little attention given to palliative care in the Netherlands. This criticism is usually made in a way (general, unsupported, denigrating) that suggests it may rest more on medical chauvinism and ideological opposition to euthanasia than on observable fact. Since so far as we are aware there are no reliable data on the matter and it has little connection with the rest of the argument in this book, we will not devote any further attention to it. See Francke et al. 1997 for a literature study of palliative care in the Netherlands.

(1) The charge that terrible things take place in Dutch medical treatment of dying patients is undoubtedly true, since such a general charge would be true of any country in the world and of many social institutions besides euthanasia.[13] Criticism that deserves serious attention must offer evidence that the Dutch are afflicted with something less ubiquitous than Original Sin. Furthermore, to get above the level of international mud-slinging, criticism must be based on more than anecdotes, uncontrollable generalities (for example, about what 'most psychiatrists' think about some issue) and surmises. And it is essential to define the kind of behavior involved carefully (so that evidence of absten-tion, for example, is not used to 'prove' the charge that 'involuntary euthanasia' is being widely practised). Yet these minimal conditions for fruitful discussion are precisely what is usually missing when this sort of charge is made. Thus a 'conclusion' such as Hendin's to the effect that "the Dutch experience teaches … that euthanasia brings out the worst rather than the best in medicine" and that "vast numbers of … patients … die inappro-priately … in the Netherlands [as a result of legalization of euthanasia]"[14] makes an implicit comparison between unsubstantiated allegations concerning the situation in the Netherlands and equally unsubstantiated, unstated surmises concerning the situa-

---

13   Compare Battin's (1994: 138) observation that arguing against Dutch euthanasia practice by invoking allegedly horrible anecdotes is like arguing against the institution of marriage by pointing to occasional cases of 'shot-gun' and other involuntary marriages.

14   1997: 214-215.

tion in the United States, and then makes an unsubstantiated guess that legalization of euthanasia accounts for the imagined difference between the two.[15]

---

15 Hendin (1994, 1997) has, of all foreign critics, probably devoted the most effort to collecting information on the Dutch situation. Unfortunately, his research methods are quite inadequate to support the sorts of conclusions he draws (the comments on Gomez' research in note 19 apply *a fortiori* to Hendin's case). The 'findings' which supposedly support his conclusions are so filled with mistakes of law, of fact, and of interpretation, mostly tendentious, that it is hard to be charitable and regard them as merely negligent. His central conclusion, to the effect that Dutch euthanasia practice has increased the power of doctors rather than that of patients, may or may not be true, but there is little in his book other than his own repeated assertion to support it. Hendin has, furthermore, been accused by a number of those interviewed by him of important errors of fact in what he claims to have learned from them, of misrepresenting their views, of breach of trust in publishing (allegedly) verbatim accounts of interviews that had been intended as off the record, and of failing to submit his account of the interviews to them for approval as they say he had promised to do. See Dworkin 1997.

Fenigsen is a Dutch rather than a foreign critic, but his article (Fenigsen 1989) is so regularly invoked as 'evidence' of how terrible the situation is in the Netherlands that a few observations are in order. No sources are given for most of his assertions; according to the *Hastings Center Report*, which published his article, this is because the sources were in Dutch. When we requested the original manuscript from *HCR*, it was obvious at a glance that the heat of Fenigsen's passionate objection to everything he calls 'euthanasia' had overwhelmed elementary considerations in dealing with matters of fact: impartiality, precision, accurate citation and critical assessment of sources, attention to representativeness, etc. No journal which holds itself to serious standards would have considered publishing such a thing (compare Spek, letter to the editor, *HCR*, November/December 1989: 50).

The largest part of Fenigsen's indictment is couched in general terms, in which a conspiracy theory of the motivations of proponents of legalization and an apocalyptic vision of Dutch public opinion find support in bizarre misinterpretations of the Dutch medical, legal and political situation. Occasionally, however, he makes assertions about identifiable instances. When these specific charges were investigated by the Medical Inspectorate at the request of the Dutch prosecutorial authorities (who were alerted by the NVVE to the fact that a number of cases of murder or manslaughter seemed to be involved), it appeared that the 6 cases Fenigsen referred to as based on his own personal knowledge had taken place a decade earlier. One had taken place in Denmark. Of the remaining 5, 4 involved abstinence and one termination of life without an explicit request (apparently a case of 'help in dying'). There seems in several of the cases to have been some carelessness on the part of the doctors involved. Fenigsen himself agreed with these conclusions of the Inspectorate. (See exchange of letters between Fenigsen and Plokker, Medical Inspectorate, North Brabant, 23 February 1990 and 29 March 1990.)

In short, Hendin and Fenigsen are both quite unreliable guides to the Dutch situation.

(2) Some critics of Dutch practice seize the psychological high ground: a request for euthanasia *cannot* be voluntary because a person cannot desire his own death. Such a request must therefore be regarded as a 'cry for help', an expression of the patient's fear of impending death or a submission to pressure from his family or his doctor. If he accedes to the request, the doctor's behavior can be disqualified in the same way as being based not on the considerations he believes are important – beneficence or respect for the patient's autonomy – but rather on his own anxieties about death, loss of control, and so forth. Hendin (1997) is a prime example of this sort of psychological reductionism. Throughout his book, he claims to 'know' better than the Dutch doctors who were directly involved (and who are his only source of information) what the 'real' reasons were for their patients' requests and what the 'real' reasons are that they did what they did. Such *a priori* knowledge liberates him from the necessity of considering carefully and open-mindedly what actually is going on. Hendin is also breathtakingly arrogant: the views of the greater part of his professional colleagues in the Netherlands (see chapter 3.5.1) are treated, in effect, as professionally incompetent, as mere psychological symptoms not worthy of serious consideration.[16]

(3) A few critics seem to accept in principle many of the arguments in favor of Dutch euthanasia practice, but reject it ultimately on the grounds that it is not, and cannot be, adequately controlled, so that its dangers outweigh its benefits. Gomez (1991) and Keown (1992, 1995) are the most responsible exponents of this position.

Gomez' general description of Dutch practice seems to have been inspired by a genuine interest in the facts, and it was at the time not far off the mark, although he was not well-informed about some crucial aspects of the Dutch situation (for example, the predominant role of general practitioners in euthanasia practice). His central theme is that euthanasia in the Netherlands is not as unproblematic as its protagonists (in the United States) would sometimes have us believe. He concludes from his study and the literature available in English in 1990 that the rules that are supposed to regulate euthanasia are

---

16   Toward the end of his book, Hendin gives away his ideological *parti pris* when he observes that "if the advocates of legalization prevail, we will lose more lives to suicide (although we will call the deaths by a different name) than can be saved by the efforts of the American Suicide Foundation and all the other institutions working to prevent suicide" (1997: 223). Hendin, who at the beginning of his book (1997: 13), had proclaimed the open-mindedness with which he undertook his study, seems here at its end to reveal its hidden agenda. One of the authors of this book (Griffiths) was among those with whom Hendin spoke when he was conducting his research in the Netherlands. The sentence quoted is especially striking if one remembers having been reassured that the American Suicide Foundation, of which Hendin is Executive Director, is a purely scientific organization, with no position one way or the other on the issues involved in the public discussion of euthanasia.

"not only … not enforced, they are probably unenforceable".[17] The most important findings on which this conclusion is based are that the reporting requirement was not being complied with (which at the time was certainly true and in fact still is) and that the voluntariness of the patient's request is questionable because of the fact that doctors are "instrumental in helping to form that volition".[18] The empirical basis for this latter conclusion, however, is far too flimsy to support it.[19] But the most essential weakness of Gomez' argument is the absence of an explicit comparison between the Netherlands and elsewhere: without a comparative analysis there is simply no basis for his (implicit) notion that there is *less* control over this sort of behavior in the Netherlands than elsewhere and, if so, that the limited legalization of euthanasia is the *cause* of this.

---

17   1991: 122.

18   1991: 123.

19   Gomez' description of the interaction between doctor and patient is based on information concerning 24 cases, collected long after the fact by a person (himself) whose grasp of the context was limited and who apparently did not speak Dutch, by means of interviews with a highly unrepresentative group of doctors who themselves were operating on the basis of memory and trying to describe subtle and complex interactions that had taken place as long as 5 years earlier, and whose English was probably not muscular enough for the task. That Gomez draws firm conclusions about the influence of the doctor on the patient's decision on the basis of this sort of information can only be described as scientifically irresponsible.

The American reader who is inclined to dismiss such criticism of Gomez' research methods as exaggerated would do well to ask himself how much confidence he would have in the conclusions of – say – a Japanese doctor who studied some controversial medical procedure in the United States by interviewing a handful of American doctors with whom he happened to come in contact about a small number cases these doctors had been involved in several years earlier (and covering only cases in which the doctors had carried out a particular procedure, not the far larger group of cases in which they had not done so). Not speaking any English, our hypothetical Japanese researcher conducted the interviews through an interpreter. Based on the interviews (and without being able to read the American literature on the subject) the Japanese researcher felt able to make vigorous assertions not only about what American doctors generally do in such cases but also about what influence this has on the patients involved (none of whom, of course, he had talked to). And from these 'findings' he came to the conclusion that American policy in the area concerned was dangerously defective. To lend his account authenticity, he larded it with local color such as the information that the 'Bibel Beld' runs across the United States from New York to San Francisco. Despite his ignorance of English, he informed his Japanese readers about the etymology of the word 'autonomy': when Americans speak of the autonomy of the patient, they refer to the patient's continued ability to drive a car ('auto'). See Gomez 1991: 91 [*Ranstaad, sic*]; 155 n. 96 [*ontluisteren*] for examples of the same sort of amusing errors.

Keown gives a useful and reasonably accurate short summary of Dutch euthanasia law and of the findings of some empirical research concerning actual practice and the effectiveness of legal control.[20] He shows convincingly what has been more extensively argued elsewhere,[21] that euthanasia cannot be effectively distinguished from other sorts of medical behavior that shortens life, such as abstinence and pain relief, where the death of the patient is often an intended result. He concludes from this that the level of medical behavior that intentionally shortens life is far higher than is generally recognized and that in many such cases the patient is not (adequately) consulted. He also concludes that current legal control over euthanasia cannot be considered effective, partly because of the permeability of its borders with other forms of medical behavior that shortens life and partly because it depends on self-reporting by doctors. Up to this point, his argument can be considered painful for the Dutch, but it is otherwise a solid one; our own conclusions in chapter 6 are much the same.

Keown then turns to the question he thinks is critical: whether the Dutch experience confirms the fear of a 'slippery slope' toward non-voluntary termination of life, a fear expressed in British and Canadian reports opposing the legalization of euthanasia. In order to make such a claim plausible, he would have to show that the total of such behavior has *increased after legalization* of euthanasia, or that it is *higher in the Netherlands than elsewhere.* Then he would have to confront the difficult task of establishing a *causal* relationship between legalization of euthanasia and increasing non-voluntary termination of life. Citing the total of non-voluntary termination of life, as revealed by Dutch research, in itself proves nothing at all. We pause to consider his argument because it is so typical of foreign criticism that claims to base itself on Dutch data.

Keown's repeated suggestion that the frequency of non-voluntary termination of life has increased in the Netherlands since partial legalization appears to be unfounded. He gives no evidence for the claim that there is "growing condonation" of non-voluntary termination of life (there is at least as much reason to suppose that under the influence of growing openness and control, such practices are becoming *less* acceptable and *less* frequent[22]).

---

20 While the argument in Keown's two articles is essentially the same, that of 1992 relies primarily on Van der Wal's early research (ultimately published in Van der Wal 1992), that of 1995 on Van der Maas, Van Delden & Pijnenborg 1992.

21 See Griffiths 1994.

22 For example: the Government and the Medical Association (KNMG) have set themselves the task of reducing the frequency of such behavior (see chapter 6.2.5 and 6.2.6), and the 1995 research seems in fact to suggest a modest decline (see table 5.2); furthermore, as far as abstinence (which Keown rightly considers equally relevant) is concerned, there are increasing indications of concern at the hospital level to ensure that the patient is involved in the decision-making (cf. Blijham & Van Delden 1996).

Keown might alternatively have supported his claim of a 'slippery slope' with an international comparison. Although he does not in fact undertake such a comparison, doing so would probably not have bolstered his argument. Although reliable data for other countries are hard to come by, as they gradually become available it seems increasingly apparent that the real difference between Dutch euthanasia policy and the situation elsewhere is not that medical behavior itself is very different: the rate of 'physician-negotiated death' seems to be roughly comparable and there is evidence of widespread, if hidden, euthanasia practice elsewhere.[23] The real difference is that in the Netherlands this behavior to a considerable extent takes place in the open and is subject to at least some legal control. And as for non-voluntary shortening of life, as far as one can tell there is nothing very unusual about the Dutch situation: abstinence and pain relief without consulting the patient seem to be widely practised elsewhere.[24] Keown's claim of a slippery slope requires him to show that the total rate of death due to these 'normal medical practices' – which he himself insists are not significantly different from what the Dutch call 'termination of life without an explicit request' – are higher in the Netherlands than they are in countries where euthanasia is entirely forbidden. He in fact does not even suggest that this is the case.

Keown's argument, which he apparently thinks condemns the Dutch approach by demonstrating a high level of non-voluntary shortening of life, is actually a boomerang. It is precisely the idea that abstinence and pain relief are *fundamentally and unproblematically different* from euthanasia and intentional termination of life without an explicit request that underlies legal policy in all other countries. If, as Keown argues, such a distinction cannot be made, then he ought to be looking closer to home for the horribles he claims to have found in the Netherlands.[25]

---

23   Recent research in the United States gives rates of assistance with suicide roughly comparable to the Dutch figure for euthanasia (see the sources cited in Dworkin et al. 1997). 'Physician-negotiated death' is estimated at about 70% of all deaths in the United States (see Kass 1993: 34; cf. Quill 1996: 199). Recent Australian research using the methods of earlier Dutch studies shows rates of euthanasia and assistance with suicide very similar to the Dutch rates (Kuhse et al. 1997).

24   Much of the 'physician-negotiated death' referred to in note 23 must involve patients who are not competent or not conscious. Studies such as Anspach (1993) and Zussman (1992), and Quill's (1996) autobiographical account of end-of-life medical practice seem to confirm this inference. See Kuhse 1997 for Australian evidence to this effect.

25   The first sentence of Keown's 1995 article reveals all the shortcomings of his position: "There is only one country in which euthanasia is officially condoned and widely practised: the Netherlands." Apart from the obvious fact of official condonation, everything in this sentence is tendentiously wrong. Almost nothing is known about the frequency of what the Dutch call euthanasia in other countries (the little that is known suggests that its frequency may not differ much from that in the Netherlands – see note 23). And much of what Keown himself regards as essentially the same as euthanasia is both officially condoned and widely practised all over the world.

In short, Keown is so anxious to prove his point that he seems to lose sight of the implications of what he is saying. He has not uncovered evidence of a slope in the Dutch data, let alone of a slippery one. What he really calls attention to is quite a different problem, namely that both in the Netherlands and elsewhere the widespread use of abstinence and administration of pain relief to shorten life calls for much more adequate regulation than it currently receives.[26]

The charges from abroad raise some fundamental questions, in particular with respect to the problem of adequate legal control, about which the Dutch themselves, as we will see, are very concerned. Unfortunately, on the whole (with the partial exception of writers like Gomez and Keown) the charges have not been made in a way which invites serious response. Imprecision, exaggeration, suggestion and innuendo, misinterpretation and misrepresentation, ideological *ipse dixitism*, and downright lying and slander (not to speak of bad manners) have taken the place of careful analysis of the problem and consideration of the Dutch evidence. It is perhaps understandable that the Dutch reaction has tended to be dismissive, since such critics do not seem to deserve respectful attention.

To a large extent, the Dutch tend simply to ignore foreign cricitism.[27] The more or less 'official' Dutch reaction, when there is one, amounts essentially to denial.[28] Denial in the

---

26   An argument essentially similar to Keown's and subject to exactly the same fundamental criticisms is made by Hendin, Rutenfrans and Zylicz (1997). Where Keown is reasonably accurate with regard to Dutch law and respectful of empirical data, however, these authors seem untroubled by whether what they say is true or not. They find evidence of a 'slippery slope' in the progression from legally sanctioned assistance with suicide to legally sanctioned euthanasia, and thence "from euthanasia for terminally ill patients to euthanasia for those who are chronically ill, from euthanasia for physical illness to euthanasia for psychological distress, and from voluntary euthanasia to nonvoluntary and involuntary euthanasia" (1997: 1720). As we will see in chapters 2 and 3.1, the first two steps on this mythical slippery slope are, as a matter of legal history, simply untrue; the third rests on a very imprecise rendition of the distinction between somatically based and not somatically based suffering (Dutch law never having permitted euthanasia for an 'illness' as such and never having required 'physical' suffering); the last suggests that 'involuntary' euthanasia has ever, under any circumstances, been sanctioned in the Netherlands, which is untrue. It is also untrue (see chapter 3.2) that the reporting procedure (either before or after the legislation of 1993) "ensur[ed]...physicians [that they] will not be prosecuted if guidelines were followed" (1997: 1721). A substantial part of these authors' 'evidence' for a slippery slope is based on anecdotes of dubious reliability or representativeness (1997: 1721-1722). In short, yet another missed opportunity to engage in serious debate.

27   Although Hendin did receive some attention in the daily press, neither Gomez nor Hendin, for example, were reviewed in Dutch professional journals except by the authors of this book (see Griffiths 1993 and Weyers 1997).

28   See e.g. Rigter, Borst-Eijlers and Leenen 1988; Rigter 1989; Aartsen et al. 1989; Van der Kloot Mijburg 1989.

first place that there has been major legal change in the Netherlands: euthanasia, it is insisted, remains 'illegal'. This position is essentially disingenuous: it relies on the fact that the articles of the Criminal Code prohibiting euthanasia and assistance with suicide have not been amended and ignores the fact that another article of the Code has been interpreted to afford a defence of justitification, so that if the relevant conditions are met, the behavior concerned is effectively *not* illegal. Denial, in the second place, that 'non-voluntary euthanasia' is taking place. In light of the evidence (see chapter 5), such a denial is only possible by insisting on the narrow Dutch conception of euthanasia, which must by definition be voluntary. Nothing is said about the large number of cases of non-voluntary termination of life that are not, in this sense, 'euthanasia' (most of them being abstinence or pain relief). Denial, most importantly, that there are problems of control. It is insisted that 'carefully and precisely drafted rules' make abuse impossible. But even a passing acquaintance with the applicable rules (see chapter 3) shows that they can hardly be described as watertight, and in any case a precise rule is quite a different matter from an effectively enforced one. It is well known in the Netherlands, and since the early 1990s this has become a subject of increasing concern, that the existing control system, depending as it does on self-reporting, cannot be regarded as adequate. This fact is simply not mentioned when foreign criticism is summarily dismissed; nor is the fact that the system, by its very nature, covers only a small part of the whole problem of medical behavior that shortens life.

Whatever the provocation, the Dutch dismissive reaction is unfortunate. The charges relating to the problem of legal control do go to the heart of the matter, even if, as levelled by most foreign critics, they do not seem to deserve the time of day. They can only be properly discussed after, in the chapters to come, we have described Dutch euthanasia practice and the legal norms and enforcement processes that regulate it. Our assessment of the strengths and weaknesses of the Dutch approach to legal control and of possibilities for improvement, will be presented in chapter 6, and in chapter 7 we will consider the relevance of all this for other countries grappling with the same underlying problems.

Intermezzo: The Dutch Health-Care System and the Care of the Terminally Ill

In this *intermezzo* we describe some features of the Dutch health-care system that are essential to an understanding of Dutch euthanasia practice and the problems associated with its regulation.[1] After a brief general introduction to the Dutch health-care system (section A) we will deal specifically with the institutions in which people in the Netherlands die (section B) and with the health-care professionals responsible for such patients (section C).

A   The Dutch health-care system

PUBLIC HEALTH

The Dutch are relatively healthy compared with the inhabitants of other countries.[2] Life expectancy at birth in 1993 was 74.0 years for men and 80.1 years for women. With an average life expectancy of 77.1 years, the Netherlands belong in Europe's top quartile. Both men and women can expect to spend about 60 years of their lives in good health.[3]

ACCESS TO HEALTH CARE

Social policy in the Netherlands reflects the country's cultural commitment to social equity and solidarity. Virtually everyone in the Netherlands is covered by health insurance.[4] In the funding of this insurance a distinction is made between 'normal' medical expenses and the 'exceptional' costs associated with long-term care or other high-cost medical treatment. Such exceptional costs are covered by a compulsory national health insurance scheme. Every person living in the Netherlands is covered by the scheme. Benefits include long-term residential and nursing care for the elderly, comprehensive psychiatric care, home-based care, and comprehensive care for the physically and mentally handicapped.

---

1   Except where otherwise noted, Schrijvers 1997 is our source.
2   SCP 1990: 21.
3   RIVM 1993: 206.
4   Recent estimates show that less than 1% of the population has no health insurance. In life-threatening situations, medical care would never be refused because the patient was not insured.

For 'normal' medical expenses, there is a compulsory public health insurance scheme applicable to all employees earning less than about 80,000 guilders per year, to social security recipients and to certain groups of the elderly. Those insured pay income-related premiums and a relatively low flat-rate premium; employers also contribute on behalf of their employees. The benefits package consists of regular medical and other care not covered by the statutory scheme for 'exceptional' care. Hospitalization and medical care by specialists, the services of GPs, paraprofessional services such as physical therapy, speech therapy, midwifery and dental care for youth, are all covered.

About 35% of the population are covered neither by the public health insurance scheme nor by specific schemes for public employees. This group includes employees earning more than the maximum amount mentioned above, self-employed persons, and owners of small businesses. Private health insurance is available for these persons; there is a standard benefit package that is almost the same as that under the public health insurance scheme.

THE COST OF HEALTH CARE

The total cost of health care in the Netherlands was 58 billion guilders in 1993, or about 10% of gross national product. In international terms, this is not particularly high: the Netherlands occupies a middle position among Western industrialized countries.[5] Intramural care accounts for about 60% of the costs of health care, the rest being divided over extramural care, pharmaceuticals, preventive care, etc.[6]

About 10% of the total cost of health care is paid for out-of-pocket by the patient; another 10% is paid by the government with funds raised through taxation. The remaining 80% is covered by insurance premiums, of which 65% are in the context of the public health insurance scheme and 15% are for private insurance.

THE ORGANIZATION OF HEALTH CARE

For purposes of health-care policy, facilities are divided into three groups: basic, primary and secondary. For our purposes primary and secondary care are the most relevant.[7] In the category of primary care are GPs, dental care, pharmaceuticals, maternity nursing

---

5   Maas & Mackenbach 1995: 261. Such comparisons are only of limited significance, since in some countries the state exercises direct influence over the total, for example because it pays for a great deal of the costs of health care or fixes the incomes of medical professionals.

6   Maas & Mackenbach 1995: 263.

7   Basic health care covers a wide variety of facilities, from school dentists to organizations occupied with labor conditions, whose activities are mainly preventive.

services, health-related social services and drug-addiction aid. Secondary facilities include hospitals and specialist care, nursing homes, psychiatric hospitals, old-age or residential homes, institutions for the mentally handicapped and foster homes and day-care facilities for the handicapped.

B   Institutions for health care and care of the elderly

Health-care institutions in the Netherlands derive historically from the activities of churches, later taken over by private organizations affiliated with the various 'pillars' of Dutch society. There were, and still are, non-denominational, Catholic, Protestant, Jewish and Humanist institutions. The recent history of Dutch health care is one of a changing relationship between government and these originally private institutions. The 'pillarization' of health care continued long after the state assumed responsibility for the financing and regulation of health care and some remains are to be found in the institutional organization of the health-care system. These can be quite important in connection with euthanasia, as we will see in chapter 5.4.2 when we examine the policies of hospitals and nursing-homes.

There are almost 750 health-care institutions that provide 24-hour nursing care in the Netherlands. Leaving aside institutions such as nursing homes for children and special institutions for the sensorily disabled, these include, in addition to hospitals and nursing homes, also mental hospitals (83 institutions with some 25,000 beds) and institutions for the mentally handicapped (139 institutions with some 35,000 beds).[8]

HOSPITALS

There were 149 hospitals with over 60,000 beds in 1995. There are 9 university hospitals in various parts of the country, 110 general hospitals providing various forms of specialist treatment and 30 specialized hospitals which limit their care to certain illnesses or sorts of patient.[9]

Originating largely in private and often charitable initiatives, almost all hospitals are still private, and all are non-profit organizations. Merger and cooperation between hospitals has been important during the last two decades with the number of general hospitals declining from 212 in 1963 to about 150 now. Since mergers often take place between two or more hospitals originally founded on different denominational principles, the 'pillarization' of hospital institutions has been declining.

---

8   *Vademecum Gezondheidsstatistiek 1996: 224.*
9   *Vademecum Gezondheidsstatistiek 1996: 224.*

Because hospitals are private institutions, they have a certain degree of freedom in determining their own policy with regard to euthanasia or other medical behavior that shortens life. However, most doctors who practise in a hospital are not employees of the hospital, and the degree of control a hospital has over doctors in private practice who have patients there is limited.

NURSING HOMES (*VERPLEEGHUIZEN*)

Nursing homes are institutions for the care and nursing of persons who no longer require hospital care but who cannot be taken care of at home, the costs being born by the public insurance scheme for exceptional medical expenses.

In 1991 there were 333 nursing homes in the Netherlands with 52,000 beds, 52% for somatic patients and 48% for psychogeriatric patients (most of them suffering from dementia). More than 90% of the persons admitted to nursing homes are over 65 years old. The average age of somatic patients is 79 and of psychogeriatric patients 83.[10] Of patients who die in a nursing home, somatic patients have spent on average 616 days there, psychogeriatric patients 1055.[11]

Like hospitals, nursing homes determine their own policy with regard to abstinence, euthanasia and related medical behavior that shortens life. Since the doctors who are responsible for patients in a nursing home are usually employed by the institution, nursing homes can generally exert far more control over life-shortening behavior than hospitals are able to do.

RESIDENTIAL HOMES (*VERZORGINGSHUIZEN*)

Admittance to a residential home (publically financed old-age homes and the like) is possible for (usually elderly) persons who because of a disability, lack of social contacts, or anxieties are not capable of living independently. Residents must, however, be able to carry out most daily tasks for themselves. They have a private home, with locked doors and a doorbell, three meals a day served at home or in the institution's restaurant, some social assistance and an alarm system. Residents pay a small income-related share of the costs of stay.

There are 1,485 residential homes in the Netherlands with about 135,000 beds. The average age of residents is 84; 80% are single, and three-quarters are women. The average length of stay is 4.5 years. Such an institution is the last home for most of its inhabitants:

---

10   Muller 1996: 11.
11   *Geriatrie Informatorium* J-4005: 17-18.

80% die in the institution, 15% are transferred to a nursing home, the remaining 5% are transferred to a hospital or elsewhere and die there.[12]

People who live in residential homes have their own personal GP (which means that in any given home a number of GPs have patients). The residents are free to organize their lives as they please, which in principle means that euthanasia or assistance with suicide is a matter between a resident and his GP, although a residential home with a strong religious orientation may find euthanasia so objectionable that it is difficult for a GP to carry it out there.

WHERE DO PEOPLE DIE?

Of the 2 milion persons over 65, 180,000 (9%) live in a residential home or a nursing home. The living situation of the rest does not differ much from that of the rest of the population. More than 80% live in an ordinary house. Some, however, move into special housing for the elderly, which comes in a variety of forms, often with some degree of common facilities. A third of this special housing is associated with a residential home or a community center.[13]

Only a rough estimate can be given of the place where people in the Netherlands die. It is assumed that more than 70% die in an institution, usually a hospital (40%), a nursing-home (15%) or a residential home (17%). About 26% are believed to die at home and 2% elsewhere.[14]

More is known about the place where persons 65 or older die. In 1995, 35% died in a hospital, 21% in a residential home, 18% in a nursing home and 26% at home or elsewhere. The change from 1970 is spectacular. In that year, 58% died outside a health-care institution and only 19% in a hospital. Most of the change took place before 1985, when 37% died in a hospital and 29% outside a health-care institution.[15]

C   Health-care professionals

The professionals involved in the care of dying patients, and the nature of their relationships with one another, vary widely from one setting to another.

---

12   Van Loveren-Huyben 1995: 11.
13   Timmermans 1997: 100-105.
14   Munnichs 1989: 10.
15   Timmermans 1997: 138.

In hospitals, apart from doctors and nurses, social and pastoral workers are usually involved, sometimes also a psychologist or psychiatrist, occasionally a physiotherapist or GP. Other specialists (e.g. anesthesiologists) are called in when needed. These various professionals tend to regard each other as a 'team' and to discuss and coordinate the various aspects of terminal care of a patient with each other; final decision-making responsibility rests, however, with the 'doctor responsible for treatment' (*behandelend arts:* attending physician).

In nursing homes, the principal professionals involved are nursing-home doctors and nurses, pastoral workers and physiotherapists. Here, too, the working relationship is conceived of as 'teamwork'; coordination of care is the responsibility of the nursing staff but ultimate responsibility for decisions concerning care is with the doctors. There is little contact with specialists (hospitals) or a patient's former GP.

In residential homes the principal professionals as far as terminal care is concerned are the home's nursing and service personnel and the inhabitants' own GPs. Coordination of care is the responsibility of the nursing home's own staff, medical treatment (including all contacts with specialists) is the responsibility of a patient's GP. Since there may be many GPs with patients in a given home, coordinating the activities of the various participants involved in the division of responsibility can be problematic and the communication of doctors with the home's staff is often considered by the latter quite inadequate.

In the case of patients who die at home, the primary professionals are the GP and the visiting nurse. Although they usually work closely together, visiting nurses often criticize GPs for excluding them from the decision-making on questions such as euthanasia. Physiotherapists, social workers and pastors are sometimes also involved, but often not in coordination with the GP, who 'just happens to come across them' when he visits the patient.[16]

DOCTORS

In 1995 there were about 28,000 doctors engaged in clinical practice (GPs, specialists and nursing-home doctors).[17] About 60% of all Dutch doctors are members of the Royal Dutch Medical Association (KNMG).[18] All practicing doctors are subject to medical disciplinary law.

---

16   Benjaminsen 1988: 22-40.
17   *Vademecum Gezondheidsstatistiek 1996:* 232.
18   See Dillmann 1996: 65.

GENERAL PRACTITIONERS (HUISARTSEN)

In 1995 there were about 7000 GPs in private practice, or about 2200 inhabitants per GP.[19] About half of all GPs are in solo-practice, 30% in duo-practice, 10% in group practice; about 5% work in a multi-disciplinary health center.[20] The proportion of partnerships, group practices and health centers is increasing rapidly. GPs who are in solo- or duo-practice always have more or less intensive contact with a number of other GPs in the immediate surroundings, with whom they form a 'substitution group' so that access to primary medical care is guaranteed for their patients 24 hours a day throughout the year regardless of an individual doctor's absence on weekends, vacations, illness, etc.

Dutch primary medical care has three major system characteristics: 'listing', 'gatekeeping', and 'family orientation'. 'Listing' means that in principle every Dutch inhabitant is registered with a GP. This guarantees patients continuity of care. Dutch GPs see three-quarters of their patients annually, averaging 4.5 contacts per patient per year. The 'gatekeeping' function refers to the fact that patients generally do not have direct access to specialists or hospital care but must be referred by their GP. The impact of gatekeeping is reflected in the low referral rate: 90% of all complaints are treated by GPs. The third characteristic, 'family orientation', refers to the fact that a Dutch GP generally serves as the personal physician for a patient's entire family. Moreover, GPs make many home visits: 17% of all contacts are visits to the patient's home.

Since the beginning of the 1990s, the relationships between GPs have become gradually more organized. In the past, apart from duo- or group practices (a recent phenomenon) the only formal contact between them was in 'substitution groups'. Recently, however, both the government and the National Association of GPs have been promoting a national organizational structure at the base of which are 'GP-groups' (in which several 'substitution groups' participate). These are responsible for the organization of substitution, continuing education, contacts with other professionals, etc.; they are also supposed to arrange for intercollegial quality control.[21] Nevertheless, GPs remain highly individualistic, and they have considerable freedom in conducting their practice. Formal control is limited, and implementation of what control there is, is weak.

GPs are the responsible doctor in about 43% of all deaths, including those of people who die at home and those of persons in residential homes.[22]

---

19   *Vademecum Gezondheidsstatistiek 1996*: 232.

20   *Vademecum Gezondheidsstatistiek 1996*: 240.

21   In J. Zaritsky's film *An Appointment with Death* (see chapter 1, note 2), there is a scene in which a GP discusses a request for assistance with suicide with his colleagues in such a 'GP-group'.

22   Compare Van der Maas et al. (1996: 1701): a GP is the responsible doctor in the case of about 40% of all deaths.

SPECIALISTS

In 1995 there were more than 13,000 specialists.[23] About three-quarters of all specialists are in private practice; 90% are connected with intramural institutions.[24] Because few of them are salaried employees, the degree of control that the intramural institutions where they work can exercise over the way they practice is limited. In particular, specialists have considerable room for policy discretion concerning terminal care, and institutional rules on the subject either respect this discretion or are not really effective (see chapter 5.4.2).

Specialists are the responsible doctor in about 40% of all deaths.

NURSING-HOME DOCTORS

'Nursing-home doctor' is a medical specialty. In 1995 there were about 800 specialized nursing-home doctors.[25] (There are, however, other doctors than nursing-home specialists who treat patients in nursing homes.)

More than most GPs and many other specialists, nursing-home doctors function as members of a treatment team, usually as its head. Most of them are employed by the institutions where they work. In particular with regard to euthanasia and other medical treatment that shortens life, their treatment discretion is more limited than that of GPs or specialists who work in hospitals.

Nursing-home doctors are the responsible doctor in about 15% of all deaths.

NURSES

In 1993 there were about 325,000 nurses working in the Netherlands. Almost 66,000 nurses work in hospitals, more than 47,000 in nursing homes and more than 54,000 in residential homes.

Nurses are also active in 'home care', a collection of support services provided partly by professionals, partly by volunteers, and intended to enable people to remain at home as long as possible. Home-nursing organizations offer a package of services, comprising nursing, support, and counselling related to illness, recuperation, disability, old age and death. About 5% of the Dutch population receive nursing care or other help at home. The elderly (70 years of age and over) are the largest group of home-nursing recipients.

---

23   *Vademecum Gezondheidsstatistiek 1996*: 232.
24   Maas & Mackenbach 1995: 256.
25   *Vademecum Gezondheidsstatistiek 1996*: 232.

Most of the costs of home-nursing care are born by the public insurance scheme for exceptional medical costs, the rest by individuals.

The nursing profession has a long tradition of professional organization. As in many areas of Dutch society, 'pillarization' plays an important role, and nurses are still largely organized along religious lines. Nurses' organizations are increasingly concerned to promote professionalization, concentrating on the following three areas: autonomy in professional practice, a voice in policy-making processes and organization of the professional group. However, in actual practice autonomy and professional responsibility are limited. The content and pace of work are largely determined by third parties. In the case of euthanasia and other life-shortening behavior, the role of nurses remains marginal.

Nurses are subject to medical disciplinary law.

PHARMACISTS

When a doctor prescribes or proposes to administer a controlled drug (which includes all drugs used as euthanatica), the drug must be supplied by a pharmacist (*apotheker*). Pharmacists are expected not to supply blindly whatever the doctor orders but to exercise some marginal control. Thus, for example, pharmacists are supposed to make sure that the proper instructions for use, warnings about side-effects, etc. are given to the patient, and to keep tabs on the various drugs prescribed for a patient (sometimes by different doctors) to ensure that the combinations are pharmacologically responsible.

There are 1500 self-employed pharmacists in pharmacies directly accessible to the public. In addition, there are some 700 pharmacists employed by the self-employed pharmacists, and another 300 who are responsible for the pharmacies of hospitals. Dutch pharmacists are organized in the Royal Dutch Society for the Advancement of Pharmacy (KNMP) and are subject to medical disciplinary law.

About 600 GPs, especially those in areas where no pharmacy is available, function as their own pharmacist.[26]

CORONERS

The Law on the Disposal of Corpses requires, before burial or cremation can take place, that a doctor attest that a person's death was due to a natural cause. If the patient's own doctor cannot do this, he must report this fact to the municipal coroner, who examines the body and decides himself whether the death was a natural one; if not, he must report

---

26   *Vademecum Gezondheidsstatistiek 1996*: 232.

the case to the local prosecutor (see further chapter 3.2). Every municipality in the Netherlands has at least one coroner. Persons authorized to practise medicine are eligible for appointment and in small municipalities a local GP in private practice is usually appointed, with several colleagues as his deputies. In larger municipalities, coroners are usually doctors in the municipal health service.

The fact that the coroner himself is a doctor can give rise to problems in connection, for example, with the reporting procedure for euthanasia. On the one hand, the coroner is required to satisfy himself of the cause of death and to provide the prosecutorial authorities with all information about the case that bears on a possible criminal prosecution. On the other hand, as a doctor he is in principle bound by the duty of confidentiality that covers the practice of medicine. When the coroner is a doctor in private practice, the independence of his judgment can be problematic (see chapter 5.3.5). There is a general consensus among those responsible for medical policy that in the future coroners should be public employees.

THE MEDICAL INSPECTORATE AND MEDICAL DISCIPLINARY LAW

The Medical Inspectorate is responsible for the enforcement of legal provisions relating to public health and the health-care system and for giving advice and information to the Minister of Health. Among other things, the Inspectors are authorized to initiate medical disciplinary proceedings.

All doctors in the Netherlands who are authorized to practice medicine, as well as other professionals involved in the health-care system (including nurses and pharmacists) are, as we have seen, subject to medical disciplinary law.[27] The primary purpose of this law is

---

27   The formulation here of the coverage of medical disciplinary law and the primary disciplinary norm is based on a new law (Law on Professions Concerned with Individual Medical Care, *Staatsblad* 1993 no. 655) that only becomes formally effective on 1 December 1997. The old law was limited to doctors, pharmacists, dentists, and midwives, and the disciplinary norm was formulated in terms of 'undermining public confidence in the profession', engaging in negligence which causes great harm to a patient, and evidencing gross incompetence.
In addition to medical disciplinary law, both civil law (malpractice and breach of contract) and criminal law bear on the behavior of medical practitioners. It is possible that for a single incident, a doctor is liable under two or even three of these bodies of law. There are agreements between the Medical Inspectorate and the prosecutorial officials concerning the division of responsibility between them. In euthanasia and related cases this means in practice that a disciplinary proceeding is held in abeyance until possible criminal proceedings are terminated. If the doctor is not prosecuted, or after his acquittal or conviction, the Inspectorate may decide to pursue disciplinary proceedings. This in fact happened in the *Chabot* case (see appendix II-2).

to guarantee the quality of medical care. Disciplinary measures can be imposed for actions or omissions that are inconsistent with the care to which others are entitled or with the demands of good medical practice. Complaints can be lodged by an Inspector, by the governing body of the institution in which the professional works, or by a person directly affected by the behavior in question. The complaint is judged in the first instance by one of the five regional Medical Disciplinary Tribunals, and appeals are to the Central Medical Disciplinary Tribunal.[28] The following measures can be imposed: a warning; a reprimand; a fine of up to ƒ10,000; suspension from practice for at most one year; revocation in whole or in part of the authority to practice.[29]

---

28 Until the new law mentioned in note 27, some appeals were to a Court of Appeals and thence to the Supreme Court.

29 See on Dutch medical disciplinary law and its functioning: Verkruisen 1993.

2   Legal Change 1945-1997[1]

Recent developments in the Netherlands regarding the legality of euthanasia and other medical behavior that shortens life are extraordinarily interesting. The subject is fundamental and it has profound existential, philosophical, and political implications. But the process itself is fascinating, too, partly because it has been so complex and partly because it has been so open. The legal norms that currently seem to be valid have not emerged from legislation nor in any simple way from judicial decisions, but from interaction between the medical profession (in particular the Medical Association), interest groups (in particular the Association for Voluntary Euthanasia), the Government, Parliament, the Health Council, the State Commission on Euthanasia, the Remmelink Commission (appointed to carry out empirical research concerning euthanasia and related practices), several groups of empirical researchers and other academic participants in the public discussion, the judiciary, the prosecutorial authorities, the medical disciplinary tribunals, the Medical Inspectorate, several political parties, a variety of social and religious organizations, the media and 'the public'.

The process of change is described in this chapter in four phases.[2] In the first period (1945-1970), euthanasia is not yet a subject of public discussion. We describe the factors that played a role in preparing the ground for the later public debate. In the second phase (1970-1982) the public becomes aware of the fact that doctors sometimes give their patients 'support in the dying process', in the sense that they either cease trying to prolong life or give death a helping hand. The idea of 'euthanasia' enters the public discussion, but it is used to refer to a variety of different sorts of behavior whose legality remains unclear to the participants in the discussion. The third phase (1982-1986) sees a fundamental legal breakthrough on two fronts. In the first place, it becomes clear that only active termination of life at the explicit request of the person concerned constitutes 'euthanasia' in the Dutch sense and that a variety of other sorts of medical behavior that shortens life fall within the scope of 'normal medical practice' and are legally unproblematic. In the second place, 'euthanasia' itself becomes generally accepted if performed

---

1   Translation by M. Griffiths.

2   Needless to say we have had to be selective in choosing what to discuss. Although this historical overview deals only with broad outlines, our aim has been to treat all the important legal cases and publications that influenced the definition and the legal treatment of euthanasia and other medical behavior that shortens life, including the formulation of the 'requirements of careful practice'.

under circumstances carefully defined both by the courts and the Medical Association. The fourth phase (1986-1997) is one in which (unsuccessful) efforts are made to codify the legal change that has taken place. Despite the failure of legislative efforts, this phase does see consolidation of the legal change, application of the new legal insights to some related problems and two major national studies of actual practice. It also sees a shift in the public discussion from the question of legitimacy to that of effective regulation.

2.1   1945-1970: How room for public debate became available

INTRODUCTION

On 11 March 1952 a doctor from Eindhoven stood trial for killing his brother, who had been suffering from advanced tuberculosis. During the weeks preceding his death the sick man had on several occasions strongly urged his brother to put an end to his misery. Eventually the doctor agreed. He told the District Court that "it was impossible for him, and he could not be expected, to ignore the claims of his conscience, which compelled him to comply with the explicit wish of his brother." He gave his brother Codinovo tablets and injected him with morphine, which led to the brother's death.

The District Court found the doctor guilty of killing on request (article 293 of the Criminal Code). Although considerations of general prevention suggested a jail sentence, the court decided to sentence the doctor to one year probation "because, as far as the Court is aware, this is the first time that a case of euthanasia has been subject to the ruling of a Dutch judge."[3] The case did not cause much commotion. The newspapers confined themselves to sober reports and the journal of the Medical Association noted but did not comment on the case.[4]

By the end of the 1960s this lack of interest had vanished entirely. A leading psychiatrist/neurologist published a book in which he sharply criticized doctors who prolong the lives of their patients at all cost. Support in the dying process in different forms was

---

3   *Nederlandse Jurisprudentie* 1952, no. 275. Before 1952 there had been three cases in which 'killing on request' was of some importance. In 1908 a man had been convicted for attempted murder of his girl-friend although he claimed she requested him to do so. In 1910 a man shot his girl-friend at her request, he said, but he was convicted for murder (Herbergs 1984: 151). In 1944 the Supreme Court nullified the ruling of the Court of Appeals, Amsterdam in a case of a man who strangled his girl-friend. In the opinion of the Supreme Court the Court of Appeals had not paid sufficient attention to the explicit request of the woman involved (*Nederlandse Jurisprudentie* 1944, no. 314).

4   *Medisch Contact* 7: 288 (1952).

the subject of radio programs and TV shows, and it was discussed in Parliament. In short, passive and active termination of life had become a topic of medical, ethical, legal, and public debate. The question to be addressed in this section is what accounts for the change.

Support in the dying process was not the only topic pitting traditional views against more modern, in particular individualistic and secular, ideas that got onto the public agenda in this period. Starting in the 1950s, sexual morality, for instance, was the subject of a great deal of public discussion. Legislation was enacted legalizing the free sale of contraceptives (1970), repealing the crime of adultery (1971), and repealing a restrictive provision on homosexuality (1971). In the same period abortion was the subject of extensive public discussion. Because the debate on the legalization of abortion shows great similarities with the later debate on euthanasia, we discuss it here in some detail.[5]

THE LEGALIZATION OF ABORTION

Articles 295 through 298 and article 251b of the Criminal Code made abortion a crime. However, in the Parliamentary debates on these articles,[6] the responsible Ministers had stated explicitly that a doctor who performs an abortion on medical grounds and does so in a medically sound fashion is not covered by their provisions.

During the 1960s social acceptance of abortion increased. In 1966 Enschedé, a prominent criminal law scholar (later a member of the Supreme Court), published a very influential article. Enschedé argued on the basis of the legislative history that a doctor who terminates a pregnancy on the basis of a medical indication falls within an implicit 'medical exception'[7] to the abortion prohibition and is not guilty of a criminal offence. He argued further that the definition of 'medical indication' is subject to change, and that in 1966 non-medical grounds could be included within its scope.[8] This view in effect decriminalizes abortion, so long as it is carried out in a medically responsible way.

Enschedé's views were widely shared. In 1969 a parliamentary debate took place on whether or not the legislation on abortion needed to be adjusted to the changed social reality. The Government proposed setting up a commission to study the issue. The Labor Party (PvdA) was not willing to await the conclusions of this study and submitted a bill

---

5   The following discussion is based on Ketting 1978; De Bruijn 1979; Outshoorn 1986.
6   The debates mentioned are those on the introduction of the new Criminal Code between 1879 and 1881 (articles 295 through 298) and on legislation of 1910 by which article 251b of the Criminal Code was amended in order to amplify the ban on abortion.
7   See further on the idea of the 'medical exception': chapter 3.1.1.
8   Enschedé 1966.

to legalize abortion. In the meantime a sort of legal vacuum had come about, in which abortion was still formally illegal but freedom of abortion was a fact. To satisfy the demand for abortion, special abortion clinics were set up.

In 1971 the Medical Association, which in 1969 had still been rather opposed to abortion, published new guidelines. These held that "the doctor's duty to give medical assistance can entail the decision to perform an abortion when he is asked to assist in an unwanted pregnancy."[9] The Association's change of direction, treating abortion on non-medical grounds as a form of 'normal medical practice' falling within the 'medical exception', meant that for practical purposes enforcement of the ban on abortion was no longer feasible.[10] After 1971, therefore, only very exceptional cases have been prosecuted, for example when abortion is performed by a non-doctor or there are special circumstances, such as a medical complication or death. There have been no convictions based on article 251b – the provision normally used – since 1974.[11] Although abortion had thus in practice been decriminalized by the early 1970s, it took five legislative proposals and a number of political crises before the legal change was finally ratified in legislation in 1982.

CHANGES IN MEDICAL PRACTICE IN THE 1960S

The general context of changing societal values, evidenced particularly in developments concerning abortion, is not the only explanation for the fact that in the early 1970s euthanasia became a topic of public debate. Developments in medical technology were also important. These developments led to questions of a medical and ethical nature fundamentally different from any that had ever been asked before. In effect, doctors had come to have the means to postpone death even when recovery is impossible. But prolonging life does not always go hand in hand with making it more bearable. Doctors found themselves increasingly confronted with the question whether they should do everything within their ability to preserve life. In medical journals this question was initially asked with regard to resuscitation: Should someone who is suffering severely and has no prospect of recovery be kept alive? Doubts concerning an unconditional 'duty to preserve life' became more and more insistent. If the answer to the duty-question is 'no', if a doctor therefore may sometimes decide not to engage in treatment that would prolong the patient's life because it would not be in the patient's interest to do so, the question soon arises whether there is difference in principle between acting and refraining from action.

9   KNMG 1971: 1025.
10   The Association's acceptance of abortion elicited objections from a few doctors. Their opinion was that the Board of the Association could not speak for all doctors and that terminating a life violates a doctor's fundamental duty. In 1973 some of these doctors founded the Dutch Association of Physicians (NAV), a 'pro-life' organization.
11   De Bruijn 1979: 239.

Apart from the changes that doctors were faced with due to developments in medical technology, the 1960s also brought about changes in views concerning the doctor-patient relationship, including the general idea of 'informed consent' and the specific question whether a dying patient should be told the truth about his condition. Because of the role of pastors, the debate on 'truth at the deathbed' was mainly conducted in confessional medical journals. Pastors were sometimes more inclined than doctors to tell a patient the truth about his condition. The pastor's role as a spiritual guide, and the Roman Catholic ritual of 'Extreme Unction', could make openness concerning the situation necessary. This openness clashed with the widespread medical opinion at the time that most people cannot accept the truth regarding their own death, and that to be open with them would cause them to lose the confidence needed to keep up the struggle for life.

THE CASE OF MIA VERSLUIS: BEFORE TERMINATING LIFE-SUPPORT A DOCTOR MUST CONSULT OTHER DOCTORS AND INFORM THE PATIENT'S FAMILY

In March of 1967 the Dutch were for the first time publicly confronted with the situation of a patient in a long and irreversible coma. The question whether such a patient should be thought of as dead or alive was widely discussed in the media. Many commentators tried to imagine whether they would want their own treatment to be continued in such a case or if they would prefer having an end put to their life.

The 21-year-old patient's name was Mia Versluis. She had had an operation under complete anesthesia on 14 April 1966 for excessive growth of the bone on her heels. During the course of the operation she probably had had a cardiac arrest, after which she was resuscitated. After the operation was over, Mia Versluis was in coma, and it appeared that she had suffered severe brain damage. Since she required artificial respiration, a breathing tube was inserted in her windpipe.[12]

Initially, the anesthetist had been optimistic about the possibility of recovery. By September 1966, however, he had lost all hope and, according to the parents of Mia Versluis, proposed to remove the tube, which was expected to lead to her death. To the outraged father this was a proposal to perform what he called 'euthanasia'. He filed a complaint with the Medical Disciplinary Tribunal against the anesthetist, who, in the father's opinion, had made mistakes during the course of the operation.[13] In the final judgment in the case the Court of Appeals, Amsterdam,[14] held that when termination of life-support is

---

12   *Nederlandse Staatscourant*, 1969 no. 55: 3-8.

13   Versluis 1970: 29-38.

14   The case had been referred to this Court of Appeals by the Supreme Court after it had ruled on the case. None of the earlier rulings was ever published.

considered, other colleagues must first be consulted on the matter, and the situation must be discussed with the family. The doctor was found guilty of behavior that undermines confidence in the medical profession. He was fined 1000 guilders and the Court of Appeals ordered that the ruling be made public in the *Official Gazette*.[15]

THE FORMULATION OF NEW IDEAS ON THE DOCTOR-PATIENT RELATIONSHIP

In 1969 the issues involved in the general debate on resuscitation and in the case of Mia Versluis in particular were formulated in an unusually provocative way by J.H. van den Berg, a psychiatrist/neurologist.[16] Van den Berg divides the history of medical technology into three periods: one of 'medical powerlessness', during which doctors had few options; one of transition; and one of 'medico-technical power'. This last period began, according to Van den Berg, in 1965. Van den Berg's argument is that medical ethics must adjust to such changes in medical technology.

> The ethical motto from the time of medical powerlessness ran thus: 'It is the doctor's duty to preserve, spare and prolong human life wherever and whenever he can.' ... The new technical power makes a new code of ethics unavoidable. This is the motto of the new ethical code: 'It is the doctor's duty to preserve, spare, and prolong human life whenever doing so has any sense.'[17]

According to Van den Berg, a doctor may passively or actively shorten life that is no longer 'meaningful'.

Van den Berg's book responded to widely felt concerns and was reprinted twenty-one times within seven years and endlessly discussed in magazines and other media. The general opinion was that Van den Berg had seriously confronted a problem of major importance. But many reviewers could not agree with the legitimacy of active termination of life. Many also found defining 'meaningful life' problematic.

Van den Berg was not the only person who expressed views in the late 1960s on the question whether or not shortening of life should be permissible. Almost simultaneously books were published by the Catholic ethicist Sporken and the lawyer Van Till. The first, dealing with the permissibility of shortening a patient's dying process, argued that

---

15   *Nederlandse Staatscourant* 1969 no. 55: 7. These are relatively heavy sanctions in Dutch medical disciplinary law (see Verkruisen 1993). Mia Versluis died on 10 November 1971 in another hospital without ever having regained consciousness.

16   An English translation of Van den Berg's book was published in 1978.

17   Van den Berg 1978: 63. This and the following quotation from Van den Berg are taken from the English translation of his book.

"active intervention leading to the termination of life" and "non-intervention when a life-threatening complication occurs" are ethically speaking not significantly different from one another. Both can be defended from a moral standpoint.[18] Van Till argued that medical actions necessary to assure the humane end of a person's life can be justified from a medical-ethical and from a legal point of view.[19]

A second issue raised by Van den Berg and by many others concerns the rights of the patient. The notion that doctors know best what is good for their patients was considered self-evident until the end of the 1950s. In the 1960s this idea was no longer unquestioned, and the balance of power between doctor and patient was increasingly a public issue. Van den Berg entitled his book *Medical Power and Medical Ethics* and ended with these words:

> My last word is for the patient himself, for in these pages I have been writing for him. With him lies the decision of in what way he is sick: knowing or not knowing. With him lies the decision of how he wants to die, nobly or unworthily. He must have the courage to say what he wants. If he perseveres he will find the doctor on his side. Yes, the doctor is for the patient and for nobody and nothing else.[20]

TO SUM UP

Two kinds of change played an important role in getting euthanasia onto the agenda for public debate: a cultural change and a change in medical technology. The cultural change can be characterized with the words secularization, individualization, and democratization. The medical-technological change greatly increased the doctor's ability to postpone death and had as a consequence that the medical imperatives 'do whatever is possible' and 'relieve suffering' no longer always went hand in hand. The ethical questions to which this technological development gave rise on the one hand, and the greater cultural emphasis on personal autonomy on the other hand, helped create the space on the public agenda within which debate on the patient's role in determining the time and manner of his death could take place.

---

18   Sporken 1969: 221-222.
19   Van Till 1970: 105.
20   Van den Berg 1978: 64-66.

2.2   1970-1982: The early stages of public debate

INTRODUCTION

Around 1970 questions concerning the sense and the legitimacy of prolonging life and the permissibility of terminating it became the subject of public debate in the Netherlands. In addition to the extensive readership of Van den Berg's book, many people watched TV shows or listened to radio programs about dying and being told the truth at one's deathbed. Symposia were organized, and 'support in the dying process' became a familiar concept.[21] The term 'euthanasia' was also heard, and starting in 1972, various organizations began ventilating their opinions on the matter. Opinion polls showed that a growing proportion of the population thought that life may sometimes (actively) be terminated and that 'euthanasia' should be legal.[22]

The term 'euthanasia' was initially used to describe a large and varied range of behavior. No consensus existed on which actions were covered by the term and which were not. This lack of conceptual consensus accounted at least in part for differences of opinion regarding the permissibility of 'euthanasia', since such opinions often concerned quite different sorts of behavior. During the period 1970-1982 a process of conceptual clarification took place, dividing behavior that generally came to be characterized as 'euthanasia' from other behavior, most of which came to be regarded as 'normal medical practice'. The process of formulating the requirements for permissible euthanasia also got under way.

THE FIRST ADVISORY REPORTS ON EUTHANASIA

Medical Power and Medical Ethics inspired a member of Parliament to propose setting up a commission to study the issues Van den Berg had raised. This proposal led the Government to request advice from the Health Council, which referred the matter to its Committee on Medical Ethics.

Before the Health Council could report, the General Synod of the Dutch Reformed Church adopted a report which concluded that 'passive euthanasia' – abstaining from life-prolonging measures for medical reasons – can be legitimate. The report also stated that if a competent patient, at the beginning of the dying process requests the doctor to stop further treatment, this wish should be respected.[23]

---

21   Ten Kroode 1982.
22   See chapter 5.1 for a summary of the results of opinion polls.
23   Generale Synode 1972.

The Committee on Medical Ethics of the Health Council did not deal with the whole issue of medical power and medical ethics but limited itself to the question of euthanasia because this topic "appears to be the most urgent". After some discussion it defined euthanasia as

> acting with the deliberate intention to shorten a patient's life or refraining from action with the deliberate intention not to prolong a patient's life, whenever this is in the patient's best interest and the patient's condition is incurable.[24]

The Committee distinguished between voluntary and non-voluntary, and between passive and active euthanasia. According to the Committee, 'voluntary euthanasia' entails the express consent of a competent patient. The Committee defined 'passive euthanasia' as "euthanasia that is performed by ceasing or not initiating life-prolonging measures and treatment" and 'active euthanasia' as "euthanasia that is performed by the use of life-shortening measures and treatment".[25] In the Committee's judgment 'active euthanasia' should not be permissible. However, it did address a few remarks to the situation of a conflict of duties. A doctor who feels he has an obligation to accede to the patient's request to use measures that will terminate the patient's life must be prepared to account for his behavior in the context of a criminal prosecution.

With regard to 'passive euthanasia' the Committee took the view that under certain circumstances a doctor can refrain from employing life-prolonging measures. The Committee had two specific situations in mind: 'voluntary passive euthanasia', when it is the patient who refuses treatment, and 'non-voluntary passive euthanasia', when the doctor considers it his medical-ethical duty to refrain from further treatment.

The Committee did not find it necessary or desirable that the law concerning euthanasia be amended.[26]

THE *POSTMA* CASE AND OTHER CASES INVOLVING VIOLATION OF ARTICLES 293 AND 294

The Committee on Medical Ethics of the Health Council had not yet completed its report when, on 27 November 1972, articles appeared in several Dutch newspapers reporting on the preliminary hearing in a criminal prosecution for euthanasia. It

---

24 Gezondheidsraad 1972: 12.

25 Gezondheidsraad 1972: 13.

26 In 1975 the Committee on Medical Ethics produced a second report, dealing with the problem of severely defective newborn babies. Again the Committee advised against amending articles 293 and 294 of the Criminal Code, but recorded its conviction that this does not imply that 'active euthanasia', in cases in which 'passive euthanasia' would be indicated, can never be justified.

appeared that Ms. Postma, a doctor, had terminated her mother's life with an injection of morphine. Ms. Postma had done this in the presence of her husband, also a doctor. The director of the nursing home where Ms. Postma's mother lived brought the matter to the attention of the Medical Inspectorate, which in turn alerted the prosecutorial authorities.

Ms. Postma's mother, a widow of 78, had been in a nursing home since a cerebral hemorrhage had left her paralyzed on one side a few months earlier. On several occasions she had asked her daughter to end her life, and she had also spoken of not wanting to live any more to her other daughter and to the nursing home's staff.

On 7 February 1973 Ms. Postma stood trial in Leeuwarden for 'killing on request' (article 293 of the Criminal Code). The Medical Inspector testified that the average doctor in the Netherlands no longer considered it necessary to prolong a patient's life endlessly. In his opinion it had become widely accepted in medical circles that when a patient is given pain relief the risk of the patient dying sooner because of this treatment can, under certain conditions, be accepted. The conditions mentioned by the Inspector were:
- the patient is incurably ill;
- he finds his suffering mentally or physically unbearable;
- he has expressed the wish to die;
- he is medically speaking in the terminal phase of his illness;
- the person who accedes to the request is a doctor, preferably the doctor responsible for treatment.[27]

The District Court pronounced sentence on 21 February 1973. It largely agreed with the Inspector's opinion. The only condition it did not accept was that the patient must be in the terminal phase of his illness.[28] The Court ruled that even though the remaining conditions had been met, it was wrong of Ms. Postma to have used an injection that was immediately lethal.[29] In the Court's opinion this was not a reasonable means to achieve Ms. Postma's goal of putting an end to her mother's suffering. Ms. Postma was given a conditional jail sentence of one week with one year probation.

---

27   *Nederlandse Jurisprudentie* 1973, no. 183: 558.

28   The Court rejected this condition because it knew of the existence "of many cases of incurable illness or accident-caused disability, combined with serious physical and/or mental suffering, where the patient is otherwise healthy and can continue living in this state for years. It is not the court's view that such suffering should be denied the relief described by the expert witness" (*Nederlandse Jurisprudentie* 1973, no. 183: 560).

29   Although it does not specifically mention the point, the ruling of the Court seems to be based on the difference between 'indirect euthanasia' (which is what the Medical Inspector had in mind) and 'direct euthanasia' (what Ms. Postma actually did).

The *Postma* case attracted a great deal of attention. It was covered extensively in the regular press. The journal of the Medical Association, *Medisch Contact*, which had ignored the earlier case of euthanasia in 1952, now devoted space to the *Postma* trial and to a general discussion about euthanasia. The Medical Association's Executive Board adopted a tentative policy position on the issues raised by the *Postma* case and by the Health Council's report. The Executive Board's position was generally the same as that of the Health Council.[30]

Aside from heightened media attention to euthanasia, opponents and advocates of the liberalization of euthanasia were starting to organize themselves. Advocates focussed mainly on societal acceptance of euthanasia. The largest organization and the only one that still exists was founded in 1973: the Dutch Association for Voluntary Euthanasia (NVVE). The Association's goal is to work toward societal acceptance of voluntary euthanasia and its legalization. The Association emphasizes the importance of the voluntary character of euthanasia. One of its most important tasks is the formulation and distribution of 'euthanasia statements' (advance directives) in which a person declares that, should an illness or accident cause such physical or mental damage that recuperation to a reasonable and dignified standard of life is impossible, he or she refuses medical treatment and wishes to have euthanasia performed.

Opponents organized themselves in associations such as the Dutch Association of Physicians and the Dutch Association of Patients. Aside from these 'pro-life' organizations there were a number of religious groups, in particular the strict Calvinist churches and the Roman Catholic Church, that opposed legalization of euthanasia. Although a few books and articles were published arguing against legalization of euthanasia, the opponents hardly ever attracted much sustained public attention.

The *Postma* case was the best known prosecution in this period of a person who killed another person at the latter's request, but it was not the only one. There were at least three other prosecutions for violations of article 293 or 294.[31] In 1969 a man strangled his incurably ill wife to death at her request. He was sentenced to seven months in jail, with a deduction of half a year for the time he had been held in pre-trial custody, and the remaining month subject to probation. In 1978 a foster son was prosecuted for strangling his stepmother to death after she had attempted to commit suicide several times without success. He was given a jail sentence of one and a half years. In 1980 the husband of a psychiatric patient who did not want to be institutionalized again was tried for having built a device that enabled her to take her own life. On appeal he was sentenced to six months in jail.

---

30   KNMG 1973.
31   Information from Herbergs 1984 and Enthoven 1988.

In none of these three cases was there any doubt that the defendant acted at the request of the person killed or that his intentions had been honest. However, in the last two cases the courts specifically ruled that it had been wrong not to call on the assistance of a doctor. The difference between these three cases and those of the Eindhoven doctor in 1952 and the *Postma* case is that the defendants in the latter cases were doctors and had access to 'gentle means'; presumably as a consequence they were punished significantly less severely.

THE REPORT OF THE MEDICAL ASSOCIATION OF 1975

In 1975 a working group of the Medical Association issued a new report on euthanasia.[32] The working group's definition is: acts or omissions intended to cause a patient's death, in his interest. The working group concluded that euthanasia in this sense can only be considered when it is voluntarily requested by the patient and there is no hope of recovery. The doctor responsible for treatment should discuss the matter with a colleague, but he must decide for himself whether and how to perform euthanasia. In most cases passive euthanasia will be the appropriate way of honoring the patient's request, and the working group considers it legitimate. But, according to the working group, "under very exceptional circumstances it can be necessary purposely to administer palliative treatment in a dosage that is too high".[33] Such active euthanasia is only acceptable in the rare situation where passive euthanasia would be permissible, but waiting passively would result in suffering that cannot be relieved in any other way. In the opinion of the working group, there is no room in the doctor-patient relationship for assistance with suicide. It also warned against the Medical Association taking an official opinion on euthanasia, "because on this subject there are as many opinions as there are doctors".[34]

A CASE OF 'INDIRECT EUTHANASIA'

In the same period a decision of the Medical Disciplinary Tribunal of Amsterdam received public attention. The doctor's behavior was labeled 'euthanasia' by the media. The case concerned a woman who had cancer and had been hospitalized because it was no longer possible to take care of her at home. The woman was increasingly short of breath and in danger of suffocating due to blockage of her tracheo-stoma. In order to avoid suffocation the blockages had to be removed many times a day. This had gone on for a long time and made it impossible for the woman to sleep normally. The doctor against whom disciplinary charges were pressed had spoken with the woman on the day she was admitted to the hospital. From that conversation it had become clear that she

---

32   KNMG 1975.

33   KNMG 1975: 10.

34   KNMG 1975: 15.

was well aware of her fatal condition. Later, the doctor had discussed the use of sleep-inducing drugs with the woman and her daughters. In the course of those discussions, explicit attention had been given to the fact that she might never awaken, since she would not notice if she began to suffocate. The woman insisted that the drugs be administered. The doctor did so. The woman fell asleep and died.

The woman's husband had, partly at the woman's own request, never been involved in the decision-making. He decided to press disciplinary charges against the doctor for having administered the drugs and for having failed to discuss the matter with him. The Medical Disciplinary Tribunal ruled that the doctor's behavior had not been incorrect, and that he was not to blame for not consulting the husband since this had been at the patient's request. This ruling was confirmed on appeal by the Central Medical Disciplinary Tribunal.[35]

THE POSITIONS TAKEN BY VARIOUS ORGANIZATIONS

The period 1970-1982 saw, in addition to some early criminal and medical disciplinary cases, the publication by various associations and political parties of their positions on euthanasia. The Humanist Society's Executive Board argued that the law should allow room for doctors to give support in the dying process in accordance with medical professional standards.[36] The right-of-center liberal party VVD took the position that both passive and active euthanasia at the patient's explicit and well-considered request should in principle be permissible, but it thought that the time was not yet ripe for amending article 293.[37] A commission of the three major Christian Democratic parties (united as CDA in 1981) deemed active euthanasia unacceptable but recognized that exceptional circumstances exist in which a doctor may feel obliged to perform it.[38]

In 1978 the NVVE's Committee on Legislation also issued a report. The Committee distinguished between passive and active, voluntary and non-voluntary euthanasia (categories recognized by the Health Council) as well as between direct and indirect euthanasia. With regard to this last distinction, it made the following remarks:

> Active euthanasia requires intentional behavior by a doctor that, whether indirectly or directly, leads to an earlier death of the patient. The distinction between active indirect and active direct euthanasia concerns the intended goal of the doctor's actions. The primary goal of indirect euthanasia is relief of the patient's suffering....

---

35   *Tijdschrift voor Gezondheidsrecht* 1978, no. 52.
36   Hoofdbestuur Humanistisch Verbond 1976.
37   Volkspartij voor Vrijheid en Democratie 1981.
38   Schroten 1979.

> The primary goal of direct euthanasia is the termination of the patient's life, in cases where this is the only way in which the doctor can put an end to his patient's suffering.[39]

As far as the permissibility of euthanasia goes, the NVVE's Committee was of the opinion that both "passive and active indirect [i.e., pain relief] voluntary euthanasia are, under certain circumstances, as a matter of actual practice and as an ethical matter quite generally accepted".[40] The Committee considered direct, active euthanasia by a doctor permissible when three conditions have been met: a fully-informed patient must have made it clear in a voluntary, well-considered, and unequivocal request that he wishes euthanasia; the patient's condition must be in the terminal phase; and the euthanasia should be performed by the doctor responsible for treatment. The Committee argued that under these circumstances direct, active euthanasia is not illegal because "voluntary euthanasia under certain circumstances is to be considered normal medical practice".[41] The Committee proposed to add to article 293 of the Criminal Code a provision that the legal doctrine of 'absence of substantial violation of the law' is applicable in such a case.

DOCTORS AND EUTHANASIA

Although the general opinion was that doctors are most qualified to perform euthanasia, doctors often did not consider themselves adequately prepared to do so. In a letter to the editor of *Medisch Contact* in 1973, for example, a doctor asked for information about the most appropriate drugs to use. Spreeuwenberg concluded from his research among GPs that those who were prepared to perform euthanasia were finding their way through "trial and error".[42] At that time the only existing source of information was Admiraal, an anesthetist who described his experiences with certain euthanatica in a chapter of a book on euthanasia[43] and in a brochure for doctors published in 1980. (See section 2.3.1 for Admiraal's trial in 1985.)

---

39 NVVE 1978: 12. The report assumes that the behavior at issue is that of the doctor responsible for treatment, or someone acting under his direct responsibility. The preference for the doctor responsible for treatment is due to the fact that only he is capable of judging whether or not the patient's condition is curable and whether or not it is in its terminal phase (NVVE 1978: 21). But the authors of the report explicitly reject the implication that euthanasia performed by someone other than the doctor responsible for treatment is impermissible under all circumstance (NVVE 1978: 6).

40 NVVE 1978: 13.

41 NVVE 1978: 7-8.

42 Spreeuwenberg 1981: 259.

43 Admiraal 1977.

During this period euthanasia in all of the varieties that were currently recognized was presumably taking place, but there was very little quantitative or qualitative information about actual practice. Some quantitative information was available from the 'Continuous morbidity registration project'. This project registered information from the practices of approximately 60 GPs. Beginning in 1976 it included requests for euthanasia. The number of such requests grew in fits and starts from 15 in 1976 to 30 in 1981.[44] Extrapolated to all Dutch GPs, this would have meant that on average a GP was confronted with a euthanasia request once every two years.

A first impression of the practice of medical behavior that shortens life was provided by some exploratory qualitative studies in the early 1980s. Spreeuwenberg (1981) interviewed 30 GPs concerning (among other things) their experience with 'support in the dying process'. Verhoef and Hilhorst (1981) did direct observation in two nursing homes. Hilhorst (1983) interviewed 42 doctors, 32 nurses and 8 pastoral workers in 8 hospitals, and Kenter (1983) described 'euthanasia' in his own practice as a GP over a period of 5 years (1976-1981).[45]

Hilhorst, the most important investigator in this period, concluded that 'euthanasia' played, as a concept, practically no role in the professionals' 'definition of the situation': "the word euthanasia was and is taboo in hospitals".[46] Clearly defined decision-making criteria or procedures were essentially non-existent. The relevant legal norms were hardly known or applied. The behavior of those interviewed and observed seemed dominated by the experience of moral tension ('the doctor helps' versus 'the doctor promotes life and not death') and by the exigencies of the concrete situation. Active, direct euthanasia was practically unanimously rejected by those interviewed, but other sorts of medical practice that shortens life (terminating or not initiating treatment; administering high doses of pain relief) were generally accepted.[47] Consultation with a second doctor took place more regularly in the hospital context than in the practice of GPs. The latter acted independently (incidentally consulting a colleague or a pharmacist), whereas in a hospital the further treatment of a patient who had expressed a wish for termination of life was discussed in a staff meeting or between the responsible doctor and the head nurse.

ATTENTION FOR ASSISTANCE WITH SUICIDE

The growing importance attached to the idea of personal autonomy brought with it interest not only in euthanasia but also in assistance with suicide. The NVVE's Committee on Legislation acknowledged in 1978 that the ethical and practical problems of

44   *Medisch Contact* 37: 1653 (1982).
45   Kenter 1983. 11 of 111 deaths in his practice were due to 'euthanasia'. In the ensuing five years the frequency was essentially the same (Kenter 1989).
46   Hilhorst 1983: 35
47   Hilhorst 1983: 87-89.

euthanasia in many ways resemble those of 'rational suicide'. But the Committee considered the subject of assistance with suicide outside its mandate. Two years later, however, both the NVVE and the Foundation for Voluntary Euthanasia (SVE) published reports in which assistance with suicide received attention. The NVVE stated that assistance with suicide should be permissible

> when the assistance is given to someone who has requested it explicitly and voluntarily, who is *compos mentis* at the time of the request, whose suffering is unbearable, and whose desire to die is of a permanent nature.[48]

The SVE argued that "rational suicide should be recognized as a worthy alternative to active euthanasia and, under certain circumstances, even as more desirable."[49] In the SVE's opinion a person who is capable of suicide should as a rule not request euthanasia but assistance with suicide.[50] Such a preference was occasionally heard from doctors as well:

> The choice of means [for the termination of life] is determined by the patient's physical condition… In order to emphasize the mutual responsibility of the patient and myself, I always try to use oral medicines.[51]

THE *WERTHEIM* CASE AND PROSECUTORIAL POLICY

In the Spring of 1981 a voluntary-euthanasia activist, Ms. Wertheim, was arrested for having assisted the suicide of a 67-year-old woman. The woman, who suffered from many ailments of both a mental and a physical nature, had on many occasions expressed her wish to die. Her GP refused to accede to her request and referred her to Ms. Wertheim. After a few meetings Ms. Wertheim agreed to help her. On the night of 19 April 1981, she mixed approximately 30 Vesparax tablets into a bowl of chocolate custard and fed it to the woman. She then gave her an alcoholic drink because she knew that this would enhance the effect of the Vesperax. Shortly thereafter the woman died.

The trial took place in Rotterdam on 17 November. The prosecutor argued that this was a case of murder, but Ms. Wertheim's lawyer claimed that only assistance with suicide had been proven, and the District Court agreed. The lawyer further argued that, even though Ms. Wertheim's conduct had violated the letter of the law, she could not be convicted, because she had not violated the purpose of the law – protection of life – the

---

48   NVVE 1980: 17.
49   SVE 1980: 61.
50   SVE 1980: 60.
51   Spreeuwenberg 1982: 268.

deceased having wanted to be released from life. Should this argument fail, her lawyer further argued, Ms. Wertheim could not be convicted because the woman had been so insistent in her desire to die that this had put Ms. Wertheim in a situation of duress. The Court's ruling on 1 December 1981 rejected both arguments.

The District Court observed that suicide is not necessarily unacceptable in all situations and that the assistance of others can sometimes be indispensable. However, in light of the prohibition of assistance with suicide in article 294 of the Criminal Code, such assistance can only be justifiable if certain requirements are met. In the Court's view, to justify assistance with suicide it must appear that:

- the physical or mental suffering of the person was such that he experienced it as unbearable;
- this suffering as well as the desire to die were enduring;
- the decision to die was made voluntarily;
- the person was well informed about his situation and the available alternatives, was capable of weighing the relevant considerations, and had actually done so;
- there were no alternative means to improve the situation;
- the person's death did not cause others any unnecessary suffering.

The assistance itself must in the Court's view meet the following requirements:

- the decision to give assistance may not be made by one person alone;
- a doctor must be involved in the decision to give assistance and must determine the method to be used;
- the decision to give assistance and the assistance itself must exhibit the utmost care, which includes: discussing the matter with other doctors if the patient's condition is in the terminal phase, or, if the patient has not yet reached this phase, consulting other experts such as a psychiatrist, psychologist or social worker.[52]

The District Court held that Ms. Wertheim had not met these requirements, and found her guilty of the offence of assisting suicide. Because a jail sentence would have been too much of a mental and physical burden for the 76-year-old Ms. Wertheim, she was given a conditional sentence of six months subject to one year probation. As a special restriction, the court ordered that she be put under house arrest for the first two weeks of her probation.

The prosecution initially filed an appeal, but after having conferred with the Procurator-General of the Court of Appeals in the Hague and the Minister of Justice, the appeal was

---

52   *Nederlandse Jurisprudentie* 1982, no. 63: 223.

withdrawn. Following this incident, the national Committee of Procurators-General decided that every case of euthanasia (article 293) or assistance with suicide (article 294) that came to the attention of a prosecutor was to be referred to the Committee for a decision on whether to prosecute. The object was to achieve national uniformity in prosecutorial policy. The conditions as formulated in the *Postma* and *Wertheim* cases were to serve as guidelines for the decisions of the Committee of Procurators-General.[53]

Soon after the decision in *Wertheim* a new case of assistance with suicide reached the courts. This case concerned a man who had brought Vesparax tablets from Switzerland for his wife, who suffered from severe facial pain from an unknown cause. The man helped his wife to take the tablets and she died. The District Court, Utrecht concluded that the conditions of permissible assistance with suicide had not been met. Among other things, other possibilities for dealing with his wife's suffering had not been adequately explored. The man was given a conditional jail sentence of six months with one day probation. "By fixing probation at one day the Court expresses its view that the conditional sentence should not be executed."[54]

TO SUM UP

In the period 1970-1982, euthanasia had become the subject of social and legal discussion and several criminal and medical disciplinary cases. Distinctions were initially made between passive, active, voluntary, non-voluntary, direct and indirect euthanasia. But the public discussion seemed to exhibit a trend towards reducing the number of meanings of the term 'euthanasia'. The central characteristic of this reduction process was that behavior that was not problematic from a moral and legal standpoint was increasingly no longer called 'euthanasia'.

A consensus was reached in this period that indirect and passive euthanasia – pain relief and abstaining from treatment – are legitimate medical behavior; they came to be regarded as 'normal medical practice'. The *Postma* case confirmed that administration of pain relief in a dosage known to be likely to cause death does not constitute a violation of article 293 of the Criminal Code. No such explicit confirmation took place with regard to abstaining from life-prolonging treatment. However, while the frequent occurrence in medical practice of such life-shortening behavior was a well-known fact, no case of passive euthanasia reached the courts. This seems indirectly to confirm that passive euthanasia was not considered a criminal offence. Aside from narrowing down the meaning of the term 'euthanasia', this decade saw the growth of a general consensus that the legitimacy of assistance with suicide depends on essentially the same criteria as that of killing on request.

---

53   *Second Chamber of Parliament, appendix, 1981-1982,* 1757.
54   *Nederlandse Jurisprudentie* 1983, no. 264.

The requirements that the person giving assistance must meet in order to avoid being guilty of the crimes of articles 293 and 294 were broadly discussed. It was generally thought that the suffering of the person requesting assistance must be permanent and irreversible and that the euthanasia request must be durable, voluntary, and well-considered. Although according to many commentators it was a prerequisite for permissible euthanasia that the patient be in the 'terminal phase', this view was not shared by the courts. There seemed to be consensus that only doctors may perform euthanasia or give assistance with suicide, and that in principle the person rendering assistance must consult with other doctors.

2.3   1982-1986: The breakthrough

As we have seen, in 1982, following the *Wertheim* case, the Committee of Procurators-General established a national prosecutorial policy on euthanasia and assistance with suicide. Prosecutions would not be brought under articles 293 and 294 if rather generally formulated requirements were met. However, it was not clear what the substantive legal grounds were for this policy. In the following period, 1982-1986, the legal basis for the legitimacy of euthanasia and the requirements for legal euthanasia were settled. The period also saw an end to uncertainty concerning the scope of the term 'euthanasia'.

2.3.1   The justification of necessity and the 'requirements of careful practice'

LEGAL DOCTRINES AVAILABLE FOR LEGITIMATING EUTHANASIA

A number of doctrinal approaches were in theory available to legitimate behavior that on its face violates articles 293 and 294 of the Criminal Code (see chapter 3.1 for a more complete discussion). In our discussion of the history of abortion, one of these has already been mentioned, namely the 'medical exception'. Enschedé repeated for the case of euthanasia the argument that had been successful during the abortion debate: articles 293 and 294 are simply inapplicable to doctors.[55]

A second defence against a charge under articles 293 and 294 could be based on the doctrine of 'absence of substantial violation of the law': the idea that behavior that violates the letter but not the purpose of the law does not constitute an offence. The NVVE had proposed in 1978 to use this doctrine in cases of euthanasia. Ms. Wertheim had invoked this defence, but the District Court, Rotterdam had rejected it.

---

55   Enschedé 1985.

A third defence that could be used to justify euthanasia is that of *overmacht* (article 40 of the Criminal Code, see appendix I-A). This defence has two variants in Dutch law: the excuse of duress and the justification of necessity. Ms. Postma, for example, invoked the defence of duress. The District Court, Leeuwarden, rejected it on the ground that a doctor can be expected to withstand pressure from patients. The justification of necessity can be invoked by a person who finds himself in a situation of conflict of duties. If a person in such a situation chooses to prefer the value that from an objective standpoint is more important, even if this means doing something that in itself is forbidden, his conduct is justifiable.

THE *SCHOONHEIM* CASE: EUTHANASIA CAN BE JUSTIFIABLE

The first euthanasia case that reached the Supreme Court concerned the GP Schoonheim who, on 16 July 1982, had performed euthanasia on a 95-year-old patient who on several occasions had asked him in a serious and insistent manner to do so. The patient was bedridden because of a fractured hip for which she had refused an operation. She could no longer walk or sit and her eyesight and hearing were deteriorating. Mentally she was in excellent shape and thus fully aware of her situation, which she found humiliating.[56] On 16 July Schoonheim talked one last time with the patient in the presence of her son, her daughter-in-law, and Schoonheim's assistant. It was obvious that she had only one desire: to die as soon as possible. Following this conversation Schoonheim acceded to her request. He injected her first with a drug that made her partly lose consciousness and then with a muscle relaxant which caused her death. That same day Schoonheim reported his actions to the police.

At the trial in April 1983 Schoonheim's lawyer argued that there was an 'absence of substantial violation of the law' and that Schoonheim had acted in a situation of *overmacht*.[57] The first defence was accepted by the District Court, Alkmaar, and Schoonheim was acquitted.[58] The prosecution appealed. The Court of Appeals, Amsterdam, rejected all of Schoonheim's defences and found him guilty, but used its discretion not to impose any punishment.[59]

On 27 November 1984 the Supreme Court ruled on Schoonheim's appeal (see appendix II-1). The Supreme Court affirmed the holding of the Court of Appeals that the doctrine of 'absence of substantial violation of the law' was not available as a defence. However,

---

56   Enthoven 1988: 95.
57   The lawyer also argued that the defendant's behavior could not be seen as 'taking someone's life' since he had been requested to act. The Court rejected this defence.
58   *Nederlandse Jurisprudentie* 1983, no. 407.
59   *Nederlandse Jurisprudentie* 1984, no. 43.

the Supreme Court concluded that the Court of Appeals had not properly considered the appeal to *overmacht* in the sense of the justification of necessity.[60] It vacated the verdict of the Court of Appeals and referred the case to the Court of Appeals, the Hague.[61]

The Supreme Court explained its decision as follows:

> [O]ne would have expected the Court of Appeals to have considered … whether, according to responsible medical opinion, subject to the applicable norms of medical ethics, this was, as claimed by the defendant, a situation of necessity.

The Supreme Court specifically referred to the patient's "unbearable suffering", including the prospect of increasing "loss of personal dignity", the risk that it might become impossible for the patient to "die in a dignified manner", and the existence of alternative ways to relieve her suffering as relevant considerations. It concluded that the approach of the Court of Appeals had not excluded

> the possibility that the euthanasia performed by defendant, according to objective medical opinion, must be considered justified, as having been performed in a situation of necessity.[62]

After securing additional evidence, the Court of Appeals, the Hague ruled that Schoonheim's defence of necessity was well-founded and acquitted him.[63] For the first time, a doctor who had performed euthanasia was found not to be criminally liable.

THE *POLS* CASE: EUTHANASIA DOES NOT FALL WITHIN THE 'MEDICAL EXCEPTION'

A second euthanasia case soon reached the Supreme Court. On 5 August 1982 Ms. Pols, a psychiatrist, had killed her friend at the latter's explicit request. The friend was 73 years old and suffering from multiple sclerosis. Ms. Pols gave her a fast-working tranquillizer in combination with a glass of port. After waiting a few hours she injected her three times

---

60 Half a year passed between the hearing of the appeal and the Supreme Court's judgment. Remmelink (Advocate-General who submitted the brief to the Supreme Court arguing that the Court should reject Schoonheim's appeal) later explained the difference between the conclusion of his brief and the Court's decision by referring to the fact that in the interim the Executive Board of the Medical Association had adopted a new policy in which it for the first time recognized the legitimacy of euthanasia performed by a doctor (Remmelink 1992).

61 *Nederlandse Jurisprudentie* 1985, no. 106. See note 6 of appendix II concerning referral to a second Court of Appeals.

62 *Nederlandse Jurisprudentie* 1985, no. 106: 459-460.

63 *Nederlandse Jurisprudentie* 1987, no. 608.

with morphine after which the friend died. That same night she delivered letters to the friend's GP and the prosecutor to inform them about her conduct. She also notified the institution where the friend had been staying.[64]

The case was tried in February 1984 in Groningen. Ms. Pols' lawyer invoked the defences of 'absence of substantial violation of the law' and of *overmacht*. The first defence was rejected, but its supporting argumentation was interpreted by the District Court as invoking the idea of the 'medical exception'. According to the Court such a defence was in theory available, but the Court rejected it here because Ms. Pols had not consulted another doctor. In the Court's opinion neither necessity nor duress had been proved. Ms. Pols was found guilty, but no punishment was imposed.[65]

On appeal all of Ms. Pols' defences were rejected. The Court of Appeals, Leeuwarden, held that the defence of *overmacht* must fail since she had put herself in the difficult situation she sought to invoke. The Court of Appeals found her guilty and imposed a conditional jail sentence of two months subject to two years' probation.[66]

On appeal to the Supreme Court, the idea of a 'medical exception' was explicitly rejected. The Court held that (by contrast with the case of abortion) it did not appear that the prohibition of euthanasia in article 293 had been intended as subject to an exception for doctors. Furthermore, contrary to the defendant's claim, there was no settled social consensus that euthanasia is a form of 'normal medical practice' that can be considered to fall within the 'medical exception'. The Supreme Court did not, however, agree with the Court of Appeals' rejection of the defence of *overmacht* in the sense of necessity.[67]

The Supreme Court referred the case to the Court of Appeals, Arnhem. This Court rejected the defence of necessity because Ms. Pols should have discussed the matter with colleagues since, among other things, she had ties of friendship with the deceased. The Court imposed the same sentence as had the Leeuwarden Court.[68] On a second appeal to the Supreme Court it was argued that the fact that Ms. Pols had not consulted colleagues should not automatically have led to rejection of the defence of necessity. The defence argued that Ms. Pols had had enough reason to believe that she had made a justifiable choice. The Supreme Court let the decision of the Court of Appeals stand.[69]

---

64   Enthoven 1988: 112-113.
65   *Nederlandse Jurisprudentie* 1984, no. 450.
66   *Nederlandse Jurisprudentie* 1985, no. 241.
67   *Nederlandse Jurisprudentie* 1987, no. 607.
68   *Tijdschrift voor Gezondheidsrecht* 1987, no. 35.
69   *Nederlandse Jurisprudentie* 1989, no. 391.

The *Schoonheim* and *Pols* cases brought much clarity with regard to the legality of euthanasia.[70] This clarity primarily concerned the grounds on which a defence could be based. The Supreme Court explicitly rejected the defences of 'medical exception' and 'absence of substantial violation of the law', but it held that a doctor can invoke the defence of *overmacht* in the form of the justification of necessity based on a conflict of duties.

THE REPORT OF THE MEDICAL ASSOCIATION OF 1984: FORMULATION OF THE 'REQUIREMENTS OF CAREFUL PRACTICE'

Aside from the fact that the doctrinal basis for legal euthanasia and assistance with suicide was settled in this period, there was also considerable clarification of the conditions with which doctors must comply. This clarification was heavily influenced by the new policy adopted by the Medical Association's Executive Board in 1984. The Executive Board explicitly stated that it was not its intention to address the question of the permissibility of euthanasia.[71] It considered euthanasia to be a fact of life. Euthanasia was defined by the Board as: "conduct that is intended to terminate another person's life at his or her explicit request".[72] As a consequence of this definition the Board was inclined to drop the distinction between euthanasia and assistance with suicide[73] and to use the same terminology and criteria for both.[74] The Board emphasized that only doctors

---

70   The Foundation for Voluntary Euthanasia (SVE) decided in 1985 to disband since its aim, securing recognition for legal euthanasia within the context of existing law, had been achieved.

71   During the discussion in the general membership meeting on the new policy, the chairman stated that the Board did not want to take a standpoint for or against euthanasia. The purpose of the guidelines was to assist those doctors who consider performing euthanasia. Debate was closed with the observation that the new policy was that of the Board, not necessarily of all Dutch doctors (*Medisch Contact* 40: 438 (1985)). The schism in the Medical Association caused by the Medical Association's position on abortion (see footnote 10) will have influenced this prudent approach.

72   KNMG 1984: 991.

73   In the 1975 report a working group of the Medical Association had, as we have seen, argued that there is no room in the doctor-patient relationship for assistance with suicide (see section 2.2).

74   The Board of the Association also decided to prepare a position paper with regard to termination of life of patients who are either not able to express a request for euthanasia or whose competence to make a request is questionable. The Board mentioned minors, prisoners, severely defective newborn babies, patients in coma and persons suffering from a mental disorder. The Board appointed the Commission on the Acceptability of Medical Behavior that Shortens Life (CAL) which delivered four reports in the period 1990-1993 and a final report in 1997 (see chapter 3.3, 3.4 and 3.5).

should be allowed to engage in actions that terminate life. The question of euthanasia was seen by the Board as one that should be dealt with within the doctor-patient relationship. It recognized that the medical profession has a collective obligation to make a "socially acceptable solution" of the euthanasia issue possible.[75]

The Board considered euthanasia performed by a doctor acceptable when the doctor has taken adequate steps to meet five 'requirements of careful practice':

1   the request for euthanasia must be voluntary;
2   the request must be well-considered;
3   the patient's desire to die must be a lasting one;
4   the patient must experience his suffering as unacceptable for him. (The Board emphasized that there are only limited possibilities for verifying whether suffering is unbearable and without prospect of improvement. The Board considered it in any case the doctor's task to investigate whether there are medical or social alternatives that can make the patient's suffering bearable.);
5   the doctor concerned must consult a colleague.[76]

THE *ADMIRAAL* CASE: A DOCTOR WHO MET THE 'REQUIREMENTS OF CAREFUL PRACTICE' WILL BE ACQUITTED

In June 1985 a doctor who had followed the 'requirements of careful practice' stood trial in the Hague for euthanasia. The case concerned the anesthetist Admiraal who on 4 November 1983 had put an end to the life of a patient who suffered from multiple sclerosis. The patient had been admitted to a nursing home in 1981 and had been in need of constant nursing care since June 1983. She had expressed her desire to end her life, but the doctor-superintendent of the nursing home refused to help her. Admiraal, who was approached through the Association for Voluntary Euthanasia, talked with the patient a number of times about her desire to die. Life was nothing but torture to her, mainly because of her complete dependency on others. After having discussed the matter with the terminal-care team of the hospital where he worked, Admiraal decided to hospitalize her there so that he could carry out the termination of life. Before Admiraal actually did so, he informed the city's Health Service and the Medical Inspector of his plans.

One of the questions raised at the trial was whether Admiraal's conduct had failed to meet the 'requirements of careful practice' since he had failed to consult an expert on multiple sclerosis, a neurologist. The District Court ruled that Admiraal had been con-

---

75   KNMG 1984: 993.
76   KNMG 1984: 994-995. In 1992 the requirement of a fully-documented written record was added (KNMG 1992: 30).

fronted by a situation of necessity, that he had carefully weighed the conflicting duties and interests against each other, and that in doing so he had made a justifiable choice. The Court saw no reason for requiring him to have consulted yet another doctor, and Admiraal was acquitted.[77]

From the *Admiraal* case it became clear that a doctor who complies with the 'requirements of careful practice' cannot be convicted for performing euthanasia. This was confirmed by the Minister of Justice who notified the Medical Association in September 1985 that doctors who comply with the 'requirements of careful practice' published by the Board of the Association in *Medisch Contact* would not be prosecuted.[78] However, the formulation of prosecutorial policy was still in a fairly primitive state. It is true that in 1982 it had been decided that every case of euthanasia and assistance with suicide that came to the attention of the prosecutorial authorities would be discussed by the Committee of Procurators-General. But since doctors did not generally inform prosecutors about such cases, the PG's were only very rarely able to assess whether a doctor had conformed to the requirements (see further chapter 5.3.5, table 5.17).

The prosecutor in the judicial district of Alkmaar seems to have been the first to design a procedure by which doctors could report euthanasia. After consultation with local doctors, the prosecutor promised that police and prosecutorial authorities would be very reticent, investigating reported cases in a reserved and low-visibility way,[79] that doctors who had abided by the 'requirements of careful practice' did not have to fear prosecution, and that a doctor who reported would be informed within 14 days if the prosecutor saw any reason for further investigation. The results of this strategy were quickly apparent. In the district of Alkmaar doctors reported eight cases of euthanasia in the last three months of 1985; in 1986 they reported 38 cases and in 1987 31. The 31 reports in 1987 amounted to a quarter of all reports nationally.[80]

---

77   *Nederlandse Jurisprudentie* 1985, no. 709.

78   A prosecution in 1987 settled beyond doubt that a doctor can indeed count on not being prosecuted as long as he has met the 'requirements of careful practice', and that a failure to consult another doctor is in itself insufficient ground for a criminal prosecution. The prosecuted doctor had given a patient lethal injections at her explicit request. When criminal charges were brought, the doctor requested the Court of Appeals, Arnhem to quash the indictment. The Court did so. In the Court's view the undisputable facts required the conclusion that prosecution of the doctor for euthanasia could not succeed, since if there were a trial it would soon become evident that the defendant had acted in a situation of necessity. The Supreme Court rejected the prosecution's appeal on the ground that the arguments given by the Court of Appeals formed a sufficient basis for its conclusions (*Nederlandse Jurisprudentie* 1988, no. 157).

79   There had been complaints in medical circles about policemen arriving at hospitals with sirens screaming, bursting in uniform into hospital wards or offices, and about the needlessly long and aggressive interrogations to which both doctors and patients' relatives were subjected.

80   See Josephus Jitta 1987, 1997; Enthoven 1988: 277.

2.3.2   The definition of euthanasia and initial proposals for legislation

INTRODUCTION

In the period 1970-1982 a general consensus had already been reached concerning the legal acceptability of so-called 'passive' and 'indirect' euthanasia. The term 'euthanasia' was less and less used to describe these sorts of medical behavior that shortens life. In the period 1982-1986 euthanasia proper came to be more precisely defined and reserved for behavior covered by article 293: termination of life at the request of the person concerned.

THE HEALTH COUNCIL REPORT OF 1982

The first step in this process was a new report of the Health Council in 1982. This report was the result of a motion adopted by the Second Chamber of Parliament in 1978 requesting that a state commission be set up to give advice on future national policy concerning euthanasia.[81] The Health Council was asked to advise on the assignment to be given this state commission. After summarizing the sorts of behavior that so far had been labeled 'euthanasia', the Council concluded that only "intentionally terminating or shortening a patient's life at his request or in his interest"[82] constitutes euthanasia. Ceasing a treatment that only postpones the moment of death, pain relief with the unintended but accepted effect of shortening life, and refraining from treatment at the patient's request are, according to the Health Council, 'normal medical practice'. The Council saw no reason to emphasize the distinction between euthanasia and assistance with suicide. "The context in which the treatment takes place seems far more important than the form assumed by the assistance in a specific case."[83]

The Council did not advise on the desirability of legislative change regarding euthanasia and assistance with suicide, limiting itself to an outline of the advantages and disadvantages of such legislative change. It did, however, call attention to the problem faced by a doctor who has performed euthanasia: is it permissible for him to file a certificate of natural death (in which case burial or cremation can take place without further ado) or must the doctor inform the coroner that death was not due to a natural cause (in which case criminal investigation is to be expected)? The Health Council observed that doctors sometimes have reasons of a practical nature for submitting a certificate of natural death, since a criminal investigation can heavily burden both the doctor and the patient's family. The Council advised that the State Commission should address this problem.

––––––––––––––

81   This motion implemented the European Council's recommendation (29 January 1976) that a national commission be set up by each member state to investigate the euthanasia question.

82   Gezondheidsraad 1982: 15.

83   Gezondheidsraad 1982: 16.

THE WESSEL-TUINSTRA BILL

Before the State Commission had finished its work, a member of the Second Chamber of Parliament, Ms. Wessel-Tuinstra of the left-liberal party D66, decided that awaiting the Commission's report would mean putting off legislative change that she considered urgent. In her opinion both the person who requested euthanasia and the doctor who agreed to carry it out, were exposed to a degree of legal insecurity that was no longer acceptable. She also found it unacceptable that the whole issue of euthanasia had been left to judges and prosecutors. Regulation of euthanasia, in her view, is a responsibility of the legislature. In April 1984 she submitted a bill providing for changes in articles 293 and 294 of the Criminal Code.[84]

Her bill (for its final form see appendix I-C-2) proposed to make euthanasia and assistance with suicide legal, as long as assistance was given in a responsible fashion "to a patient whose condition is terminal or to a patient whose physical or mental suffering is unbearable".[85] A number of conditions were formulated in the bill. The request must be voluntary and well-considered. The decision to end the patient's life must be made by a doctor who has convinced himself that the patient and his request meet the various requirements. The doctor must keep a written record of the case and must report his act to the proper authorities. Parliamentary action on the bill was postponed until after the State Commission's report.

THE STATE COMMISSION ON EUTHANASIA

On 19 October 1982 the State Commission on Euthanasia was installed (its chairman Jeukens was a member of the Supreme Court). Its assignment was to report on future national policy concerning euthanasia and assistance with suicide, with an emphasis on legislation and its implementation.[86] The Commission's installation had been opposed in advance by advocates of euthanasia. In their opinion the only purpose of the Commission was to postpone needed legislative reform. Whether these fears were justified at the time or not, the fact is that the State Commission succeeded in moving euthanasia to the top of the political agenda.

In the summer of 1985 the State Commission produced its report.[87] The Commission defined euthanasia as "intentionally terminating another person's life at the person's

---

84 *Second Chamber of Parliament 1983-1984*, 18 331, no. 2 and 3.

85 In 1986 this text was changed to make its terms congruent with those of the State Commission: 'a situation of hopeless necessity' (compare appendix I-C-2).

86 Staatscommissie 1985: 12.

87 The report consisted of a majority report and a minority report in which two members rejected any legalization of euthanasia. The majority report included minority views on some subjects, such as the requirement that the dying process have commenced (see below).

request".[88] For the Commission the patient's request was essential. This definition makes the term 'euthanasia' congruent with the behavior prohibited in article 293.

The State Commission organized public hearings where interested persons and organizations could state their views on euthanasia and assistance with suicide. During these hearings there was practically unanimous agreement with the distinction made by the Health Council between 'euthanasia' and other medical behavior that shortens life and with the position that abstinence and pain relief, even when death is the expected result, constitute 'normal medical practice'. Such agreement certainly did not exist with respect to the question whether euthanasia and assistance with suicide are morally or legally acceptable. Views on possible changes in articles 293 and 294 varied widely.

The transcripts of the hearings show the range of arguments current at that time. The statements of advocates of legalizing euthanasia and assistance with suicide generally rely on the right of personal autonomy. Opponents can be divided into two categories. There are those who invoke religious authority (the most important claim is that life belongs to God and is only given temporarily to human beings). And there are opponents who advance secular arguments against liberalization: euthanasia and assistance with suicide are in conflict with medical ethics; the 'right to life' imposes on the state a duty to protect human life; it is impossible to determine whether a request is voluntary; and liberalization of voluntary euthanasia will lead inexorably to social practices we all abhor (the 'slippery slope'). (See chapter 4.2 for a more extensive treatment of these arguments.)

The Commission urged the Government and Parliament to clarify the legal situation concerning euthanasia and assistance with suicide. In its opinion legislation was essential to accomplish such clarification. Like the Supreme Court, the Commission considered the 'medical exception' and the doctrine of 'absence of substantial violation of the law' not applicable to the case of euthanasia. As far as the justification of necessity was concerned, the Commission sought to define criteria to determine when a patient's situation is such that it would be reasonable and acceptable for a doctor, faced with the patient's request to terminate his life, to claim that he was confronted with a conflict of duties. The Commission was unable to reach a complete consensus on what the nature of the patient's situation must be. A majority agreed on the requirement that the patient must be suffering 'hopelessly' (*uitzichtloos*: without prospect of improvement; senseless), although this suffering could be either physical or mental. A minority wanted to add the requirement that "the dying process must irreversibly have set in".[89] After formulating these requirements concerning the patient's situation, the Commission emphasized that

---

88   This definition is much like the one Leenen, a member of the State Commission, had already formulated in 1977 (Leenen 1977: 80).

89   Staatscommissie 1985: 59.

"the termination of life must be performed by a doctor in the context of careful medical practice, and sufficient procedural control must be guaranteed."[90]

The Commission saw no significant difference between killing on request and certain forms of assistance with suicide. If a doctor gives the patient lethal medication which the patient himself takes, the case should, in the Commission's view, be treated in the same way as killing on request.

The State Commission proposed a legislative revision of article 293 (see appendix I-C-1 for the text of the State Commission's proposal). The revised article provides that euthanasia is legal when performed by a doctor in a medically responsible way, at the request of a patient who is in a situation of 'hopeless necessity' and when certain 'requirements of careful medical practice' have been met. The Commission formulated the following requirements:

1   the patient must be informed about his condition;
2   the doctor must have convinced himself that the patient's request was made voluntarily and after serious consideration;
3   the patient and the doctor must agree that there are no alternative ways of dealing with the patient's condition;
4   the doctor must consult with a doctor designated by the Minister of Health.

The Commission proposed that a doctor who fails to comply with the requirement of consultation or who files a certificate of natural death after performing euthanasia or assistance with suicide should be guilty of a specific criminal offence, the remaining requirements being conditions of legal euthanasia. The Commission further proposed that the doctor should report having performed euthanasia or assistance with suicide to the district prosecutor. Such a report should be accompanied by a statement in which the doctor explains how he has met the criteria and a statement by the doctor who was consulted.

The State Commission also proposed adding a new section to article 293 in which euthanasia proper would be distinguished from the so-called 'false forms of euthanasia'. Four such 'false forms' were specified in the State Commission's proposal: not initiating or stopping treatment either at the request of a patient or in a situation in which the treatment is medically futile, not treating a secondary illness or disorder in case of a patient who has permanently lost consciousness, and hastening the moment of death as a subsidiary effect of treatment that is necessary to relieve suffering.

---

90   Staatscommissie 1985: 125.

Besides recommending changes in article 293, the State Commission proposed to add a new article. This article (292b) would provide that termination of the life of a person who cannot make his wishes known is forbidden, except in the case of a doctor who in a medically responsible way terminates the life of a person who is in an irreversible coma and whose medical treatment has been stopped because it was futile. Here, too, the doctor is required to consult with a doctor designated by the Minister of Health.

EUTHANASIA IS NOT A 'NATURAL' CAUSE OF DEATH

The reports of the Health Council and of the State Commission called attention to the need to create an adequate system of control over euthanasia practice. This problem, which later on came to dominate the entire public debate, was first addressed by asking whether a doctor can properly file a certificate of natural death after performing euthanasia.[91] The majority opinion was that euthanasia cannot be considered a 'natural' cause of death.

In 1985 a criminal case began in Rotterdam which definitively settled this issue. The case concerned a doctor who on 15 December 1983 had ended a patient's life in a nursing home at her explicit request. He filed a death certificate stating that the cause of the patient's death had been natural. The doctor was tried for euthanasia and for submitting a false certificate (article 228(1) of the Criminal Code, see appendix I-A). The doctor's defence to the euthanasia charge was based on the justification of necessity. The District Court agreed and found him not guilty of euthanasia. The doctor's lawyer also invoked the justification of necessity as a defence to the second charge. She argued that the doctor was in a situation of conflict of duties: on the one hand his duty to the surviving relatives and the other patients in the nursing home for whom reporting the death as a non-natural one would have entailed additional grief and agitation, on the other his duty not to file a false certificate. Confronted with the choice of two unattractive options, he chose the less harmful one. The Court did not agree. In its opinion, filing a false certificate undermines legal control of termination of life. The doctor was sentenced to a fine of 500 guilders, half of which was made conditional.[92] On appeal, the Court of Appeals, the Hague agreed with the District Court. It also rejected the defendant's reliance on his oath of secrecy: this oath gives a doctor the right to remain silent, but not to give false infor-

---

91   Enschedé had argued that a certificate of natural death may be filed in situations where the cause of death is not a criminal offence. To this he added the consideration that a doctor must sometimes file such a certificate since he would otherwise violate his obligation of professional secrecy (Enschedé 1985).

92   *Tijdschrift voor Gezondheidsrecht* 1985, no. 44.

mation.[93] In December 1987 the Supreme Court upheld the decision of the Court of Appeals.[94] As we will see in chapter 5.3.5, there have subsequently been a number of prosecutions and convictions for this offence.

TO SUM UP

In the period 1970-1982 there had been considerable discussion about how to define 'euthanasia'. This question was given a definitive answer in the period 1982-1986. In the same period important steps were also taken to legalize euthanasia and assistance with suicide under specific conditions. It became established in a series of court decisions that, when a patient who is suffering unbearably and hopelessly makes a voluntary and well-considered request, a doctor who accedes to the request, if he conforms to the 'requirements of careful practice' and makes his behavior controllable by not filing a certificate of natural death, is not guilty of a crime. The specific contents of the 'requirements of careful practice' had also been worked out in some detail. However, this clarification work did not end the public discussion on euthanasia. Legislation had still not been adopted to regularize a practice that had come to be considered legally acceptable, and the problem of termination of life without the patient's request, put on the agenda by the State Commission, remained to be seriously addressed.

2.4   1986-1997: Efforts to codify emerging practice in legislation; broadening the subject of debate

INTRODUCTION

By 1986 it had become clear what 'euthanasia' means as a matter of Dutch law and what legal doctrine is available to legitimize behavior by doctors that on its face violates articles 293 and 294 of the Criminal Code. Moreover, a bill had been submitted to Parliament which proposed to legalize euthanasia subject to a number of requirements and the State Commission had recommended legislation along the same lines. Such legislation was supported by a substantial majority in Parliament. One might have thought that the legalization of euthanasia by doctors was imminent. As we will see, this expectation did not materialize.

---

93   *Nederlandse Jurisprudentie* 1987, no. 756.
94   *Tijdschrift voor Gezondheidsrecht* 1988, no. 13.

The State Commission had put an end to the discussion about the definition of 'euthanasia',[95] but at the same time it put termination of life without an explicit request onto the public and political agenda. Termination of life without an explicit request had also emerged as a subject of discussion within the Medical Association. The legitimacy of assistance with suicide to patients whose suffering is not physical but mental also received attention in the period 1986-1997.

POLITICAL RESPONSES TO THE REPORT OF THE STATE COMMISSION

In early 1986 the Government, a coalition of the Christian Democrats (CDA) and the right-of-center liberal party VVD reported to Parliament its tentative conclusions in light of the State Commission's report. The Government was inclined to the view that the time was not yet ripe for legislation concerning euthanasia. Nevertheless, should Parliament be of a different view, the Government indicated in a 'tentative draft of a bill' (*de Proeve*) what sort of legislation would be acceptable to it. In effect, the Government proposed to add to Wessel-Tuinstra's bill the additional limitation that euthanasia would only be legal in a situation in which there was "a concrete expectation of death". The Government thereby adopted the position of the minority within the majority of the State Commission.[96] An explicit if limited role was accorded to the immediate family of the patient: added to the 'requirements of careful practice' was the requirement that the doctor must consult with the patient concerning their inclusion in the decision-making. The Government also proposed to add a new section to article 293 specifying, as the State Commission had advised, those forms of medical behavior that shortens life that do *not* fall under its prohibition.[97]

Parliament, confronted with the Wessel-Tuinstra bill, the Government's alternative, and a number of more or less fundamental proposed amendments, decided to refer the matter to the Council of State for advice. The Council of State advised that the public discussion on euthanasia had not yet reached the point at which it was desirable to try to specify in the Criminal Code when euthanasia is permissible.[98] The Council nevertheless did advise adding to the Criminal Code a provision making explicit that abstention and pain relief are not covered by articles 293 and 294 and, in separate legislation outside the

---

95   Which is not, of course, to say that other uses disappeared from popular discourse. There, the term 'euthanasia' sometimes has an astonishingly extensive meaning. The city of Groningen recently distributed a poster concerning the local tax on dogs, advising owners that one way of establishing that one no longer has a dog is by submitting a veterinary's "euthanasia statement".

96   See footnote 87 above.

97   *Second Chamber of Parliament 1985-1986*, 19 359, no. 2.

98   *Second Chamber of Parliament 1985-1986*, 18 331, no. 43.

Code, specifying a number of minimum procedural and administrative requirements that a doctor would have to meet before being allowed to invoke the defence of necessity.

In January 1987 the Government notified Parliament that it would look into the possibility of a limited bill as advised by the Council of State. But first it proposed to ask the Health Council for advice concerning the 'requirements of careful practice'. The Council answered in March 1987. It re-emphasized the importance of fully informing the patient, of ensuring that his request is voluntary, well-considered and durable, of consultation, and of full record-keeping. The Council suggested that an advance directive could replace the patient's current request if the patient was no longer able to express his wishes. The family should be involved in the decision-making, unless the patient had a serious and well-founded objection that was regarded as valid by the doctor and the consulted expert. In the case of patients under 16, still subject to legal guardianship, the Council regarded it as essential that the doctor discuss the request with the immediate family, but even in such cases recognized that there might be exceptional situations.[99]

The Government also asked the Committee of Procurators-General for its views concerning the advice of the Council of State, from the point of view of effective law-enforcement and doctrinal consistency with the rest of the criminal law. On 28 April 1987 the Procurators-General reacted very negatively to the advice of the Council of State and the Government's draft bill.[100] They objected to the device of a 'negative definition of an offence' (the specification of behavior *not* included in article 293) and to specifying requirements for the defence of necessity outside the Criminal Code. They also pointed out that so long as euthanasia remains a criminal offence, the proposed requirement that the doctor must file a certificate of non-natural death seemed to violate the privilege against self-incrimination.

At the very end of 1987 the Government submitted a revised bill under which essentially nothing in the Criminal Code would be changed.[101] Instead of changing articles 293 and 294 the bill would have added two provisions to the Law on Medical Practice:[102] (1) the exclusion of death due to termination or non-initiation of treatment and to pain relief from the scope of articles 293 and 294, and (2) minimum procedural and record-keeping requirements that a doctor who performs euthanasia would have to meet. According to these requirements the doctor should assure himself that the patient's request is explicit and serious, informed and voluntary, he should consult with the

---

99 Gezondheidsraad 1987: 6.
100 *Second Chamber of Parliament 1986-1987*, 19 359, no. 8.
101 *Second Chamber of Parliament 1987-1988*, 20 383, no. 2 and 3.
102 This law was replaced in 1993 by the Law on Professions Concerned with Individual Medical Care (see the *Intermezzo*).

patient's family or other intimates (unless the patient objects to this) and with another, independent doctor, and he should keep a complete, written record.[103] It would be up to the prosecutors and the courts to determine to what extent these provisions outside the Criminal Code were relevant to the defence of necessity.

THE REACTION OF THE DUTCH ASSOCIATION FOR VOLUNTARY EUTHANASIA

In April 1989 the Dutch Association for Voluntary Euthanasia (NVVE) published an extra-parliamentary bill as an alternative to the Government's bill. The gist of the NVVE bill was that euthanasia and assistance with suicide by a doctor would be removed from the Criminal Code.[104] A provision was to be added to the Law on Medical Practice to the effect that medical care requires a doctor to limit the physical and mental suffering of the patient. Within the framework of this limiting of suffering, a doctor would be entitled, at the request of the patient, to assist him to die. The usual 'requirements of careful practice' were provided. The NVVE bill also provided that a doctor need only certify that the patient died from a cause that according to the doctor did not give rise to any objection to giving permission for burial or cremation.[105] The NVVE bill sought in effect to provide a legislative foundation for the 'medical exception'.[106]

PRELUDE TO A NATIONAL STUDY OF MBSL

In May of 1989, before Parliamentary consideration of the Wessel-Tuinstra bill and the most recent version of the Government's alternative was complete, the center-right Government (CDA and VVD) fell and was replaced by a center-left Government (CDA and PvdA). During the formation of the new Government, the parties agreed that further legislative treatment of euthanasia should await the findings of a Commission appointed to conduct research into the extent and characteristics of current euthanasia practice.[107]

---

103 There were also special provisions permitting the honoring of a written request (not more than 5 years old) of a patient no longer capable of expressing his wishes, and dealing with euthanasia requests by minors (whose legal representatives must be included in the decision-making and must agree to euthanasia).

104 The NVVE proposed to add to the articles 293 and 294, after the words "a person who," the words "other than as the doctor responsible for care". Article 293, for example would read: "A person who, other than as the doctor responsible for care, takes the life of another person at that other person's express and earnest request is liable to a term of imprisonment of not more than four years or a fine of the fourth category." (NVVE 1989)

105 NVVE 1989.

106 Compare De Wit 1989: 1.

107 *Second Chamber of Parliament 1988-1989*, 21 132, no. 8 (coalition agreement): 47.

The Commission Appointed to Carry out Research Concerning Medical Practice in Connection with Euthanasia (referred to as the 'Remmelink Commission' after its chairman, who at the time was Advocate-General at the Supreme Court) was installed on 18 January 1990. Its research was supposed to provide insight into "the state of affairs with respect to acts or omissions by doctors which shorten the life of a patient, with or without an explicit and serious request".[108]

In November of 1990 the Minister of Justice announced a reporting procedure for euthanasia.[109] This had been arrived at after negotiations with the Medical Association, which had conditioned its support for the intended research of the Remmelink Commission on clarification of the procedure to be followed by doctors for reporting cases in which they have carried out euthanasia. In broad terms the new reporting procedure was based on the assumption that a doctor who has performed euthanasia or assistance with suicide may not file a certificate of natural death but must notify the coroner of what he has done (see further chapter 3.2.)[110] At the same time, the Procurators-General issued instructions governing the investigation by the police of reported cases. The gist of these instructions was that the whole investigation should be as discrete as possible. Thus, for example, when visiting a doctor in the course of an investigation, the police should not be in uniform nor drive a marked police car. They should also be as considerate as possible of the feelings of the next of kin.[111]

THE *STINISSEN* CASE: ARTIFICIAL FEEDING IS MEDICAL TREATMENT

At the end of 1990 the Dutch were confronted again with a dramatic case of a person in irreversible coma (see section 2.1 on the earlier case of Mia Versluis). In June 1987 Gerard Stinissen had brought a civil action in the District Court, Almelo asking for a judgment that further treatment of his wife Ineke could be stopped. Ineke Stinissen had been in coma since March 1974 as a result of a medical mistake during a Caesarian delivery. Already in 1976 Gerard Stinissen had asked the nursing home where his wife was being kept alive to allow her to die. The nursing home refused, first because they were opposed to taking an 'active' decision to let a patient die, but later on because they were unsure of their legal position.

Stinissen requested the Court to order that the artificial feeding of his wife be stopped, that possible complications not be treated, and that the nursing home confine itself to care aimed at the relief of suffering. Stinissen argued that medical treatment was futile

---

108 *Second Chamber of Parliament 1989-1990*, 20 383, no. 13: 2.
109 *Second Chamber of Parliament 1990-1991*, 21 800, no. 23: 2.
110 *Medisch Contact* 45: 1303 (1990).
111 *Medisch Contact* 45: 1304 (1990); compare section 2.3 and note 79 on the earlier policy in Alkmaar.

and that the patient could not be considered to have given consent to it. The Court ruled that the artificial feeding of Ms. Stinissen should be considered medical treatment and therefore fell within the authority of a doctor to terminate futile medical treatment. But it considered the doctor's decision to keep Ineke Stinissen alive legitimate and refused to intervene.[112]

In 1989, on appeal, the Court of Appeals, Arnhem likewise rejected Stinissen's request that the artificial feeding be stopped. The Court argued that judgments concerning medical treatment should be made by doctors. The Court of Appeals did however confirm the ruling of the District Court that the artificial feeding should be considered medical treatment.[113]

After the Court of Appeals' decision, Ineke Stinissen's doctor decided to stop the artificial feeding.[114] Ineke Stinissen died on 19 January 1990.

THE REPORT OF THE REMMELINK COMMISSION AND THE GOVERNMENT'S REACTION

The Remmelink Commission delivered its report in September 1991. The research of Van der Maas, carried out under the authority of the Remmelink Commission, finally put an end to more or less wild speculations concerning the extent of euthanasia. It appeared from this research that about 1.7% of all deaths (2300) per year were due to euthanasia and 0.2% (400 deaths) to assistance with suicide. The research also revealed that in 0.8% (1000 deaths) the life of a patient was ended without the patient having made an explicit request for this (see further chapter 5.3 on the findings of this research).

Politically speaking, the essential function of the Remmelink Commission was the same as that which the State Commission had failed to perform: to pacify the euthanasia discussion. Whether or not such a pacificatory function was consciously intended,[115] it was certainly fulfilled. Although the results of the research can support a variety of interpretations and conclusions, the Commission's report consistently chooses the politically unproblematic interpretation and draws the politically reassuring conclusion. The general tenor of its report is that – leaving aside some lapses in observance of the 'requirements of careful practice' – the current situation in the Netherlands gives no occasion for

---

112 *Tijdschrift voor Gezondheidsrecht* 1987, no. 50.

113 *Nederlandse Jurisprudentie* 1989, no. 909.

114 The Dutch Association for Patients (a 'pro-life' organization) brought a civil action to force the doctor to continue the artificial feeding of Ms. Stinissen. The District Court ruled that the plaintiff had no standing to sue (*Kort Geding* 1990, no. 32). The Court of Appeals confirmed this ruling (*Nederlandse Jurisprudentie* 1990, no. 470).

115 There is no reason to attribute any such intent to the members of the Commission, let alone to the researchers.

political concern. The reception of the report can best be characterized as a collective sigh of relief that there was apparently no real problem. The Labor Party (PvdA) – long supporters of the Wessel-Tuinstra bill – were promptly able to agree with the Christian Democrats (CDA), with whom they had formed a Government in 1989, that no substantial legislative change was required.

The Government gratefully seized the opportunity offered it by the report of the Remmelink Commission. On 8 November 1991 it published its formal reaction to the report.[116] The research done for the Commission had demonstrated, the Government concluded, that "medical practice in connection with the end of life is characterized by great conscientiousness and responsibility".[117] With very rare exceptions, doctors exhibit the "greatest possible care" before coming to the decision that the situation of necessity that justifies euthanasia is present. Such decisions take place in circumstances in which "medically speaking the patient must be considered beyond hope".[118] The Government noted the Commission's conclusion that however good the treatment of pain is, this will not always replace the need for euthanasia, among other things because pain is not always the most important kind of suffering that leads to a request for euthanasia.

For the sake of the necessary external control over medical decisions concerning euthanasia, the Government proposed to maintain the existing provisions in the Criminal Code, as interpreted by the courts. The nature of the defence of necessity as a justification for departure from the general norm precludes, the Government argued, the formulation in legislation of the conditions under which the defence will succeed.

The Government proposed to withdraw the bill of 1987 and to substitute a new one, which did no more than put a legal foundation under the reporting procedure in effect since 1990.[119] As the Remmelink Commission had advised, this procedure would now also be applicable to cases of terminating life without an explicit request. The 'requirements of careful practice' would be incorporated in the reporting procedure.[120]

THE LEGISLATION OF 1993

The legislation ultimately adopted in 1993 and currently in effect was an amendment to the Law on the Disposal of Corpses.[121] It makes a technical change in the legal status of the forms to be used for reporting the death of a patient. Pursuant to the new Law a

---

116 *Second Chamber of Parliament 1991-1992,* 20 383, no. 14.
117 *Second Chamber of Parliament 1991-1992,* 20 383, no. 14: 2.
118 *Second Chamber of Parliament 1991-1992,* 20 383, no. 14: 2
119 *Second Chamber of Parliament 1991-1992,* 22 572, no. 2 and 3.
120 The Government also proposed to continue support for research into the treatment of pain and to strengthen the support services for patients who choose to die at home.
121 Wet op de lijkbezorging, art. 10 s. 1, *Staatsblad* 643, 1993.

special form was prescribed for cases of euthanasia, assistance with suicide and termination of life without an explicit request. This form[122] consists largely of a list of 'Points requiring attention' to be covered in the doctor's report, which more or less correspond to the various elements of the 'requirements of careful practice' laid down in the case law. In this indirect way the Dutch Parliament can be said to have addressed itself to the legitimacy of euthanasia and, via a back door, to have ratified what the courts had long since done. Technically speaking, the legislation does not affect the legality of euthanasia at all. (See appendix I-B for the text of the Law and the 'Points requiring attention'.)

THE *CHABOT* CASE: ASSISTANCE WITH SUICIDE IN CASES OF NON-SOMATIC SUFFERING

The next important legal development was in 1994, when a case of assistance with suicide given to a person whose suffering was not based on a somatic condition reached the Supreme Court.[123]

---

122 *Staatsblad* 688, 1993, effective 1 June 1994.

123 Two earlier cases deal with the question of legitimacy of assistance with suicide to patients whose suffering is not somatic. The first case concerned a woman who for many years suffered from severe depressions. Medical treatment appeared to be pointless, and her doctors, a psychiatrist and a GP, decided to assist her with suicide. They supplied her with lethal drugs and were prosecuted for assistance with suicide. They moved to dismiss the indictment, arguing that they had followed the 'requirements of careful practice'. The Court of Appeals, the Hague, held that it was not clear if in cases of non-somatic suffering the 'requirements of careful practice' are the same as in cases of physical suffering, but that in any event the doctors had not consulted an independent doctor. The Supreme Court affirmed this decision (*Nederlandse Jurisprudentie* 1991, no. 789). The doctors stood trial in Rotterdam. The District Court found that the request of the woman had been voluntary, well-considered and lasting. The Court ruled that the doctors could invoke the defence of necessity and acquitted them in spite of the Court's opinion that it would be desirable in cases of non-somatic suffering to consult another independent doctor (*Nederlandse Jurisprudentie* 1992, no. 664). The Court of Appeals, the Hague, also acquitted the doctors (*Tijdschrift voor Gezondheidsrecht* 1993, no. 52).

In the second case a pediatrician was prosecuted in 1991 for supplying lethal drugs to a 25-year-old patient suffering from *anorexia nervosa* (the case is known from John Zaritsky's film *An Appointment with Death*, see chapter 1, note 2). The pediatrician moved to dismiss the indictment arguing that he had followed the 'euthanasia protocol' of his hospital. He also invoked the defence of necessity. The District Court, Almelo considered the patient's suffering unbearable, saw no hope for recovery and judged the patient's request voluntary and well-considered. In the Court's opinion the doctor had followed the 'requirements of careful practice' and had been in a situation of necessity. The indictment was dismissed. (*Tijdschrift voor Gezondheidsrecht* 1992, no. 19.)

On 28 September 1991 the psychiatrist Chabot, at her request, supplied Ms. B with lethal drugs. She consumed the drugs in the presence of Chabot, a GP and a friend and died shortly thereafter. Chabot reported her death the same day to the local coroner as a suicide which he had assisted.

Briefly, the facts were as follows (see appendix II-2 for the decision of the Supreme Court and a fuller statement of the facts). Ms. B was 50 years old. Over a period of several years she had undergone a series of traumatic experiences that had deprived her of all desire to continue living. Psychiatric treatment had had little effect, and she had made one serious suicide attempt. She was referred to Chabot by the Association for Voluntary Euthanasia. After extensive discussions with her, he concluded that there was no question in her case of a psychiatric disorder or a major depressive episode. Her psychic traumas were in principle susceptible to psychiatric treatment (which would, however, have been long-term and with limited chance of success), but Ms. B consistently declined therapy. In Chabot's opinion, Ms. B was experiencing intense, long-term psychic suffering, the suffering was unbearable and hopeless for her, and her request for assistance with suicide was well-considered. He consulted a total of seven experts. Most of them agreed with his assessment of the situation and of the treatment perspectives (none of them considered it necessary to examine Ms. B).

The District Court, Assen,[124] and the Court of Appeals, Leeuwarden,[125] found the defence of necessity well-founded. On appeal, the Supreme Court reaffirmed its earlier judgments that euthanasia and assistance with suicide can be justified if

> the defendant acted in a situation of necessity, that is to say … that confronted with a choice between mutually conflicting duties, he chose to perform the one of greater weight. In particular, a doctor may be in a situation of necessity if he has to choose between the duty to preserve life and the duty as a doctor to do everything possible to relieve the unbearable and hopeless suffering of a patient committed to his care.[126]

The Court rejected the argument of the prosecution that this justification is not available in the case of assistance with suicide given to a patient whose suffering is non-somatic and who is not in the 'terminal phase'. It agreed with the holding of the Court of Appeals "that the wish to die of a person whose suffering is psychic can be based on an autonomous judgment". However, the Court concluded that in the circumstances of the case there was insufficient proof to support the defence of necessity, since there was no

---

124 *Tijdschrift voor Gezondheidsrecht* 1993, no. 42.
125 *Tijdschrift voor Gezondheidsrecht* 1993, no. 62.
126 *Nederlandse Jurisprudentie* 1994, no. 656: 3154.

statement from an "independent medical expert who has at least seen and examined the patient himself". Although, the Court observed, failure to consult a colleague – whether or not the latter examines the patient – does not in an ordinary case foreclose the defence of necessity, in the case of suffering that is not somatically based, evidence of consultation including actual examination of the patient is essential. The judgment of the independent colleague should cover the seriousness of the suffering and the prospects for improvement, the alternatives to assistance with suicide, and the question whether the patient's request was voluntary and well-considered, "without [the patient's] competence being influenced by his sickness or condition". In passing, the Court observed that "there can in principle be no question of lack of prospect of improvement if there is a realistic alternative to relieve the suffering which the patient has in complete freedom rejected."[127] Chabot was found guilty of the offence of assistance with suicide (however, no punishment was imposed).

REPORTS ON PROBLEMATIC CATEGORIES OF MBSL

Between 1990 and 1994 the Commission on the Acceptability of Medical Behavior that Shortens Life (CAL) of the Medical Association (see footnote 74 above) produced four provisional reports on the legitimacy of terminating life without an explicit request or in cases where the patient's competence is questionable. Two of these reports concern patients who are not able to make a request at all: severely defective newborn babies (CAL 1, 1990) and patients in a long-term coma (CAL 2, 1991). The third report concerns demented patients who are not entirely competent during the entire course of the decision-making (CAL 3, 1993), and the fourth report considers the legitimacy of assistance with suicide in the case of psychiatric patients (CAL 4, 1993). (See chapter 3.3, 3.4 and 3.5 on these reports.) A fifth problematic category was put on the public agenda in the same period by a former member of the Supreme Court, Drion. He argued for the right for persons over 75, under very limited circumstances, to be supplied with a 'pill' with which they could choose their own moment of death and thus avoid being exposed to a situation of physical or mental deterioration (see further chapter 3.5.2).

Except for including it in the reporting procedure, the Government had addressed no attention to the problem of patients not capable of expressing their will, put on the political agenda by the State Commission and the *Stinissen* case, and dealt with in the early 1990's in the CAL reports. In 1994, however, the Minister of Justice decided, against the advice of the Committee of Procurators-General, to prosecute two doctors for having actively terminated the lives of severely defective newborn babies.

---

127 See chapter 3.5.1, notes 179 and 192, on the difficulty of interpreting the expressions "complete freedom" and "realistic alternative".

THE *PRINS* AND *KADIJK* CASES: TERMINATION OF LIFE WITHOUT AN EXPLICIT
REQUEST IN THE CASE OF SEVERELY DEFECTIVE NEWBORN BABIES

On 26 April 1995 the gynecologist Prins stood trial in Alkmaar for murder, for having on 22 March 1993 terminated the life of a three-day-old severely defective baby. The medical team responsible for the baby, in consultation with her parents, had earlier decided to cease further medical treatment and in particular not to operate on her *spina bifida* because such surgery was considered medically futile. This decision made the baby's death inevitable, but it was not certain how long her dying would take. The baby was suffering unbearable pain which could not effectively be treated. The doctors and the parents decided to give the baby a lethal injection. Prins properly reported his act to the local coroner.

Prins acknowledged at his trial that he had put an end to the baby's life but he argued that this could not be called 'murder'. Further, he invoked the defence of absence of substantial violation of the law. In case these defences should fail, he invoked the defence of necessity. The District Court rejected the first and the second defences but held that active termination of life without an explicit request by the person concerned can be justifiable if certain requirements are met. Prins' defence of necessity was accepted because

a.   the baby's suffering had been unbearable and hopeless, and there had not been another medically responsible way to alleviate it;
b.   both the decision-making leading to the termination of life and the way in which it was carried out had satisfied the 'requirements of careful practice';
c.   the doctor's behavior had been consistent with scientifically sound medical judgment and the norms of medical ethics;
d.   termination of life had taken place at the express and repeated request of the parents as legal representatives of the newborn baby.[128]

Prins was acquitted. On appeal, the Court of Appeals, Amsterdam, agreed with the holdings of the District Court.[129]

On 26 April 1994 the GP Kadijk ended the life of a baby who had lived for 24 days. The baby suffered from an incurable congenital disorder that was bound to prove fatal, and her parents had decided, in consultation with her doctors, to care for her at home until she died. It was decided to omit all further medical treatment except for relief of suffering. When the baby's suffering grew worse and it became apparent she would probably

---

128 *Nederlandse Jurisprudentie* 1995, no. 602: 2878.
129 *Nederlandse Jurisprudentie* 1996, no. 113. The Court of Appeals did not discuss requirement (d).

die in an unacceptable way, Kadijk decided together with the parents to give the girl a lethal injection. Kadijk reported the death of the child as 'not natural' to the coroner.

Kadijk stood trial for murder in Groningen on 13 November 1995. The District Court rejected the request of the prosecutor to dismiss the case on the ground that the reporting procedure is in violation of the privilege against self-incrimination. It also rejected the defendant's request to dismiss the case on the ground of abuse of the power to prosecute to secure legal development rather than to secure a conviction. After having also rejected other defences (Kadijk claimed that the behavior was not 'murder', and he invoked the defence of the 'medical exception'), the Court accepted the defence of justification due to necessity.[130] The District Court's decision was affirmed on appeal (see appendix II-3 for the judgment of the Court of Appeals).

A SECOND NATIONAL STUDY OF MBSL

In 1994 a new Government (PvdA, VVD and D66) had been formed in which, for the first time in modern Dutch political history, none of the confessional parties was represented. It came as a great disappointment to many when the Government announced that it did not intend

> to introduce legislation to delete euthanasia from the Criminal Code. The way in which the Law on the Disposal of Corpses is working will be carefully assessed, with special attention to the reporting procedure; the relationship between the reporting procedure in the case of termination of life on request and of termination of life without a request, and prosecution policy, will also be examined. This evaluation will be completed within two years.[131]

In light of the Government's position, the NVVE decided it was necessary to keep up the pressure for legislative reform. In April 1996 it published a new proposed bill on euthanasia (see appendix I-C-3 for the text of the NVVE bill). The gist of the proposed revisions of articles 293 and 294 of the Criminal Code is that euthanasia and assistance with suicide by a doctor are not illegal when performed in accordance with the 'requirements of careful practice', which are to be included in the Criminal Code. The NVVE bill would also add a new article which makes it legal to supply a person who is not currently suffering, but who does not want to undergo physical or mental deterioration, the means for a 'gentle death'. The NVVE seeks hereby to legalize the so-called 'Drion pill'.

---

130 *Medisch Contact* 51: 199-203 (1996).
131 *Second Chamber of Parliament 1993-1994*, 23 715 no. 11 (coalition agreement): 32.

The results of the research promised by the Government in 1994 became available at the end of 1996. As we will see in chapter 5.3, the results generally confirm the picture presented by the research for the Remmelink Commission in 1991, and the political message – that with regard to medical practice in connection with euthanasia and assistance with suicide there is not much reason for great public concern – was essentially the same. However, the new research directly addresses the question of the effectiveness of the reporting procedure, and here the burden of the findings, as we will see in chapters 5 and 6, is more problematic: the rate of reporting, while improved, is still rather low, and it seems that the more dubious cases (and in particular cases of termination of life without an explicit request) are hardly being reported at all. The problem of effective enforcement of the legal rules concerning euthanasia thereby became a central concern in the public debate. The Medical Association and the NVVE argued that legal insecurity resulting from the failure to adopt legislation legalizing euthanasia is the cause of the problem. The Government, on the other hand, argued that the problem lies in the distaste of doctors for having their behavior assessed by lawyers, and proposed that cases reported by doctors should be examined, in the first instance, by regional assessment committees composed largely of doctors. All these proposals are discussed extensively in chapter 6.

TO SUM UP

In the period 1986-1997 a variety of efforts were made to codify the results reached in the courts in an earlier period. All of these stranded, not always for want of majority support in Parliament but as a result of the exigencies of forming coalition governments. In the end, the only legislation that could be passed did nothing more than place the already functioning reporting procedure on a firmer legal footing. When for the first time a Government was formed in 1994 that consisted exclusively of parties that had earlier supported legislative legalization, this Government nevertheless turned out to have little enthusiasm for burning its fingers on the issue and proposed to postpone legislation until after new national research, including an evaluation of the reporting procedure.

In the same period, and as a direct consequence of the legislative stalemate, two major national studies were made of euthanasia and other medical behavior that shortens life. The results will be extensively discussed in chapter 5. Stimulated in part by the findings of this research, the public debate – having in an earlier period been narrowed down to euthanasia and assistance with suicide – was widened again to include other sorts of medical behavior that shortens life. First in reports of several medical professional bodies and shortly thereafter in the case law, the problems of assistance with suicide in the case of psychiatric patients and of shortening of life of severely defective newborn babies and of long-term coma patients began to receive serious attention. Toward the end of this period, in particular after the results of the second national survey became available, the public discussion focussed increasingly on the problem of effective regulation, a matter that receives extensive attention in chapter 6.[132]

2.5   Concluding remarks on the process of legal change

At the end of the 1960s euthanasia and assistance with suicide, which never before had received much public attention in the Netherlands, had become subjects of public debate. In section 2.1 we concluded that two kinds of change played an important role in bringing this about: a cultural change and changes in medical technology. These two changes alone, however, cannot account for more recent developments in the Netherlands regarding the legality of medical behavior that shortens life.

The lack of ideological confrontation between opponents and advocates of legalization of euthanasia is remarkable and is reflected in the fact that in this chapter almost no attention has been paid to the opponents. Partly this is because only a few opponents wielded the pen, and those few were mostly ignored. But more important is the political atmosphere in the Netherlands. Even though the period of 'pillarization' has come to an end, the solution generally sought for dealing with political disagreement over a matter of fundamental principle remains one of avoidance of frontal conflict whenever possible. Avoidance is accomplished by postponement of decision-making or by 'depoliticizing' the issue involved as much as possible (see the *Prologue*). Political decisions can often be postponed by appointing advisory commissions, and as we have seen, much use has been made of this technique by successive Dutch Governments.

'Depoliticizing', the art of representing political questions which risk polarization as if they can be solved in an objective, politically neutral way, is reflected in the early separation of euthanasia and assistance with suicide from the whole complex of medical behavior that shortens life. The effect of this separation was that political and legal decisions could be taken in stages. First the less controversial sorts of MBSL were recognized as 'normal medical practice'. Then MBSL that could be justified in terms of the principle of autonomy were liberalized. And finally the limits of shortening life without an explicit request were explored. We are not suggesting that 'depoliticization' is a conscious strategy. It is rather that the characteristic way the Dutch political system operates avoids

---

132 A recent institutional development should be mentioned here. In 1993 the KNMG had made a number of proposals for experimental projects intended to increase the willingness of doctors to report cases of euthanasia. One of these proposals was for a 'support center' in Amsterdam to which doctors can turn for information and advice in advance from a specially trained doctor, who is also available for formal consultation. This center recently began operation. See Dillmann et al. 1997.

frontal confrontations wherever possible and requires politicians to try to find some common ground that is widely shared on which to base important political decisions. Frequently that common ground can be found in a small part of some larger problem.

'Depoliticizing' has not only been a feature of public, political debate: professional groups have also avoided ideological discussions. They have focussed their attention on procedures and rules of careful practice. The Medical Association, which has played an important role in the process of change, has been very cautious. For a long time the Association took no position on euthanasia. Even in 1984, when it stated that euthanasia was part of the doctor-patient relationship, it avoided the question whether it was permissible. As a result of this careful policy, euthanasia and assistance with suicide were made subjects of open discussion within the profession. The Association's recognition in 1984 that the profession was responsible for euthanasia and assistance with suicide opened the way for a measure of decriminalization. This recognition was also very important for the public debate because it was made by a professional group in which the Dutch in general have great confidence.

One consequence of the tendency toward conflict avoidance has been that the process of change has gone rather slowly. Successive Governments never put much pressure for quick results on the Health Council or other advisory commissions. The motion requesting a state commission, for example, was adopted in 1978. The Government decided first to ask the Health Council to give advice on the assignment to be given this commission. This advice took three years, and then the work of the State Commission took another three years. However frustrating it has been for some participants in the public debate, this slowing down has not been without its benefits. The State Commission still had not finished its work when the Supreme Court ruled on the *Schoonheim* case. In this way the State Commission's advice and the judgment of the Supreme Court were mutually reinforcing. In the meantime the public, the medical and legal professions and the political elite were given time to adjust to changes which, at least partly as a result of the passage of time, had in the meantime acquired wide support throughout Dutch society.

The legal vacuum created by the deliberate pace of political decision-making has been filled by the courts, which have accepted the task of reconciling the conflict between the explicit prohibition of euthanasia and assistance with suicide in the Criminal Code and the increasingly apparent fact that these MBSL are widely practiced and enjoy general public support. In a sense, the courts have thereby usurped the constitutional role of the legislature, but the latter has not protested. On the contrary, the Government itself (which in a parliamentary system is directly answerable to the legislature) has frequently and openly made use of the courts to secure legal development. And Parliament itself has exhibited only respect for what the courts have done.

Looking back on the process of legal development, it is remarkable to see that already in the *Postma* and *Wertheim* cases the conditions under which euthanasia is legitimate and the essential contents of the 'requirements of careful practice' were already in place. Limitations that were later proposed and then abandoned, such as the 'terminal phase' and the assumption that non-somatic suffering cannot justify euthanasia or assistance with suicide, had already been rejected in those first decisions.

Exploiting the possibilities of the casuistic approach made available by the justification of necessity, Dutch courts and prosecutors have been able to emphasize the uniqueness of each individual case, thereby leaving a maximum of legal room within which doctors can make decisions in situations where shortening of life is at issue and be open about what they are doing. Both the courts and the prosecutorial authorities have from the beginning made it clear that they are inclined both to follow the medical profession itself in fashioning rules concerning justifiable euthanasia and to leave a great deal of latitude in individual cases to professional judgment.

In addition to professional groups, advisory bodies and the Association for Voluntary Euthanasia (which, because of its very moderate approach, has often been able to exercise considerable influence behind the scenes), there are also some individuals whose role has been important. It is thanks to individual doctors that the practice of shortening of life came out of the closet and subjected itself to public scrutiny, debate and, ultimately, control. Doctors came forward of their own accord, made the facts of their life-shortening behavior public, and subjected their behavior to the hazards of criminal prosecution. Without their idealism and courage it seems unlikely that Dutch legal development in this area would have progressed as quickly and effectively as it has.

3   The Current Legal Situation

In chapter 2 we have described the process of public debate and legal change that has led, over a period of almost 30 years, to the current state of affairs in Dutch law concerning euthanasia and related forms of medical behavior that shortens life. The purpose of the present chapter is to describe in a detailed and accurate but non-technical way what that law is.[1]

The chapter consists of two parts. The first two sections deal with matters on which legal development has fairly run its course and the applicable legal rules can be stated with some certainty. After dealing in section 3.1 with the substantive legal rules concerning various sorts of medical behavior that shortens life, we will describe in section 3.2 the existing system of legal control over this sort of medical behavior – the so-called 'report-ing procedure' – together with the problems that the technical legal basis of that regime implies with respect to the scope and the effectiveness of control.

The second part of the chapter (sections 3.3, 3.4, and 3.5) deals with unsettled questions, with the law in motion. Here, there are many points on which it is not easy to formulate current law in terms of settled rules, although the general contours of emerging law are on the whole quite clear. The treatment is therefore different: more discursive and more dependent on what appear to be the fundamental values and concerns underlying the course of legal development. On many questions we can predict with some confidence what the law 'is' (is becoming), but to do so we must often rely on a certain amount of legal hunch. An example of this is our prediction that the law governing medical behav-ior that shortens life in the case of coma patients (in the absence of an advance directive or other indication of the patient's wishes) will generally follow the development that has already taken place in the case of severely defective newborn babies, relying heavily on the 'priority principle' according to which 'active' termination of life can usually only be justified after – and as an extension of – a decision to let the patient die by abstaining from further treatment.

Needless to say, at a number of places such a division between the law that is settled and the law that is coming breaks down, either because there is an unsettled issue in a context

---

1   For general introductions in English to Dutch (criminal) law, see Blankenburg & Bruinsma 1994; Chorus et al. 1993. For a translation of the Dutch Criminal Code see Rayar & Wadsworth 1997.

of legal rules that have otherwise become well settled, or because there is a fixed point in a context that is otherwise in a state of rapid development. Whether and under what circumstances a legal preference for assistance with suicide as against killing on request will emerge is an issue of the first sort; making a prediction depends on how one interprets things happening at the cutting edge of legal development. The requirement of consultation is an example of the latter sort of issue: under what circumstances 'active' termination of life without an explicit request will ultimately be regarded as legal is not yet entirely clear, but it is quite clear that consultation of a second, independent doctor who himself examines the patient will in any case be required.[2]

A note to the reader. To a non-lawyer, especially the first part of this chapter (section 3.1) may seem about as dense as a tax code. That is because the subject is complicated and the Dutch have been engaged for a number of years in a kind of national project to regulate it carefully and in all of its aspects. The detail is important in itself – there is after all nothing trivial about the subjects dealt with. But it is in particular important as part of the overall argument of this book: the evidence assembled in this chapter shows as no generalization possibly could, how earnestly the Dutch have taken the task of regulating medical behavior that shortens life. If nothing else it puts the lie to the suggestion sometimes heard to the effect that the Dutch have substituted a sort of sloppy 'tolerance' and a naive faith in doctors for serious legal control (often thought by such critics to reside *par excellence* in criminal codes). We would like to ask you to bear with us, to do your best, and to feel entitled to skip a footnote once in a while.

---

2   A. Josephus Jitta observes (letter of 26 May 1997) in this connection that, based on his prosecutorial experience with some 500 cases in the period 1988-1994, the medical situation of the patient is almost never a matter of doubt and therefore not of discussion between the consulting and the consulted doctor, and furthermore is usually well documented. Consultation therefore concerns primarily the voluntariness and well-consideredness of the request. To the extent that this is the case (compare chapter 5.2 and 5.3.1), consultation might seem *less* indicated in cases where there is no request. However, in our view the principal function of consultation is not the 'second opinion' but rather control: another (expert) person knows what the situation was before the patient died. From that point of view, consultation is *more* essential in the case of termination of life without an explicit request.

3.1   A summary of current law concerning medical behavior that shortens life

3.1.1   'Normal medical practice', the 'medical exception' and a 'natural death'

In principle, intentionally causing injury or death is an offence under one or more of a number of provisions of every criminal code. Nevertheless, in everyday medical practice behavior regularly occurs that is more or less certainly known and expected – and in that legal sense, 'intended' – to have such a result: the dentist who causes pain by drilling in one's teeth, the surgeon who amputates a leg, the oncologist who gives one chemothera-py. While such behavior violates the literal terms of the criminal law, it also falls within the scope of the legal authority to practice medicine. As such it constitutes 'normal med-ical practice' and is taken to be covered by an implicit 'medical exception' to the criminal offences that protect life and bodily integrity. The death of a patient due to such 'normal medical practice' – for example, during open-heart surgery or as a result of intensive use of pain-killing drugs – is considered a 'natural death' and can be reported as such to the coroner by the responsible doctor (which means in practice that no further official inves-tigation of the death will be undertaken). These three legal terms – medical exception, normal medical practice, and natural death – are the foundation stones of the Dutch sys-tem of legal control over medical behavior that shortens life.

The concepts themselves will be discussed extensively in the course of this book, espe-cially in chapter 6 in connection with the effectiveness of legal regulation of medical behavior that shortens life. But it is important to be aware that – while remaining largely implicit – they afford the underlying structure of the legal analysis presented in this chapter. The essence of that structure is as follows. The 'medical exception' applies to that behavior of doctors that constitutes 'normal medical practice', that is to say, behavior that doctors are generally authorized to perform based on medical indications and according to professional (technical and ethical) norms. However, there are other sorts of behavior that doctors are also legally authorized to perform, behavior based not on 'medical' indi-cations nor regulated by professional norms but defined and regulated directly[3] by the law. In the past, abortion was believed to be an example of both sorts of medical behav-ior. Medically-indicated abortion fell within the category of 'normal medical practice' and thus within the 'medical exception'. As the demand for abortion for non-medical reasons grew, legal standards applicable to such abortions had to be sought outside the

---

3   Indirectly, of course, all professional norms – at least, all those that derive from the legal authority to practice medicine – are 'legal', but much of their formulation and enforcement is in practice delegated to some extent to the profession itself (although Dutch medical discipli-nary law, for example, is predominantly 'legal' both substantively and procedurally). It is incorrect to describe professional control as 'turning the matter over to doctors'.

scope of 'normal medical practice'. The abortion reform law of 1984 permits doctors to perform such abortions under specified (non-medical) conditions. Similarly, euthanasia (and termination of life without an explicit request) falls at present outside the category of 'normal medical practice' (and the 'medical exception') and therefore, to the extent it is legal at all, the standards applicable to its performance are legal and not medical standards.[4]

3.1.2   The concept 'medical behavior that shortens life' (MBSL)

With the benefit of hindsight it is clear that one of the most important contributions of the report of the State Commission on Euthanasia (1985) was to clarify the definition of 'euthanasia' (see chapter 2.3.2). In the Dutch public and legal discussion 'euthanasia' now refers exclusively to *behavior that terminates the life of another at the request of the person concerned.*

A solution to the resulting problem of defining the larger category of behavior, within which euthanasia is a distinct sort, has been worked out over the last few years in a sort of dialogue between Van der Maas and his colleagues, appointed by the Government to carry out the first national survey in 1990,[5] and the Commission on the Acceptability of Termination of Life of the Medical Association (CAL – see section 3.3 of this chapter on the CAL reports). In its first report the CAL had defined the general category of 'behavior that terminates life' in terms of the *purpose of the intervention*.[6] Van der Maas and colleagues found a definition in terms of behavior whose purpose is the death of the patient too narrow. They proposed, instead, the term 'medical decision concerning the end of life' (MDEL), defined as including "all decisions of doctors where the purpose is to hasten the death of the patient or where the doctor takes account of the likelihood that the death of the patient will be hastened".[7]

---

4   See Leenen 1994: 135ff, 278-279; 1996: 35ff, 99ff, for this analysis of the concept of 'normal medical practice' and application of the analysis to abortion and euthanasia. Enschedé's argument – successful in the case of abortion (see chapter 2.1) – took a different position: he argued that 'social indications' could, under modern conditions, be taken to fall within the scope of the concept of a 'medical indication'.

5   Van der Maas et al. 1991.

6   CAL 1: 4.

7   Van der Maas et al. 1991: 13-14. A number of objections can be made to the term MDEL: what needs to be defined is not *decisions* but *behavior*; the relevant decisions are only partly 'medical' (e.g. when the patient refuses further treatment); the behavior does not 'concern' the end of life, it brings it about; the behavior does not necessarily take place in the context of the 'end of life' – the patient need not necessarily have been 'dying'.

Starting with its second report, the CAL has emphasized not the doctor's purpose but his *responsibility for the results of the intervention*: 'behavior that terminates life' was defined in the second report as "behavior of doctors that causes the death of the patient".[8] In the third report, 'behavior that shortens life' takes the place of 'behavior that terminates life' (the latter being restricted to the situation in which a euthanaticum is used). Death is not necessarily the reason the doctor does what he does, but having "foreseen and accepted" that result, the doctor is responsible for bringing it about.[9] Since most of the patients involved are near to death anyway, the improved definition of the whole family of behavior of which euthanasia is a part emphasizes precisely what it is that the doctor is responsible for: not so much the fact of death as the moment at which it occurs, not so much his purpose as what he has reason to expect.

The concept of 'medical behavior that shortens life' (MBSL) that emerges from the process of conceptual development just sketched covers the following legal categories. (Quantitative data on the various sorts of MBSL is to be found in chapter 5.)

THE PATIENT REFUSES (FURTHER) LIFE-PROLONGING TREATMENT

A competent patient[10] has the legal right, for whatever reason, to refuse (further) treatment, even if the treatment is (in the opinion of the doctor) indicated and necessary to continued life. It is not relevant that the patient exercises this right in order to shorten his life; nor is it relevant that the doctor (or anyone else) agree with the patient's decision.

In the not very distant past Dutch doctors tended to be rather authoritarian and the law accepted this, but as in other countries where the idea of 'informed consent' has acquired general acceptance, the patient's essentially unqualified right to self-determination in this regard is no longer subject to doubt. It may be a right whose exercise is not always made easy for the patient, but as a matter of legal principle the doctor who imposes treatment on a patient without his consent is without question guilty of a number of medical disciplinary, civil and even criminal offences.

Because of the limited conditions under which euthanasia is legal and a variety of other difficulties that may stand in the way of a person who wishes to die, it has recently been noted by several observers in the Netherlands and elsewhere that cancer patients and

---

8   CAL 2: 3.
9   CAL 3: 9.
10   CAL 3 and 4 consider the problem of refusal of treatment by only partly competent persons (in the case of senile dementia and psychiatric patients) – see sections 3.4 and 3.5.1 below. Blijham & Van Delden (1996) argue for a presumption of competence in connection with the role of the patient in decision-making with respect to reanimation. See also note 174 (p. 145).

elderly people suffering from dementia can and do 'let themselves die' (*versterven*) by starvation and dehydration (abstaining from food and/or drink). Especially when done in cooperation with a sympathetic doctor and with appropriate symptomatic relief, the method is alleged to be a not unpleasant one, at least for the elderly. It is probably in fact a way that many people in the past have died.[11]

It is when it is not the patient himself but someone else who seeks to exercise the right to refuse treatment on his behalf that legal difficulties arise. The fact that a person is not at the relevant moment himself capable of exercising the right to refuse treatment does not necessarily entail a forfeiture of its benefit. For one thing, he may have done so in the past by means of an 'advance directive'. Recent legislation in which the autonomy of the patient with respect to medical treatment is guaranteed provides explicitly that a written 'advance directive' binds the doctor, although it is not entirely clear what the exact scope and limitations are of this binding force.[12] The same legislation provides that appointed representatives and close relatives of the patient can exercise the right on his behalf;[13] presumably they must thereby take account of the known wishes and general outlook of the person concerned. There is still much room for legal clarification and refinement of basic principles that are now generally accepted. Some of the issues are discussed further at various places in this chapter.

The doctor who, at the request of the patient (or his surrogate), abstains from treatment that is necessary for the preservation of life is not regarded as having killed the patient, in the sense of the homicide offences mentioned above. The patient's death is considered

---

11   On 'letting oneself die' see Chabot 1996; see also section below. For an indication of the magnitude of the phenomenon, see chapter 5.3.1 note 49. See also notes 10 and 16.

12   *Wet op de geneeskundige behandelingsovereenkomst* [Law on Contracts for Medical Treatment], which became effective on 1 April 1995 as artt. 7:446 ff. of the Civil Code. Art. 450 section 3 provides that if a patient 16 or older, who "cannot be considered capable of coming to a reasonable assessment of his interests" has made a written declaration to the effect that he refuses treatment under certain circumstances at a time when he was competent to do so, both the doctor and a representative of the patient are bound to follow his instructions. The doctor may only override the patient's refusal if he considers that there are 'well-founded reasons' for doing so (that is, substantial reason to suppose that the patient himself would have wanted the treatment in question). See generally on this law: Sluyters & Biesaart 1995.

13   Art. 465 of the law referred to in the previous footnote accords such representatives a substantial status in the decision-making with regard to treatment. As in the United States, there have been a number of cases concerning the right of the family of coma-patients and of severely defective babies to refuse treatment on behalf of the person concerned. For discussion of these cases see Leenen 1994: 314-322. See section 3.3.1 on 'surrogates'.

due to a 'natural' cause, which means that, by contrast with euthanasia, no special legal controls obtain.[14]

'NORMAL MEDICAL PRACTICE'

Two other sorts of medical behavior that shorten life are likewise essentially non-controversial. They are deemed to fall within the scope of the 'normal medical practice' that a doctor is authorized to perform. The death of the patient is considered 'natural', with the consequences for control just mentioned. Outside the medical profession itself there has not been much debate on these sorts of MBSL and the complex issues of control that they involve. As we will argue in chapter 6.3.3, it seems important that the 'requirements of careful practice' that have been worked out over the last decade for euthanasia also come to apply, *mutatis mutandis,* to these less controversial sorts of MBSL.

1   Use of drugs to alleviate pain or other symptoms even though the dose used will more or less certainly hasten the moment of death.

It is generally accepted that shortening the dying process in a way that leads to a 'death without suffering' (*zachte dood*) can be a legitimate subsidiary objective of the administration of pain relief.

2   Not initiating, or terminating, life-prolonging treatment when this is 'medically futile' [*medisch zinloos*], either in the sense that the treatment has no chance of success or that it would be (or has become) disproportionate to any benefit for the patient.

The only real controversy concerns the extent to which the doctor's decision to abstain can be based on 'quality-of-life' considerations (see further section 3.3.1).

What constitutes 'medical treatment' in this connection has in recent years been the subject of considerable discussion. It is now clear that artificial administration of food and drink is 'medical care' that can be terminated.[15]

---

14   Civil and general medical disciplinary law does, of course, apply. Thus doctors are subject to general requirements of informed consent, record-keeping and the like. See Sluyters & Biesaart 1995: 33ff, 62ff.

15   See the *Stinissen* case (chapter 2.4); Leenen (1994: 315-317) distinguishes between the case in which giving a patient food and drink are part of normal nursing care (the withholding of which would be the offence defined in article 255 of the Criminal Code) and the case, as in *Stinissen,* in which the artificial aspect of administration of food and drink is predominant.

A doctor is not required to accede to a patient's (or his representative's) insistence on treatment the doctor considers futile. On general principles it would seem that he must at least inform the patient or, in the case of a non-competent patient, the family or others responsible for the patient, of the fact that he proposes to abstain from treatment he considers futile, if only so that they can seek a second professional opinion.[16]

Unless based on the patient's request, 'Do Not Resuscitate' instructions and other advance decisions not to administer life-prolonging treatment under specified conditions also fall in this category. It has recently been argued in connection with a hospital protocol for such decisions that the greater the role that proportionality or 'quality-of-life' considerations play, the greater the role of the patient (or his representative) in the decision-making should be.[17]

TERMINATION OF LIFE

The final category of MBSL is termination of life, which encompasses what used to be called 'active, direct euthanasia' (see chapter 2.2, 2.3.2). 'Termination of life' could be operationalized as the use of euthanatica[18] were it not for the residual possibility of non-pharmacological methods of terminating life (such as the 'plastic bag method') and the continuing if declining use of morphine.[19]

Termination of life is either voluntary or non-voluntary, depending on whether or not it is done at the explicit request of the person concerned. As we will see in section 3.3.1 and chapter 5.3.2, in many cases of non-voluntary termination of life there is reason to sup-

---

16   See Leenen 1994: 312-313. In 1994 the family of an Alzheimer patient complained to the prosecutorial authorities that a doctor had ceased artificial administration of food and drink without consulting them, allegedly in violation of article 255 of the Criminal Code (failure to care for a person for whose care one is responsible); the treatment was recommenced (see Leenen 1994: 317, n. 155). A recent case involving an Alzheimer patient who almost died in a nursing home as a result of application of the home's policy of abstaining from further artificial hydration under certain circumstances, but who recuperated when his family had him transferred to a hospital, has called national attention to the frequency of such practice and to the importance of good communication with the family. The man's daughter complained to the prosecutorial authorities who, after consulting the Medical Inspector, decided not to prosecute. See NVVE 1997 for a collection of newspaper reports concerning this case and, more generally, the phenomenon of 'letting oneself die' [*versterven*] (see also note 11 above).

17   Blijham & Van Delden 1996.

18   Compare CAL 3: 9 for such an operationalization.

19   The view that the use of morphine for termination of life is unprofessional is based in part on the resulting confusion as to what the doctor 'really' did: termination of life or pain relief.

pose that the person concerned would have wanted it if he had been able to express a will at the critical time; in the remaining cases, nothing is known about the will of the patient and termination of life is based on what are taken to be his interests. Although the expression 'involuntary euthanasia' (meaning: involuntary termination of life) is sometimes tendentiously used by critics of Dutch law to describe situations in which the termination is non-voluntary, there is in fact no room in Dutch law for termination of life *contrary to* the will, express or presumed, of the person concerned. Such behavior by a doctor would be simple murder and is no more tolerated in the Netherlands than anywhere else. There seems no reason to suppose it in fact occurs more frequently in Dutch practice than elsewhere. It does not fall within the category MBSL.

Voluntary termination of life is either euthanasia or assistance with suicide. It is a crime under articles 293 and 294 of the Criminal Code. The circumstances under which it may nevertheless be legally justifiable are discussed in the following section. Non-voluntary termination of life is known in the Dutch discussion as 'termination of life without an explicit request'. It amounts to murder or manslaughter (articles 289 and 287 of the Criminal Code). The circumstances under which it may nevertheless be legally justifiable are discussed in sections 3.3 and 3.4.

Figure 3.1 summarizes the various categories of MBSL:

Figure 3.1 The different sorts of MBSL

sort of MBSL		legal category	basis of legitimacy	legal status
refusal of treatment		**refusal of treatment**	autonomy of patient	criminal and civil prohibitions on invasion of bodily integrity
'normal medical practice'		**abstinence**	futility; interest of patient; (presumed) will of patient	authority to practice medicine
		pain relief	interest of patient; (presumed) will of patient	
'termination of life'	voluntary	**euthanasia**	autonomy of patient	justification of necessity
		assistance with suicide	autonomy of patient	
	non-voluntary	**termination of life without an explicit request**	interest of patient; (presumed) will of patient	

3.1.3 'Euthanasia'

Article 293 of the Dutch Criminal Code (see appendix I-1) provides that a "person who takes the life of another person at that other person's express and earnest request" is guilty of a serious offence. This is what is considered 'euthanasia' in the Netherlands. 'Euthanasia' is thus on its face illegal but, as we have already seen in chapter 2, it can under specific conditions be legally justifiable. Killing a person *without* his 'express and earnest request' (non-voluntary termination of life) may or may not be justifiable, but it is not 'euthanasia'. It is known in the Dutch discussion as 'termination of life without an explicit request'. Prosecutions in such cases (a number of which will be considered later on in this chapter) are generally for murder or manslaughter.

By contrast with euthanasia, assistance with suicide would not be an offence at all but for article 294, since suicide itself is not an offence. Nevertheless, despite their distinct treatment in the Criminal Code[20] and the fact that they carry rather different penalties, Dutch law, as we have seen in chapter 2, generally makes no distinction between the two as far as the justification available to a doctor is concerned. As elsewhere in this book, we will in this chapter often use the term 'euthanasia' for both except where the difference is relevant. Section 3.1.4 considers the question whether distinct legal treatment would be desireable.

As we have seen in chapter 2, the older Dutch literature made a distinction between 'passive' and 'active', and between 'direct' and 'indirect' euthanasia. The State Commission, however, successfully insisted on the distinction between euthanasia proper and what it called 'false forms of euthanasia'. Abstaining from treatment that the patient does not want or that is medical futile ('passive euthanasia') and death due to pain relief ('indirect euthanasia') are no longer considered 'euthanasia' at all.

The well-known Dutch criminal law scholar and former Supreme Court judge Enschedé argued some years ago that euthanasia, like other *prima facie* violations of the criminal offences protecting life and bodily integrity, is subject to an implied 'medical exception'.[21] But as we have seen in chapter 2.3.1, this argument was rejected by the Dutch Supreme Court in 1986.[22]

---

20 Their legislative histories are in fact quite different (see Smidt 1891), and neither of them was enacted with an eye to medical practice, which was for Enschedé an important argument in favor of recognizing a 'medical exception' (see chapter 2.1, 2.3.1).

21 See chapter 2.1 (abortion), 2.3.1 (euthanasia). See Leenen 1994: 278-279 for criticism of this position.

22 *Nederlandse Jurisprudentie* 1987, no. 607. Compare the decision of the Court of Appeals in the *Kadijk* case (appendix II-3), similarly rejecting the 'medical exception' in the case of termination of life without a request.

The Dutch courts had, apart from the 'medical exception', only a limited number of doctrinal tools available to them by means of which some opening for legal euthanasia could be created. One was the idea of 'absence of substantial violation of the law' [*ontbreken van de materiële wederrechtelijkheid*], of which the essence is that the legislator, in defining the offence, had another sort of situation in mind. Although the Supreme Court once accepted such a defence (in 1933[23]), the Dutch courts have been loath to honor it, its invocation by a defendant generally being regarded as an invitation to judicial legislation. Although euthanasia defendants have regularly raised the defence, arguing that in the circumstances of euthanasia or assistance with suicide by a doctor the essential purpose of the criminal prohibition is not violated, the courts have resolutely rejected the appeal.[24]

Another doctrinal tool that defendants have invoked is the excuse of duress: the patient's appeal to the doctor, it being argued, having overwhelmed the latter's ability to conform to the law. The courts have made short shrift of this defence, dryly observing that it is precisely the task of the doctor to be able to resist this sort of pressure from patients.

The doctrinal tool finally accepted by the courts is that of justification due to necessity, as provided for in article 40 of the Criminal Code.[25] Article 40 provides that an actor is not guilty of an offence if it was "the result of a force he could not be expected to resist [*overmacht*]". Since 1923 this provision has been interpreted to include the defence that the act took place in a situation of necessity in which the actor made a justifiable choice between two conflicting duties. (The text of article 40 can be found in appendix I-A.) The doctor confronted by the request of a patient who is unbearably and hopelessly suffering can, the courts have held, be regarded as caught in a situation of conflict of duties. On the one hand, there is the duty to respect life, as formulated in articles 293 and 294. On the other hand, there is a duty that has been variously formulated as one to reduce suffering or to respect the 'personality' (autonomy) of the patient.[26] If, in this situation of conflict of duties, the doctor chooses a course of action that, considering the norms of medical ethics, is 'objectively' justifiable, the Supreme Court held in 1984 in the *Schoonheim* case (see appendix II-1) that he is not guilty of an offence.

The requirements of a substantive and of a procedural or professional character that must be met by a doctor who carries out euthanasia or gives assistance with suicide have become fairly clear. Some of these have been formulated by the courts in the context of

---

23 *Nederlandse Jurisprudentie* 1933, no. 918.

24 See e.g. the opinion of the Supreme Court in the *Schoonheim* case (appendix II-1).

25 Confusingly, both the justification of necessity (conflict of duties) and the excuse of duress are based on article 40, which on its face seems only to deal with duress in the sense of an excuse.

26 See appendix II-2, note 29.

criminal prosecutions,[27] others in a variety of other legal sources, in particular proposed legislation, existing legal rules, and the reports and position-papers of various organs of the medical profession.[28] Since our interest here is in the whole of the law (including the law that is in the process of emerging), the minor differences between the various sources are not essential. The following requirements are now generally accepted:

SUBSTANTIVE REQUIREMENTS

The essential substantive conditions of legal euthanasia concern the patient's request, the patient's suffering, and the doctor-patient relationship.

1   The patient's request must, in the terms of article 293, be 'express and earnest'. Absent such a request, the behavior concerned is not euthanasia but murder. The request requirement is operationalized as follows:

–   the request must be explicitly made by the person concerned;[29]
–   the request must be voluntary (not the result of undue external influence);[30]

---

27   See Leenen (1994: 291-294) for treatment of the requirements specifically rooted in this case law.

28   The most important current sources for the law with regard to euthanasia are the decisions of the Supreme Court in the *Schoonheim* and *Chabot* cases (appendix II-1 and II-2), the 'Points requiring attention' included on the form to be used in reporting euthanasia (see appendix I-B), and the most recent version of the official guidelines of the Medical Association (KNMG 1995, which includes the 'Points requiring attention' in an appendix).

29   This requirement is to be found in all formulations of the law concerning euthanasia since the report of the State Commission in 1985 (see chapter 2.3.2). For an example of its application in practice, see the decision of the District Court, Haarlem, in which the Court rejects the defence that not murder (as charged) but euthanasia was involved, emphasizing the difference between a patient's expression of a desire for the end of life and an explicit request to the doctor to terminate life. *Tijdschrift voor Gezondheidsrecht* 1986, no. 34.

30   This requirement is included in all formulations of the requirements for euthanasia (cf. the decision of the Supreme Court in the *Chabot* case, appendix II-2). See NVP 1997 (discussed in section 3.5.1 below) for consideration of voluntariness as a requirement distinct from that of well-consideredness; see also KNMG 1995.

–   it must be well-considered: informed, made after due deliberation and based on an enduring desire for the end of life (evidenced for instance by its having repeatedly been made over some period of time);[31]
–   the request should preferably be in writing or otherwise recorded.[32]

The requirement of a voluntary and well-considered request is actually only a variant of the general requirement of informed consent required in the case of a competent patient for all medical treatment. If there is a difference in the case of euthanasia, it lies in the oft-heard suggestion that the initiative should come from the patient himself, whereas in the case of other MBSL the doctor can suggest and even recommend a given course of action.[33]

2   The patient's suffering must be 'unbearable' [*ondraaglijk*] and 'hopeless' [*uitzicht-loos*] (in the sense of 'without hope for improvement').[34] This requirement is further operationalized as follows:

–   the suffering need not be physical (pain etc.) nor is a somatic basis required;[35] non-physical suffering can include such things as the prospect of inhuman deterioration [*ontluistering*] and the possibility of not being able to die in a 'dignified' way;[36]

---

31   See, e.g., the 'Points requiring attention'; KNMG 1995. See CAL 3 and 4 and NVP 1997 (discussed in sections 3.4 and 3.5.1 below) for extensive consideration of the requirement of well-consideredness in the case of patients suffering from dementia or a psychiatric disorder. The problem of competence of patients suffering from a somatic disorder has received relatively little attention (but see NVP 1997, §§ 6.4 and 6.5).

32   See the 'Points requiring attention'; KNMG-afdeling Enschede 1987: 667 ('preferably record-ed in writing or with a dictaphone'). See however NVP 1997 for the position that a written request may sometimes be undesirable.

33   From time to time, however, one also sees suggestions that a conscientious doctor may make a patient aware of the possibility of euthanasia (compare chapter 5.3.1 note 54). However this may be, considering the complexities of human communication and the fact that in most cases no one else will have been present, it seems doubtful that a strict rule requiring patient initiative would be enforceable.

34   On the whole, these are treated together as a single requirement, and the patient's subjective experience of his suffering is regarded as largely determinative (although it must be 'under-standable'). In 1995 the Committee of Procurators-General proposed to 'objectify' the suffer-ing requirement by separating the two components, but the Minister of Justice refused to allow this (see chapter 5.3.5).

35   See Leenen 1994: 293-294. The Medical Association earlier took the position that non-physi-cal suffering must at least be based on a somatic condition (KNMG 1992). In light of the Supreme Court's decision in the *Chabot* case (appendix II-2), it seems clear that this is not required (see also KNMG 1995).

36   See e.g. the decision of the Supreme Court in the *Schoonheim* case, appendix II-1.

- if the patient's suffering is based on a somatic condition, other possibilities[37] for treating the condition or relieving the suffering must have been exhausted or have been rejected by the patient (it is well-established that in such a case the patient's exercise of the right to refuse treatment does not preclude a request for euthanasia based on the resulting suffering[38]);
- if the patient's suffering is not based on a somatic condition, there must be no realistic possibility of treatment.[39]

It is not clear to what extent anticipation of a fate one does not want to undergo (e.g. confinement to a nursing home, or further mental deterioration) can by itself meet the requirement of unbearable suffering, nor whether euthanasia can be carried out on a demented patient who is not currently suffering from the dementia but who in an earlier advance directive requested it in such circumstances (see section 3.4).

---

37 See note 192 below for the possibility that these are not necessarily limited to *medical* possibilities.

38 Leenen 1994: 292. In one case, for example, the defence of necessity was allowed (in a situation of somatic suffering) despite the patient's refusal of treatment with psychopharmaca (Supreme Court, 27 November 1984, *Nederlandse Jurisprudentie* 1985, no. 106; Court of Appeals, The Hague, 10 June and 11 September 1986, *Nederlandse Jurisprudentie* 1987, no. 608). This situation seems in fact to be fairly common in practice, patients refusing life-prolonging treatment (e.g. cytostatic treatment) and requesting euthanasia; some patients apparently refuse palliative treatment, on the ground that they do not want to endure the diminished awareness that accompanies it, and request euthanasia instead. See however note 193 for a limiting case in which refusal of treatment may stand in the way of euthanasia.

39 See section 3.5.1 and the decision of the Supreme Court in the *Chabot* case (appendix II-2) on the question of refusal of treatment in the case of non-somatically based suffering.

3   Only a doctor may legally perform euthanasia.[40] In principle this should be a doctor who has an established treatment-relationship with the patient [*behandelend arts*].[41] No individual doctor is under an obligation to perform euthanasia, but a doctor who is conscientiously opposed should refer the patient to another doctor.

It was until recently sometimes supposed that the patient must be in the 'terminal phase' of his illness, although the Medical Association has since 1984 rejected such a requirement as medically meaningless, and the courts rejected it from the very beginning (see the *Postma* case, discussed in chapter 2.2). The former Minister of Justice's more or less one-man insistence on this limitation led to a number of prosecutions in late 1993 which were at the time generally believed to have significantly reduced the willingness of doctors to report euthanasia as such. However this may be, it is clear since the decision in the *Chabot* case (see chapter 2.4, 3.5.1 and appendix II-2) that no such limitation applies.[42] In fact, it is possible that the person requesting euthanasia may not necessarily have to be 'ill' at all (see section 3.5.2).

If for legal purposes, within the context of the defence of justification to a criminal charge, the requirement of a 'terminal phase' plays no role, it does not follow that it is irrelevant as a matter of legal policy. As we will see in chapter 6.3.2, one of the advantages

---

40   This restriction is included in all statements of euthanasia law – see, e.g., the legislative proposals of the State Commission on Euthanasia, Wessel-Tuinstra and the NVVE (appendix I-C). The KNMG guidelines of 1992 (KNMG 1992 – incorporated by reference in KNMG 1995) provide that the euthanasia must be carried out by or (if it takes place over a longer period) under the direct responsibility and supervision of the responsible doctor. A number of cases hold the defence of justification not available to lay persons (see chapter 2.2; *Tijdschrift voor Gezondheidsrecht* 1986, no. 22; 1990 no. 5). It is also not available to nurses (*Tijdschrift voor Gezondheidsrecht* 1988, nos. 1, 65; *Nederlandse Jurisprudentie* 1995, no. 477; 1996 no. 61).

41   This restriction is generally accepted although it is difficult to find specific authority for it (see e.g. Leenen 1994: 292). In 1994 there was a small political tempest in connection with several 'travelling euthanasia doctors', as they were disparagingly called, who made their services available through the Association for Voluntary Euthanasia to patients whose own doctors had failed to honor their requests. The Minister of Justice answered parliamentary questions about the practice by reporting the results of research both in prosecution files and by the Medical Inspectorate. It appeared that only a very small number of doctors were involved and that in some of these cases either criminal or medical disciplinary proceedings had been brought. The Minister expressed the view that in the case of a doctor other than the patient's own doctor, there is no doctor-patient relationship and it "would be difficult to invoke the defence of necessity". *Second Chamber of Parliament 1994-1995, appendix*, no. 301.

42   See also Leenen 1994: 293.

of a decriminalized approach to control over euthanasia is that it would permit a more fine-tuned approach to the considerations relevant to a doctor's behavior. In such a context, the extent to which the patient's life is shortened by euthanasia may well influence the extent, for example, to which he should insist on exploring treatment alternatives or should engage in more than the minimum consultation.

A final substantive requirement that is sometimes suggested but appears not yet to have been accorded any legal status is that euthanasia should not be performed if the patient is receiving life-prolonging treatment that has not yet been discontinued. In other words, abstinence should have priority over administration of euthanatica.[43] The idea is essentially the same as the 'priority principle' that has been proposed in the case of termination of life without an explicit request (comatose patients, newborn babies, etc. – see section 3.3.1).

PROCEDURAL AND PROFESSIONAL REQUIREMENTS ('REQUIREMENTS OF CAREFUL PRACTICE')[44]

In addition to the substantive conditions of legal euthanasia, the doctor who performs euthanasia must meet a number of procedural requirements.

1   The doctor must take adequate steps to satisfy himself with respect to the substantive requirements set out above. (Although often so formulated, it is not clear that this is really an additional requirement.)

2   He must formally[45] consult at least one other doctor with respect to the patient's condition and life-expectancy, the available alternatives, and the adequacy of the request (voluntary, well-considered, etc.).[46]

---

43   Compare KNMG 1975: 11; see the similar suggestion in Zwaveling 1994.
44   See generally KNMG 1995; 'Points requiring attention'. See the Glossary for the Dutch term 'zorgvuldigheidseisen'.
45   The Medical Association distinguished as early as 1984 between informal discussion with other doctors (especially those with whom one works or who are involved in treating the patient concerned) and a "formal assessment in advance of the merits of the request for euthanasia," for which it proposed the creation of local committees of 3-5 doctors to carry out such assessments (KNMG 1984). Nevertheless, it has only recently become clear that what the requirements of careful practice contemplate is not merely an informal discussion of the case but a formal 'consultation' (see KNMG 1995).
46   See Leenen 1994: 292; 'Points requiring attention'; various legislative proposals (appendix I-C). Compare note 2 above for the subjects actually dealt with in consultation.

– the consultant should in principle be 'independent' (not a subordinate, a member of a joint practice, a colleague in a group practice of specialists, or a doctor involved in the treatment of the patient);[47]
– in the case of a patient apparently suffering from a psychiatric disorder the consulted doctor should be a psychiatrist;[48]
– if the patient's suffering is of non-somatic origin, the consultant must himself examine the patient,[49] and in other cases he should do so;[50]
– the consultant should make a written report, that becomes part of the medical dossier of the patient.[51]

It seems in effect to be part of the consultation requirement that the consultant agree with the decision of the responsible doctor.[52] [53]

---

47 See 'Points requiring attention'. The Medical Association (KNMG 1995) further expresses a preference for a doctor who does not work in the same institution, especially in the case of smaller hospitals. From time to time the opinion is heard that in the case of GPs, the consultant ought not to be a fellow-member of a local substitution-group of GPs. The KNMG observes that if the case involves problems requiring special expertise, more than one consultant may be required (KNMG 1995).
There have been a number of proposals over the years to formalize the consultation procedure, for example by appointing specially qualified doctors to perform the function (see the State Commission's proposal for doctors appointed by the Minister of Health, appendix I-C-1; the KNMG's proposal for assessment committees, note 45 above).

48 See CAL 4: 36-37; NVP 1997: §4.1; 'Points requiring attention'; NVVE-bill (appendix I-C-3).

49 See the decision of the Supreme Court in the *Chabot* case (appendix II-2).

50 See KNMG 1995; 'Points requiring attention'.

51 See KNMG 1995.

52 See KNMG 1995, which regards it as necessary, if the consultant disagrees, to consult a second doctor (who should be apprised of the negative judgment of the first doctor). If the judgment of the second consultant is also negative, a doctor should not approach still other consultants until one of them agrees with him, but should reconsider his own opinion. NVP 1997 takes a similar position.

53 A case currently under investigation by the prosecutorial authorities and the Medical Inspectorate raises a new issue in connection with consultation: how long before the euthanasia can this take place, and in particular can it take place when the patient's suffering is not yet unbearable (in the case concerned, the consultation took place two months before the euthanasia)? The doctor involved considers such a practice preferable to consultation at the last minute when the patient is already suffering unbearably, since the patient is in a better position to express his wishes clearly to the consultant. See *Het Parool*, 19 July 1997; 'Open letter to the Medical Inspector, South Holland,' *Medisch Contact* 52: 776-777 (20 June 1997).

3   The doctor should discuss the matter with the immediate family and intimate friends [*naasten*] of the patient (unless the patient does not want this or there are other good reasons for not doing so).[54]

4   The doctor should discuss the matter with nursing personnel responsible for the patient's care and, if a nurse is involved in the request for euthanasia or in carrying it out, she should be included in the decision-making.[55]

5   The doctor should keep a full written record of the case (including information concerning the above elements).[56]

6   The termination of life should be carried out in a professionally responsible way and the doctor should stay with the patient continuously – or be immediately available – until the patient dies (except possibly, for good reasons, in the case of assistance with suicide if careful arrangements are made, including the availability of the doctor if needed).[57]

7   Death due to euthanasia may not be reported as a 'natural death' (in effect, the doctor must report himself as having committed what *prima facie* is a serious criminal offence) (see section 3.2).

If the above requirements for the legally permissible performance of euthanasia have been clear for about the last 10 years, there has been less clarity over how, exactly, they are to be enforced. The substantive requirements for justifiable euthanasia are enforced

---

54   See 'Points requiring attention'; KNMG 1995; but cf. Leenen 1994: 292.

55   See 'Points requiring attention'; in the case of psychiatric patients, at least, this requirement has a "mandatory character" (CAL 4: 37). For the situation in which a nurse is somehow directly involved, see KNMG 1992, 1995.

56   See 'Points requiring attention'; KNMG 1995. See for a recent case in which one of the failures of which the doctor was accused was failure to maintain an adequate dossier, District Court, Amsterdam, 1 April 1997 (*Makdoembaks*).

57   See Leenen (1994: 294); 'Points requiring attention'; KNMG 1985. Among the failures of which the doctor was accused in a recent case was the use of an inappropriate euthanaticum (insulin) and failure to remain with the patient until her death (District Court, Leeuwarden, 8 April 1997 (*Schat*)). The requirement of continuous presence, as formulated by the KNMG, does not seem to take account of the use of 'slow' methods of euthanasia such as morphine in which some part of the execution must necessarily be in the hands of nurses, it being hardly feasible for the doctor to be present the whole time. In a recent disciplinary case the tribunal was of the opinion that the doctor must maintain control over the euthanaticum until the moment of administration (Leenen 1994: 294) but presumably this does not apply in some cases of assistance with suicide.

through the criminal law. Without the patient's voluntary and well-considered request, the behavior is not a potentially justifiable case of 'euthanasia' but a *prima facie* (though, as we will see in sections 3.3 and 3.4, possibly justifiable) case of murder or manslaughter. Recent prosecutions for termination of life without an explicit request (newborn babies, coma patients, and 'help in dying' – see sections 3.3.2, 3.3.3 and 3.3.4) have in fact been prosecutions for the latter two offences. If the euthanasia is not performed by a doctor, the case falls under articles 293 or 294 but is not justifiable (except perhaps under extreme circumstances). Euthanasia in the absence of unbearable and hopeless suffering is not presently regarded as legally justifiable (see however section 3.5.2).

It was for some time unclear to what extent conformity with the 'procedural' requirements ('requirements of careful practice') is necessary for a successful defence to a criminal charge. It seems now to be settled that deviation from these requirements does not necessarily stand in the way of an appeal to the justification of necessity. Such a development was to be expected, since it would be disproportionate to convict a doctor for homicide when the euthanasia itself was otherwise unobjectionable and what he is really accused of is inadequate consultation, record-keeping or the like. The 'requirements of careful practice' are generally enforced in medical disciplinary proceedings (although it seems that in a case of multiple violations of the 'requirements of careful practice' the courts will hold that the defence of justification is not available[58]).

THE PATIENT'S RIGHT TO EUTHANASIA

As we have seen, the legal regulation of euthanasia has taken the form of a justification, available only to doctors, for what otherwise is a violation of two explicit provisions of the Criminal Code. A consequence of this is that the patient, even when his case meets all of the legal requirements, has no 'right' to euthanasia: if he finds a doctor willing to perform it, the doctor can legally do so, but no doctor has any obligation to accede to his request, however well-founded. In fact, all participants in the public debate have been insistent from the beginning that no doctor can ever be required to carry out euthanasia, and a small number of Dutch doctors are in fact for various reasons unwilling to do so.

In these circumstances the availability of euthanasia to a patient is largely a function of who the doctor responsible for his treatment happens to be. It is presumably rare that this doctor was specifically selected for his willingness to perform euthanasia.[59] However, the doctor responsible for treatment does have a duty to give his patient accurate and

---

58   See the *Makdoembaks* and *Schat* cases, referred to in notes 56 and 57.

59   Furthermore, as Van Overbeek (1996) has shown, a patient may have very good reasons for not changing his doctor despite the fact that the doctor makes clear that he is not willing to perform euthanasia.

full information and, if he himself is unwilling to accede to a legitimate request, to make this clear to the patient and to cooperate in a referral of the patient to another doctor. The Medical Association describes these duties as 'requirements of careful practice', putting them on the same footing as the requirements applicable to a case in which euthanasia is carried out.[60]

Given the monopoly of the medical profession over euthanasia – a position the Medical Association has insisted on from the outset – it has been argued that even though no individual doctor is obliged to perform it, the profession as a whole is bound to ensure the availability of euthanasia to eligible patients.[61] In this context, the existence of institutional policies prohibiting euthanasia (see chapter 5.4.2) is particularly problematic. It seems pretty clear that a patient whose request meets all the legal criteria sometimes experiences great difficulty in finding a doctor willing and – in light of the limitation to doctors with an established treatment relationship – legally able to carry it out.[62] The whole complex of problems surrounding the availability of euthanasia has yet to receive adequate legal attention.

THE LEGAL POSITION OF THIRD PARTIES

The legal position of nurses is in a highly unsatisfactory state. The only thing that is quite clear is that they may not perform euthanasia or other MBSL on their own.[63] Straightforward application of the criminal law rules relating to accessories would seem in some cases to make the liability of a nurse who participates in carrying out euthanasia dependent on the justifiability of the doctor's behavior. If the doctor's behavior is justified, so is that of the nurse. But if what the doctor did is a crime, the nurse may well fulfill the requirements for being an accessory.[64] To the extent they do not ignore nurses altogether, proposals for legislative legalization tend to treat the liability of the nurse in the same

---

60   See KNMG 1995; compare Staatscommissie Euthanasie 1985: 104. See Van der Wal, Siemons & Verhoeff 1994 on the problem of referral after refusing a request for euthanasia, including the suggestion (earlier made by the chief Medical Inspector) that the requirements of informing the patient and cooperating in a transfer can, if necessary, be enforced through medical disciplinary proceedings. The NVP (1997: § 2.2) takes the position that a psychiatrist who has conscientious objections does not have to refer a patient himself, but he must explain his position to the patient and inform him of the possibility of being referred back to his GP.

61   See Griffiths 1987: 691; cf. Blad 1996: 425-428.

62   See e.g. Van Overbeek 1996.

63   See note 40 above.

64   See Leenen 1994: 295.

way.[65] Such a situation seems legally intolerable since a nurse's independent responsibility for what takes place will generally be quite limited.

The extent to which a nurse can carry out some or all of the actual administration of euthanatica (or, for that matter, of other MBSL, such as discontinuing life-support) is quite unclear. As we will see in chapter 5.3.1, the practice was fairly common, at least until recently, especially in hospitals. The Medical Association takes the position that nurses should not be involved in the actual administration of euthanatica but qualifies this if the method used takes a considerable amount of time.[66]

In 1995 a nurse was prosecuted for her role in a case of euthanasia that met all the requirements except that the doctor, while present and supervising, acceded to the patient's request that the nurse (a personal friend of the patient) be allowed to administer the euthanaticum. The doctor was not prosecuted, but the nurse was convicted of unjustifiable euthanasia and sentenced to probation.[67] Perhaps this conviction is an anomaly, but as things stand it seems that a nurse can be convicted of euthanasia when the substance of the matter is that the doctor violated one of the rules of careful practice – assuming, that is, that it was wrong for the doctor to have delegated the actual administration.

Pharmacists (*apothekers*) are likewise involved in euthanasia, in the sense that they are the source of the lethal drugs used by doctors. They have, however, been assured by the prosecutorial authorities that if a doctor is prosecuted for illegal euthanasia the pharmacist who supplied the means will under normal circumstances not be prosecuted as an accessory; and the Pharmaceutical Inspectorate has taken the position that the pharmacist must discuss the matter with the doctor concerned, but he does not have to investigate whether the doctor is acting in conformity with the legal requirements.[68] The Royal Dutch Association for Pharmacy (KNMP) has for some years had a number of 'requirements of careful practice' that a pharmacist who is asked by a doctor to supply euthanatica should follow. These include:

– there must be a written request from the doctor and this must meet the requirements of and be maintained in the pharmacist's records in the same way as a request that falls under the legislation concerning narcotic drugs;

---

65 See the legislative proposals of the State Commission and of the NVVE; article 293b in the bill of Wessel-Tuinstra is a notable exception (all of these are in appendix I-C).

66 KNMG 1992. The Medical Association and the professional organization of nurses agree that a nurse is entitled to decline any involvement in euthanasia if she has conscientious objections.

67 *Nederlandse Jurisprudentie* 1996, no. 61 (Court of Appeals, Leeuwarden).

68 See KNMP 1994: 18.

- the request must include the patient's name unless there are very clear reasons for not doing so and anonymity does not undermine the possibility of tracing the euthanaticum or otherwise pose a danger of misuse;
- the pharmacist must secure from the doctor information on those aspects of the case that are relevant for the pharmacist;
- the pharmacist may consult another pharmacist so long as he does not thereby breach the confidentiality owed to doctor and patient;
- he must not permit his staff to be involved in the preparation or delivery of the euthanaticum;
- the euthanaticum must be properly labelled and the label should include the instruction to the doctor to return the container and any unused drug to the pharmacist;
- a pharmacist may refuse to supply euthanatica, but if he does this as a matter of principle it would be wise for him to inform the doctors in his vicinity of this.[69]

Apart from criminal liability, pharmacists are subject to medical disciplinary law and to the disciplinary rules of their Association. So far as is known, there has never been any sort of proceeding against a pharmacist in connection with euthanasia.[70]

There is no doubt that lay persons cannot legally perform euthanasia or give assistance with suicide,[71] but the possibility of their involvement under the responsibility of a doctor has received little or no attention.[72] In the case of involvement in suicide by non-doctors, the issue can arise as to what constitutes 'assistance'. In a recent case involving the 'plastic bag' method, the defendant[73] advised the deceased as to the method, was present at the time, and told him when to pull the bag over his head. The courts held that while the assistance prohibited by article 294 does involve actual presence at the time of the

---

69   KNMP 1994: 18-19. These criteria were first formulated in 1984 and revised in 1987. From a journalistic account of an informal 'network' of pharmacists and GPs in Amsterdam in the mid-1980s, it appears that many of these requirements were being rather systematically violated. In particular, everything was done secretly, outside of working hours, with no prescription or other written registration of what transpired. As was common at that time, the death was reported as a natural one. See A. Scherphuis, 'Artsen en apothekers zijn met hun euthanasie 'netwerk' de politiek allang voor [Doctors and pharmacists are with their euthanasia 'network' way ahead of politicians],' *Vrij Nederland*, 14 February 1987.

70   Information received from the KNMP.

71   See note 40 above.

72   The NVVE-bill provides for euthanasia "done by or in close consultation and cooperation with a doctor"; assistance with suicide, however, is only legal if done by a doctor (see appendix I-C-3).

73   Defendant was a doctor but maintained that she had not acted as such.

suicide, more than that is required. Even 'moral support' or 'merely giving information' are in themselves not enough. The defendant, however, was considered to have gone further than this: what she did amounted to giving the deceased an 'instruction'.[74]

3.1.4 Euthanasia versus assistance with suicide

Unlike the situation elsewhere in the world, one of the most characteristic features of euthanasia practice in the Netherlands is that from the beginning of the public discussion until very recently there has been no suggestion of a legal preference for assistance with suicide over euthanasia in the narrow sense of killing on request.[75] The justification defence worked out by the courts does not distinguish between killing on request and assistance with suicide, and as we will see in chapter 5.3.1, killing on request is much more common than assistance with suicide.

The Dutch preference for killing on request reflects the way in which euthanasia law has developed in the Netherlands (see chapter 2). By contrast with the situation in, for example, the United States, this development began not so much with a demand for 'patients' rights' as with the insistence by doctors, supported after some initial hesitation by the Medical Association, that under limited circumstances euthanasia is a legitimate medical procedure. The issue was legally formulated not so much in terms of what patients have a right to demand as in terms of what doctors are authorized to do.[76] For many doctors it has seemed an integral part of the doctor's responsibility, once he has decided that the life of a patient should be terminated, to carry out the decision himself.

The possibility that the requirements for the justification of necessity in the two cases may be different has received little explicit attention in the Dutch public discussion. From time to time there have been suggestions in the literature of a preference for assis-

---

74 The decision to this effect by the Court of Appeals, The Hague, was upheld by the Supreme Court (*Tijdschrift voor Gezondheidsrecht* 1993, no. 24; 1994 no. 65; *Nederlandse Jurisprudentie* 1996, no. 322).
   The proposed legislation of the NVVE (see appendix I-C-3) retains only 'incitement' and 'procuring the means' in article 294, thereby eliminating the criminal liability of lay persons who merely 'assist'.

75 See Leenen 1994: 296 (the two are "essentially the same" and despite the fact that two different articles of the criminal code are involved, "there is no reason to distinguish between them in a case of assistance due to severe suffering"). The State Commission proposed to treat them as one (Staatscommissie Euthanasie 1985: 62-63) and legislative proposals since then (with the partial exception of that of the NVVE) have followed suit (see appendix I-C).

76 See Griffiths 1987: 690-691.

tance with suicide, but this is probably a minority view and in any case has had little effect on practice.[77] The fact that there may be important reasons for affording assistance with suicide a preferred position has only recently begun to attract attention. It can be argued that there is an extra guarantee of the voluntariness and seriousness of the patient's request when he has to perform the final act himself, and less emotional burden on the doctor when a patient capable of administering the lethal drug to himself does not impose the moral burden of doing so on his doctor.[78]

Recently there have been some signs of change that may be harbingers of a future preference for assistance with suicide. To begin with, committees of the Medical Association and of the Netherlands Association of Psychiatrists, in reports on the situation of psychiatric patients who want a doctor to help them die (see section 3.5.1 below), assume without discussion that in such a case what would be involved is assistance with suicide. The decision of the Dutch Supreme Court in the *Chabot* case seems to share this assumption. The discussion of various forms of euthanasia for the non-'sick' and the non-'suffering' (see section 3.5.2) is likewise in terms of assistance with suicide.

The Medical Association has recently adopted new guidelines in which a careful preference is expressed for assistance with suicide whenever this is possible.[79] If one may hazard a guess, it would be that over the course of the coming years assistance with suicide

---

77   See chapter 2.2. An early report of the Health Council (Gezondheidsraad 1982) is an exception to this generalization, but the proposal there to decriminalize assistance with suicide and to retain the prohibition of euthanasia except in cases in which the patient is not capable of carrying out suicide had no influence on subsequent legal development. Compare Benjaminsen 1988 (the research in Utrecht referred to in chapter 5 note 1): a number of doctors interviewed and the one hospital with a formal policy had a preference for assistance with suicide where possible, but in fact it hardly ever took place. See chapter 5.2, note 18, for an apparent preference among GPs for assistance with suicide if the patient's suffering is less 'unbearable'.

78   Doctors are occasionally heard to complain of the moral pressure put on them by patients who are perfectly capable of carrying out their desire to die themselves, for example by ceasing to take medications that they know are essential to keep them alive. Van der Wal and Van der Maas (1996: 173) report that about half of all doctors say they are of the opinion that if a patient is capable, assistance with suicide is to be preferred, among other things as less emotionally burdensome for the doctor. Zwaveling (internist on an intensive care ward of a university hospital) argues that "euthanasia may be good for the patient but it is bad for the doctor" because of the psychological burden it involves (1994). He also argues that the autonomy of the patient's desire for death is better assured if the patient carries out the final act himself. He suggests that decriminalization of assistance with suicide and a more extensive use of abstinence could help keep the rate of euthanasia to a minimum.

79   KNMG 1995: 7-9.

will come to be regarded as preferred practice whenever there is not a clear reason for euthanasia (e.g. the inability of the patient to administer the fatal drugs himself). So far, however, there are no signs of this in actual practice; in fact, as we will see (table 5.2), the frequency of assistance with suicide relative to euthanasia actually *declined* slightly between 1990 and 1995.

It would probably be a mistake, moreover, to exaggerate the brightness of the line between the two sorts of behavior and to put too much weight on it as a ground for substantially different sorts of legal treatment. Assistance with suicide varies from, on the one end of the spectrum, behavior scarcely distinguishable from euthanasia (in the presence of the doctor, the patient opens the valve on a lethal intraveneous drip), through the intermediate 'normal' situation in which the doctor prepares the drugs to be used and gives them to the patient to take in his presence, to the opposite extreme of a situation in which the doctor makes pills available to a patient who may or may not use them at some future time. It is doubtful that this whole range can be dealt with as one regulatory category, distinct from euthanasia. In other words, it is probably wiser to retain the current legal situation in which killing on request and assistance with suicide are, from the point of view of the justification of necessity, not distinguished, and to seek via professional protocols – or perhaps simply by way of advice and education – to promote a general preference for letting the patient take as much as possible of the responsibility not only for the decision but also for actually carrying it out. In a system of decriminalized control, as we will see in chapter 6.3.2, it would be possible to make subtler distinctions than are now possible within the criminal law justification of necessity, and to encourage the use of assistance with suicide whenever, considering all the circumstances, it is to be preferred.

Assistance with suicide can, as we have seen, pose problems with respect to one of the 'requirements of careful practice': the requirement that the doctor be present at the moment the patient uses the drugs the doctor has supplied. There are some obvious considerations in support of such a requirement: maintaining control over the availability of euthanatica, ensuring the effective and humane carrying out of the suicide and timely reporting of the death to the coroner.[80] On the other hand, there are also some important reasons for not (always) insisting on the presence of the doctor. Some doctors, for example, have described their own practice of giving dying cancer patients a supply of lethal drugs to keep next to their bed in case their suffering should become unbearable, the doctor's position being that the mere availability of such control is such a relief to the patient that he can concentrate his thoughts and his energy on other matters and in fact

---

80   See note 57 above for the general rule requiring presence.

usually never uses the drugs at all.[81] In such circumstances, insistence that the doctor be present may in fact work unnecessarily to increase the number of cases of assisted suicide.[82] The whole idea of a 'pill' for the elderly, to allow them to decide for themselves when they no longer wish to go on living (see section 3.5.2), is of course inconsistent with a general requirement that the doctor be present.

3.2   The reporting procedure

The system of legal control over euthanasia and termination of life without an explicit request, which we will examine with an eye to its actual functioning in chapter 5.3.5 and will analyse with regard to its effectiveness in chapter 6, is based on the doctor's duty to report a patient's death as the result of a non-natural cause.

As we have seen in chapter 2.3.2, beginning as early as 1985 at the local level, and since 1990 at the national level, the prosecutorial authorities, in cooperation with the Medical Association, have worked out a special procedure for investigating cases in which a doctor reports a death as euthanasia. The prosecutorial authorities have also over the years made it increasingly clear that a doctor who reports a case of euthanasia as such and whose behavior meets the criteria for permissible euthanasia as developed by the courts will not be prosecuted; the result of this policy is that very few reported cases are in fact prosecuted (see chapter 5.3.5).

Elsewhere in this book we speak rather loosely of the doctor's 'duty' to report the death as a 'non-natural' one. This is what the legal situation amounts to in substance. However, this is the place to describe the applicable legal rules more precisely.

The Law on the Disposal of Corpses (*Wet op de lijkbezorging*[83]) requires the city clerk's permission for a funeral or cremation. Such permission is granted if the doctor responsible for treatment files a death certificate on which he certifies that the patient died from

---

81 See Schaepman & Scherphuis, 'Euthanasie' (*Vrij Nederland* 10 and 17 October 1987) for such a practice of a specialist in cancer of children (the patients involved were adolescents). Although there was some public commotion resulting from his revelation, so far as we know no prosecution or disiciplinary complaint was brought against him.

82 Compare the argument for not requiring presence in the case of patients suffering from a psychiatric disorder, section 3.5.1 below.

83 *Staatsblad* 1991: 133.

a 'natural cause'.[84] If the doctor is not convinced that the death was a natural one, he must notify the coroner, who inspects the body of the deceased, and makes his own judgment about the cause of death. If the coroner is convinced that the death was a natural one, he files a death certificate; otherwise, he reports the case to the local prosecutor, who must decide whether to notify the city clerk that he has no objection to burial or cremation.

Certifying a death due to euthanasia or termination of life without an explicit request as a 'natural' death is a distinct criminal offence (under article 228(1) of the Criminal Code – see appendix I-A), for which there have been a number of prosecutions.[85]

Based on these legal requirements, what is generally referred to as the 'reporting procedure' (*meldingsprocedure*) was agreed upon in 1990 between the Ministry of Justice and the Medical Association (see chapter 2.3.2). In 1993 the reporting procedure acquired a statutory basis in an amendment to the Law on the Disposal of Corpses and an accompanying Order in Council. (See appendix I-B for the text of the Law and the Order in Council.)

What the 1993 legislation, in a technical legal sense, does is authorize the Ministers of Justice and of Health to provide by Order in Council for the form on which euthanasia, assistance with suicide and termination of life without an explicit request are be reported by the coroner to the local prosecutor.[86] The form issued pursuant to this legislation includes a list of 'Points requiring attention' (*aandachtspunten*) on which the doctor who

---

84 What exactly amounts to a 'natural cause', is a matter of some confusion and disagreement. In the legislative history of the relevant provisions of the Law on the Disposal of Corpses, an acknowledgement that the term 'natural cause of death' cannot be precisely defined is followed by the reassurance that in practice it will be sufficiently clear. "Not only death due to intentional or negligent acts of others is not-natural, but also death due to suicide, even if this is the natural result of mental illness, as well as death due to an accident or external violence, even if this is not attributable to human fault." (*Second Chamber of Parliament 1951-1952*, 2410, no. 3: 7). The operational definition in prosecution practice is said to be that a 'natural' death is 'one that comes from within', in which case not only euthanasia but a large number of other medically caused deaths would have to be considered 'non-natural'; deaths due to pain relief or to abstention are, under such a criterion, arguably not 'natural', although they are universally so regarded.

85 In 1987 the Supreme Court rejected the idea that the justification for euthanasia also applies to violation of this article (see chapter 2.3.2). See chapter 5.3.5 for some incidental prosecution data.

86 Actually, the legislation does even less than this, since such authority to promulgate the reporting forms already existed. The new law merely gives this authority a higher legal status accompanied by a slightly different procedure for exercising it.

brings such a death to the attention of the coroner must supply information (see appendix I-B for the text of the 'Points requiring attention'). On the whole, these follow the existing substantive and procedural requirements. On a few points the 'Points requiring attention' suggest requirements that do not entirely correspond to existing formulations of the 'requirements of careful practice' (for example, that the request should be in writing). The exact status of the items about which the form requires information is not entirely clear, and in any case the courts and prosecutors will not necessarily regard these items as defining the contours of a successful defence of necessity.

In reaction to the findings of the 1990 research, the new reporting procedure was made applicable not only to euthanasia but also to termination of life without an explicit request. This was much to the dismay of proponents of legal euthanasia, who have always insisted on voluntariness as the essence of euthanasia and did not want it to become confused with non-voluntary practices. The Government emphasized that the research had revealed the extent of this sort of MBSL and that it was important to subject it to control, but that the fact it was covered by the reporting procedure in no sense implied that it would not be criminally prosecuted.[87] In fact, as we will see in chapter 5.3.5, hardly any such cases have been reported; the Government has recently proposed to separate the two reporting procedures (see chapter 6.2.5).

One final aspect of the reporting procedure requires attention: its uneasy relationship to the privilege against self-incrimination.[88] Serious concerns about this were raised in 1987 by the Committee of Procurators-General in connection with the advice of the Council of State on pending legislative proposals concerning euthanasia (see chapter 2.4). During the Parliamentary consideration of the legislation of 1993 similar concerns were voiced.[89] But until recently the question was not raised by defendants in criminal prosecutions, apparently because they sought vindication on the merits.[90] As far as we are aware, the issue was first raised in court by the prosecutor in the *Chabot* case, but because he did not do so formally the court did not deal with the matter. The same prosecutor took the unusual step in the *Kadijk* case of formally requesting the court to dis-

---

87   See *First Chamber of Parliament 1992-1993*, 22 572, no. 275a: 4ff.

88   The privilege – known in continental legal discourse as the *nemo tenetur* principle – is binding on the Dutch legislator and courts as an aspect of the right to a 'fair trial' guaranteed by article 6 section 1 of the European Convention for the Protection of Human Rights and Fundamental Freedoms. See Wöretshofer 1996.

89   See *First Chamber of Parliament, 1992-1993*, 22 572, no. 275a: 23-24; *First Chamber of Parliament 1993-1994, Proceedings*, 10-392.

90   Information from E.Ph.R. Sutorius, lawyer for the defendant in many recent cases concerning medical behavior that shortens life.

miss the prosecution for violation of the privilege.[91] The District Court regarded the question as immaterial since at the time the doctor had reported, the statutory reporting procedure was not in place (the Court appeared to ignore the fact that the requirement of reporting was not created by the new legislation but had always been immanent in the doctor's duty to report a case of euthanasia as a 'non-natural death'). The Court of Appeals (see appendix II-3) made equally short and unsatisfying shrift of the matter, holding that since the defendant had "made clear from the beginning ... that he wished to account for his behavior" no problem of self-incrimination was involved.

The result of all this is that the problem of self-incrimination, unmistakeably involved in the reporting procedure, has still to receive authoritative legal attention. In the public discussion it tends to get brushed off by those who defend the procedure with the observation that if the doctor has met the various requirements, reporting does not involve incriminating himself – which is true, but irrelevant, since it is the doctor who has *not* met all the requirements who is at issue. If the issue is cleanly raised,[92] the solution will presumably depend on the extent to which an administrative requirement connected with the disposal of corpses and imposed upon doctors in connection with their professional activities falls under the exception for general bookkeeping and record-keeping measures even though (1) it has a central place in the process of criminal investigation and enforcement of a specific crime, and (2) it involves a potential defendant supplying not merely some information that might be used at some time in a criminal prosecution but all the elements of a crime that the authorities have committed themselves to prosecute if it is brought to their attention. The seriousness of the offence involved is presumably also relevant. In situations in which the doctor's behavior does not clearly fall within the established terms of the justification of necessity, the reporting procedure thus

91　This led to an unfortunate but revealing incident. When her attention was called by a question in Parliament to what the prosecutor had done, the Minister of Justice took the position that his behavior was in violation of her instructions to prosecute the case. He later received a formal ministerial reprimand. The incident received considerable attention in the press at the time, in which the central point of contention was the Minister's assertion of authority to control the course of individual criminal prosecutions all the way down to the level of the legal position asserted by a prosecutor in court.

92　This is not as easy as one might think. The doctor who reports and is prosecuted can be met with the reaction of the Court of Appeals in the *Kadijk* case (in effect, that he waived the privilege by reporting). The doctor who falsely reports euthanasia as a natural death is prosecuted for filing a false death certificate (article 228(1) of the Criminal Code); if he then raises the issue of self-incrimination he can expect to be told that the privilege gives no license to lie. The theoretical possibility of not reporting at all is dealt with in note 93.

seems vulnerable to serious legal challenge.[93] As we will see in chapter 6, the procedure is fundamentally ineffective anyway, so a court decision holding it in violation of the European Convention should be welcomed as an invitation to the Government to come up with a more serious way of enforcing the law in this area.

3.3   The CAL and NVK reports: law *in statu nascendi*

To this point we have been treating matters on which the law is generally fairly well settled. Now we turn to matters on which it is not. Here, the law is in a state of becoming, and judgments about what it *is* are necessarily based to some extent on judgments about what it *will be*.

In 1985 the Medical Association appointed a Commission on the Acceptability of Medical Behavior that Shortens Life (CAL) to report on the legitimacy of various MBSL in the case of not (entirely) competent patients. The CAL issued four interim reports in the period 1990-1993 (CAL 1-4).[94] In the same period, the Dutch Association for Pediatrics (NVK) issued a report on MBSL in the case of severely defective newborn babies (NVK 1992). Recently, the Dutch Association for Psychiatry (NVP) issued a report on assistance with suicide in the case of psychiatric patients (NVP 1997). In the complex interaction process characteristic of legal developments concerning MBSL in the Netherlands (see chapter 2), these reports, while perhaps not possessing formal 'legal' status, almost certainly point the way in which legal change can be expected to occur. In some cases (severely defective newborn babies and psychiatric patients) the central ideas of the reports have already been confirmed in judicial decisions. While the details of the ultimate legal regime may differ from the position taken in the reports, it seems safe to assume that the general tenor of emerging law is to be found there.

---

93 Compare Wöretshofer 1996. Knigge (1997), however, argues that there is no self-incrimination problem because, while there is a duty not to report falsely, a doctor has no affirmative duty to report anything more than his own inability to file a certificate of natural death (any further duty would involve breach of the doctor's duty of confidentiality, which is why the legislator chose a construction that does not impose an affirmative duty). If the doctor so notifies the coroner, it is up to the latter and the prosecutorial authorities to investigate the case themselves. In Knigge's view, all the reporting procedure does is give the doctor an opportunity to avoid such further investigation. A doctor might thus in theory be able to avoid the problem of self-incrimination by not reporting the death as a 'natural' one but also not qualifying it as euthanasia (or termination of life without an explicit request). In most cases, however, his moral duty toward the family of the deceased (who need a death certificate in order to bury or cremate the body) will preclude this course.

94 A final, comprehensive report integrating the four interim reports was recently adopted: KNMG 1997. Since it is the interim reports that have played a role in legal development to date, we have used them as the basis for the discussion in this chapter.

This section deals first with the general approach of the reports, then with the specific situations of severely defective newborn babies and coma patients, and finally with the more general idea of 'help in dying' that seems to emerge from these reports and other recent developments. The special problems of the demented elderly will be dealt with in section 3.4. Section 3.5 discusses the CAL and NVP reports on assistance with suicide in the case of psychiatric patients, as part of a discussion of the more general problem of non-somatically based suffering.

3.3.1 The legitimacy of decisions to shorten life in the absence of a competent request

In the case of euthanasia and of abstaining from life-prolonging treatment at the request of the patient, the legitimacy of the doctor's behavior depends upon the patient's request. It is the absence of this source of legitimation that is troublesome in the case of non-competent patients such as babies and the comatose. If the life of the patient is dependent upon initiating or continuing a life-prolonging treatment and the patient has not (competently) declined further treatment, how can a decision to withhold or termi-nate such treatment be legitimate? In many cases more or less objectively 'medical' crite-ria supply the answer: further treatment would have no chance of success, would involve a burden to the patient disproportionate to any possible benefit, or (because of other medical problems from which the patient suffers) cannot succeed in restoring a minimal level of functioning. Decisions grounded on the idea of 'medical futility' (*medisch zinloos handelen*) in this narrow sense can be regarded as being bound by medical-professional standards.[95] But can a decision to forego treatment be based on the essentially non-med-ical judgment that the patient's future 'quality of life' will be so limited that he is better off dead? On what basis could anyone, particularly a doctor, be authorized to make such a decision for a patient?

In the American literature a basic structure for the analysis of this question has emerged, one that is also latent in emerging Dutch law. A non-competent patient enjoys the same fundamental right to refuse (further) treatment that accrues to a competent patient. For the exercise of this right, however, resort must be had to a 'surrogate decision-maker', who can be either the doctor or a representative (family or friend or appointed represen-tative) of the patient. This surrogate can base a decision on behalf of the non-competent patient on one of two grounds: evidence concerning what the patient himself would have wished in the circumstances ('substituted judgment') or a judgment as to the 'best interests' of the patient.[96] There is growing room in Dutch law for the 'substituted judg-

---

95   See Leenen 1994: 309-310.

96   The 'substituted judgment' and 'best interests' approaches merge into one another to the extent that specific evidence concerning what the patient would have wanted is not available and recourse must be had to what a 'reasonable person' in his position would have wanted.

ment' approach with a representative, family member or close friend of the patient as preferred surrogate decision-maker;[97] but on the whole, the legal discussion to date has largely been within the framework of a 'best interests' approach with the doctor as surrogate decision-maker.[98]

The problem of the doctor's authority to ground a MBSL in 'quality of life' considerations can be avoided in many cases by means of a substituted judgment approach or, when that approach is not available (newborn babies), a 'best interests' approach with the family (parents) as surrogates. Nevertheless, there remain cases in which the doctor of necessity must decide. To exclude 'quality of life' considerations in such cases would imply that the law requires the doctor – in the absence of authorization by the patient or a representative – to act as if blind to all but the medical consequences of his behavior. Such an interpretation of the idea of medical futility seems remote from reality. No sensible person would want a doctor to devote himself exclusively to biological life with no consideration for the things that make life worth living, so it can safely be assumed the law does not require any such thing.

The reports of the CAL and the NVK share a common approach to the problem of the legitimacy of medical behavior that shortens life, one that puts the problem of the relationship between 'quality-of-life' considerations and the concept of medical futility in a different light. Their argument is premissed on a fundamental point of departure. In effect, the reports stand the ethical problem of non-treatment on its head. The problem of legitimacy concerns not the artificial *shortening* of life but rather its artificial *prolongation*. If (further) treatment that is essential to prolong life cannot be legitimated, no additional legitimation for 'shortening' it by abstaining from the treatment is necessary. And in the case of a non-competent patient, the legitimacy of such treatment cannot be based, as is usually required, on the patient's consent.

Once having posed the question of legitimacy in this way, the reports invoke a time-honored principle of medical ethics: *in dubio abstine* (when in doubt, abstain). The doubt that brings this principle of non-intervention into play can derive from the limited chance of success of an intervention, from a lack of proportionality between intervention and result, or from the limited value to the patient of the additional life to be won. Quality-of-life considerations can give rise, in other words, to sufficient doubt about the legitimacy of (further) intervention that a doctor ought not to engage in it, at least not on his own authority.

---

97   See the provisions of the new Law on Contracts for Medical Treatment (note 12 above).

98   See Kooij 1996 for this analysis. She shows that American courts have, on the whole, preferred the 'substituted judgment' approach, with family, etc., as the surrogate decision-maker (differing on such things as the sort of evidence required) while the English courts have opted for the doctor as surrogate and the 'best interests' approach. Dutch law, she argues, is in the process of moving from the English to the American approach.

In particular, in the case of very premature babies and comatose patients the dramatic increases over the past decades in the technical possibilities for keeping a patient artificially alive have led, the CAL and NVK reports argue, to a systematic departure from the principle *in dubio abstine*. For a number of reasons – most importantly, to win time in order to make a fully informed diagnosis – doctors have come to apply the contrary principle: *in dubio fac* (when in doubt, act). If there seems to be any chance at all of a favorable outcome, the doctor initially deploys all available means to keep the patient alive. If the patient does not die but the medical intervention leads to a situation that, if it had been foreseen from the beginning, would not have been thought to justify a decision to intervene, then the doctor is confronted with a choice between continuing treatment that (with the benefit of hindsight) has been without legitimation from the beginning and ought not to have been commenced, or applying *in dubio abstine* retroactively, as it were. The latter course often implies that one cannot limit oneself to 'passive' non-intervention; one must 'actively' intervene to put an end to life-prolonging treatment.

> Only on the condition that an intervention with which one has begun ... can later be stopped, is it possible to assure that it is not medical technology, but medical-ethical norms that have proved their value over the years ('in dubio abstine' and 'primum non nocere'), that define the character of medicine and ... guarantee the well-being of the individual patient.[99]

Medical intervention on the basis of *in dubio fac* thus entails a special responsibility, and the doctor who begins a life-prolonging treatment on this basis must be prepared to take the responsibility for discontinuing it when it becomes clear that further treatment cannot benefit the patient. The CAL and NVK reports regard the line of thought to this point as essentially non-controversial.

The CAL and NVK next argue for the less well-settled position that artificial administration of food and drink are medical interventions that require legitimation. This sort of intervention, they conclude, is not significantly different from other forms of artificial prolongation of life. The consequence of this position for comatose patients and for most severely defective newborn babies is clear: the absence of legitimation for prolonging life may justify abstaining from (further) artificial administration of food and drink, which will inevitably lead to the patient's death.

The CAL further insists on the 'priority principle': life-terminating treatment (use of euthanatica) should only be considered *after* life-prolonging treatment has been termi-

---

99   CAL 2: 27.

nated. If the patient does not die in a humane way after life-prolonging treatment has been stopped, the doctor should intervene to ease the process of dying. Since,

> the death [of the patient] has already been accepted [when the decision to terminate treatment was made] ... administration of drugs in a fatal dosage can be indicated ... as a form of 'assistance in dying' [*stervensbegeleiding*].... [For some doctors the death of the patient is] part of the intention with which one began the process (terminating treatment and then giving adequate 'help in dying' [*stervenshulp*]).[100]

The combined implication of these points of departure is that in almost all cases the patient will die quickly, and (except for possible 'help in dying') there will be no occasion for 'active' administration of euthanatica. The situations in which the legitimacy of 'active' termination of life – as to which, by contrast with discontinuing life-prolonging treatment, the medical profession is described by the CAL as divided – needs to be considered, are thereby reduced to a minimum.

Abstaining from (further) life-prolonging treatment because of serious doubt as to the benefit for the patient meets far fewer ethical or legal objections, at least in the Netherlands, than using euthanatica to terminate the life of a patient whose prospects are unacceptable. Standing the problem of legitimation on its head, as the CAL and NVK reports do, seems an effective way to defuse an area of medical ethics and law that otherwise could give rise to the same kind of political controversy as has characterised euthanasia. Putting the emphasis on the legitimacy of prolonging life also focusses the discussion where it on the whole belongs: on the ethical and practical consequences of the increasing medical-technical possibilities for prolonging biological life long beyond the point that doing so is sensible or humane.

But is standing the problem of legitimation on its head anything more than a rhetorical trick? The whole argument stands or falls with the status of the principle *in dubio abstine* and the underlying idea that (passive) non-intervention requires less legitimation than ('active') intervention (compare chapter 4.1.1). The reports say nothing about the ethical foundations of the principle; it is simply invoked as a sort of medical-ethical axiom. One might support its application here by arguing that the prospect of a 'life not worth living' is an insufficient basis for 'presumed consent' to further treatment[101] or, alternatively, for concluding that the patient's 'interest' justifies it. However this may be, so long as people

---

100   CAL 2: 35. As we have seen in chapter 2.3.2 (see also section 3.3.3 of this chapter), the State Commission on Euthanasia adopted the same principle in its treatment of the problem of coma patients. Unlike the Remmelink Commission (see section 3.3.4), the CAL does not draw the seemingly inescapable conclusion of its argument: that 'help in dying' constitutes 'normal medical practice' and the death of the patient is a 'natural' one that can be reported as such (see CAL 1: 23, CAL 2: 45). See the Glossary for the terms *stervensbegeleiding* and *stervenshulp*.

101   Compare CAL 2: 39.

of otherwise conflicting views on the legitimacy of medical behavior that shortens life can find common ground in the principle, it affords a basis for the development of norms to govern medical practice in this area.[102] As we will see in the following sections, the position of CAL and NVK seems in fact to underlie current legal developments with regard to the regulation of decisions to terminate or not to initiate life-prolonging treatment and, in that connection, to administer 'help in dying', both in the special cases of severely defective newborn babies and coma patients, and for non-competent patients more generally (see section 5.3.4).

3.3.2 Severely defective newborn babies (and late abortion)

Two of the reports mentioned above deal with the problems of medical behavior that shortens life in the case of severely defective newborn babies. One was prepared by the Commission on the Acceptability of Termination of Life of the Medical Association (CAL 1, 1990), the other by the Dutch Association for Pediatrics (NVK, 1992). Both are the fruit of intensive discussion with and among neonatologists and are intended to reflect the views of the entire professional group. The positions taken in the two reports are very similar.[103]

As we will see in chapter 5.3.3, of slightly over 1000 babies per year who die in their first year, more than half die as the result of abstinence, about half the time accompanied by

---

102 It is clear from the CAL reports that the extent to which the *in dubio abstine* principle can give rise to specific treatment protocols with a more or less binding character varies from one medical situation to another. For some situations – such as long-term coma – criteria for abstaining from (further) life-prolonging treatment can be given in concrete, quantitative terms (see section 3.3.3) . This is not (now) the case for senile dementia, which is presumably the reason that the CAL in that situation relies primarily on the figure of the 'presumed will' of the patient (see section 3.4). Both the CAL and the NVK treat the situation of seriously defective newborn babies as comparable in this respect to that of the senile demented (see section 3.3.2). There are, however, neonatologists who argue that specific quantitative criteria should determine whether life-prolonging treatment of premature babies is appropriate (duration of pregnancy and body weight); below this limit, any life-prolonging treatment would require special legitimation. A weak point in both reports is the failure to consider this possibility. The information collected by the CAL reveals that Dutch academic hospitals set varying minima, from 23-24 to 26 weeks, despite the fact that the prognosis for these babies is extremely poor. The ethical and legal problems with which the CAL is concerned would presumably be far less frequent if neonatologists were restrained by clear-cut norms in the application of *in dubio fac.*

103 The NVK report is one of the most careful and thorough contributions to date to the Dutch political and legal discussion on the legitimacy of medical behavior that shortens life.

pain relief expected to hasten death and quite regularly including what seems to amount to 'help in dying' (some 80 cases per year).

The discussion in neonatology essentially concerns the question whether and when a life-prolonging treatment can be discontinued. Abstinence from the beginning – according to the principle *in dubio abstine* – is rare, at least in neonatal intensive care units. At the outset all available technical possibilities are used to save the life of the baby until a reliable diagnosis can be made.

The reports recognize two basic reasons for abstaining from or discontinuing life-prolonging treatment: the prognosis that the baby has 'no real chance of survival' (treatment would have no chance of success: *kansloos medisch handelen*) and the prognosis that the baby has a 'limited chance of a life worth living' (treatment would be pointless: *zinloos medisch handelen*).[104] In both cases the legitimation for (further) artificial prolongation of life is absent. The idea of a 'life worth living' is further operationalised in terms of the child's expected ultimate level of functioning in a number of distinct respects: the possibility of communication (verbal and non-verbal); suffering (physical and otherwise); dependency on others; autonomy; and personal development.[105]   According to the reports, Dutch pediatricians are virtually unanimous in the view that refraining from further prolongation of life is legitimate if the baby's prospect is one of a 'life not worth living' (*onleefbaar leven*).

The only point of disagreement among neonatologists concerns 'active' termination of life with lethal drugs. The NVK report distinguishes three situations: (a) as a result of life-prolonging treatment that is no longer necessary the child has survived, but in a condition that, if it had been foreseen at the beginning, would have led to abstaining from life-prolonging treatment; (b) discontinuation of life-prolonging treatment has led to a situation of unacceptable suffering; (c) independently of any earlier life-prolonging treatment the baby has serious defects that are consistent with life but not with a life worth living. In situations (a) and (b), some neonatologists would consider the use of euthanatica legitimate while others would not, but both positions are generally considered legitimate. The CAL itself considers use of lethal drugs morally acceptable in situation (b) even when this is done preventively to avoid unnecessary suffering.[106] Situation

---

104 The NVK proposes this pair of concepts as an improvement on the established term 'medically futile' (*medisch zinloos*) that confusingly lumps the two rather different situations together (NVK: 23-24, 29-39). See also CAL 1: 6-7. Van der Wal and Van der Maas, in their recent report on research carried out at the behest of the Government, explicitly adopt the terminology of the NVK (1996: 182-183).

105 CAL 1: 15; NVK: 31-32.

106 CAL 1: 11.

(c) is highly exceptional, among other things because of the possibility of abstaining from fairly routine forms of life-prolonging treatment such as artificial administration of food and drink. The profession is divided on the question whether termination of life with euthanatica can ever be legitimate in this situation.[107]

Both reports emphasize the importance of the views of the parents. According to the CAL, if the prognosis is that the baby has no real chance of survival, there is "no real problem of choice and the views of the parents can therefore play only a marginal role". Nevertheless, careful practice requires "that in all cases the wishes of the parents [with respect to 'help in dying' or the moment of death] … be ascertained, and if possible honored". If the prognosis is of a 'life not worth living' – in which case the capacity of the family to deal with the situation is relevant – "the views of the parents must receive much more weight … than seems currently in many cases to be accorded". This "of course" does not mean "that the parents can dispose freely over the life of their child…. [T]he decision[108] should primarily be based on the expected physical and/or mental handicaps of the newborn baby and the minimum values that have been established therefor." In cases in which these 'minimum values' do not unequivocally indicate the proper course of action, it is appropriate for the doctor to adopt a "modest" position and "in principle to give the views of the parents a very important role" in the decision-making.[109]

The role of the parents and the importance of careful communication with them receives even greater emphasis in the report of the NVK. The wishes of

> thoughtful parents for whom the interests of the child are a central consideration…
> [should] be taken very seriously. A doctor who thinks parents are not being suffi-
> ciently careful or are not serving the best interests of the child (which after all is pri-
> marily entrusted to them), bears the burden of proof.[110]

If the doctor is of the opinion "that the parents' wish (for example: not to operate) is clearly inconsistent with the child's interests" and there is consensus in the profession on this, then the procedure for temporary removal of parental custody should be used.[111] Subject to that legal outer limit, the NVK seems (almost) to recognize parents as holders of decisive *rights and powers* and not merely as sources of *important considerations* to be taken into account by the doctor.

---

107 NVK: 48-53.

108 Reference is apparently to the decision of the doctor.

109 CAL 1: 16-17.

110 NVK: 39.

111 NVK: 55. As in other legal systems, Dutch law provides for temporary assignment of custody to a guardian if a parent's refusal of medical care is not in the 'best interests of the child'. See Leenen 1994: 147.

Neither report explicitly considers the implications of the legal capacity of the parents as guardians of their child. At least as far as decisions to abstain from (further) life-prolonging treatment are concerned, it would seem that the parents, deciding on behalf of their child, can in principle refuse treatment for any reason the child itself would be entitled to consider, subject to the outer limits of parental authority. This argument from legal principle is reflected in the new Law on Contracts for Medical Treatment,[112] article 465(4) of which requires a doctor to comply with the parents' instructions unless to do so would be incompatible "with the care expected of a good [doctor]". The historical paternalism of the medical profession does not seem to have caught up with the law on this matter.

Two recent cases (see chapter 2.4; see appendix II-3 for the judgment in the *Kadijk* case) have clarified the controversial issue of 'active' termination of life in the case of severely defective newborn babies. In each case, the baby suffered from very serious defects and was not expected to live long; in each case a decision to abstain from further life-prolonging treatment had already been taken; in each case the doctor, in consultation with the parents, had decided to administer euthanatica to save the baby from a painful and inhumane death. The doctors concerned (one gynecologist and one GP) had scrupulously followed all of the 'requirements of careful practice' and had reported the deaths as 'not natural'. The Minister of Justice ordered prosecutions (for murder), deeming the two cases suitable vehicles for securing legal clarification. In both cases, the doctors were acquitted by both the respective District Courts and Courts of Appeals. The responsible prosecutorial officials saw no grounds for an appeal to the Supreme Court. The upshot of these cases seems to be that the law on the matter is essentially that recommended by CAL and NVK: if the parents agree, 'active' termination can be justifiable to put an end to further suffering in the case of a severely defective newborn baby, where essential life-prolonging treatment has been stopped in order to let the baby die, but death (while imminent) does not take place immediately.[113]

A closely related sort of MBSL that has not played much of a role in the public discussion deserves mention here, namely that of last-trimester abortion. Dutch abortion law permits abortion only until the foetus can reasonably be considered capable of surviving outside the womb, and this is interpreted to mean 24 weeks (minus an uncertainty factor of 2-4 weeks); once the foetus is in that sense viable, killing it is considered killing a person.[114] If serious, non-treatable defects are first diagnosed later in the pregnancy than

---

112 See note 12 above.

113 It is arguable that the baby's death could be reported as a 'natural' one in such a case (see note 100 above); the CAL, however, insists that reporting as a non-natural death is required in all cases in which euthanatica are used to terminate life.

114 See Leenen 1994: 138-139.

this and the woman urgently requests an abortion, the responsible doctor is confronted with a dilemma similar to that of termination of the life of a newborn child.

The Dutch Association for Obstetrics and Gynecology (NVOG) has adopted a position paper for such situations that is largely derived from that of the NVK.[115] If the foetus can only be expected to survive after birth for a short time or not at all, the criterion of viability is not met, and abortion is in the opinion of the NVOG probably legal. If the foetus has a chance of survival, but only if given life-prolonging treatment, and this would lead to a 'life not worth living', or if the baby might live without life-prolonging treatment but in circumstances such that active termination of life would be considered legitimate, the NVOG considers abortion acceptable.[116] The NVOG proposes a number of procedural rules of careful practice generally similar to those for other MBSL. The NVOG takes the position that the doctor must report the death as a 'non-natural' one.

Although there have been a number of cases reported to the prosecuting authorities (see chapter 5.3.3), we know of no court decisions clarifying the law on this point.

3.3.3   Coma (PVS) patients

The second CAL report (CAL 2, 1991) deals with long-term coma (often referred to as 'persistent vegetative state' – PVS), defined as a severe form of loss of consciousness in which all communication and normal movement are impossible.[117]

In the Netherlands, about 1000 patients per year experience a coma that lasts longer than 6 hours; of these, about 100 per year ultimately fall into a long-term coma.[118] The longer the condition lasts (the age of the patient and the traumatic or non-traumatic cause of the coma also being important variables) the greater the chance that the coma will prove to be irreversible or that it will be followed by permanent and serious physical and mental handicaps.

---

115 NVOG 1994.
116 If the foetus survives the abortion, the NVOG observes that the NVK guidelines suggest that life-prolonging treatment should not be commenced, and recommends that gynecologist and pediatrician should have agreed on this course of action before the abortion.
117 CAL 2: 5-7. In 1994 the Health Council issued a thoughtful and carefully-researched report on patients in a 'vegetative state' (Gezondheidsraad 1994); on the whole, the positions taken are very similar to those of the CAL.
118 CAL 2: 9.

The CAL describes current treatment policy in the case of long-term coma on the basis of the literature and discussions with a number of those directly involved. Treatment is primarily directed at keeping the patient alive. By contrast with seriously defective new-born babies, treatment policy is generally not influenced by the unfavorable prognosis. A number of factors seem to be responsible for this, among them the personal opinions of those directly concerned (the attachment of nursing personnel and family members to the patient can be important) and the religious principles of the nursing homes involved. The CAL observes that "non-medical and subjective motives ... [appear to play an important role] in connection with life-prolonging behavior" and "there does not appear to be any consensus concerning ... the applicable criteria."[119] But the nature of the medical situation is also an important explanation for the fact that putting an end to life-prolonging treatment is so rare. As time passes, the certainty of the prognosis increases, but often also the patient's independence of the more intensive forms of life-prolonging treatment (such as artificial respiration). Only ceasing artificial feeding remains as an option, and the acceptability of this is sufficiently controversial that it seldom occurs. Termination of life with euthanatica encounters even greater resistance from those involved in treatment decisions. At most they wait for an unrelated medical problem such as an infectious disease to present the opportunity for abstinence.

Apart from an unfavorable prognosis, the most important reason, in practice, for abstaining from (further) life-prolonging treatment is the presence of a written 'advance directive' [*schriftelijke wilsbeschikking*] or information concerning the 'presumed will' of the patient. These are accorded significant weight, especially in non-religious institutions (although if there are objections on the part of the family to carrying out the patient's will, these apparently often prevail). The opinion of the Commission is that the will of the patient should be accorded a "crucial and determinative role" in the decision-making, whether or not the "personal opinions" of family and close friends, or of the doctors, happen to concur. If the patient has not explicitly consented to life-shortening treatment in advance, a doctor may justify his intervention on the basis of the patient's 'presumed will', for instance by consulting family and close friends about this, but the express will must take precedence.[120]

For cases in which no 'will' of the patient can be ascertained, the CAL argues that the point of departure in the decision-making should be "the question whether continued life-prolonging treatment is legitimate". The Health Council justifies reversing the question of legitimacy in this situation as follows: life-prolonging treatment requires the consent of the patient, but this can in the circumstances only be a 'presumed consent'; the assumption that the patient would consent is no longer reasonable when further treat-

---

119 CAL 2: 20.
120 CAL 2: 15-20; 37-40.

ment serves no "convincing purpose that is relevant for the patient" (i.e. prolongation of a vegetative state without hope of recovery).[121] The CAL's approach is slightly different. It argues that "a continuing (limited) biological life without consciousness … is an insufficient condition to legitimate further treatment."[122] Since the preceding medical treatment is partly responsible for the patient's situation,

> one cannot invoke as a justification for continued treatment the mere presence of life.… For one has oneself contributed to the specific situation in which this life now is. One is therefore at least partly responsible for that situation. That the patient is alive is of course relevant and of great importance, but it is not a **sufficient** reason for continuing treatment.[123]

Continuing treatment simply to prolong a limited biological life is inconsistent with "human dignity", both because "one [thereby] may be doing something that the person in question would not have wished" and "because one prevents the dying process from coming to an end".[124]

Waiting for a complication or an unrelated medical problem from which one can let the patient die implies – incorrectly, in the view of the CAL – that maintaining the patient in a comatose situation does not itself entail intervention. "The question whether the life-prolonging treatment should be continued always comes first. 'Waiting' (that is, continuing treatment) is only acceptable as the outcome of an explicit decision, based on the meaningfulness of the treatment."[125]

The CAL suggests a limit of about 1 month for traumatic and 6 months for non-traumatic coma as the point at which the chance of recovery is too slight and the risk of permanent serious handicap in the case of recovery too great to justify further life-prolonging treatment.[126]

The 'priority principle' implies that use of euthanatica to terminate life should only be considered once it has been decided to discontinue the existing treatment, including artificial feeding. One has thereby in fact already accepted the death of the patient, so

---

121 Gezondheidsraad 1994: 46.
122 CAL 2: 22.
123 CAL 2: 25; boldface in original.
124 CAL 2: 25-26.
125 CAL 2: 28.
126 In the final, integrated report (KNMG 1997), guidelines of 12 months in the case of trauma and 3-6 months in the case of non-trauma are proposed, based on more recent international studies. Compare Gezondheidsraad 1994: 37-39.

that, as we have seen above, use of euthanatica to avoid further suffering in the dying process may be legitimate. The State Commission on Euthanasia had proposed in its 1985 report to make an exception for the case of irreversible coma to the "central principle" that "intentional termination of life without a request therefor from the person concerned cannot be allowed". The Commission reasoned on the basis of the priority principle: termination of life is only possible after "treatment that according to current medical knowledge is futile" (that is, "cannot lead to any improvement in the situation of the patient") has been stopped. The legitimacy of active termination of life lay, in the Commission's view, in the 'inhuman deterioration' [*ontluistering*] that the patient would undergo once artificial feeding is stopped.[127] It is not clear why the State Commission did not recognize a similar legitimation in the case of severely defective newborn babies and other unconscious patients.

When the medical situation of the patient does not itself indicate the appropriate course of action, the views of the family are as important as those of parents in the case of severely defective newborn babies. The CAL recognizes that nursing personnel, too, can be "an important source of information" and can play a "valuable role" in a careful decision-making process; they should be included in all discussions in the medical team. If, once the views of all parties involved are known, the conclusion to be reached is not clear, it is "essential" that the responsible doctor consult an experienced, independent colleague.[128] These passages concerning the role – both procedurally and substantively – of the family, nursing personnel and an independent colleague are rather vague. Sometimes it seems that if the decision to be taken is clear, the responsible doctor can act without consulting anyone: that the participation of the others is only necessary in cases of doubt. At other places one reads that the participation of the other parties is of great importance. The general approach of the CAL would seem to imply that the doctor is in any event bound to ascertain from the family and nursing personnel information relevant to the 'will' of the patient. However this may be, the 'requirements of careful practice' are becoming so well-settled throughout MBSL practice that it seems highly unlikely that they will be any less stringent here than in other situations.

In early February of 1992 the Committee of Procurators-General announced its decision, with which the Minister of Justice agreed, not to prosecute a specialist who had ended the life of a 70-year-old, irreversibly comatose patient. The man had been found lying unconscious on the street, brought to hospital and reanimated (*in dubio fac*). It

---

127 State Commission 1985: 44-46. The Health Council assumed that cessation of artificial administration of food and drink generally leads to a 'peaceful death' (Gezondheidsraad 1994: 13); this is presumably the reason that it did not consider the legitimacy of use of euthanatica in such cases.

128 CAL 2: 39-42.

then appeared that he had had a heart attack that had resulted in severe brain damage from which the chance of recovery was negligible. Since continuation of treatment was considered futile, artificial respiration was stopped in the expectation that the patient would quickly die. This did not happen, but the man's breathing was irregular and in the opinion of the doctor he was suffering severely. After extensive consultation with colleagues, the doctor came to the conclusion that 'active' termination of life with a euthanaticum was unavoidable. In answering questions in Parliament about the decision not to prosecute, the Minister of Justice said that this was based on "the combination of concrete, special circumstances, which in this case would have led to a successful defence of [necessity]". The PGs were of the view, the Minister emphasized, that their decision in this case created no "precedent".[129]

In light of the recent cases dealing with 'active' termination of life in the case of newborn babies (see section 3.3.2), it seems very likely – despite the Minister's insistence that no precedent was being set – that the decision not to prosecute accurately reflects current Dutch law. The 'priority principle' seems to have been applied precisely as intended, and the decision to allow the patient to die by abstaining from further treatment was thus the essential decision, the administration of euthanatica a merely derivative one.

3.3.4 'Help in dying'

'Intentionally' and 'actively' shortening the life of a person without his explicit request is *prima facie* murder. Until recently, all participants in the Dutch public discussion seemed to agree on two propositions: such behavior is surely criminal, and it has nothing to do with euthanasia. At most the possibility of a justification in truly extraordinary circumstances was grudgingly acknowledged. Nevertheless, as we have seen in the preceding two sections, the realities of medical practice have recently overtaken the public discussion.

While anticipated as far as coma patients are concerned in the State Commission's report of 1985,[130] the problem only really entered the public debate with the publication of the results of the first national survey of MBSL in 1990. It appeared that Dutch doctors were

---

129 *Second Chamber of Parliament 1991-1992, appendix*, no. 394. From a newspaper account of the case (*de Volkskrant* 14 February 1992) the following additional facts appear: The decision was preceded by intensive discussions with the family and the patient's GP to ascertain what his wishes would have been. Two independent doctors were consulted, and the responsible doctor discussed the case with nursing personnel and with the deceased's 'spiritual advisor'. He informed the coroner of his proposed action beforehand and reported the case afterwards.

130 See appendix I-C-1. See also the brief of Remmelink as Advocate-General in the *Pols* case (Supreme Court, 21 October 1986, *Nederlandse Jurisprudentie* 1987, no. 607: 2126-2127).

terminating life without an explicit request at a rate of about 1000 cases per year. In 1995 the rate was about the same. (See chapter 5.3.2 for the relevant data.)

The Remmelink Commission (see chapter 2.4), which supervised the 1990 research, came to the conclusion that at least some part of this practice should be regarded as 'help in dying': administration of euthanatica to speed up the dying process in the case of a patient whose bodily functions are successively and irreversibly failing.[131] The Commission regarded 'help in dying' as 'normal medical practice', so that the patient's death can be reported as a 'natural' one (that is, due to the condition from which the patient was already dying). It seems likely that 'help in dying' has long been rather standard medical practice. However, the suggestion was received in Parliament with expressions of outrage,[132] and nothing much has been heard of it in the public discussion since.

Nevertheless, as we have seen in the preceding two sections, there is growing acknowledgement that some forms of termination of life without an explicit request can indeed be justified under specified circumstances and subject to a regulatory regime ('requirements of careful practice') similar in most respects to that for euthanasia. In the early 1990s, authoritative reports from within the medical profession began to suggest this. Recently, in court decisions described in sections 3.3.2 and 3.3.3, the position taken in these reports was confirmed with regard to severely defective newborn babies and coma patients.

In a recent case, the principles involved in the case of newborn babies and coma patients received a more general application, perhaps signalling a rebirth of the idea of 'help in dying'. The defendant, a urologist, was prosecuted for manslaughter for having ended the life of a patient with a euthanaticum. The defence was necessity in the sense of conflict of duties. The patient had been admitted to hospital for optimal pain relief while awaiting death from prostate cancer that had spread to the bones and was no longer treatable. He was suffering continuously, seriously and without prospect of improvement and himself considered the situation unbearable and hopeless. From the outset, a non-reanimation decision was taken. To relieve the patient's pain, increasing doses of various drugs were tried, but without success. Use of morphine was decided upon after discussion with the family (in light of the risk that this would hasten the moment of death), but this, too, proved insufficient even after the dosage was greatly increased. An anesthetist was consulted and advised using another drug to keep the patient unconscious until he died. Shortly after this was administered, the patient ceased breathing for several minutes and appeared to be dying. When the patient nevertheless recommenced breathing, the doctor administered a euthanaticum: he considered it inhumane to allow the patient to

---

131 Commissie Remmelink 1991: 15, 32, 37.
132 See Gevers 1992.

regain consciousness (especially since brain damage might have occurred in the period in which breathing had stopped), and it was not possible at short enough notice to get a new dose of the drug used to render the patient unconscious. The District Court concluded that the defendant had acted in a situation of necessity in which "after balancing the conflicting duties and interests, he had made a choice that objectively considered, and in light of the specific circumstances of the case, could reasonably be regarded as justifiable." The doctor was acquitted of the charge of manslaughter.[133]

In short, current law is that at least some part of the practice of termination of life without an explicit request, revealed in the surveys of 1990 and 1995, can legally speaking be regarded as justifiable. Without explicitly referring to it, the courts seem to have adopted the 'priority principle' argued for in the reports mentioned above: the essential decision that the patient should be allowed to die is taken in the context of abstinence from (further) life-prolonging treatment, and only thereafter is 'active' intervention with lethal drugs justifiable as a form of 'help in dying'. If such help in dying were to become accepted as 'normal medical practice', application of the priority principle could considerably reduce the frequency of euthanasia and termination of life without an explicit request.

3.3.5   Assessment of the approach of the CAL and NVK reports

The most important contribution of the CAL reports to legal development concerning medical behavior that shortens life probably lies in the insistence that the question of the legitimacy of life-*prolonging* behavior has priority over the question of the legitimacy of life-*terminating* behavior. Intractable problems concerning the role of 'quality of life' considerations in the decision-making become much less intractable when the question of legitimacy is stood on its head in this way. The 'priority principle' based on this approach has begun to bear fruit in court decisions. The distinction made by the NVK between life-prolonging treatment that has no chance of success and treatment that can-

---

133 District Court, Almelo, 28 January 1997. He was also acquitted for lack of evidence of a subsidiary charge of euthanasia. He was convicted for having submitted a false report of a natural death and fined *f* 5000. The Court explained this relatively heavy fine by observing that defendant had violated the trust that doctors enjoy in such cases, suggesting that the false report was intended to avoid a possible criminal prosecution. This latter suggestion seems dubious in light of the evidence (see chapter 5.3.2) that many doctors consider the death in such circumstances a 'natural' one, as indeed did the Remmelink Commission. In a somewhat similar case, also in Almelo, almost 10 years earlier, a doctor was convicted of murder and given a suspended sentence, but in that case the doctor had violated most of the 'requirements of careful practice' (consultation, investigation of alternatives, administration by the doctor himself) (*Tijdschrift voor Gezondheidsrecht* 1988, no. 43).

not lead to a 'life worth living' (as operationalized by the NVK), together with its insistence that life-prolonging treatment can be as lacking in legitimacy in the latter as in the former case, has proved very influential. Apart from developments in the case law, these reports are the most important contributions to the public discussion of MBSL since the report of the State Commission in 1985.

3.4   The demented elderly

About 8500 persons are admitted per year to psycho-geriatric institutions and about 8000 per year die there. In 1990 there were more than 15,000 persons in nursing homes with dementia as primary diagnosis. The total number of persons in the Netherlands with a demential syndrome is estimated at 100,000.[134] Both in a quantitative sense and, as we will see, substantively as well, the problem of MBSL in the case of senile dementia raises problems of a dramatically different order of magnitude from those we have considered so far.

The patients concerned are not entirely non-competent during the entire course of the decision-making. Rather, they gradually, and with periods of remission, but nevertheless inexorably and irreversibly, lose competence. The large number of patients involved, their age,[135] and the institutional setting likewise have profound consequences for medical practice and for its legal regulation.

In describing current treatment practice in the case of severely demented patients, the CAL (by contrast with its two earlier reports on severely defective newborn babies and on coma patients), was not able to provide more than vague generalizations. The absence of clear criteria and established procedures is striking. Written protocols hardly exist and, to the extent that institutions have treatment policies, these are not generally available and are not made known at admission.[136]

Two forms of life-prolonging treatment are of particular importance in the case of severely demented patients: use of antibiotics and artificial feeding. The crucial point in the decision-making concerns the initiation of treatment for a life-threatening condition.

---

134 See CAL 3: 14-15. On MBSL in the case of demented patients, see also NVV 1997, which discusses many of the same issues as CAL 3. The possibility of 'letting oneself die' (*versterven*) is, however, not discussed, and as far as competence is concerned this report argues that competence to refuse life-prolonging treatment should have to meet a stricter standard than competence to consent to it – which seems a peculiar position when one considers that one and the same decision is involved.

135 Alzheimer's disease is responsible for 50-70% of all dementia. Alzheimer's is primarily a disease of the elderly. Its incidence is about 3.2% of persons 70 or older and 10.8% of persons 80-89. (CAL 3: 14)

136 CAL 3: 21.

The considerations taken into account are the chances for recovery or improvement, the additional burden of the treatment itself, the views of the family and (if ascertainable) the views or wishes of the patient. Life-prolonging treatment is discontinued on the basis of similar considerations, but some doctors limit such discontinuance to the 'dying phase'. Most doctors consider artificial feeding a medical intervention that can be discontinued. Pain relief is only used when medically indicated, although accelerating the dying process is accepted as a secondary effect. Active termination of life does not occur.[137]

In current practice, the patient's wishes play only a limited role in the decision-making, although the wish of a patient who, for example, repeatedly pulls out the feeding tube is generally respected. 'Advance directives' are still rare and are usually couched in general terms. The doctors concerned are of the view that such a document "can never take the place of the doctor's judgment about the patient's situation", although they are prepared "to take its contents into consideration". In practice, advance directives play essentially no role in the decision-making.[138]

In the Commission's view, two questions are of central importance in assessing the acceptability of life-shortening treatment for these patients: Under what circumstances is life-prolonging treatment no longer legitimate? And what is the relevance of the remaining capacity of the patient to participate in the decision-making, and how can the wishes of the patient be ascertained? In connection with the second question there is also the problem of patients who "in an early stage of dementia make requests that are consistent with their preceding way of life and personality" but who, when the dementia is more severe, resist effectuation of their earlier request[139] or do not appear to be suffering unbearably.[140]

The Commission takes the position that the competence of the patient is not a matter of all or nothing. The remaining autonomy of the patient should be respected as much as possible, and in this regard the patient's determination and the family's judgment should be taken into account. The mere fact that his wishes seem unwise is no reason to ques-

---

137 CAL 3: 19. According to the national surveys of 1990 and 1995 (see table 5.4) about two-thirds of all deaths for which nursing-home doctors are responsible involved a MBSL, roughly equally divided over abstinence and pain relief. The CAL makes no comment on the fact that there is apparently a far higher level of death due to MBSL in nursing homes than one would expect from the Commission's findings.

138 CAL 3: 22-23. Compare the findings for the United States of Teno et al. 1997a, 1997b.

139 The CAL seems with this offhand reference to suggest that it is conceivable that an earlier euthanasia request be carried out on a resisting patient. As far as we are aware there is no one in the Dutch euthanasia discussion who would defend such an idea.

140 CAL 3: 24-25.

tion a patient's competence. The balance of positive and negative effects of the patient's choice is important: when a patient whose remaining life expectancy is limited refuses food and drink, this should be respected even if the patient has hardly any remaining competence. Refusal of pain-killers or of food by a patient whose dementia is still only moderate could lead to the opposite conclusion. "The criterion used to determine competence … should be more demanding to the extent that the consequences are more serious."[141]

The legitimacy of life-prolonging treatment should, according to the Commission, be judged from a number of perspectives. In the first place, the patient's express wishes should be "determinative" if the patient is competent to indicate what he or she wants. If not, the question whether medical treatment is legitimate must be answered on other grounds. The "presumed will" of the patient is in that connection the most important "guideline". This can be ascertained either from an 'advance directive' or, if none is available, the patient's "concept of his life as a whole" can be reconstructed with the help of his family and close friends and nursing personnel.[142]

If an express or 'presumed' will does not give a decisive answer, then a judgment concerning the legitimacy of life-prolonging treatment must be based on the burden for the patient of the treatment in question and the expected positive effects: in other words, on what the doctors and the close relatives and friends of the patient consider to be in his interest. The Commission considers these factors a specific operationalization of the concept of 'futile medical treatment' in the context of treatment decisions with respect to severely demented patients.[143] Elsewhere, the Commission observes that a decision based on such factors does not imply a "judgment about the quality of life of the patient concerned, but primarily one concerning the added value or the point of medical treatment".[144] In the last phase of severe dementia,

> the legitimacy of further treatment … ceases. The demented patient would be reduced … to a number of still intact physiological functions. Since improvement can no longer be achieved, the dying process would simply be drawn out: treatment in such circumstances brings the patient into an inhumane situation and keeps him in it longer than necessary.[145]

As in its report on long-term coma patients, the Commission emphasizes the importance of the 'priority principle' in the decision-making: consideration of the legitimacy

---

141 CAL 3: 26-31.
142 CAL 3: 32-33, 60.
143 CAL 3: 32-35.
144 CAL 3: 50.
145 CAL 3: 36-38.

of life-terminating treatment is only appropriate after the conclusion has been reached that (further) life-prolonging treatment is not legitimate and it has been stopped.[146]

The Commission appears to attach far more weight to an 'advance directive' or appointed representative than is common in current practice, and it expects an increasing use of such instruments in the near future.[147] But the Commission's support for this way of involving the patient's own will in the decision-making is qualified. The "opinion" of the appointed representative, for example, "should be accorded ... great weight," but the representative must be able to "make it plausible that his/her instructions really represent the patient's wishes". And if the patient has provided that "he or she does not want to be subjected to certain treatments ... then *in general* this wish should be respected" [italics added]. Elsewhere the Commission observes that at the moment of writing such an 'advance directive', a person can hardly "imagine what the later situation will be like" (but qualifies this remark with the observation that the same applies to doctors and relatives and friends who are called upon to take decisions for the patient). At the end of its treatment of 'advance directives', the Commission is not prepared to go further than the proposition that if such a written request is clear and current enough, "and in addition ... the appointed representative (if any) of the patient confirms its contents, then a doctor is obliged to respect it."[148] In this, it seems to fall short of the requirements laid down in the Law on Contracts for Medical Treatment, that became effective in 1995 (see section 3.1.3).

The legitimacy of euthanasia pursuant to an 'advance directive' in which the patient requests it in the case of severe dementia – something the Commission expects to occur more frequently in the future – raises two questions: whether serious dementia meets the criteria for euthanasia (as these have been worked out in the Dutch case-law), and how the doctor is to decide that the moment has come for carrying out the request.

The key problem with respect to the criteria for euthanasia is that the patient's request in an 'advance directive' is not based on contemporaneous suffering but on the prospect of becoming severely demented. In all probability a severely demented patient does not suffer from the dementia itself. Unlike the case of euthanasia there is thus no situation of 'necessity' arising out of a "direct and intensive contact with the patient, who experiences his/her situation as unbearable". If dementia is accompanied by some other condition that does cause serious suffering, or if carrying out an 'advance directive' to terminate

---

146 CAL 3: 50.

147 CAL 3: 35.

148 CAL 3: 38-43. The Commission also notes that positive requests for a particular form of treatment – for example, generous use of pain relief – should be honored so long as they do not conflict with the professional standard.

artificial feeding places the patient in an unacceptable situation, then some members of the Commission consider euthanasia legitimate; others would "want to limit themselves to relieving the patient's suffering, accepting as a secondary effect that this might lead to an earlier death".[149]

Despite its reservations, the Commission concludes by observing that, if the prospect of severe dementia did not satisfy the criteria for euthanasia, it would never be possible to honor an 'advance directive' requesting it. The Commission considers such a "categorical conclusion – considering the extent of the loss of dignity [*ontluistering*] associated with advanced dementia – not easy to defend".[150]

The second problem with an 'advance directive' requesting euthanasia is that it requires the doctor to decide *when* to carry out the patient's request. In a normal case of euthanasia, it is the patient's 'concrete request' that determines the time termination of life takes place. But carrying out euthanasia on the basis of an 'advance directive' requires the doctor to determine the moment at which the patient's criteria have been met. "The doctor becomes responsible for a not unimportant part of the patient's decision." The CAL considers that this "cannot necessarily be expected of a doctor". In fact, the objection is probably fatal to the prospects of euthanasia pursuant to advance directive on any significant scale.[151] The situation is perhaps less difficult – at least for the doctor – if the patient has appointed a representative who can determine when the moment has come.[152]

As far as termination of life with euthanatica on the basis of a 'presumed will' is concerned, the Commission does not go further than the observation that it is not impossible for such a will to be "convincingly reconstructed". Whether termination of life can be legitimated on such a basis the Commission leaves to further discussion. However, if the reconstruction satisfies the strictest demands and, apart from severe dementia, the patient is also apparently suffering severely from other disorders, the Commission considers termination of life legitimate (it does not expect the situation to occur frequently).[153]

In the absence of an 'advance directive' or a 'presumed will', termination of life can only be legitimated in terms of the seriousness and duration of suffering: there would have to be a situation of necessity "in which the patient's situation is inconsistent with human

---

149 CAL 3: 45-46.
150 CAL 3: 42-48.
151 See also Keizer, cited in Holsteyn & Trappenburg (1996: 10-11), for the virtual impossibility that a doctor could honor an 'advance directive' requesting euthanasia under specified, future conditions.
152 CAL 3: 46-47.
153 CAL 3: 48.

dignity". The dementia itself is in any event an insufficient condition. It would have to be demonstrated that termination of life is not in violation of the '(presumed) will' of the patient. Family and friends would have to consider termination of life acceptable. The Commission concludes that the legitimacy of terminating life under such circumstances is so complex a question that it does not feel able to take a position on it at present. If, however, the conditions stated are not met, then it is certainly not legitimate.[154]

In short: it is much too early to predict with any confidence how the law is going to develop on this matter. It seems unlikely that in the case of senile dementia 'active' termination of life with euthanatica, except in the form of 'help in dying' after the termination of life-prolonging treatment, will ever play more than a marginal role: the patient who requests it is of doubtful competence, 'advance directives' (even when accompanied by appointment of a representative) present too many seemingly insuperable problems, and termination of life with no request at all is hard to justify except under exceptional circumstances. The most important MBSL in these cases will continue to be abstinence. The most important legal developments will therefore probably concern the binding force of 'advance directives' or of instructions from an appointed representative in which life-prolonging treatment (including artificial feeding and hydration) is refused.[155]

3.5   Euthanasia in the absence of somatic suffering

Much of the discussion further on in this section assumes that for purposes of the regulatory regime applicable to euthanasia and assistance with suicide a distinction can be made between somatically based and not somatically based suffering. It is generally recognized that a distinction between 'physical' and 'mental' suffering would be untenable, since all suffering is 'mental' and all of it involves impairment of functioning. The question here is a slightly different one: whether suffering can be differentiated in terms of its source.

The question is less important than it once seemed,[156] since its relevance for regulation was significantly reduced by the holding of the Supreme Court in the *Chabot* case (see sections 2.4, 3.5.1 and appendix II-2) to the effect that not somatically based suffering

---

154 CAL 3: 49.

155 See note 11 on refusal of food and drink [*versterven*].

156 See the position of the KNMG of 1984 and the nurses' organization 'Nieuwe Unie' of 1992 (KNMG 1992: 47), rejecting euthanasia in the absence of a somatic source of the patient's suffering.

can support a valid request for assistance with suicide. However, as the *Chabot* case also makes clear, the distinction does remain relevant for the consequences of the patient's refusal of treatment and for the substance of the consultation requirement and the consequences of inadequate consultation. It is therefore worth raising the issue whether the distinction deserves the status still accorded it.

What ultimately is the intrinsic significance of the somatic/non-somatic distinction? Euthanasia or assistance with suicide in a case of suffering of somatic origin usually involves a shortening of life on the order of days or weeks (see table 5.11), although in the case of a few conditions such as MS, AIDS, and paraplegia, it may be much more than that. The shortening of life involved in a case of non-somatic suffering will usually be far greater. The Supreme Court in *Chabot* presumably had this in mind in referring specifically to the requirement of 'proportionality' in the case of a patient whose suffering is non-somatic and who has refused a realistic alternative to assistance with suicide: the burden for the patient of treatment less easily outweighs the benefits when the life to be won is significant. Is this, then, a reason to distinguish cases of somatic and of non-somatic suffering so far as the defence of necessity is concerned?

Not all cases of non-somatic suffering involve a substantial remaining life expectancy. It is not clear that this was true in the *Chabot* case. The various experts Dr. Chabot consulted were agreed that Ms. B was likely to attempt suicide again within a month if not given assistance. The argument that a patient's life expectancy should be considered in isolation from his suicidality was specifically rejected by one of these experts as irrelevant, since in that case the patient would be a different person.[157] So the distinction somatic/non-somatic is not necessarily congruent with the problem of proportionality.

The idea that in cases of non-somatic suffering there is more reason to doubt whether the patient's request is voluntary and well-considered does not, on further inspection, support the distinction: a patient suffering from somatic causes may also suffer from diminished competence, and the competence of patients whose suffering is non-somatic need not necessarily be in question at all. In short, the distinction is not congruent with the problem of competence.

Euthanasia or assistance with suicide in the case of non-somatically based suffering may entail serious problems of establishing after the fact that the patient was suffering unbearably, was competent, and wanted to die. This seems an obvious reason for wanting to impose special procedural requirements in cases of non-somatic suffering. Cancer is the main occasion for euthanasia in the Netherlands, and cancer leaves a substantial

---

157 Compare CAL 4: 15, 36.

trail of corroborating evidence behind. Where x-rays, laboratory reports and autopsy evidence of (probable) suffering and a (likely) request are lacking, the reports and the testimony of other doctors who examined the patient can be particularly important. Nevertheless, as the *Chabot* case illustrates, the distinction somatic/non-somatic is not always congruent with the need for such corroborating evidence: there was in fact a wealth of corroboration concerning the situation of Ms. B.

Finally, whatever the merits or demerits of the distinction between somatic and non-somatic suffering, it seems questionable whether it can be made to stick in practice. Increasingly, psychiatric conditions that used to be considered entirely non-somatic in origin are being found to include biological factors in their etiology. Instead of a sharp line there seems to be a considerable grey area that is gradually effacing the formerly distinct categories on either side. In short, it seems unlikely that the distinction somatic/non-somatic can be made to do the major work that its role to date in the public discussion and in legal development demands.[158]

3.5.1 Persons whose suffering is due to a psychiatric disorder

As we have seen (section 3.1.4 above), Dutch law has generally made no distinction between killing on request and assistance with suicide as far as the justifiability of the doctor's behavior is concerned and the 'requirements of careful practice' that apply. Nevertheless, in connection with suffering not based on a somatic condition it is almost universally assumed that what is at issue is assistance with suicide.[159]

Of a total of about 1600 suicides per year in the Netherlands, about half are by persons with some psychiatric history (45% have been institutionalized at some time); about 250

---

158 As we will see in chapter 6.3.2, a system of decriminalized control could deal with differences in proportionality and the other differences of degree that may sometimes be associated with the difference between somatically and not somatically based suffering far better than can a system of criminal control.

159 See CAL 4; NVP 1992; Van der Wal & Van der Maas 1996: 202; *Chabot*, appendix II-2.

of these are persons who are institutionalized at the time.[160] Psychiatric disorders are reported by doctors as the most important illness of the patient in about 1% of all cases of euthanasia (and in 14% of the cases in which euthanasia is refused). Psychiatrists are regularly consulted by non-psychiatrists in connection with requests for euthanasia, usually in cases involving a somatic disorder. Dutch psychiatrists receive some 320 serious requests for assistance with suicide per year; some 2 to 5 of these are granted, in more than half of which the patient is also suffering from a fatal somatic disorder (see chapter 5.3.4).

The terminological confusion that suffuses the preceding paragraph is characteristic of the legal and ethical discussion.[161] Under the misleadingly simple label 'psychiatric patients' lurk situations that pose some quite different problems: (1) *psychiatric patients*[162] who seek assistance with suicide *from a psychiatrist* because of *suffering due to their psychiatric disorder*, including as a special case persons *voluntarily or involuntarily institutionalized* with a psychiatric disorder; (2) persons who seek assistance with suicide *from a non-psychiatrist* because of a *psychiatric disorder*; (3) persons who seek the *assistance of a psychiatrist* in committing suicide although they have *no psychiatric disorder and also are not suffering based on a somatic condition*; (4) persons who request assistance with suicide *from a psychiatrist* because of *suffering due to a somatic condition*; (5) persons who request euthanasia because of a somatic disorder, but whose *competence is in doubt* because of a (suspected) psychiatric disorder.

In this section we are concerned with persons whose suffering is due to a psychiatric disorder, whether or not they are 'patients', whether or not they are under treatment by a psychiatrist, whether or not they are institutionalized, and whether or not it is a psychia-

---

160 CAL 4: 9; for data on total suicides per year see CBS, *Statistisch Jaarboek* 1997: 439. Psychiatric patients account for far more than their share of suicide: their frequency is 10 times that of the population as a whole, and 30-40 times higher if only institutionalised patients are considered. About half of all suicides are by persons who have some psychiatric history. Only an estimated 5% of all suicides appear free from serious psychiatric disorder.
The CAL data are a decade old and in some respects the situation is now different; for the most recent data on suicide see Kerkhof 1996. Among other things, it appears that by 1993 half of all suicides were by persons currently under treatment for a psychiatric condition and 75-80% had had such treatment at some time. Since the total number of suicides has been declining in the Netherlands, Kerkhof interprets these data as indicating greater success on the part of the institutions and doctors concerned in coming in contact with the population at risk.

161 See e.g. Van der Wal & Van der Maas 1996: 202-203.

162 Both the CAL and the NVP identify a 'psychiatric patient' as someone being treated by a psychiatrist for a 'psychiatric disorder' (CAL 4: 3-6; NVP 1997: § 1.5).

trist who is asked to render the assistance. The possible importance of the latter questions will emerge in the course of the discussion. The special situation of persons with no disorder at all who approach a psychiatrist (or another doctor) for assistance with suicide is considered in section 3.5.2. The problem of persons whose suffering is somatic but whose competence is in question was touched on in section 3.1.3.

Until the beginning of the 1990s (despite indications to the contrary in some early judicial decisions – see for example the *Wertheim* case discussed in chapter 2.2) it was quite widely supposed that legitimate euthanasia or assistance with suicide requires 'physical suffering' and a 'terminal illness' and that it is not available for persons whose suffering is based on a psychiatric disorder. The Health Council's *Advice on Suicide* of 1986 observed that the competence of a psychiatric patient is not always problematic, but the Council was divided on the question whether non-somatically based suffering alone could afford sufficient legitimation for assistance with suicide.[163] The Medical Association concluded in its policy statement of 1991 that "a somatic condition or pain" is generally required and that it is "doubtful whether a [psychiatric] patient can be considered capable of making a well-considered and entirely voluntary request".[164] After the Medical Association and the Ministry of Justice had agreed, in late 1990, on a procedure for doctors to report cases of euthanasia, the National Inspectors for Public Health and for Mental Health stated in 1991, in a joint letter to all doctors, that this procedure was not applicable to psychiatric patients because a psychiatric condition could never afford a basis for assistance with suicide.[165]

The letter of the Inspectors led to a great deal of criticism, including questions in Parliament. In its answer to these, the Government disavowed the categorical position of the Inspectors. In 1993 the Inspector for Mental Health brought out a report concluding that exceptional situations are possible in which assistance with suicide at the request of a psychiatric patient could be legitimate; the letter of 1991 was withdrawn.[166] In the meantime, the Dutch Association for Psychiatry (NVP) had issued a report rejecting the idea that a psychiatric disorder necessarily affects the patient's competence and adopting the position that assistance with suicide for such patients does not differ in principle – and need not be judged in a different way – from euthanasia in all other cases.[167]

Beginning in the mid-1980s, the courts had been confronted with a number of cases in which these issues were presented. With the exception of one decision of the Central

---

163 Gezondheidsraad 1986.
164 KNMG 1992: 30.
165 See Legemaate 1993: 758-759.
166 See Legemaate 1993: 759.
167 NVP 1992.

Medical Disciplinary Tribunal that led to the letter of the Medical Inspectors mentioned above, the judgments seemed to allow room for assistance with suicide in the case of psychiatric patients (see chapter 2.4). By 1994 all these developments appeared to have arrived at a tentative resolution. In November 1993 the CAL published the fourth in its series of discussion-papers: *Assistance with Suicide in Psychiatric Practice* (CAL 4), in which it accepted the legitimacy of assistance with suicide for psychiatric patients. In May 1994 the Dutch Supreme Court rendered its decision in the *Chabot* case, which resolved various questions in favor of the legitimacy of assistance with suicide for persons whose suffering is based on a non-somatic disorder. Finally, the Dutch Association for Psychiatry recently produced a tentative draft of a report, *Assistance with Suicide in the Case of Patients with a Psychiatric Disorder* (NVP 1997); its arguments and conclusions are generally similar to those of the CAL.[168]

From the foregoing sketch of recent Dutch developments it is clear that there are two specific questions involved in the legitimacy of assistance with suicide at the request of a psychiatric patient: the question of competency to make a request and the question of non-somatic suffering. The reports of the CAL and the NVP deal with both questions.

COMPETENCE

The CAL rejects the "categorical approach" of the Inspector for Mental Health to the question of competence: "The position that psychiatric patients in general are not competent is ... untenable." The CAL argues that the patient's "actual present competence, not the psychiatric disorder" should be decisive. However, if psychiatrists question the competence of their patients, this is not a matter of "prejudice" but of experience in practice that "treatable conditions ... can give rise to temporary suicide wishes or attempts". The doctor must try to distinguish between "a request that is really meant as such, and one that may well be the symptom of some temporary or treatable condition". The CAL thus situates the problem of assistance with suicide at the request of psychiatric patients at the point of tension between two competing objectives: promoting the welfare of the patient (which may sometimes require paternalistic measures) and respect for the autonomy of the patient.[169]

The CAL takes the same position as in the case of dementia (see section 3.4): competence is a matter of more or less. Furthermore, in the case of some conditions, relatively 'good'

---

168 Because the version available to us at the time this book went to press was not yet the final published version, all references are to section numbers in the final report. See the list of literature at the end of this book for further information on this report.

169 CAL 4: 3-8.

periods may alternate with relatively 'bad' ones.[170] The patient's competence can be assessed with the help of a number of criteria, varying from being able to 'express a choice' to being able to 'make a decision on the basis of a rational thought-process'. The Commission's position is that if "there is no longer a treatment perspective, the patient is suffering severely and unpreventably, and the patient emphatically and repeatedly expresses the wish to die," it is not necessary that the patient meet "the strictest possible standards of competence". The patient must, however, meet the criterion of "actual understanding of information with respect to the choice".[171]

The approach of the NVP is slightly different. It is presented as an exegesis of the requirements for justifiable euthanasia in the specific case of psychiatric patients: the patient's request must be 'voluntary and well-considered'. A 'voluntary request' is defined as one "free from coercive influence by others"[172] and a 'well-considered' request is one that involves a 'clear choice' for death and in which the patient is able to receive and understand the relevant information, to assess the considerations for and against the choice and to give an explanation for that choice and to take account of the consequences his suicide will have for others. The NVP observes that a psychiatrist must be alert to the danger that "primitive inclinations and drives" that the patient is not consciously aware of may play a role in his choice, but it rejects the idea that all psychiatric patients lack the normal human capacity for a well-considered request.[173] The patient's request must also be based on an "enduring desire for the end of life", and in the case of a psychiatric patient this means that the request must be made "over a period of *at least several months*, in a well-considered way, repeatedly, and in the presence of others".[174]

---

170 This gives rise to the problem – similar to that in the case of 'advance directives' – that the competent decision (during a 'good' period) and the unbearable suffering (during a 'bad' one) may not occur at the same time. The CAL considers assistance with suicide during a 'good' period in principle legitimate (CAL 4: 14). But carrying out a written request, made during a 'good' period, during a period that the patient is not competent is "in general" not acceptable: one must wait until the patient is competent again (CAL 4: 38-39).

171 CAL 4: 14-15, 18-21.

172 NVP 1997: § 3.1.1.

173 NVP 1997: § 3.1.2.

174 NVP 1997: § 3.2 (italics in original). The NVP rejects a requirement of a written request, out of concern that such a request might tend to commit the patient to the request (*ibid.*). The District Court, Assen (10 October 1997) was recently confronted with the case of a man of 81, in a nursing home recovering from a hip fracture, whose wife had died while he was in the home, and who as a result of refusing to eat was expected to die. A proceeding for involuntary commitment to a psychiatric institution was brought and the evidence showed that although the man knew perfectly well what he was doing, his wish to die was the result of a treatable psychiatric disorder. The Court ordered commitment for the unusually short period of 3 months to see whether he could be helped by treatment.

SUFFERING

The CAL argues that it is "not meaningful to distinguish between types and causes of suffering". What is important is "the individual (psychic) experience" and the possibility of "influencing actual suffering with the help of appropriate medical-therapeutic means". In the CAL's view, it is the treatment perspective that is the central factor in the legitimation of assistance with suicide at the request of psychiatric patients. If there is no longer a treatment perspective, the principal legitimation of medical treatment – "alleviating … suffering or eliminating it through cure" – is absent.[175] Under these circumstances it

> becomes meaningless … to interpret the patient's wish for death as the result of a psychiatric condition. That may well in fact be the case, but since we have no further possibility of letting the patient continue to live without the condition, and without the wish for death, we will have to change our perspective. The patient, his life-history, his condition and his wish for death are ultimately one existential whole. It is this actual person who must be our measure when we consider what action is appropriate.[176]

TREATMENT PERSPECTIVE

The CAL and the NVP are agreed that the requirement that the patient's suffering be 'without prospect of improvement' requires the absence of a 'realistic possibility of treatment', which is taken to exist when, according to current medical opinion, there is a treatment that offers hope of improvement, within a reasonable time, and with a reasonable balance between the expected results and the burden for the patient.[177] The NVP seems to be slightly more restrictive than the CAL in specifying that a 'reasonable time' in any case must be long enough to carry out a "complete psycho-pharmacological protocol together with a protocolled psychotherapeutic treatment directed at a specific complaint". The NVP is emphatic that a patient can only be considered untreatable when every realistic possibility of treatment that "current medical-scientific opinion deems indicated" has been tried without success, and these treatments must reflect the "state of the art".[178]

The psychiatric patient's refusal of treatment, unlike that of a patient whose suffering is based on a somatic condition, thus precludes assistance with suicide if the preferred

---

175 CAL 4: 36.
176 CAL 4: 14.
177 CAL 4: 20; NVP 1997: § 3.3.3.
178 NVP 1997: § 3.3.3.

treatment offers "a reasonable chance of success within a reasonable period".[179] The CAL does remark in this connection that "expectations with respect to treatment may be based more on hope than on knowledge and experience," with the possible consequence that "the suffering of the patient is pointlessly prolonged". The NVP notes that an improvement in psychiatric terms will not necessarily always be experienced by the patient as reducing his suffering, and in such a case refusal may be acceptable.[180] Ultimately, the existence of a treatment perspective must weigh more heavily than the suffering of the patient.[181]

Why a patient whose suffering is somatically based but perfectly treatable – for example, a patient with diabetes – should be allowed to refuse treatment and still qualify for euthanasia, whereas a patient whose suffering is non-somatically based cannot, has nowhere been satisfactorily explained. Nevertheless, almost everyone (CAL, NVP, Supreme Court) seems to be agreed on the distinction.[182]

INSTITUTIONALIZED PATIENTS

The CAL and the NVP are agreed that an involuntarily committed patient should in principle be discharged before assistance with suicide is given.[183]

The NVP considers particularly difficult the problem of institutionalized suicidal patients for whom there is no treatment perspective but only one of continued physical

---

179 CAL 4: 21, 40; NVP 1997: § 3.3.4; *Chabot*, appendix II-2. The *obiter dictum* of the Supreme Court, that treatment refused "in complete freedom" would preclude assistance with suicide, is endorsed by the NVP. The expression is peculiar: in the first place because in human affairs there is no such thing as 'complete freedom', and in the second place since it seems paradoxically to imply that a patient whose rejection of treatment is *less* than free does *not* thereby disqualify himself for assistance with suicide.

180 It does insist, however, that "when indicated, biological psychiatric treatments, because of their relatively quick effects and the fact that side-effects are seldom serious, can in no case be refused".

181 CAL 4: 39-40.

182 The NVVE is an exception: it rejects the requirement that a psychiatric patient must accept treatment (NVVE 1996: 29). See chapter 6.3.2 for the possibilities of fine-tuning the relevance of refusal of treatment in the context of a decriminalized control regime.

183 CAL 4: 42; NVP 1997: § 6.1. Neither the CAL nor the NVP consider whether it is necessary to inform the committing court of the proposed release, although prevention of suicide may have been the main reason the court ordered the commitment in the first place. The NVP also considers the case of persons involuntarily confined as a result of a criminal conviction: for a variety of reasons assistance with suicide can only be contemplated after their involuntary confinement is at an end.

restraint and who are suffering unbearably from a psychiatric disorder that precludes a well-considered request. "One is confronted by the limits of what psychiatry has to offer." The choice, in the view of the NVP, is between giving assistance with suicide even though not all the requirements have been met (and thus running the risk of a criminal prosecution), or following the "less official route" and letting the patient leave the institution, knowing that he will probably commit suicide. The NVP regards the former course as 'preferable'; for the CAL the latter course is "indefensible": the risk is too great that such a suicide will take place in a way that the patient and those exposed to it ought not to have to undergo.[184] The CAL in fact considers this risk a specific legitimating factor in the case of psychiatric patients. There is a group of patients who "with great conviction and tenaciousness seek death" and who "end their lives in a hard and violent way that can be traumatic for those confronted with it." "The chance of such an outcome should be taken into account in deciding how to react to a request for assistance with suicide by a psychiatric patient."[185]

NON-PSYCHIATRISTS

Neither the CAL nor the NVP considers it in principle impossible that a non-psychiatrist – for example, the patient's GP – give assistance with suicide in the case of a psychiatric patient. If the doctor who receives the request is not himself a psychiatrist, he should discuss the case intensively with the patient's psychiatrist(s) (in particular to establish that further treatment is regarded by them as futile) and consult two independent psychiatrists.[186]

CONSULTATION

Because of the special susceptibility of psychiatric patients to suggestion and influence, and the danger that the psychiatrist, too, may be influenced in his judgment by unconscious motives,[187] CAL and NVP argue that an especially high degree of care is required in these cases. In the case of a psychiatric patient there should be consultation with one, and in difficult cases more than one, independent psychiatrist (or other doctor); the consulted doctors must have examined the patient themselves.[188]

---

184 NVP 1997: § 6.1; CAL 4: 21-22.

185 CAL 4: 15.

186 CAL 4: 36-37; NVP 1997: § 6.4.1.

187 The NVP discusses at some length the problem of unconscious motives that can affect the judgment of the psychiatrist (NVP 1997: § 3.4).

188 CAL 4: 37; NVP 1997: § 4. The 'Points requiring attention' pursuant to the reporting procedure (see appendix I-B) contemplate consultation with one doctor and at least one other person "with knowledge of the psychological condition of the patient", both of whom have examined the person concerned, in a case of a "patient … suffering from a psychiatric disorder".

The most important questions to which the consultant(s) should address themselves are "the patient's competence, the treatment perspective, and the problem of counter-transference"; the NVP adds to this the patient's enduring desire for death and the unbearability of his suffering.[189]

OTHER 'REQUIREMENTS OF CAREFUL PRACTICE'

Other health professionals (GPs, nursing personnel, psychologists) should, according to CAL and NVP, be included in the decision-making. There must be "good and convincing reasons … not to inform the family and close friends" (in order to limit their suffering as much as possible), and their judgment can in particular be of importance in connection with the question of competence.[190]

The NVP argues that there can be good reasons for the psychiatrist not to insist on being present when the patient commits suicide; and giving the patient the euthanaticum for use within a prescribed period (such as a week) can be a way of keeping the patient from feeling 'obliged' to go through with the suicide. In such cases, however, specific agreements must be made covering the continued availability of the psychiatrist, the place the suicide is carried out, etc., and the GP and close relatives or friends must be notified.

The NVP devotes extensive attention to the importance of careful and complete record-keeping and in this respect goes further than the 'Points requiring attention' pursuant to the reporting procedure, covering all aspects of the case from the initial request through the ultimate carrying out of the suicide.[191]

THE *CHABOT* CASE

In its decision in 1994 in the *Chabot* case (see chapter 2.4 and appendix II-2), the Dutch Supreme Court addressed several of the issues involved in the foregoing discussion. The Court's decision answers four important questions:

a. Can assistance with suicide be legally justifiable in the case of a patient whose suffering does not have a somatic basis and who is not in the terminal phase? The Court holds that it can be.
b. Can the wish to die of a person suffering from a psychiatric sickness or disorder legally be considered the result of an autonomous (competent and voluntary) judgment? The Court holds that it can be.

---

189 CAL 4: 42-43; NVP 1997: § 4.2. See note 52 above on the question how binding the consultant's opinion is on the doctor who requests it.
190 CAL 4: 15, 19, 28, 33, 36-7, 37-8, 41; compare NVP 1997: §§ 5.1, 5.2.
191 NVP 1997: § 7.

c. Can the suffering of such a person legally be considered 'lacking any prospect for improvement' if he has "in complete freedom" refused a "realistic alternative to relieve the suffering"?[192] The Court holds that in principle it cannot be.[193]

d. What are the legal requirements of consultation in such a case, as far as the defence of necessity is concerned? The Court holds that in the case of not somatically based suffering, the requirement of consultation (specifically, that the consultant examine the patient) is not merely a 'procedural' rule enforceable in disciplinary proceedings, but a condition of the justification of necessity. The different treatment of the consultation requirement in the situation of non-somatic suffering follows, in the view of the Supreme Court, from the "extraordinary care" required in such cases.

We have purposefully included the term 'legal' in each case to emphasize something that non-lawyers tend to forget: the decision of the Court concerns a number of legal terms and norms (in particular, those of the criminal law), not psychiatric or other terms or theories. There are, of course, psychiatrists who as a matter of professional opinion deny the very possibility of a 'voluntary' or 'balanced' request for suicide. As far as the criminal law is concerned, the Court follows the CAL and the NVP in rejecting such a categorical approach. The Court's holding does not address the more specifically professional concern, discussed below, for the delicate and dangerous nature of the psychiatrist-patient relationship, with its problems of transference and counter-transference (misplaced anger, need for control), of blackmail ('if you don't agree to help me, I will do it in a horrible way'), etc.[194]

---

192 The Court's opinion is not entirely clear on whether the "realistic alternative" to which it refers is limited to *medical* possibilities. The brief of the Advocate-General had in fact suggested that 'social' possibilities should be explored. Both CAL and NVP share this view: "Other than medical possibilities … of reducing the suffering" should also be exploited; but in that case "responsibility for [dealing with the suffering] … is entirely outside the competency of the doctor" (CAL 4: 36); the NVP includes among the interventions that must be tried: "social interventions that could make the suffering more bearable" (NVP 1997: §3.3.3). The implications of these remarks for what the doctor must do are not entirely clear. See also note 179 on the idea of refusal in 'complete freedom'.

193 In the *Chabot* decision this was *obiter dictum*. The rule was applied shortly thereafter in another case which suggests how complicated the question can be. In that case, the District Court, Haarlem (*Tijdschrift voor Gezondheidsrecht* 1994, no. 48), concluded on the basis of expert testimony that there were realistic possibilities for dealing with the patient's suffering which, while it was due to paralysis caused by several strokes, was treated by the Court as essentially non-somatic in character. The Court held that the doctor had too readily accepted the patient's refusal of any alternative to assistance with suicide.

194 The risk of transference and other psychological threats to the medical integrity of the psychiatrist's decision-making is of course equally present when the decision is to *refuse* assistance with suicide, a point often overlooked in arguments against assistance with suicide by psychiatrists.

After the decision in the *Chabot* case, the Ministers of Justice and of Health promptly announced a revision of the prosecutorial guidelines to reflect the holdings of the Supreme Court, and 11 of the 15 pending prosecutions (involving non-somatic suffering or patients not in the 'terminal phase') were dropped.[195]

KILLING ON REQUEST OR ASSISTANCE WITH SUICIDE?

Strictly speaking only assistance with suicide, not euthanasia, was at issue in the *Chabot* case and, while it does not suggest any difference in the justifiability of the two, the Court does seem to take for granted that in the case of psychiatric patients assistance with suicide and not euthanasia would be at issue. Both the CAL and the NVP similarly assume, as we have seen, that only assistance with suicide is appropriate in the case of psychiatric patients.

If, as we have argued in section 3.1.4, assistance with suicide should (and will) enjoy a preferred status, especially because of the additional guarantee of voluntariness that it affords, this may afford an explanation for the implicit assumption that psychiatric patients should be given assistance with suicide and not euthanasia. From the point of view of societal control over what the doctor does, the most troubling aspect of these cases is, after all, the problem of the lack of material evidence to support the doctor's assertion that the patient's request, right up to the last moment, was voluntary and based on 'unbearable and hopeless' suffering. If to this consideration we add the unspoken assumption that persons suffering from a psychiatric disorder are generally capable of carrying out the act themselves, whereas persons suffering from a somatic disorder frequently are not, we seem to have an adequate explanation for at least a general rule of thumb. If correct, such an explanation would seem to entail that the rule applies not only to psychiatric patients but to all cases of non-somatically based suffering. The explanation also implies that in the case of a psychiatric patient *not* capable of carrying out a suicide[196] the law will accept euthanasia as legitimate.

WHY PSYCHIATRISTS?

The CAL and the NVP have addressed the questions, whether assistance with suicide should be available for persons suffering from a psychiatric disorder and whether and how psychiatrists should be involved in the decision-making. What neither the CAL nor

---

195 See *Staatscourant* no. 179, 19 September 1994:1. In a recent case, the District Court, 's Hertogenbosch (31 July 1997), applied the criteria of the *Chabot* case and acquitted a psychiatrist. The psychiatrist was, at the explicit request of the patient, not present at the time she took the euthanaticum, but was continuously available.

196 See NVVE 1997 for some anecdotal evidence concerning cases of persons whose mental disorder deprived them of the capacity for the necessary planning. A.J. Tholen has suggested to us the example of a psychiatric patient who is paraplegic after a suicide attempt.

the NVP address is the question why a psychiatrist should be involved in rendering the assistance. There seem to be opposing professional views on this question. On the one hand there are those who emphasize the importance of a psychiatrist being able honestly to assure a (potential) patient that he is in principle willing to give such assistance, as a necessary condition of getting a treatment relationship established, on the basis of which it may be possible to forestall a suicide. On the other, there are those who argue that entertaining the possibility of assistance with suicide would be fatal to a therapeutic relationship. As, for example, with the possibility of a sexual relationship, it is something that must be categorically excluded lest it corrupt the therapeutic possibilities not only of the psychiatrist who permits it in his own practice but also (by affecting the expectations of patients) of those of his colleagues who do not. On the latter view, there is not necessarily anything wrong with assistance with suicide, but it must be given by anyone *except a psychiatrist.*

The medical and psychiatric professions in the Netherlands have, as we have seen, on the whole taken a less restrictive view of the limitations of the relationship between psychiatrist and patient than some psychiatrists (especially outside the Netherlands) consider appropriate. Nevertheless, by contrast with other developments in connection with MBSL, the decision in the *Chabot* case – and more particularly, what Chabot had done – provoked a rather polarized debate among psychiatrists in the Netherlands.[197] What is involved here seems not so much a legal issue as one of competing professional views among psychiatrists. It does not seem necessary for the law to take a position on one side or the other of an internal professional debate.

3.5.2   The legal horizon: assistance with suicide by the non-'sick' and the non-'suffering'

The legitimacy of a doctor giving assistance with suicide to a person whose non-somatic suffering is not due to a psychiatric disorder has much in common with the case of a person whose suffering is based on a psychiatric disorder, except that the competence of the person concerned is not at issue. If assistance with suicide in the case of a psychiatric patient can be legitimate, this would seem to apply *a fortiori* in the case of a 'rational suicide', unless the presence of an 'illness' is considered critical.

Assistance with suicide in a case of non-somatic suffering such as that of Ms. B in the *Chabot* case is only in a residual sense 'medical'.[198] Although Chabot himself is a psychia-

---

197 See Koerselman 1994; articles collected in NVVE 1995; appendix II-2, note 45.

198 The Supreme Court did apparently regard Ms. B as in some sense 'sick', although Chabot himself makes it quite clear that he did not (see *Chabot*, appendix II-2, part 2; Chabot 1996: 153). He himself raises the question whether help of the sort he gave need be restricted to doctors.

trist and the Supreme Court obviously considered it essential that he was a doctor, nevertheless the principled basis on which Dutch euthanasia law rests seems with the decision in the *Chabot* case to have taken a hesitant step away from the doctor-centered approach that has dominated legal development up to now and toward giving somewhat greater weight to the *principle of autonomy* (see chapter 4.3 on the balance between the various principles underlying legal policy concerning euthanasia).

Looked at in this way, the decision in *Chabot* may later be seen as having opened the way to a legal development that accepts assistance with suicide to persons who are not 'sick' at all (e.g. very elderly persons who are incapacitated in various ways and simply 'tired of life') and to persons who are not suffering at the time the request is made but, in anticipation of future deterioration, want to be in a position to choose the time of their death in advance of becoming incapacitated and dependent. There is, of course, nothing inevitable about such a development, and the mixture of partly conflicting legal principles on which Dutch euthanasia law (and the decision in *Chabot*) rest (see chapter 4.3), affords more than enough basis for choosing not to go that route. But the argument from autonomy wins unmistakeably in weight from the Supreme Court's decision in *Chabot*.

'Rational suicide' has begun over the past few years to occupy a place in the Dutch public discussion concerning medical behavior that shortens life. This seems likely to be an area of important legal development in the future. A number of situations can be distinguished:

–   A person who is not psychiatrically 'sick' suffers unbearably as the result of a traumatic experience, and there is no treatment acceptable to the person concerned or with so favorable a prognosis that its benefits can be considered to outweigh the burden to the patient. (This was the situation in the *Chabot* case, at least on Chabot's view.)

–   As a result of old age, with the accompanying physical deterioration, dependency, loneliness, etc., a person is 'tired of living': life as such has become unbearable. Such cases – in which the prosecuting authorities decided not to prosecute doctors who rendered assistance – have been described in the literature.[199]

–   Although a person is not currently suffering, the prospect of dementia, physical deterioration, dependency, confinement to a nursing home, etc. is unacceptable; the person concerned wishes to choose his or her own moment of death in order to

---

199 See Chabot 1992 and Weisz 1994. See sections 3.1.2 and 3.4.4 on the possibility that such persons can make use of the absolute right of the patient to refuse all treatment (including administration of food and drink) and hence 'let themselves die' (*versterven*).

avoid being exposed to such a situation. As we have seen in chapter 2.4, Drion has suggested that, under very limited circumstances, elderly persons should have the right to be supplied with a 'pill' with which they could accomplish this at a time of their own choosing.[200]

It would be foolhardy to wager a prediction on the direction or the speed of legal development in these cases.[201] So far, it does not seem that Drion has succeeded in helping to de-medicalize assistance with suicide by shifting the focus of attention away from the doctor and toward the right of an individual to decide for himself. However, it is worthy of note that the newest draft euthanasia bill of the Dutch Association for Voluntary Euthanasia (NVVE 1996) allows for assistance with suicide (by a doctor!) on no other condition but that the request be well-considered.

3.6   Conclusion

The substance of Dutch law concerning MBSL is pretty well settled on most of the major problems that have been subjects of public discussion and legal development, with the important exception of 'advance directives' requesting euthanasia in the case of dementia and the whole area of not somatically based suffering. Leaving aside for a moment the huge category of 'normal medical practice' (abstinence and pain relief), not currently regarded as problematic, the essential structure of legal control consists of the following elements:

– a prohibition (euthanasia, murder, etc.);
– a justification, available only to doctors, under clearly-defined circumstances (unbearable and hopeless suffering plus a request, or application of the 'priority principle');
– procedural 'requirements of careful practice' (consultation, proper administration, record-keeping, etc.);
– the duty to report the death as a non-natural one (except, perhaps, in the case of 'help in dying').

There are some residual problems concerning the way in which the 'requirements of careful practice' are enforced (criminal or disciplinary proceedings), the scope of the

---

200 Drion 1992. For a variety of practical reasons, Drion proposed to limit this to single persons over 75.

201 One technical problem to be solved is the requirement that the doctor involved be responsible for the patient's treatment. In the case of a person who is not 'sick', there can in the nature of things not be such a doctor.

idea of 'help in dying', the application of the notion of a 'natural death', the liability of nurses and other non-doctors for their participation in euthanasia or assistance with suicide, the precise contours of the role of parents, family and friends, etc.

As far as legal regulation is concerned, it is abstinence and pain relief – not euthanasia, assistance with suicide or even termination of life without an explicit request – that seem to present the most pressing problems. These sorts of medical behavior that shorten life are, as we will see in chapter 5.3.1, every bit as 'intentional' as euthanasia, they often are not at the request of the person concerned (who frequently, for example, is unconscious), and they involve vastly larger numbers of patients. Furthermore, they are distinguished from the controversial sorts of MBSL in terms of legal concepts (action versus omission; intentionality) that, as we will see in chapter 4.1, are intrinsically problematic, and as we will further see in chapters 5 and 6, make effective control over 'active, intentional termination of life' essentially impossible. Despite such good reasons to subject them to public control, they remain largely unregulated, both substantively and procedurally.

However, the biggest problem with which the Dutch are now confronted does not so much concern the legal rules as their effectiveness in practice. This is partly because of the conceptual inadequacies just mentioned and the exclusion of abstinence and pain relief from the scope of legal control, but more importantly it is a consequence of the very structure of the current control regime, based on a criminal prohibition and self-reporting. This problem will be addressed directly in chapter 6, after we have looked at the conceptual difficulties of the present control regime and the conflicting principles on which it is based in chapter 4, and the available empirical information in chapter 5.

4   The Terms of Debate since 1982

The central question around which the political euthanasia debate revolves is: to what extent and on what basis should the state become involved in the relationship between someone who wishes to die and someone who, at the request of this person, brings about his death or provides assistance to this end? More specifically, should the state legally prohibit a doctor from honoring a patient's request for help to end his life? Within the Dutch euthanasia debate, a variety of arguments for and against the legalization of euthanasia have been advanced. The most important of these will be presented in section 4.2. This will be followed in section 4.3 by an analysis of the Dutch euthanasia debate in which we will consider the various arguments and examine whether there is common ground in terms of which the opposing positions might be reconciled.

But first, attention must be given to a fundamental presupposition of the euthanasia debate: the idea that there are valid reasons to distinguish 'euthanasia' from shortening of life as a result of 'normal medical practice'. This idea has, as we have seen in chapter 3, led to two different legal control regimes, applicable to the two sorts of life-shortening behavior. In section 4.1 we will conclude that the basis for the distinction is not adequate to support such widely different legal treatment.

4.1   Distinguishing euthanasia from other MBSL

As we have seen in chapter 2.3.2, during the early 1980s the Dutch debate concerning the shortening of life in a medical context concentrated on euthanasia in a narrow sense: intentional life-shortening behavior by someone other than the person involved, at his request. Euthanasia proper was distinguished from the so-called 'false forms of euthanasia'. Not euthanasia but 'normal medical practice' was said to be involved if death is a result of (a) not beginning or ceasing a treatment that is 'medically futile', (b) not beginning or stopping medical treatment because the patient does not want it, or (c) administering pain-killing drugs.

Euthanasia is prohibited by article 293 of the Criminal Code while 'normal medical practice' with life-shortening consequences is uncontroversial as far as both criminal and medical law are concerned. When such shortening of life is the result of not beginning or ceasing treatment because the patient refuses (further) treatment, the doctor's behavior is not criminal because a patient who is of sound mind has the right to refuse treatment.

The other two forms of 'normal medical practice' with life-shortening consequences fall under the heading of the 'medical exception' and are therefore not subject to the criminal law (see chapters 2.2, 2.3.1, and 3.3.1). It is thus very important that the dividing line between euthanasia on the one hand and 'normal medical practice' with life-shortening consequences on the other can be clearly drawn. If this is not possible, it will not be clear which life-shortening behavior is criminal and which is not. This section will examine whether or not a distinction can be made and whether or not the basis for the distinction is morally relevant.

The distinction between euthanasia and 'normal medical practice' has become generally accepted in the context of the Dutch euthanasia debate, but in fact there has been little discussion devoted to it.[1] Discussion of the foundations of the distinction has occurred primarily in the international philosophical literature. In this literature the possibility and the importance of the distinction between euthanasia and normal medical practice with life-shortening consequences are founded on two underlying dichotomies: the first is between *killing* and *letting die* and the second between the *intentional* and the *non-intentional shortening of life*. The importance of these two underlying distinctions is defended as follows:

– shortening of life as a result of not beginning or ceasing treatment that is medically futile or not (any longer) desired by the patient is classified as 'letting die' and is, by contrast with euthanasia (a form of 'killing'), morally less objectionable or even acceptable; and
– shortening of life as a result of administering pain-killing drugs is distinguishable from euthanasia by the absence of an intention to cause death, and is therefore morally less objectionable or even acceptable.

In the following sections we examine these two claims closely.

4.1.1   Killing versus letting die

The distinction between 'killing' and 'letting die' is based on the so-called *acts and omissions doctrine*. This doctrine holds that

> failure to perform an act, with certain foreseen bad consequences of that failure, is morally less bad than to perform a different act which has identically foreseeable bad consequences.[2]

---

1   See however Van Till 1970; Staatscommissie 1985: 201ff; De Beaufort & Dupuis 1988; Dupuis 1994.
2   Glover 1977: 92.

This idea has an honorable pedigree.[3] Nevertheless, its moral relevance can be questioned. The arguments for the distinction are as a general matter untenable, or they do not apply in the medical context. The five most important of these arguments will be reviewed here.

(1) The first argument in defense of the distinction is that in the case of killing the death of the patient is 'caused' by the doctor. Letting die, by contrast, allows Nature to take its course, which leads to a 'natural death' (in which some recognize the hand of God).[4] This argument has the plausibility of popular wisdom and, as is often the case with such wisdom, cannot stand up to analysis. There is no such thing as 'the cause' of a particular state of affairs. Any given occurrence is always the outcome of a complex intermingling of circumstances. Excluding omissions from such a complex is completely arbitrary and assumes exactly what needs to be proved.[5]

(2) A second argument is to the effect that 'killing' always implies that death is a desired result, at least as a means of reaching some further goal (for example, relieving the patient's suffering), while this need not be the case in a 'letting die' situation. But in fact any motive a person can have for killing can equally well be a motive for letting die. The thought that in the case of letting die death, in itself or as a means to an end, is not desired is incorrect: there are, for example, each year in the Netherlands some 17,600 such deaths, the intended results of abstinence from life-prolonging treatment (see table 5.2).[6]

(3) A third argument refers to a supposed difference in moral weight between two general duties everyone in principle has: the duty not to harm and the duty to help. It is argued that killing is a violation of the duty not to harm and letting die is at worst a violation of the duty to help (premise 1). Because our moral intuition is that the first duty is of

---

3   See Rachels 1986: 106.

4   The Dutch criminal law scholar Enschedé has observed that preoccupation with euthanasia and neglect of the other MBSL seems to reflect a latent Christian objection to suicide: the supposed 'intention' of the doctor permits the patient's death in the case of the other MBSL to be ascribed to a terminal condition that was already present rather than to human agency (Enschedé 1986a).

5   Compare Rachels 1986: 115. Most actions that are part of the complex of factors leading to a particular result can easily be described as omissions. A pedestrian may die from being hit by a motorist who was not looking where he was going and did not brake on time because he did not see the pedestrian soon enough, and the City Council may have contributed by allowing the motorist's visibility to become limited by postponing cutting back bushes growing along the side of the road.

6   Compare Kuhse 1987: 123ff.

greater moral weight than the second (premise 2), it can be concluded that killing is morally worse than letting die.

Both premises of the third argument are problematic. As far as the first premise is concerned, it is unclear why letting die can never be considered as inflicting harm (especially if we accept that omissions can be a cause of a person's death – see above). The doctor who lets Mr. X die because he has confused him with another patient Mr. Y for whom a non-reanimation decision had been taken certainly does inflict harm on Mr. X. It is therefore possible that letting die involves violation of the duty not to harm. Furthermore, it is possible that shortening of life, regardless of whether it is regarded as killing or as letting die, does not always amount to inflicting harm. It may be regarded as in the patient's interest if, for example, it is the only way to relieve unbearable suffering.[7] Finally, there are situations conceivable in which letting die inflicts more harm than killing: for example in the case of a dying patient suffering serious untreatable pain, when letting die would prolong his misery.

The second premise is based on the assumption that the duty not to harm weighs more heavily than the duty to help. However, the reason more weight is often attributed to the duty not to harm lies in the fact that fulfillment of the duty to help often asks more of the actor than fulfillment of the duty not to harm. The duty not to murder your neighbor, for example, is more absolute than the duty to help provide food for children in the Third World because the latter is much more demanding.

In the case of shortening of life in a medical context, the argument that the duty not to harm outweighs the duty to help is particularly unconvincing. The moral weight of the duty to help is determined by whether or not there is a special relationship between the person who is able to offer help and the person in need of help. In a medical context there most certainly is such a special relationship. Whether looked at as a matter of the contractual relationship between doctor and patient or as a general obligation resting on doctors as a consequence of the authority to practice medicine,[8] the essence of the doctor-patient relationship is the doctor's duty to treat the patient. Furthermore, the burden for a doctor in fulfilling the duty to help a patient is far less than it would be for a lay person, since the doctor possesses the necessary medical expertise.[9]

It follows that the third argument also fails.

---

7   The *principle of beneficence* is in fact one of the most important arguments in favor of the legalization of euthanasia: see section 4.2.2.
8   See also article 255 of the Criminal Code in appendix I-A.
9   Compare Feinberg 1984: 164; Rachels 1986: 116.

(4) The next argument is that there is a distinction of certainty of outcome between killing and letting die: by contrast with killing, someone who allows a patient to die leaves open the possibility, for example, that a third party may intervene, which is supposed to reduce the first actor's responsibility for the death.[10] This argument may be generally true. But it is not a good reason for making the distinction in a medical context. A doctor who lets a patient die does so in the expectation that a third party will not intervene. The doctor responsible for a patient's care knows that in principle only he is authorized to make treatment decisions.[11] And, in general, those in a doctor's immediate surroundings will, at least as far as the sorts of 'abstinence' that are broadly accepted as legitimate are concerned, share his view of the case and therefore not be inclined to intervene.

(5) Finally, it is frequently stressed that the aim of medicine and therefore a doctor's first duty is to preserve life and that killing a patient directly conflicts with this duty.[12] Only in a case where further medical treatment would be futile is allowing a patient to die not considered to be in conflict with this duty because in such a case the doctor has done all he could reasonably have done to save the patient's life. It is, however, not clear that any such basic 'aim of medicine' can be defined. Preventing inhuman suffering and respecting the autonomy of the patient could equally well be considered basic aims of medicine. Such considerations do not amount to an independent argument for the distinction between killing and letting die. What a doctor's duty is, is precisely what is at issue. Now that the idea is increasingly accepted that in certain circumstances death may be in a patient's interest, it is dogmatic simply to assert that a doctor should strive for continuation of life.[13]

The conclusions concerning the distinction between killing and letting die that can be drawn from this discussion are as follows. It is doubtful whether the distinction has general moral relevance. But however that may be, within the medical context its importance is limited. This has to do mainly with the duty a doctor has to his patient. This duty makes the doctor morally accountable for everything that happens to the patient for whose care he is responsible. It is the doctor's ability to influence the situation which

---

10   A variant of this fourth argument points out that death is the *certain* result of killing, whereas it is only a *possible* result of letting die.

11   To ensure that his decision to let the patient die is not frustrated, a doctor may inscribe 'NTBR' (not to be reanimated) on the patient's chart, with the express purpose of preventing life-extending treatment from being administered by someone else.

12   The Hippocratic Oath is often invoked in this connection: see Amundsen 1987.

13   Compare Veatch 1981: chapter 1; Rachels 1986: 118ff.

constitutes his responsibility, not the nature (killing or letting die) of what he does.[14] In all cases of life-shortening treatment the possibility and the duty to exert influence are in principle present. Whatever sort of life-shortening behavior is involved, a doctor has to do *something*, even if that something is limited, for example, to giving instructions to nursing staff. And a doctor, even if he chooses to abstain (and hence let die), always remains responsible for what happens to the patient after this decision, for example for administering pain killers if needed. He may never use the idea of a 'mere omission' as an excuse for abandoning a patient to his fate.

In short, the distinction between killing and letting die cannot be clearly drawn and does not afford sufficient ground for the argument that there is an important moral or practical difference between euthanasia and 'normal medical practice' resulting in the shortening of life.

4.1.2   Intentionally shortening life

The third form of death due to 'normal medical practice' from which euthanasia is generally thought to be clearly distinguishable is death as a result of the use of pain killers. This is not regarded as controversial, since it is assumed it is not the doctor's intention to cause the death of the patient but rather to alleviate pain; the death of the patient is considered an 'undesired side-effect'.[15] This approach raises two questions. First, how must the distinction between the intentional and the non-intentional shortening of life be understood? And second, is the distinction morally relevant?

The idea that in the case of a death as the result of administering pain killers the doctor's intention is not to cause the death of the patient, which is merely an undesired side-effect, is linked with the so-called *doctrine of double effect*. The roots of this doctrine originate in the teachings of Thomas Aquinas and to this day form part of the moral teachings of, for example, the Roman Catholic Church.[16] Because medical ethics have historically been strongly influenced by Roman Catholic moral teaching, the doctrine of double effect has played a major role in medical ethics.

The doctrine of double effect developed in connection with the Judeo-Christian *principle of the sanctity of human life*. This principle absolutely forbids the intentional termina-

---

14   Compare Hart 1968: 122; Harris 1985: 30. See also Staatscommissie 1985: 205; Fahner 1988: 817; Leenen 1994: 276.

15   Compare Staatscommissie 1985: 27. See also Van der Wal & Van der Maas 1996: 41.

16   Compare Fisher 1995.

tion of innocent human life.[17] The so-called *doctrine of innocence* can be used to justify the death penalty and killing in self-defence or in wartime.[18] But there are other cases where causing death is also considered permissible. The doctrine of double effect keeps cases that, on grounds of moral intuition, are not considered morally reprehensible outside the scope of the principle of the sanctity of human life.[19]

The doctrine of double effect holds that behavior that has both a good and a bad effect can, despite the bad effect, be morally permissible provided

1   the behavior itself is not intrinsically wrong (that is: considered separately from its consequences);
2   the actor intends only the good effect, not the bad one;
3   the bad effect is not a means used to bring about the good effect; and
4   the good effect outweighs the bad effect.[20]

In order to ensure that the outcome of the doctrine of double effect corresponds with moral intuition, the term 'intention' in the second condition is interpreted in a special, narrow way. This can be understood as follows. Behavior can have three sorts of consequences: consequences desired for themselves; consequences desired as a means toward a result that is desired for itself; and consequences that are side-effects of the behavior. According to the narrow conception of the intentional, only the first two are to be considered 'intended', while side-effects are 'merely foreseen'.[21] The doctrine of double effect rests, therefore, on the distinction between 'intention' and 'foresight of consequences'.

Adherents of the doctrine of double effect conclude that shortening life as a result of alleviating pain is morally permissible because, although it can be foreseen, death in such a case is not desired either for itself or as a means of achieving the goal of alleviating suffering.[22] What is desired is the alleviation of the patient's suffering. His death is not a

---

17   See Kuhse 1987: 7. Compare Ferngren (1987: 34) on the 'Christian concept of imago Dei' that "provided the basis for the belief that every human life has absolute intrinsic value as a bearer of God's image and an eternal soul for whom Christ died".

18   Compare Rachels 1986: 12: "[A] person is 'innocent' unless he has by his own misconduct forfeited his right that others should not kill him. Using this criterion we can understand why criminals, murderers, and enemy soldiers are said not to be innocent."

19   The applicability of the doctrine of double effect is not limited to behavior that shortens life. In this sense the doctrine is more general than the principle of the sanctity of human life.

20   See Rachels 1986: 16; Kuhse 1987: 91. In connection with problematic aspects of the doctrine of double effect, several different versions have been developed: see Marquis 1991.

21   See Hart 1968: 120; Kuhse 1987: 89.

22   See, for example, Finnis 1995: 27.

means to achieve that goal, and administering the same drug to cause the patient to die *in order to put an end to his suffering* would not be permissible.[23]

There is an important objection to the distinction between 'intention' and 'foresight': it is questionable whether the distinction can be made in the clear-cut way that adherents to the doctrine of double effect suppose. There are two problems: first, it seems on careful analysis to be impossible to distinguish those results of an act that are merely 'foreseen' side-effects from those that are a 'means to an end'; and second, the idea that 'intent' requires more than mere 'foresight' makes intentionality a purely subjective concept.

The problem of distinguishing side-effects from means can be illustrated by two well-known abortion cases, the *hysterectomy case* and the *craniotomy case*. Abortion performed by removing the cancerous uterus of a pregnant woman with the aim of saving her life (the first case) is considered morally permissible by adherents of the doctrine of double effect. Crushing the skull of a foetus caught in the birth canal with a view to the same life-saving goal (the second case) is not. In the latter case, the argument goes, the death of the foetus is a means of saving the woman's life, while in the first case it is only an unavoidable and undesired side-effect.

But why should we consider the foetus' death from a crushed skull in the craniotomy case a (desired) 'means' of saving the pregnant woman's life, but not its death from the removal of the mother's uterus in the hysterectomy case? At this point, the argument for the doctrine of double effect boils down to the opinion that what the doctor does in the first case, but not in the second, 'is' the actual killing of the foetus.[24] This argument is a pure *ipse dixit*. The two cases have in common the only two apparently relevant circumstances: the death of the foetus is a *foreseeable consequence* of what the doctor does and a *necessary condition* for his success in saving the woman's life.[25]

That the way the actor's behavior is described plays a crucial role in the application of the doctrine of double effect becomes even clearer if we consider another case, that of the hero who throws himself onto an exploding grenade in order to save other human lives. Sacrifice of his own life leads to no reproach from adherents of the doctrine of double effect. His death is not considered a means of preserving the lives of others (in which case it would be a reprehensible suicide, a violation of the principle of the sanctity of human

---

23 Ceasing treatment that is disproportionately burdensome, even if this will probably cause the patient to die is, according to adherents of the doctrine of double effect, also morally permissible. Shortening the patient's life is not considered a means of ending the burden to the patient but as a merely anticipated side-effect.

24 See Kuhse 1987: 100.

25 See Hart 1968: 123.

life) but a 'mere side-effect'.[26] They believe that what the hero in fact 'does' must be described as 'throwing himself on the grenade' and not 'killing himself to save others'. It thus appears that the *way an act is described* determines which of its effects are to be considered means and which side-effects. If the sacrifice is to be sanctioned by the doctrine of double effect, then the act of sacrifice must be described in such a way that the result-that-may-not-be-desired (the hero's death) does not figure. That the hero could be sure that under the circumstances his death was inevitable does not matter.

The fact that the way behavior is described is so determinative undermines the doctrine of double effect since behavior can always be described in several ways, depending on which effects one is concerned with. Like the heroic soldier, what a doctor 'does' can be described as 'putting the patient out of his misery' (with death as a side-effect) or as 'killing him to end his suffering' (with death as a means). It is in principle arbitrary to regard either of these possible descriptions as preferred. That which in a particular description of a case is presented a means to an end thus cannot be conclusive with respect to the 'intention' of the actor. The relationship between what an actor intends and what is to be regarded as a 'means' or a 'side-effect' is precisely the reverse of what the doctrine of double effect assumes. It is not whether something is a 'means' that determines what an actor intends, but what he intends (as an end) that determines the appropriate way of describing his behavior and hence those consequences of his behavior that can be designated as means or as mere side-effects. Which of all the effects foreseen by the actor are 'intended' can therefore not be ascertained independently of what he has in mind. To be tenable, the doctrine of double effect would have to distinguish permissible and impermissible actions not on the basis of what the actor *does*, but on the basis of *a mere interior state of mind*.[27]

Could the adherents of the doctrine of double effect accept the conclusion that the moral permissibility of behavior that, as a foreseeable effect, involves the death of another person, depends on what the doctor considers to be his motive at the moment he causes the patient's death? A doctor would then be able to determine the permissibility of his behavior simply by reassessing his own motives.[28] Such a position has two drawbacks. In the first place it judges not the permissibility of behavior but the *character of the actor*. In the second place it is impossible for *human beings and human institutions* to establish what

---

26 Compare this case with that of the person who commits suicide in order to escape from depression, for example. This is not considered permissible: death is 'desired' as a 'means' to relieving suffering.

27 Compare Kuhse 1987: 159.

28 Compare Williams 1957: 322: If the doctrine of double effect "means that the necessity of making a choice of values can be avoided merely by keeping your mind off one of the consequences, it can only encourage a hypocritical attitude towards moral problems."

the actor's motive is. This is possibly not an issue from the point of view of Roman Catholic teaching; after all, God sees everything. However, for purposes of secular morality and legal control, making the responsibility of an actor dependent on his motive is unacceptable. It would undermine every possibility of effective control by making those responsible for control dependent on information possessed only by those whose behavior is to be controlled. It comes as no surprise that the criminal law rejects the idea of liability based on motives and subjective intentions known only to the actor, taking instead all consequences of his behavior that the actor could foresee as constituting his 'intention'.[29]

Ultimately, only the proportionality criterion of the fourth condition of the doctrine of double effect seems capable of withstanding analysis.[30] The moral permissibility of a course of action depends on the relation between its good and its bad consequences. An actor is responsible for all of those consequences that for him were foreseeable.[31] As far as the doctor's intention is concerned it is unclear why 'normal medical practice' in the form of pain killing with shortening of life as a foreseeable result should be considered in itself morally less problematic than euthanasia. The same applies to abstinence that will foreseeably lead to death.

4.1.3   Conclusion

In this section we have seen that the moral distinctions that are supposed to underlie the different legal treatment of euthanasia and of other forms of intentional shortening of life (distinctions between 'killing' and 'letting die' and between the 'intentional' and the 'non-intentional' shortening of life) seem to be both untenable and morally irrelevant.

The conclusion to be drawn from the foregoing discussion, at least as far as the public debate over the regulation of euthanasia is concerned, is as follows. The distinction

---

29   Compare Hart 1968: 117ff; Enschedé 1986b: 39; Hazewinkel-Suringa & Remmelink 1996: 201ff.

30   Applying the narrow conception of the intentional to the second condition of the doctrine of double effect makes the third condition redundant: compare Marquis 1991: 520. The same objection that is fatal to the second condition also undermines the first condition: there is no such thing as 'the behavior itself', distinguished from its consequences: there are only *different descriptions* of behavior. Compare Davis 1991.

31   Compare CAL 3: 8, quoted in chapter 3.3; Rachels 1986: 95: "Remember that the rightness or wrongness of an act is determined by the reasons for and against it.... The intention you would have, if you decided to cease treatment, is not one of the things you need to consider. It is not among the reasons for or against the action."

between euthanasia and intentionally causing death as a result of 'normal medical practice' is not a good starting point for a system of legal control of life-shortening behavior in a medical context. Both euthanasia and intentional death resulting from 'normal medical practice' must in principle be judged according to the same criteria. In this section we have shown that the responsibility of a doctor for shortening the life of a patient should not depend on the 'nature' of his behavior nor on the subjective 'intention' he has, but on his responsibility for what happens to the patient. Whether behavior that shortens life violates his duty to the patient depends on the reasons for or against the behavior, and in particular the advantages and disadvantages it has for the patient. Apart from that, the responsibility of the doctor should depend on whether he could have foreseen the patient's death and on the extent to which he was in a position to influence the processes that led to that death.

4.2   The most important arguments since 1982

We have seen in chapter 2 that at the end of the 1960s euthanasia became a topic of public debate. In the first phase of that debate, the argument concentrated on the moral permissibility of shortening of life by doctors. In the 1970s the discussion focused on defining and distinguishing different sorts of life-shortening behavior. It was not until the end of the 1970s that discussion turned to the question of legal policy. From that last perspective the primary question is not whether euthanasia is to be considered an acceptable course of action for an individual and his doctor, but whether it is legitimate for the *state* to permit or to restrict euthanasia, and if so how and under what circumstances.

This latter question was first posed in the political forum when in 1978 Parliament asked the Government to

> request advice about future government policy with regard to euthanasia from a State Commission set up for this purpose.[32]

As we have seen in chapter 2.3.2, this request resulted in a preparatory report of the Health Council and, ultimately, in a report of the State Commission on Euthanasia.[33] The subject of these reports was whether it would be advisable to amend articles 293 and 294 of the Criminal Code that specifically forbid euthanasia and assistance with suicide.

The reports of the Health Council and the State Commission seemed to offer excellent starting points for a debate of high quality on legal policy. However, such a debate never

---

32   *Second Chamber of Parliament 1978-1979*, 15 300, no. 26.
33   Gezondheidsraad 1982; Staatscommissie 1985.

actually took place. Instead, politics were more or less overtaken by judicial decisions: halfway through the 1980s the Supreme Court interpreted the existing provisions of the Criminal Code in a way that left room for euthanasia under specific conditions. The discussion of legal policy thereafter stayed more or less within the bounds of the legal solution adopted by the Supreme Court.

The question of the legal permissibility of euthanasia having been solved in a way that proved generally acceptable, attention shifted in the second half of the 1980s to more practical matters. From that time on, the question was not so much whether or not euthanasia should be legally permissible, but how it can best be *regulated*. The focus of concern has been, in particular, on the question how conformity with the 'requirements of careful practice' can be achieved. The debate on fundamental matters of legal principle was thereby pushed to the background.[34]

In this section we confine ourselves to a presentation of the arguments that have in fact been made. Attention will first be paid to the three arguments of principle that have figured in the public discussion: the *principle of autonomy*, the *principle of beneficence*, and the *right to life*. After that two practical arguments that have played a role in the public discussion will be dealt with: the *slippery-slope argument* and *control arguments*. A critical assessment and exploration of the various positions in the context of the question whether they can be reconciled with each other will be postponed to section 4.3.

4.2.1   The principle of autonomy

The principle of autonomy is one of the most important arguments of those who are in favor of the legalization of euthanasia. At first sight, this seems strange. The issue in the euthanasia debate is not whether an individual has the freedom to end his own life (suicide never having been illegal in Dutch law), but whether a *doctor* can legally give him assistance in doing so. On closer examination, the appeal to the principle of autonomy involves a slightly more complex argument than appears at first sight. Threatening the doctor with criminal punishment puts an obstruction in the way of a patient who wants (or needs) his doctor's help to end his life. The appeal to the principle of autonomy thus amounts to the claim that the state must not do anything that obstructs the exercise of what is regarded as a fundamental freedom.

Appeal to the principle of autonomy is not meant as an appeal to an existing legal right. Those who make use of the argument use it either as a moral principle considered to be

---

34   This generalization is less applicable to problems of termination of life of persons considered not (fully) competent than it is to euthanasia proper.

of such heavy weight that it must be taken as a starting point for the regulation of euthanasia, or as a legal principle already implicit in the law as a whole. As a moral principle the principle of autonomy is widely accepted in medical ethics.[35] As a legal principle it has been frequently invoked in the Dutch euthanasia debate. The Health Council regards it as a "basic idea of a modern legal system" that the autonomy of every adult member of society must be respected as much as possible. A "legitimate public regulation … must be directed toward the realization of individual interests as defined by those concerned." According to the Health Council this principle entails that, leaving aside the necessity of guarding against abuses, the state is not entitled to protect legal rights (such as the right to life) when the individual concerned does not want such protection. The state should restrict itself to creating conditions under which individuals can exercise their autonomy. One of these is the opportunity to die a good death and to receive help if one wants it.[36]

The legal philosopher Soeteman endorses this argument. He observes that human dignity is invoked by both supporters and opponents of the principle of autonomy, but that they interpret human dignity differently. Supporters of autonomy think that an individual should be entitled to define his own conception of human dignity: Soeteman refers to this as a 'tolerant' interpretation of human dignity. Opponents, on the contrary, want to impose a particular conception of human dignity on their fellow citizens. Soeteman argues that only the tolerant interpretation of human dignity corresponds to Dutch law, while the 'moralistic' interpretation of the opponents has no legal support. A tolerant interpretation of human dignity can, Soeteman believes, be the foundation for a principle of autonomy that applies, among other things, to euthanasia.[37]

Leenen, author of the influential *Handbook of Health Law*, is emphatic on this point. According to him, the principle of autonomy is a natural right of human beings, not derivative from the state or the community:

> The foundation of the right to decide for yourself is the principle of the free, autonomous human being who has an inherent dignity that deserves unconditional respect, and who is entitled to dispose over his own life.

Leenen argues that the principle of autonomy is reflected in a number of fundamental rights laid down in the Dutch constitution, such as for instance the freedom of religion,

---

35 Beauchamp & Childress 1989:68ff; Dupuis 1994:47-64.
36 See Gezondheidsraad 1982: 64-68 and 74-77. The arguments quoted here and elsewhere in this chapter are not the position of the Health Council itself. In its preparatory report the Health Council did not formulate a final conclusion of its own, but limited itself to an inventory of different arguments for and against euthanasia.
37 Soeteman 1986: 61ff.

the right to privacy and the right to inviolability of the body. This last right includes the right to refuse medical treatment.[38] Leenen argues that,

> The individual right of autonomy is the basis of the right to make decisions about the end of one's life. That fundamental value would be violated if others (the state, the doctor) could continue a person's life against his will, which would make that life one without freedom and autonomy. That would entail a lack of respect for the person concerned and would force him to violate the dictates of his conscience.[39]

The proposed amendment to articles 293 and 294 of the Criminal Code submitted by Wessel-Tuinstra in 1984 was largely based on the principle of autonomy. The accompanying Memorandum included the following passage concerning the task of the state with regard to euthanasia:

> [The state] must, departing from the generally accepted norm of protection of life, create space for an individual's decision to determine the limits of that protection as far as his own life is concerned, subject to the state's specific responsibility to strengthen the legal position of the vulnerable and the quality of medical and other assistance [*hulpverlening*].[40]

Wessel-Tuinstra's bill had the support of the majority of the Second Chamber of Parliament halfway through the 1980s, but as we have seen in chapter 2.4 it was, for reasons having to do with coalition politics, never adopted.

In the case law, the principle of autonomy plays a more limited role than it does in the public debate. That is understandable in light of the fact that the courts cannot simply ignore articles 293 and 294 of the Criminal Code, articles that seem on their face inconsistent with such a principle. Nevertheless, in 1983 the District Court in Alkmaar held that in connection with the increasing societal acceptance of autonomy with regard to the ending of one's own life, euthanasia (by a doctor) fell within the doctrine of 'absence of substantial violation of the law'. However, the Court of Appeals reversed this decision,

---

38   That the right to inviolability of the body must be seen as based on the principle of autonomy is reflected, according to Leenen, among other things in the legislative history of the most recent constitutional revision of 1983 (Leenen 1994: 38).

39   Leenen 1994: 31, 22ff, 43, 262. Leenen observes (*id.*, 260) that opinions concerning euthanasia differ, but that "in the case of moral disagreement on a subject such as euthanasia legal rules should respect everyone's opinion to the extent this is possible.... The current prohibitions of euthanasia and assistance with suicide in the Criminal Code are inconsistent with [this fundamental principle]."

40   *Second Chamber of Parliament 1983-1984*, 18 331, no. 3: 12-13.

and on this point the Supreme Court agreed. In the *Schoonheim* case, the Supreme Court held that the principle of autonomy cannot support the conclusion that euthanasia is not a substantial violation of the law (see chapters 2.3.1 and 3.1.3, and appendix II-1). In the same judgment the Court concluded that euthanasia by a doctor may, under certain circumstances, be justifiable as a correct choice between conflicting duties. But it is not clear that respect for the autonomy of the patient is one of those conflicting duties: in the *Chabot* case the Court referred explicitly to the duty concerned as one requiring a doctor to do everything possible to alleviate the intolerable and incurable suffering of a patient in his care.[41]

The supporters of autonomy with regard to the termination of life do not assert that autonomy is without its limits. Their view is that its exercise should not lead to damage to others, and they believe that the legalization of euthanasia will not have this as a consequence, provided that sufficient legal protections are in place. They accept, for example, that the law must ensure that a request for euthanasia is truly voluntary. In the words of Leenen:

> The legislator should … not impose a particular moral opinion on the population, but when a decision has such far-reaching consequences as the termination of life with the assistance of another, he must enact rules to guarantee the voluntariness of the request and to eliminate the risks due to the fact that another person, the doctor, is involved.[42]

According to Soeteman, the requirement of 'unbearable and hopeless suffering' offers the necessary protection:

---

41 See appendix II-2, section 3.1. Schalken concludes, however, in his note to the *Chabot* judgment (see appendix II, note 3): "It would be more accurate to describe the emergency situation as a conflict between the duty to preserve life and respect for the wishes of the patient to end his life." This interpretation is linked to a note by Mulder (*Nederlandse Jurisprudentie* 1987, no. 608) that expressed the view that the doctor must "weigh the respect owed to the personality of the patient against [the duty to preserve life, as provided for in article 293]. In extreme cases respect for the personality of the patient will weigh more heavily than respect for [the preservation of life] and in this way [the patient's] wish for termination of life will be honored." According to Den Hartogh (1996: 167), however, a duty to respect the autonomy of the patient can never result in a conflict of duties because "the duties that correspond to the principle of autonomy are all negative duties, duties of a non-interfering nature, none of them requires provision of positive help".

42 Leenen 1994: 300.

It can function as part of a pragmatic operationalization of the condition that it must be reasonably clear that there was nothing wrong with the request…. The requirement of unbearable and hopeless suffering is a plausible one in this connection because it ties the permissibility of euthanasia to situations in which the wishes of the person involved can be reasonably understood.[43]

4.2.2   The principle of beneficence

A second argument in support of the legalization of euthanasia is based on the principle of beneficence.[44] This principle imposes a duty, within limits, to act on behalf of another. Applied to suffering, and in this variant sometimes called the *principle of mercy*, the principle imposes the duty to alleviate pain or ease suffering. The principle of beneficence can be considered an independent ground for legalization of the termination of life, but it can also be invoked in support of autonomy. In the latter case it is argued that patients in general know best whether or not continuation of life is in their interest. The duty to act on behalf of the patient is thus best served by allowing him to decide for himself.

The principle of beneficence is not recognized as a general proposition in Dutch law. But because the Dutch Supreme Court has accorded medical-ethical norms a prominent place in its euthanasia decisions, beneficence has played an important role in the process of legal change with regard to termination of life. The duty of a doctor to alleviate 'unbearable and hopeless suffering' has, via the justification of necessity recognized by the Supreme Court, become the principal legal basis for the legalization of euthanasia and assistance with suicide.[45]

As a medical-ethical principle beneficence is fairly non-controversial. From ancient times the principle has been given great weight in medical ethics, more so than the principle of autonomy.[46] Prevention of damage to the patient and the promotion of his interests are a doctor's central duties, and if necessary he may be quite paternalistic in effectuating them.[47] Traditionally, it has been regarded as a corollary of the principle of beneficence that a doctor must do everything possible to postpone death.[48]

---

43   Soeteman 1986: 69. See also Leenen 1994: 301.

44   The principle of beneficence is here interpreted as including the *principle of non-maleficence*. It has been argued (for example by Beauchamp & Childress 1989: 121) that these two principles must be distinguished, the latter weighing more heavily than the former. For discussion of that idea see section 4.1.1.

45   Most recently in the *Chabot* case: see appendix II-2.

46   See Beauchamp & Childress 1989: 112.

47   See Brennan 1991: 36.

48   See Veatch 1981: chapter 1; CAL 1: 10, CAL 2: 23; Dupuis 1994: 28.

Despite this history, the principle of beneficence has recently begun to play an important role in arguments in support of the legalization of euthanasia. The traditional interpretation of beneficence has come under pressure in recent decades. As we have seen in chapter 2.1, as a result of medical-technological developments there has since the 1960s been growing awareness that medical treatment does not always serve the patient's interest. Strict adherence to the aim of preservation of life is, therefore, not always desirable. Doing everything possible to postpone death amounts to submission to the 'tyranny of technology' by which it is not the patient's interest but medical-technical possibilities that determine how the patient is treated.[49] When the (continued) use of medical technology entails damage to the patient, life-prolonging medical treatment is increasingly seen as in conflict with the principle of beneficence.[50]

Such a position inevitably raises the question whether there are criteria that could be used to determine whether continued life is in the patient's interest. As mentioned above, it is generally accepted that a patient in general knows best whether continued life is in his interest. This is why there are in principle no such criteria needed for patients who are competent. As regards patients who are not (fully) competent, a distinction must be made between those patients who previously were competent (comatose or senile patients) and patients who have never been competent (seriously defective newborn babies). In the first case, life-shortening decisions can often be made on the basis of an explicit expression of will, for example in the form of an advanced directive, made when the patient was competent. If such an explicit expression of will cannot be relied on, one must work with the idea of the presumed will of the patient.[51]

If there is no indication of any (presumed) will of the patient, the situation of formerly competent patients and of patients who were never competent is similar: the so-called *best interests standard* must be brought into play. As we have seen in chapter 3.3.2, the CAL and the NVK argue that life-prolonging treatment is no longer in the best interests of a severely defective newborn baby when such treatment cannot lead to a 'life worth living'. With regard to long-term comatose patients, the CAL argues that continuation of treatment is only justified if there is a chance of a return to consciousness and if a minimum quality of life is then to be expected (see chapter 3.3.3).

Apart from abstinence from (further) life-prolonging treatment that is not in the patient's interest, the principle of beneficence can be invoked to justify termination of life, although such use of the principle is much more controversial. Continued life may arguably not be in the interest of the patient either when the patient, although not

---

49   Dupuis (1994: 41) refers to this as the moral fallacy that 'What can be done, must be done.'

50   Compare CAL 1:10.

51   Compare Jacobs 1987.

dependent on life-support, is still alive as a result of medical treatment that did not lead to an acceptable situation, or when the patient's situation is not the result of any medical intervention but nevertheless involves hopeless suffering or (the prospect of) an unacceptably low quality of life. In both cases it can be argued that the principle of beneficence supports termination of life in the patient's interest. An example of the former situation is a newborn baby whose life has been saved by heroic medical intervention, but whose prospects in life are so poor that if one had foreseen this outcome from the outset one would not have regarded intervention as justifiable. As we have seen in chapter 3.3.2, the CAL and the NVK argue that in such a case beneficence may justify (active) termination of life. But this conclusion can also obtain where the doctor bears no responsibility at all for the patient's deplorable situation. The CAL suggests, for example, that if a very senile patient is in a situation of extreme distress, and termination of life does not conflict with an earlier express will nor with a presumed will, "a reason for terminating life can possibly be based on the intention to end a situation that obviously conflicts with human dignity."[52]

4.2.3   The principle of the sanctity of life

The idea of an inalienable right to life derives from the principle of the sanctity of human life, the ancient and originally religious principle that forbids the intentional termination of life, regardless of whether or not this is requested (see section 4.1.2).

The appeal to a 'right to life' is the most important argument of principle raised against the legalization of the termination of life in a medical context in the Dutch euthanasia debate. The right to life is not only a fundamental moral right, it is specifically guaranteed in article 2 of the European Convention for the Protection of Human Rights and Fundamental Freedoms and article 6 of the International Covenant on Civil and Political Rights. These international treaties are fundamental law in the Netherlands, binding both the courts and the legislator.

The idea that the right to life, protected in these treaties, sets limits on the scope of the principle of autonomy can be expressed in different ways. The Health Council argued, for example, that the right to life implies a lack of duty on the part of the state to promote autonomy at the expense of life because

> [i]n a democratic state the government has a duty to guard and protect the inviolability of human dignity.... Human life cannot be considered in isolation from human dignity. One of the fundamental rights of a human being is the right to life. The government's responsibility is to protect human life from invasion by third parties.[53]

---

52   CAL 3: 51-52; compare chapter 3.3.4.
53   Gezondheidsraad 1982: 78ff.

In 1984, the legal philosopher and later Minister of Justice Hirsch Ballin went further than this. Dropping the restriction to 'invasion by third parties', he contended that there "definitely is an opposition between … a right to dispose of one's own life and the right to life" guaranteed in the two treaties just mentioned. Hirsch Ballin's view is that autonomy with respect to the ending of life would be inconsistent with the 'integrity of the person'. He concludes with this rhetorical question:

> With other fundamental rights, such as freedom of movement, freedom of the press and freedom of religion, there are good reasons why, even if one does it out of free will and thinks that this is in one's best interest, a person cannot legally alienate these rights as against other persons. Should one be able to do so with the right to life?[54]

The most extensive consideration of the relevance of the right to life is to be found in the minority report of the State Commission. In the majority report attention to article 2 of the European Convention was limited to the observation that the article requires "great care … in making euthanasia no longer a crime". It is partly for this reason that the State Commission advised limiting legalization to cases in which the doctor judges that there is a 'situation of hopeless necessity'.[55]

In response to this, the minority of the State Commission argued that authorizing a doctor to perform euthanasia necessarily implies authorizing him to act on the basis of a quality-of-life judgment, which would be inconsistent with the human dignity protected by the right to life:

> A decision … to terminate a life and/or the request to do so includes, logically and necessarily, *another* judgment, namely that because of the suffering *life itself* … has, everything considered, if it is not ended, become pointless.

A doctor may not make such a judgment, because

> the dignity of the human being [does] not allow others to accept a person's judgment on the pointlessness of his remaining life…. People must refrain from such a judgment because it would deny … *the dignity of the human person* … as expressed by the Universal Declaration of the Rights of Man.[56]

---

54   Hirsch Ballin 1984: 183ff.
55   Staatscommissie 1985: 37-38; see appendix I-C-1 for the text of the State Commission's proposed legislation.
56   Staatscommissie 1985: 243ff. Compare Klijn 1985; *Second Chamber of Parliament 1984-1985*, 18 331, no. 6: 9.

The idea that the right to life sets limits on autonomy is also reflected in the legislative history of article 293 of the Criminal Code. The Government observed at the time (1886) that, while the patient's consent cannot make a killing legitimate, it does fundamentally change its character:

> [T]he law … no longer punishes the assault against a certain person's life, but the violation of the respect due to human life in general – no matter what the motive for the act may be. Crime against human life remains, crime against the person is absent.[57]

Many different arguments have been made against appeals to the right to life. Leenen argues that a human person is more than a mere biological creature and therefore

> respect for life means respect for humanness in all its aspects, thus also for the autonomy of the person and human dignity.

As far as article 2 of the European Convention is concerned, Leenen argues that

> The individual fundamental rights such as article 2 of the European Convention for the Protection of Human Rights and Fundamental Freedoms protect against the state, and also, if we assume horizontal working, against other individuals. Individual rights do not limit a person's autonomy with regard to himself. Fundamental rights do not limit the freedom of the person concerned.[58]

The legal philosopher Soeteman, among others, argues that the comparison made by Hirsch Ballin between the right to life and other basic rights as a basis for his position that the right to life is inalienable is a lame one.

> The duty to live does not follow automatically from the right to life. Inalienability does not change this, because inalienability means essentially that one may not and cannot dispose of the right, which is something different from disposing of life itself.[59]

---

57   Smidt 1891: 463; this passage was cited by the Supreme Court in the *Schoonheim* case (appendix II-1). Mulder (*Nederlandse Jurisprudentie* 1987, no. 607) observed in connection with this passage: "The legislator obviously attached value to life, even if it no longer has any value for the individual. A doctor is obliged to protect life as a public good. His treatment of the patient is in part in service of the community."

58   Leenen 1994: 261.

59   Soeteman 1986: 59. See also Alkema 1978: 47ff; Van Haersolte 1985: 68; Van Dijk & Van Hoof 1990: 245.

Finally, in light of the discussion in section 4.1 it would seem that a consistently applied right-to-life argument would require the conclusion that 'normal medical practice' with intended life-shortening results is not permissible. However, those who invoke the right to life do not draw this conclusion.

4.2.4   The slippery-slope argument

A practical argument frequently raised against the legalization of euthanasia is that even if euthanasia itself is perhaps acceptable, legalizing it will inevitably lead to practices that are not. There are two versions of this 'slippery-slope' argument: a logical or conceptual version and an empirical or causal version.

According to the logical version, legalization of euthanasia logically implies the legalization of other forms of termination of life that are morally unacceptable. It is argued, for example, that those who argue for the legalization of euthanasia on the basis of the principle of autonomy have no argument against legalization in cases in which the patient is not suffering, or that those who argue for legalization of euthanasia on the basis of the principle of beneficence must also support termination of the lives of patients who have not requested it, such as severely deformed and acutely suffering newborn babies. It is also argued that the criterion of 'unbearable and hopeless suffering' is an insufficient barrier against euthanasia at the request of a patient whose suffering has a non-somatic cause. These examples make clear that the logical version of the slippery-slope argument presupposes that the forms of termination of life allegedly implied by legalization of euthanasia are obviously unacceptable.

The logical version of the slippery-slope argument is invoked in the minority report of the State Commission to counter the standpoint of the majority that euthanasia can be legalized provided it is limited to a 'situation of hopeless necessity'. In the eyes of the minority, the majority (which considered the patient's request a necessary condition for, but not the legitimizing basis of euthanasia) could not answer

> the question why free will, if this is not really the source of legitimation, must always be a condition sine qua non. There seems to be no reason why the situation of necessity would not be allowed to 'overrule' this condition under certain circumstances.

In addition, there is the problem of operationalising the idea of a 'situation of hopeless necessity':

> The problem of discriminating between suffering and suffering, between 'not yet serious enough' and 'just serious enough', and of answering the patient's question how bad it has to be and how long he has to wait, cannot be solved by those respon-

sible for treating him and thus leads to erosion [of the norm]. It calls into being a dynamic process that will lead, willy nilly, to a greater and greater expansion of direct termination of life.

This argument strengthened the conviction of the authors of the minority report that euthanasia can never be permissible.[60]

Although its conclusions can be disputed, the minority report does call attention to the fact that confusion about the foundations of legalization of a particular form of termination of life can lead to difficult situations. De Beaufort emphasizes this problem:

> Proponents of euthanasia who, under certain circumstances, also consider non-voluntary euthanasia to be justified, can get themselves into a predicament. They obviously cannot rely on the principle of autonomy but must appeal to the principle of beneficence. If, at the same time, they maintain that voluntariness is *always* a necessary condition for the permissibility of euthanasia, or even for being able to speak in terms of 'euthanasia' – as they sometimes seem to do – they are inconsistent.[61]

The empirical version of the slippery-slope argument holds that the legalization of a desirable form of termination of life will lead in fact to a sort of erosion of norms, so that ultimately forms of termination that are currently considered undesirable will come to be accepted as more or less unproblematic. Legalization of euthanasia will, for example, so undermine our sense of the sanctity of human life that we will eventually not object to certain sorts of non-voluntary termination of life. And where termination is now still linked to the interests of the person involved (as for instance in the case of defective newborn babies), later on the interests of others will come to be decisive. The Health Council formulates this concern as follows:

> A danger lurks in the possibility that the freedom to engage in euthanasia will lead to a certain routine and habituation, which raises the danger that required standards of care will not always be adhered to in making judgments whether or not euthanasia or assistance with suicide is in fact indicated. Even those who have a high regard for the medical profession do not suffer from the illusion that every doctor will always be able to resist the direct or indirect pressure that can be inflicted on him by third parties.[62]

In short, we will adhere less and less precisely to our norms with regard to matters of life and death.[63]

---

60   Staatscommissie 1985: 251-252.
61   De Beaufort 1987: 18.
62   Gezondheidsraad 1982: 72.
63. Compare Dessaur & Rutenfrans 1986: 109ff; Keown 1995.

In this connection De Beaufort points out that

> the big problem in discussing the empirical version of the slippery-slope argument about euthanasia is that hard evidence for these predictions, or for the denial thereof, cannot be given. The discussion frequently amounts to little more than an exchange of contradictory assertions, many recriminations and few arguments.[64]

According to Leenen there is

> no basis for the assumption that by permitting euthanasia society will come to accept the termination of life without a request as normal. Reference is often made in this connection to Nazi Germany during the Second World War. The situation under German fascism cannot be compared with that of the democratic Netherlands. In the Netherlands euthanasia is a matter of human rights, and the [patient's] request is crucial; in Nazi Germany human rights were denied, and lives were terminated in large numbers without the request and against the will of those involved.[65] Murder under the pretense of euthanasia cannot be treated as if it were the same thing as a person's own decision to end his life because of acute suffering. Experience does not lend much support to the risk of a slippery slope. The argument was, for example, often used in the discussion concerning the legalization of abortion. The domino theory proved unfounded. The Netherlands has a law permitting abortion, and one of the lowest abortion rates in the world.[66]

One variant of the empirical version of the slippery-slope argument is the claim that legalization of euthanasia will undermine public confidence in the medical profession. The concern is that a patient will no longer feel secure that a doctor for whom it is (legally) possible to administer life-terminating treatment can be counted on to do everything possible to preserve the patient's life.[67] According to others, however, there is no indication whatever that legalization will undermine the doctor-patient relationship. On the contrary, Leenen argues:

---

64 De Beaufort 1987: 21.

65 Compare Griffiths 1987 for the observation that the slippery-slope argument based on the Nazi experience is paradoxical: the danger in that case was from the state, whereas it is that same state to whom opponents of legalization look for *protection* of human life. He suggests that budgetary concerns of the state are probably the source of the greatest danger to the norms concerning medical treatment of dying patients.

66 Leenen 1994: 262-263. See also De Beaufort 1987: 25ff. It is often argued that the approximately 1000 cases of non-voluntary termination of life that take place annually in the Netherlands are proof of the slippery slope. In fact, however, as we argue in chapter 7 (see also Leenen 1994: 270), closer examination of this category shows that this is not the case.

67 See, for example, the State Commission's minority report: Staatscommissie 1985: 262.

> The possibility of open communication about euthanasia contributes to the rela-
> tionship between patients and doctors. The doctor's promise that if the time arrives
> he will administer euthanasia often brings peace of mind to the patient who is con-
> templating his death; fear of having to endure a horrible death is thereby reduced. It
> is doctors pulling out all the stops to preserve patients' lives against their will that has
> undermined confidence in medicine.[68]

The empirical version of the slippery-slope argument assumes that the values that are at
stake are better protected by a *criminal* prohibition of euthanasia than they can be by
other (legal or non-legal) means.[69] It is therefore important to consider the slippery-
slope argument in conjunction with the cluster of arguments to be discussed in the next
section: the control arguments.

4.2.5 Control arguments

An important argument against the legalization of life-terminating behavior claims that
it is in practice not possible to ensure that the rules designed to guard against abuse will
be adhered to. It is argued, for example, that it is not possible to know for certain whether
the request of the patient was truly voluntary:

> An important question concerning the voluntariness of the request to die is how such
> a condition for euthanasia or assistance with suicide is to be interpreted. There are two
> possibilities: (1) the voluntary nature of the request is assumed, unless there are good
> reasons to doubt it, and (2) the voluntary nature must be proven. In the first case it is
> hard to see how a watertight arrangement can be designed, such that no single case of
> non-voluntary euthanasia can occur. In the second case the condition of voluntari-
> ness becomes a practically insurmountable obstacle, because there can always be some
> doubt whether the person involved made a completely free decision.[70]

The conclusion often drawn from such uncertainty is that the 'safest' choice should be
made and the categorical prohibition of any sort of termination of life maintained.
Euthanasia may, on this view, sometimes be morally acceptable, but the instruments of

---

68   Leenen 1994: 263-264.
69   Compare the minority report of the State Commission (Staatscommissie 1985: 271): "Crimi-
     nal law is not the only means of legal protection, but can in certain circumstances be neces-
     sary. If a law has ceased to be effective, it can be a good idea to look for other means." The
     entire minority report is, however, permeated by the thought that the criminal prohibition of
     euthanasia is actually effective.
70   Gezondheidsraad 1982: 71. Compare *Second Chamber of Parliament 1984-1985*, 18 331, no. 6: 8.

the criminal law are too crude to be able to make the moral distinctions required, so it is better not to legalize it at all:

> Legalization of euthanasia and similar decisions means that the state must try to formulate something that cannot be expressed in legal terms. A whole complex of subtle and interdependent factors and motives cannot be transformed into general rules.[71]

Proponents of legalization have not been convinced by this argument. They have countered that there can be effective guarantees (a written request, waiting periods) that confirm the autonomy of the patient's request.[72] Furthermore, they argue that it is wrong to assume that it is always necessarily a greater evil wrongly to let someone die than it is wrongly to make him go on living. Nor can it be assumed that in the case of legalization the number of the former sort of mistake will be bigger than the number of the latter sort in the case of continued prohibition, while it is precisely the ratio between the two that is relevant.

Finally, as with the empirical version of the slippery-slope argument, the control arguments take for granted the effectiveness of the criminal prohibition of euthanasia. But since the 1980s it has been clear that euthanasia has in fact been practised for a long time. To quote the Health Council once again:

> The state forbids euthanasia and assistance with suicide, but in practice doctors do perform euthanasia under certain circumstances, and they do in certain cases supply the means with which a person can kill himself, without in fact exposing themselves to criminal prosecution. This situation is objectionable in several respects. The fact that doctors who, in certain cases, are prepared to perform euthanasia and to assist with suicide, and who actually do so, are not exposed to criminal prosecution is simply a result of the fact that they give their help 'behind closed doors', so that no charges can be filed against them. All this leads to disingenuous representations of what has taken place that are completely uncontrollable. When medical practice takes place out of public view, furtively, it is impossible to know whether the doctor acts conscientiously.
>
> [Such a] situation is also confusing and uncertain for those seeking help. It is not clear what is and is not allowed and to whom they can ultimately turn. It is the doctor who decides when a request for help is a cry of distress and when it is a well-considered request for a humane death; the uncontrollability and arbitrariness of the decision-making can continue unchecked.[73]

---

71 Trappenburg 1991: 532.
72 See Gezondheidsraad 1982: 77; Leenen 1994: 264.
73 Gezondheidsraad 1982: 86-88.

The bill introduced in Parliament in 1984 by Wessel-Tuinstra was motivated in significant part by the need to do something about feelings of insecurity caused by the uncontrollability to which the Health Council called attention:

> The bill submitted by the undersigned only proposes to bring something that (at least in the Netherlands) has been taking place for a long time and that is regarded as acceptable both by large groups in the population and by the judiciary, out of the criminal context, to make it controllable, and at the same time to increase the legal security of all those involved. Also for those who do not want euthanasia.[74]

This interpretation of the Dutch situation was confirmed by the research of Van der Maas in 1991 and that of Van der Wal and Van der Maas in 1995 (see chapter 5.3). The chasm between the criminal prohibition and actual practice makes clear that the criminal law is not an effective control regime in the case of euthanasia and other life-shortening behavior of doctors. In short, there is an important control argument *for* decriminalization: this is desirable, not so much because it is 'in principle' better but because it is a necessary condition of a more effective system of control, one that will do a *better* job than the criminal law in protecting values shared by the proponents and opponents of euthanasia. In chapter 6 we pursue this line of thought further.

4.3   A fundamental difference of opinion?

Notwithstanding the divergent views discussed in the previous section, there is general consensus in the Netherlands as to the legal permissibility of euthanasia. Although the foundation for this consensus is not clear, the Dutch euthanasia controversy is in fact substantially settled. In this section we attempt a closer evaluation of this consensus. The most important opposing arguments in the debate will be reconstructed, and we will examine on what basis the opposing positions could be reconciled.

4.3.1   *The nature of a question of legal policy*

The central question in the euthanasia debate – the authority of the state to regulate (or not regulate) euthanasia – is one of legal policy. Such questions must be distinguished from moral and from legal questions. A moral question is concerned with what an individual or group 'may' (or 'may not') do, and although law may be relevant to such a question, it is not finally determinative. The questions whether (assuming euthanasia is not a criminal act) a patient may request euthanasia and whether a doctor may in such a case

---

74   *Second Chamber of Parliament 1983-1984*, 18 331, no. 9: 32.

co-operate in performing it are moral in nature. The answer is dependent on moral theory. A legal question concerns the content of currently valid legal rules. Whether the proper interpretation of the relevant provisions of the Criminal Code is that a doctor who performs euthanasia at the request of a dying patient is guilty of a criminal offence is a legal question. The answer depends on what sources of law are considered authoritative and how these are to be understood. Questions of legal policy, finally, are concerned with what the law *should* be. The opinion that the prohibition of euthanasia, as set out in the Criminal Code, should be revised to make euthanasia by doctors legal is an opinion on a question of legal policy.

The importance of these distinctions becomes clear in the context of two fundamental principles on which Dutch constitutional law is based: the *separation principle* and the *principle of the rule of law*. The separation principle holds that the 'public domain' and the 'private domain' must be kept separate and that considerations relevant within a person's private domain cannot be simply transferred to the public domain as a basis for legal policy. The principle of the rule of law holds that the judiciary, among other agents of state power, must base its decisions exclusively on existing law.

Both political and legal practice show that these distinctions are not without their difficulties. The creation of law in the political arena is not a value-free enterprise. It always presupposes an underlying moral position. Something similar applies to adjudication. What in a concrete case is 'law' is not always clear. Sometimes the law offers no definitive answer and judges have to take refuge in what were previously 'non-legal' norms.[75]

The euthanasia debate shows how difficult it can be to honor the two principles. The positions adopted by participants in the legal policy debate have often been based on considerations of personal morality. And the norms of medical ethics have played an important role in judicial decisions concerning the legality of euthanasia (see chapter 2.3.1 and appendix II-1 and II-2). It seems that moral and legal questions (and answers) can be distinguished but not *kept separate* from questions of legal policy. This raises the question which normative standpoints are and which are not relevant to the creation of legal rules. In other words: what restrictions apply to the considerations invoked in the formulation of a standpoint on a question of legal policy?

The first requirement of legal policy is one of coherence. The way in which euthanasia is legally regulated must not be purely *ad hoc* but must be grounded on general principles of legal policy. This approach has the advantage that the conclusions reached derive their weight in part from the fact that they have a certain general validity, because they are based on considerations that are not only relevant for the regulation of euthanasia but also for other problems of legal policy.

---

75 Compare Dworkin 1985: chapter 1.

If every participant in a debate on legal policy tries to base his position on general principles, this does not in itself guarantee that all controversy can be resolved. In the first
place, there is no complete consensus on the principles concerned. Furthermore, the
scope of the principles is not fixed. Finally, the principles are not sacrosanct: a system of
law is never 'finished', and legal culture, like culture in general, is continuously in motion.
The last two factors imply that the expectation that every participant in the debate
should be able to deduce his position on euthanasia from his general position on legal
policy – assuming he has one – is ill-founded. For such a specific position on a question
such as euthanasia functions as a crystallization and also, to a certain extent, a test of the
principles concerned. There is always a reciprocal relationship between, on the one hand,
a person's position regarding the legal permissibility of euthanasia, for example, and, on
the other hand, his position on what are to be considered the general principles of the
legal culture to which he belongs.[76] A lack of consensus on legal policy concerning
euthanasia could be a result of the fact that the point of equilibrium between their general and their specific positions is not the same for everyone.

4.3.2   A quest for common ground

Dealing with a controversy such as that concerning the legal permissibility of euthanasia
on the basis of arguments means searching for *common ground*. However, it is not necessarily the case that Dutch legal culture includes general principles of legal policy that
afford such common ground.

The Netherlands, like other modern Western nations, is in a constitutional sense liberal
and democratic. The freedom of the individual plays a key role in the constitutional
order. To protect this freedom, the state's power is limited. Such limitation is partly procedural: public decision-making is subject to the requirements of democratic government. The limitation is also substantive in the sense that the state's power is restricted by
the separation principle mentioned above. This separation principle has over the centuries led to the recognition of specific individual constitutional rights that guarantee
the individual a domain of private activity free from state interference. Connected with
this is a view of criminal law in which there is less and less room for the enforcement of
moral values as such.

---

76   In Rawlsian terms (Rawls 1972: 20) one could say that in an ideal debate, the concrete posi-
      tion on a specific question of legal policy of every participant is in *reflective equilibrium* with
      his view of the general principles of legal policy of his legal culture. Achieving such an equi-
      librium will be more difficult for one participant than for another, dependent on the tension
      that exists between the elements that must be reconciled. The outcome will partly depend on
      how much weight is accorded to the respective elements of the equilibrium. A 'fanatic' is a
      person who attaches disproportionate weight to a concrete position, too little to general prin-
      ciples.

We have already noted that it is not always clear what the scope is of any given general principle of legal policy. This observation applies to the separation principle. There is general consensus that the state must respect *some* boundary between the public and the private domain. However, since it is not clear exactly what the considerations are that underly the separation principle, it can in particular cases be debated whether the principle requires respect for the freedom of the individual where this is not required by specific constitutional rights.

In legal philosophy two basic views concerning the separation principle can be distinguished: a (strictly) liberal vision and a more conservative one.[77] In the liberal vision the state's power is restricted as a matter of principle,[78] and there is a *presumption of liberty* that applies to every form of public regulation.[79] This presumption of liberty holds that every restriction of not otherwise protected individual freedom must be justified by considerations of greater weight; those who argue for such a restriction have the 'burden of proof'. More conservative thinkers believe that the reasons for restricting the power of the state are merely practical. They point to the importance of the surrounding society for the moral forming of the individual and in that connection are prepared to afford the state a wide latitude to concern itself with moral matters.

There are good reasons to suppose that the Dutch legal order, at least as far as immaterial moral questions are concerned, is characterized by a (more or less strict) liberal interpretation of the separation principle. Such indications can be found, for example, in the way the political controversy over the question of abortion was resolved, in the freedom generally (and non-controversially) accorded to the individual on matters such as homosexuality and pornography, and in the legislative history of the most recent revision of the constitution.[80] The question is then whether the liberal interpretation of the separation principle (the 'liberal paradigm') affords sufficient common ground for the euthanasia debate.

In the next section we attempt in two stages to reconstruct the opposing views in the Dutch euthanasia debate. In this way we seek to establish how much common ground is latently present and whether this common ground fits within the liberal paradigm. The conclusion to which we come is that the Dutch euthanasia controversy can only be resolved to a limited extent on the basis of the liberal paradigm, because, among other reasons, even most supporters of the legalization of euthanasia accept restrictions on individual freedom that do not correspond with that paradigm.

---

77   Compare Musschenga, Voorzanger & Soeteman 1992.

78   The restricting principles of the liberal paradigm will be discussed in section 4.3.3.

79   Compare Feinberg 1984: 9: "Liberty should be the norm; coercion always needs some special justification."

80   See Leenen 1994: 38ff; Gezondheidsraad 1982: 64-67; Soeteman 1986: 63.

4.3.3 The appeal to tolerance

In section 4.2 we have seen that the sharpest principled opposition in the euthanasia debate is between the principle of autonomy and the principle of the sanctity of human life. The first principle implies that a competent individual has a right to decide when he has had enough of life and that a doctor who accedes to such a person's request for termination may appeal to the patient's right if accused of killing him. The second principle is thought by some to imply an inalienable right to life that obliges the state to maintain the criminal prohibition on euthanasia, by others to require much stricter legal limits on euthanasia than the principle of autonomy would allow.

The value of autonomy is thus apparently opposed to the value of the sanctity of human life. May the law offer protection to one of these values, to the exclusion of the other? Is there an argument available that could convince supporters of the value *not* (completely) protected by the law? A number of important arguments can be offered in favor of autonomy: apart from the fact that autonomy can be considered worthwhile in its own right, people in general know best what is in their interests, while community pressure on the individual involves the infliction of suffering. But these arguments are for many adherents to the principle of the sanctity of human life not sufficient to induce them to alter their standpoint.

The legal philosopher Dworkin has argued that the American abortion and euthanasia controversies are not characterized by opposition between autonomy and the sanctity of human life, but that those who argue for individual freedom of choice want individuals to be free to follow their *own interpretation* of the sanctity of human life.[81] According to Dworkin the American Constitution protects the individual's right to follow his own interpretation of the sanctity of human life.[82] However, an appeal to a legal document seems unlikely to convince those who on the basis of their interpretation of the sanctity of human life completely reject euthanasia; they will argue for another interpretation of the Constitution.

---

81   Dworkin (1993: 34) distinguishes between a conservative and a liberal interpretation of the sanctity of human life. "[L]iberal opinion, like the conservative view, presupposes that human life itself has intrinsic moral significance, so that it is in principle wrong to terminate a life even when no one's interests are at stake." In Dworkin's view, life is valued 'intrinsically' if and to the extent someone has 'invested' in it. Liberals attach relatively more value to the human 'investment' (especially that which has been done by the person whose life is concerned), conservatives relatively more to the 'investment' of Nature (God). (Dworkin 1993: chapter 3.)

82   Dworkin 1993: 166ff. Compare with regard to euthanasia Dworkin et al. 1997.

An appeal to the *principle of tolerance* might offer a solution here.[83] According to this principle the state must be neutral as between the different conceptions of morality present in society and the values on which these conceptions are grounded.[84] This neutrality concerns the motives on which legal rules may legitimately be based: the motive may not be to favor certain values above others. The neutrality that, according to the principle of tolerance, must guide state action is thus a 'neutrality of justification'. Neutrality of justification means in the case of euthanasia that the rules of criminal law with regard to termination of life may not be intended to favor the position either of supporters of the principle of autonomy or of supporters of the sanctity of human life.

The neutrality of justification that is implied by the principle of tolerance must be distinguished from 'neutrality of outcome', which would require the state to take care that state action does not in practice favor any single conception of the good.[85] Where one of the principles involved is the principle of autonomy, application of the principle of tolerance clearly is not neutral with regard to the resulting outcome. If the law is to respect the principle of autonomy just as much as the principle of the sanctity of human life, it can only do so by leaving matters to individual choice: seeking to enforce the sanctity of human life with the aid of the criminal law would amount to *legal moralism*, which conflicts with the principle of tolerance.[86] Application of the principle of tolerance thus leads in practice to autonomy, even if the motive of the legislator is neutral.

The neutrality that must characterize the behavior of the state does not imply that the freedom of choice required by the principle of tolerance is without limitations. According to the liberal view, the power of the state may be mobilized when this is indicated by the so-called *harm principle*, which holds that the freedom of an individual is limited to behavior that does not cause harm to others.[87] The harm principle can be invoked to

---

83   As remarked in section 4.3.1, legal questions can be distinguished but not separated from questions of legal policy. Dworkin's legal argument is based on a specific view of legal policy in which the idea of tolerance plays an important role (compare Dworkin 1993: 167-168).

84   Compare Dworkin 1985: 191ff; Mendus 1988; Musschenga, Voorzanger & Soeteman 1992.

85   Compare Rawls 1993: 183; in more detail, Raz 1986: 114ff.

86   Legal moralism is the view that it can be morally legitimate to prohibit conduct on the ground that it is inherently immoral, although it does not cause any harm (Feinberg 1984: 27). The form of legal moralism involved here is called *strict moralism*: moralism directed to the enforcement of what is considered to be 'true' morality, and must be distinguished, among other things, from *moral conservatism*: the idea that preserving a way of community life, including the maintenance of conventional morality, is legitimate (Feinberg 1988: chapter 29-30).

87   This principle was proposed by John Stuart Mill (1993: 78) in the last century and expounded in the so-called *enforcement of morals* debate, in which legal regulation of questions such as prostitution, homosexuality and pornography played a central role. Compare Hart 1963; Devlin 1965; Dworkin 1977.

legitimize a legal prohibition of euthanasia to the extent that allowing euthanasia would lead, for example, to non-voluntary termination of life. But because there is no proof of a causal connection between the two (see section 4.2.4), the harm principle does not, in the case of the euthanasia controversy, permit absolute restriction on individual autonomy, although it does permit procedural protections designed to insure voluntariness.

Because the principle of tolerance does not guarantee neutrality of outcome, and in fact in the case of euthanasia does not produce it, it itself requires a powerful defence. Without this, supporters of the principle of the sanctity of human life, in seeking to balance their specific legal policy position on the permissibility of euthanasia and their view on what are to be considered the general principles of legal policy, will attribute more moral weight to the sanctity of human life than to the principle of tolerance.

There are, however, a number of strong arguments to be made against such a rejection of an appeal to the principle of tolerance. The principle of tolerance is a so-called 'meta principle', a principle of a higher order that mediates between other principles such as the principle of autonomy and the principle of the sanctity of human life. It cannot be set aside because its results in a particular case are unpalatable to the adherents of one of the principles between which it mediates. The history of the wars of religion during the sixteenth and seventeenth centuries, out of which the principle of tolerance emerged, illustrates this point. Freedom of worship, the historical basis of modern constitutional liberalism, developed in connection with efforts to bring an end to these wars. Such religious freedom violated the deeply-held convictions of most of the participants. If the latter had gone on appealing to their convictions as overruling the principle of tolerance, the religious wars would never have come to an end.

This pragmatic foundation of the principle of tolerance went hand in hand with the more principled consideration that religious persuasion is no true 'persuasion' if it does not come about freely.[88] Later, the idea of moral skepticism, according to which every individual must be free to follow his own idea of morality since there are no ultimately

---

88   The argument that none of the means of regulation that the state has available are able to impose 'genuine religious beliefs' is central to Locke's famous *A Letter on Toleration*. It should be noted that the principle of freedom of conscience that emerged at the end of a period in which, for example, religiously motivated intolerance was considered normal, originally had a *theological* basis: every individual must be able to follow his conscience, since this is God's messenger, *even if* the individual thereby sometimes 'strays'. Rawls (1993: 58ff) broadens the scope of Locke's argument by demonstrating that genuine non-religious (moral) convictions also presume that they are freely held.

decisive arguments in favor of one specific idea, emerged. Finally, Rousseau and Kant argued for the intrinsic value of tolerance, based on the respect that we owe to others.[89]

In short, constitutional liberals argue that the principle of tolerance affords sufficient common ground for settling questions of legal policy such as the euthanasia controversy in a way that corresponds with the basic assumptions of the existing legal system: an unqualified prohibition of euthanasia does not belong in the Criminal Code because the neutrality of the state requires that every competent individual be permitted to make decisions about his own death and the state must not interfere with this so long as the exercise of this autonomy causes no harm to others.[90]

4.3.4 Respect for life

Although opposition between the principles of autonomy and of the sanctity of human life is an important aspect of the Dutch euthanasia debate, there are good reasons to assume that this opposition alone does not adequately characterize the debate. We will suggest here that the Dutch euthanasia controversy is influenced to an important extent by what one might call concern for *respect for life*. If this suggestion is right, it follows that appeal to the principle of tolerance cannot entirely settle the controversy and some further common ground is needed.

There are a number of reasons in support of the view that the opposition between the principle of autonomy and the principle of the sanctity of human life does not adequately characterize the Dutch euthanasia debate. Some of these concern the position of the supporters and others that of the opponents of legalization of euthanasia. To begin with the former: most supporters in fact accept only a *restricted* autonomy. The patient's request alone is not considered a sufficient basis for legal euthanasia. The case law has always imposed additional requirements, which have also been accepted in the political forum, in public opinion (see chapter 5.1) and, by and large, in the literature. The most important of these is the requirement that there must be 'unbearable and hopeless suffering'.

---

89 Compare Dent 1988. There are also other arguments that have been made in favor of tolerance. Mill, for example, supports his plea for tolerance with a reference to the *value of diversi-
ty* and the *value of truth* (Mill 1993: chapters 2 and 3). Dworkin (1985: 191) argues that the
idea of the fundamental equality of persons requires the moral neutrality of the state and thus
the principle of tolerance.

90 Compare, for example, Soeteman's argument, described in section 4.2.1.; and Leenen 1994:
260: "Those who support a prohibitive law that corresponds with their own opinion are acting in a rather paradoxical way because they claim for themselves something they do not wish
to permit to another."

Imposing additional requirements does not necessarily conflict with the principle of autonomy. It might be justified on the grounds of so-called *weak paternalism*, the view "that the state has the right to prevent self-regarding harmful conduct ... *when but only when* that conduct is substantially non-voluntary, or when temporary intervention is necessary to establish whether it is voluntary or not."[91] But it is not clear that the criterion of 'unbearable and hopeless suffering' can be defended as necessary to insure the patient's autonomy.[92] That seems contrived, because it is not clear why wanting to die when one is not suffering unbearably and hopelessly would imply a *less* autonomous decision, and because imposing the requirement of 'unbearable and hopeless suffering' cannot be regarded as a 'temporary intervention' to investigate the voluntariness of someone's decison.

That the patient's request is insufficient ground for the legality of euthanasia reflects the more general fact that in criminal law the *volenti principle*, which holds that an act to which a person consents cannot be considered 'injury' to him (*volenti non fit iniuria*), is not generally applicable.[93] From this perspective it is not surprising that the Supreme Court has rejected appeals to autonomy (see section 4.2.1). Another indication that a request is generally considered insufficient justification for the termination of life can be seen in the objections that were raised to the proposal of a former member of the Supreme Court, Drion, to provide elderly people with a 'suicide pill' on request (see chapters 2.4, 3.5.2). These objections were not merely of a practical nature.[94]

The second reason for believing that the opposition between the principle of autonomy and the principle of the sanctity of human life does not adequately characterize the Dutch euthanasia debate has to do with the position of the opponents of legalization. It seems unlikely that most of these opponents unconditionally subscribe to the principle of the sanctity of human life, since the assumptions that underlie that principle are not plausible and unremitting application would have consequences most of them would think undesirable.

---

91   Feinberg 1986: 12. Weak paternalism must be distinguished from *hard paternalism*, that "will accept as a reason for criminal legislation that it is necessary to protect competent adults, against their will, from the harmful consequences even of their fully voluntary choices and undertakings" (*idem.*).

92   See, for such a defence, Soeteman 1986; compare section 4.2.1.

93   Compare Den Hartogh 1996: 154. See the legislative history of article 293 for explicit rejection of the *volenti* principle.

94   Compare Van Holsteyn & Trappenburg 1996, whose survey of public opinion shows that the weight that Dutch conventional morality attaches to the right to decide for oneself with regard to the end of one's life is not unlimited (see chapter 5.1.).

The principle of the sanctity of human life forbids, as shown in section 4.1.2, the intentional termination of innocent human life. Adherents to the principle oppose euthanasia and other forms of intentional shortening of life in a medical context because they consider every form of human life equally and intrinsically valuable, regardless of the value the life has to the person concerned or to others. According to the doctrine of double effect, this principle is compatible with the shortening of life as a result of administering pain relief or abstaining from futile treatment.

In section 4.1.2 we saw, however, that the doctrine of double effect does not provide a reliable test for distinguishing between death due to euthanasia and death due to such 'normal medical practice'. Only the doctrine's proportionality criterion survived critical analysis. It follows from this that proponents of the principle of the sanctity of human life have to choose between two positions. The first is so-called *vitalism*, that holds that the preservation of (even merely biological) human life must *always* be striven for.[95] If taken consistently, this position dictates that, for example, terminal cancer patients, irreversibly comatose patients and severely defective newborn babies must be kept alive as long as possible.[96] As far as medical practice is concerned, there seems to be essentially no one who seriously wants to take this radical position. Besides, since proponents of vitalism do not consistently apply a biological criterion (which would require them to argue for similar protection of at least all animal life) it seems that the vitalist position boils down to the idea that human life is intrinsically valuable because a human belongs to the species *homo sapiens*. Such an arbitrary preference for one species amounts to *speciesism*, which is essentially the same sort of moral mistake as racism.[97]

The other possibility for adherents to the principle of the sanctity of human life who accept death due to 'normal medical practice' as legitimate, is to accept that medical behavior that shortens life is at least in part justified in terms of patient autonomy and, as far as incompetent patients are involved, in terms of the interests of the person concerned, which implies accepting the necessity of quality-of-life judgments.[98] Since the

---

95   See Kuhse 1987: 203.

96   And also that the death penalty and killing in self-defence or in wartime are not permissible.

97   Compare Singer 1985: 76; Kuhse 1987: 212; Singer 1994: 173.

98   Compare section 4.2.2. Compare Kuhse 1987: 208: "The sanctity-of-life doctrine, in denying the moral relevance of quality-of-life considerations, cannot raise … questions [about how to make quality-of-life judgments] to a theoretical level. In practice, this means that the medical profession is, in the absence of such standards, faced with an anarchy of values and meaning." Singer (1994) points out that making quality-of-life judgments has been common medical practice for some time in many countries (America, England, Australia), where it already enjoys a degree of (implicit) legal sanction. Recent Australian research (Kuhse et al. 1997) supports this claim.

doctrine of double effect is not an adequate guide to medical decisions that shorten life, and since medical practice cannot be understood in terms of a vitalistic interpretation of the principle of the sanctity of human life, one has to assume that most of those who invoke the principle of the sanctity of human life *in fact* do not take it as an absolute guide to the justifiability of medical behavior that shortens life.

Since the principle of autonomy and the principle of the sanctity of human life alone cannot account for the positions of the supporters and the opponents of legalization of euthanasia, our thesis is that both the restrictions on autonomy that the supporters consider necessary and the objections of many opponents to (further) legalization derive from one and the same concern: respect for life. The *principle of respect for life* functions as an alternative for the liberal paradigm's harm principle. Where according to the liberal paradigm every form of shortening of life that does not cause harm to others must be tolerated, the principle of respect for life allows only those sorts of shortening of life that show respect for life.

So far, the concept of 'respect for life' has not been well articulated or developed, and what we here say about it is rather tentative. However, the essence of the idea of 'respect' is clear enough. To respect something means to show regard (esteem) for it. But within a certain range, there is room to balance the value of life against other values such as autonomy. The principle of respect for life is thus different from the principle of the sanctity of human life, that, according to its proponents, must be interpreted in an absolute way.

Respect for life has two aspects that are relevant with regard to legal policy: a 'paternalistic' and an 'environmental' aspect. The paternalistic aspect reveals itself in the fact that in the Dutch euthanasia debate euthanasia is in principle only allowed on the basis of a *combination* of the principle of autonomy and the principle of beneficence. Euthanasia can only legally be performed if continuation of the life of the patient concerned is no longer in his interest. A person is generally free to determine whether further life is in his interest, but this freedom is not unrestricted.[99] Although he is allowed to act on his own

---

99   Compare Den Hartogh (1996: 155), who points out that the limitations thereby imposed on autonomy to a large extent can be understood in terms of aspects of the value of autonomy itself. To the extent that the principle of autonomy is based on the idea that people generally know themselves what is in their best interests, only the intrinsic value of autonomy is opposed to well-being. It is only these two that have to be balanced: "My argument is that the balance will tip more in the first direction [paternalism] the more the damage granting the requested help causes, the more difficult it is to heal, and the better third parties are able to judge it. High scores on these dimensions are often rightly to be expected in the case of professional behavior. It is thus not coincidental that the *volenti* principle has little weight in the professional ethics of the classical professions."

conception of the value of his life, in which he may value the biological side of life more than the mental side, or vice versa, he is required to show 'respect' for his life, in the sense of acting after due deliberation and in a way comprehensible to others. On the other hand, the principle of autonomy is also limited in the sense that shortening of life *without* a request can be acceptable in limited circumstances, for example in the case of 'help in dying' (see chapter 3.3.4).

The environmental aspect of respect for life concerns what can be called the 'moral environment' of a community. Members of a community share an interest in "maintaining a moral environment in which decisions of life and death are taken seriously and treated as matters of moral gravity."[100] Respect for life concerns the context within which decisions to shorten life can be regarded as *morally* autonomous, a matter of which the requirement of an explicit and well-considered request does not take account. On this view, it is not only the economic and interpersonal circumstances under which decisions concerning termination are made that are important in assessing such decisions.[101] The general moral environment is also important, and maintaining a healthy one, in which moral autonomy can flourish, can be considered a legitimate concern of the state. Illustrative of this concern for the moral environment is the fact that participants in the debate frequently argue that euthanasia must always be regarded as a *problem*. They warn of the dangers of moral indifference that might follow from unrestricted adherence to the principle of individual autonomy.

The key question of legal policy is, ultimately, whether respect for life is a legitimate foundation for criminal prohibitions in a liberal state.[102] As far as the paternalistic aspect of respect for life is concerned, prohibition would amount to *legal paternalism*, according to which it is a good reason in support of a prohibition that this is probably necessary to prevent harm to the actor himself.[103] Such legal paternalism would imply a weakening of the presumption of liberty that is not acceptable within the liberal paradigm.[104]

As far as the environmental aspect of respect for life is concerned, enforcement would also seem to conflict with the liberal paradigm, which in principle only permits criminal prohibitions necessary to protect individual rights and interests.[105] The harm principle,

---

100 Dworkin 1993: 168. Compare Postema 1992.

101 Compare Rozemond 1995; Schalken 1995.

102 Dworkin (1993: 167ff) argues that concern for what is here called the environmental aspect of respect for life weighs heavily enough to legitimize state action, but that it counts for little against the interest of an individual in his autonomy.

103 See Feinberg 1984: 26.

104 See Feinberg 1986.

105 See Mill 1993; and currently, among others, Feinberg 1984-1988.

discussed above, is based on that position. But in addition to individual interests, there are so-called *social goods* that may call for protection. Social goods consist of *public goods* and *collective goods*. A public good is an interest that (nearly) every member of a society, more or less coincidentally, shares; a collective good is an interest individuals have as members of a specific community.[106] Public goods can be reduced to individual interests, and legal protection of public goods against *public evils* can therefore be based on the harm principle. Collective goods cannot be reduced to individual interests.[107] Legal protection of collective goods is therefore problematic in the liberal paradigm.

To the extent that respect for life can be regarded as a public good, prohibitions can be based on the harm principle. But it seems rather artificial to characterize a change in the social environment in which decisions concerning life and death are being taken as an injury to individual interests. Perhaps this is not impossible, but it does require the concept of 'harm' to be so extended that it is probably no longer acceptable to a strict liberal. The alternative is to regard respect for life as a collective good. But in that case the argument for legal protection is at odds with the liberal paradigm since it boils down to *moral conservatism*.[108]

---

106 Compare Soeteman 1992: 180: "We value [collective goods], partly at least, because they are characteristic for our community, because our community, that we value, values them. These shared values are essential in creating a community out of an assemblage of persons. Collective goods constitute a community." The language spoken in a specific community is an example of a collective good.

Another example of a collective good is a taboo against, for example, killing. Compare Dworkin (1993 : 149) with regard to abortion: "It is not true that an individual woman's decision to have an abortion affects only herself (or only herself and the fetus's father), for individual decisions inevitably affect shared collective values. Part of the sacred is a sense of taboo, and it is surely harder to maintain a taboo against abortion and to raise one's children to respect it, in a community where others not only reject it but violate it openly."

107 Soeteman 1992: 180: "[I]t is wrong to reduce the collective values to values of individual persons. Of course, it is individuals who share the collective values... But they do so because they have an interest in this particular kind of community, with which they identify."

108 Moral conservatism is the view that it is legitimate to limit liberty by means of legal coercion in order to prevent drastic change in a group's way of life, including changes of moral attitudes within the group (Feinberg 1988: 39). It is not clear how serious the objection stated is. The moral attitudes concerned are fundamental ones since they regard life and death, and the enforcement of this part of group morality might therefore be less problematic from a liberal perspective. Compare Hart's *moral minimum* (Hart 1967).

The apparent conclusion of this discussion is that the Dutch euthanasia debate cannot be adequately described in terms of the liberal paradigm alone. Many participants in the debate in fact refer more or less implicitly to the so-called 'communitaristic' school of thought, that warns against a 'reductionist' image of man in which the individual is seen as a creature whose interests amount to little more than protection of his exercise of autonomy. They plead for greater attention to communal influences and interests.[109] Perhaps it would contribute to the debate if such references were made more explicit.

4.3.5 Conclusion

In this section we have argued that the question of legal policy that is central to the euthanasia debate concerns the authority of the state to regulate euthanasia. Such a question must be answered in terms of general principles of legal policy. At the same time we have seen that what these principles precisely require must be made specific in a process in which their content reciprocally influences and is influenced by the position a given participant assumes with regard to the legal permissibility of, for example, euthanasia. We took as a starting point for our discussion the 'liberal paradigm' that, in the Netherlands, is widely subscribed to as far as legal regulation of immaterial moral questions is concerned. We have examined the extent to which this paradigm offers common ground on which the different participants in the euthanasia debate can engage in fruitful debate over legal policy.

We have seen that the Dutch euthanasia debate is characterized by a number of oppositions. It can only to a certain extent be described in terms of the opposition between the principle of autonomy and the principle of the sanctity of human life. This is true, among other things, because a large majority of the participants in the debate (opponents and supporters of a limited legalization) seem wary of placing exclusive emphasis either on autonomy or on the sanctity of life.

Two conclusions can now be drawn. In the first place, the presumption of liberty has in the Dutch debate been subject to concessions that so far have not been convincingly accounted for. Either the Dutch legal system is not as liberal as was previously thought, or it must be shown that the positions taken can be reconciled with the liberal paradigm.

---

109 Compare Mulhall & Swift 1997. Sutorius (lawyer in many leading euthanasia cases) expresses the following 'Burkian' concern (in Dam 1996: 584): "There is also another possibility, one that frightens me. Namely, that death becomes an option, a possible choice. People can choose to continue living or to stop living. Just as in Seneca's time, it is again a virtue to think: it is my time, I'm going. If this possibility materializes, then we are now witnessing a cultural 'turning point' that worries me."

In the second place, our sketch of the terms of the Dutch debate has made clear why a shift from a principled to a pragmatic perspective took place in the Dutch debate halfway through the 1980s (see section 4.2). The oppositions that characterize the debate are, as it happens, only relative. Most participants discuss the issues in more or less the same terms. Both supporters and opponents of (further) legalization are concerned with the social climate in which decisions pertaining to termination of life are taken and with the protection of patients' interests. And since the differences between them are, as we have seen, connected with that social climate and those interests, it is understandable that a pragmatic approach to the controversy, in which the best possible social control of practice and the highest possible quality of decision-making are the focus of attention, has come to characterize the entire debate.

5   What is Known about Medical Practice and its Regulation?

Earlier chapters have dealt with current Dutch law concerning euthanasia and other MBSL, with the process of legal change that led to this set of legal arrangements and with some of the fundamental concepts in terms of which the debate over legal change has been waged. The bulk of this chapter (sections 5.2 and 5.3) considers what is known about the actual practice of MBSL and the way its various sorts are currently regulated. Detailed and reliable empirical data have become available over the past 10 years, especially as a result of two major national studies commissioned by the Dutch Government, both of which were touched on in chapter 2.[1] However, we begin (section 5.1) with an overview of the public opinion polls that have been conducted over the course of the last 30 years. The chapter ends with discussions of some other recent research on special aspects of the problem (section 5.4). In the final section (section 5.5) the results of all this research are summarized and the implications for the political debate on how to regulate euthanasia practice are considered.

A note to the reader: Even though the data presented in this chapter are but a small fraction of what is available as a result of the research discussed, and even though they will be presented in a simplified and non-technical way,[2] this chapter is rather dense, and reading straight through may seem heavy going. Those who are less interested in matters of detail and are willing to take our interpretation of the data on faith may want to skim through the chapter looking for things that particularly interest them and to rely for the rest on the summary in section 5.5.

---

1   In addition to the national surveys treated extensively in this chapter, one local research project deserves mention. It concerned the care of terminal patients and euthanasia in Utrecht and was carried out on behalf of the city of Utrecht. The first report (Benjaminsen 1988) deals with the institutional facilities for the care of terminal patients and the way which, within these facilities, euthanasia requests are responded to. The second (Melief 1991) deals with the same questions at the level of individual health-care professionals. The results are on the whole similar to those of the national research and therefore do not require separate discussion. Where they appear to afford additional information or a different perspective, this will be noted.

2   Many percentages are not given at all (especially where N is small), or only in rounded-off form; all indications of statistical significance and the like have been omitted.

5.1   Public opinion concerning euthanasia and other MBSL

Public opinion polls since 1975 consistently show that a large majority of the Dutch population believes that doctors in principle should be permitted to carry out euthanasia. A majority of all important religious and political groups share this opinion.

For almost half a century polls have investigated the opinion of the Dutch public concerning euthanasia.[3] These polls tend to suffer from one or another of the sorts of defects characteristic of opinion polling. In particular, 'euthanasia' is often inadequately defined or distinguished from other MBSL, and the formulation of the question posed often leaves much to be desired and in any case differs from one poll to the next without the poll-takers apparently being aware of the different things they are asking (whether the respondent might consider euthanasia, approves of it, thinks a doctor should accede to a patient's request, thinks the law should allow it, etc.). The result of all this is that the results are difficult to interpret or compare. The first poll was conducted in 1950 and the question posed was: 'If a person is suffering from a painful and incurable illness and the patient and the family request it, should a doctor be allowed painlessly to hasten the moment of death?' 54% of the respondents were opposed to allowing this, but 55% of the non-religious respondents were already in favor.[4]

Since 1966 the Social and Cultural Planning Bureau (SCP) has polled Dutch opinion using the same question:[5] 'Should a doctor give a lethal injection at the request of a patient to put an end to his suffering?' The results are as follows:[6]

Table 5.1 Results of SCP-polls 1966-1991

year	yes	depends	no
1966	40	12	49
1970	53	24	24
1975	51	32	16
1980	52	36	12
1985	55	33	12
1991	58	33	9

---

3   For a discussion of some of these polls see Catsburg & De Boer 1986; Holsteyn & Trappenburg 1996: 51-53; Blad 1996: 390-401.

4   Hessing et al. 1996: 161.

5   Source for the text of the question: telephonic contact with SCP.

6   See SCP 1992: 475 and Van der Maas et al. 1995. A very small and otherwise uninteresting 'do not know' category has been eliminated for the sake of simplicity. The results of the SCP polls are available in graph-form (and in more detail for 1966 and 1991) in English in Van der Maas et al. 1995; see also for discussion in English of these and some other polls, Hessing et al. 1996: 161ff.

As the SCP polls show, the greatest change in public opinion had occurred by about 1975. Since the middle of the 1970s, a majority of the Dutch population has consistently been 'in favor of' euthanasia; the percentage of unqualified opponents has declined from about 25% in 1970 to about 10% in 1991.[7]

The general trend can be observed for all the various segments of the population whose opinion has been separately measured. There are essentially no differences between men and women. Younger people are slightly more positive than older people. Supporters of the non-confessional (social-democratic and liberal) parties (PvdA, D66, VVD) have long been strongly positive, whereas a positive majority among the Christian Democrats (CDA) only emerged in the mid-1980s. A majority of persons who report no religious affiliation were already supportive in 1966 (28%: 'no'), and they remain the most supportive group (in 1991, 3%: 'no'). A majority of Catholics were opposed in 1966 (55% 'no'), but by 1991 Catholics were essentially indistinguishable from the rest of the population. Dutch Reformed are now only slightly less supportive than the general population (16%: 'no'), and the stricter Calvinists (*Gereformeerd*) are least supportive of all (34%: 'no').[8]

According to the SCP, there is every indication that with regard to euthanasia, as with a variety of other issues, a process of cultural diffusion has taken place. Until the middle of the 1960s, values were rather traditional throughout the country. Beginning in the cities a process of modernisation set in, and traditional attitudes toward a variety of issues (marriage, sexuality, emancipation of women, homosexuality, abortion, euthanasia, political protest) began to change. The winds of change began somewhat later in the less urban areas of the country. In the case of euthanasia, convergence set in only from about the beginning of the 1990s. At present, there is little remaining difference between the urban and rural population.[9]

Holsteyn and Trappenburg recently published an extensive study of Dutch public opinion, not only on euthanasia but also on a number of other MBSL.[10] As far as euthanasia is concerned, their results generally confirm what had been found earlier. In 1995, about 10% were of the opinion that euthanasia should 'always be forbidden', whereas 64% considered that it should 'always be allowed' on the request of the patient. Some 80% of

---

7   According to Van der Wal & Van der Maas (1996: 234-235), citing SCP 1996, the degree of acceptance of euthanasia increased until 1991 and since then has remained stable or even slightly declined. The published SCP data do not appear to support this latter suggestion.

8   Most of the above data are taken from Van der Maas c.s. 1995: 1413; for the data on political party affiliation see NVVE 1988.

9   SCP 1996: 516-525.

10   Holsteyn & Trappenburg 1996. The results quoted below are to be found throughout their book.

those who answered the question thought that the doctor in a case described in the questionnaire (based on a widely shown television film of an actual case of euthanasia[11]) had done the right thing; half of those who disagreed did so on grounds having to do with the particular circumstances of the case.

The results on some other MBSL, whose legal status has been discussed in chapter 3.3, 3.4 and 3.5, are as follows (the results given are for the outspoken opposite opinions; the in-between category accounts for the rest of those who answered the respective question):[12]

SEVERELY DEFECTIVE NEWBORN BABIES

- 80% consider it acceptable for a doctor to cease life-prolonging treatment (artificial respiration) of a seriously defective baby who is certain to die anyway (the request of the parents is considered essential by a large majority); 6% are under all circumstances opposed.

- 71% consider it acceptable, if the baby does not die quickly and is in great pain, for the doctor to give the baby a lethal injection (again, the request of the parents is considered essential); 14% are opposed.

- 46% consider active termination of life acceptable if the baby is severely defective and will be very severely handicapped (here, too, the parents' request is essential); 26% are opposed.

- 15% consider it acceptable for the parents of a baby with Downs Syndrome to refuse an operation for a life-threatening defect; 66% are opposed.

COMA PATIENTS

- 60% consider it acceptable to cease artificial feeding of a patient in a permanent coma at the request of the family; 16% are opposed (36% consider an advance directive essential and only 29% consider that the doctor may terminate a futile treatment on his own authority).

- 34% agree that the doctor may administer a lethal injection to hasten the process of dying; 38% are opposed.

---

11   M. Nederhorst, *Dodelijk verzoek* [Death on Request], documentary television film, first broadcast on 20 October 1994.

12   The percentages given here are after exclusion of the answer: 'no opinion'.

PSYCHIATRIC PATIENTS

–   24% consider it acceptable for a psychiatrist to assist a severely depressive person with suicide; 45% are opposed.

SENILE DEMENTIA

–   33% consider euthanasia acceptable in the case of a person with senile dementia who requests it, while 31% do not; the figures become 44% and 24% if the request was made before the person became demented; 25% consider it only acceptable if a family member agrees.

THE ELDERLY WHO WISH TO DETERMINE THE TIME OF THEIR DEATH

–   29% consider it acceptable that the elderly be permitted to have their doctor prescribe a lethal pill for them that they can take whenever the prospects of life (e.g. institutionalization) become too unattractive; 48% and 42%, respectively, consider the danger of misuse or the risk that old people will consider themselves unwanted too great; 26% are opposed.

Holsteyn and Trappenburg analyse the reasons their respondents gave for their opinions on the various questions. They conclude that the most important explanation lies in a person's attitude toward the idea of personal autonomy on such matters. With the exception of the case of the baby with Downs Syndrome (where the results were the other way around), those who believe there is such a right are much more likely to support the various MBSL (even in the case in which the right must be exercised by a parent or other family member). Attitudes toward the principle of beneficence – in particular, whether a respondent considers it the primary role of a doctor to relieve the patient's suffering or to keep him alive – are of some, but not major importance. Sex, age and educational level are only marginally and variably relevant. Weekly church attendance is generally associated with opposition to the various MBSL. It is also very strongly associated with a person's attitude toward autonomy (4% of those who have never had a religious affiliation reject the idea of personal autonomy, as against two-thirds of those who attend church). But according to Holsteyn and Trappenburg, the autonomy effect remains even when religious affiliation is held constant.[13]

---

13   Chabot has recently argued (*Trouw*, 25 January 1997) that the results of the national studies in 1990 and 1995 show a shift over the last 5 years within the overall category of medical behavior that shortens life toward those sorts in which the role of the patient is most prominent (euthanasia and abstaining from treatment at the request or with the agreement of the patient). He concludes that, "The patient's role in deciding how he wants to die is making some gains against the increased power of doctors over the last fifty years to postpone the moment of death."

5.2   The first national survey: euthanasia by GPs and nursing-home doctors

Until 1990, the available quantitative data on euthanasia in the Netherlands were fragmentary, often impressionistic and anecdotal, and of unclear general validity. Especially foreign estimates of the number of cases per year tended to be tendentious extrapolations on a slender base and they varied widely: from 5,000 to 20,000 cases per year.[14]

The first serious effort[15] to establish national frequencies was made by Van der Wal and a number of colleagues. The research concentrated primarily on GPs (and therefore upon deaths at home), on the assumption that they are responsible for the lion's share of euthanasia, but it also covered nursing-home doctors. The data cover the period 1986-1990 and derive from mail surveys, and for some aspects of the research from prosecutorial files.

A methodological caveat: Critics often express the concern that the research to be discussed in this chapter may *understate* the extent of medical behavior that shortens life. We know of no reason to suppose this is a serious problem (although as we will see, the *characterization* of that behavior is highly problematic). On the other hand, Admiraal[16] has suggested that, to the extent morphine is used as a euthanaticum (and as we will see in section 5.3.1, despite all the reservations that have been expressed about such use this was, while declining rapidly, until recently quite widespread), doctors may unwittingly *overstate* the number of cases in which their administration of this drug causes the death of the patient. Admiraal argues that many doctors attribute far more lethal potency to morphine than it in fact has, and therefore ascribe deaths to it that actually were due to the patient's underlying disease. The rate of death due to pain relief may well be subject to a similar inflation.

---

14   Van der Maas 1992: 179. One problem with many early estimates was the variable meaning of the term 'euthanasia'.

15   In 1985, Van Wijmen conducted a survey of a national random sample of GPs and specialists (Van Wijmen 1989). The response was rather low, and the research suffered from a lack of conceptual clarity that makes interpretation of the findings problematic. About four-fifths of the respondents indicated a willingness, in principle, to accede to a request for euthanasia (that it was illegal was mentioned by only 2 doctors as a reason for their unwillingness). The level of willingness to give assistance with suicide was lower than that for killing on request: the respondents seem to have associated requests for assistance with suicide with psychiatric problems. Slightly over half the respondents had received at least one request for euthanasia in both 1983 and 1984; three-quarters stated that the frequency of requests was fairly stable over the years. About two-fifths indicated that they had performed euthanasia in 1983; the rate for 1984 was about the same; only 9 respondents had ever reported a case of euthanasia as such. Two-fifths stated that they had at least once terminated life without a request (the question posed did not, however, adequately distinguish administration of a lethal drug from termination of treatment).

16   1983: 965.

EUTHANASIA AND ASSISTANCE WITH SUICIDE BY GPS[17]

In the period 1986-1990, all but 2% of GPs *discussed* euthanasia or assistance with suicide with at least one patient per year: 61% did so with 1-5 patients, 20% with 6-10,
another 16% with 11-50, and 1% with more than 50 patients per year. On the other
hand, a quarter of the doctors had not had a single *explicit request* in the four years covered by the research; 56% averaged less than one request per year and only 1% received
as many as four. Per year, about 5,000 requests were received by some 6300 GPs (the
number of requests per year seemed to be rising); 23% of these requests were for assistance with suicide.

By 1990, lightly fewer than half of all GPs (48%) had never *performed* euthanasia or assistance with suicide; 47% had done so at least once within the previous four years (the
highest number was 17 times). A quarter of the doctors did so one or more times per year
(only 1% as often as 3 times per year). The total number of cases per year for all GPs in the
Netherlands was about 2,000 (about a quarter of these assistance with suicide). About
40% of all explicit requests were honored (this varied considerably, from 47% in 1986 to
35% in 1989). There were indications of an uneven geographic distribution of euthanasia, with an especially high frequency in the highly urban western part of the country.

Almost 85% of the cases of euthanasia involved a patient whose primary diagnosis was
cancer. Euthanasia or assistance with suicide was most frequent in the age-group 65-69;
below 30 and above 85 it was rare.

According to the GPs, the patient was (very) seriously suffering physically in more than
90% of the cases and mentally in more than two-thirds.[18] There was no correlation
between the two sorts of suffering. The most commonly mentioned kinds of (very) serious suffering were 'general weakness or tiredness' (85%), 'dependency or helplessness'
(74%) and 'loss of dignity or degeneration' (59%). Pain was a cause of (very) serious suffering in 57% of the cases, especially those involving cancer (63%); but in 27% it was not
a major cause of suffering and in 16% not a cause of suffering at all.

---

17   See Van der Wal 1992 for most of the data discussed below. Some of the most important find-
     ings of this research are summarized in English in Van der Wal et al. 1992a and 1992b. The
     survey of GPs covered almost half of those in the province of North Holland (including Ams-
     terdam, as well as the judicial district of Alkmaar, where the most well-established procedure
     for reporting euthanasia to the prosecutor's office existed at the time – see chapter 2.3.1) and
     10% of those in the rest of the country. The response-rate was 67%.

18   The less 'unbearable' and 'hopeless' the doctor considered the patient's situation, the higher
     the proportion of assistance with suicide, suggesting "that the patient is given ... more
     responsibility for ending his life" (1992b: 139).

Pain was the most important reason for the patient's request in only 5% of the cases. Not being able to eat or drink was mentioned in 51% of the cases (especially in the case of throat or stomach cancer). Other commonly mentioned sorts of (very) serious suffering included 'invalidity' (49%), 'shortness of breath' and 'fear of suffocation' (36% and 20% – often mentioned together), 'nausea' and 'vomiting' (31% and 22% – ditto), 'fear' (31%) and 'depression' (25%).

In general, the substantive criteria for euthanasia (voluntary request, unbearable and hopeless suffering) seemed to govern actual practice, whereas the procedural requirements did not, except in the minority of cases that were accurately reported as euthanasia. In only a third of all cases was the patient's request in writing. In almost half of all cases no written record of any sort was made.

Three-quarters of the doctors sought a formal consultation with another doctor (a quarter of these consulted more than one doctor); the doctor consulted was almost always either a close local colleague or a specialist involved in the treatment of the patient concerned. Of the doctors who did not formally consult, about a third had at least some discussion with a colleague. Twelve percent did not discuss the decision with any other health-care professional, including nurses. Consultation concerned primarily the seriousness of the patient's suffering and the voluntariness and well-consideredness of the request. The consulted doctor saw the patient about half the time, and the second opinion was in writing about a third of the time.[19]

In two-thirds of the cases the patient was receiving nursing care, but in a third of these cases the doctor did not discuss the situation with the nurse concerned.[20] It was rare (10%) for the nurse to be present at the time of performance. Incidentally (4%) it was the nurse who administered the lethal drugs, almost always in the presence (sometimes intermittent) of the doctor.[21]

Before 1986 a death resulting from euthanasia or assistance with suicide was almost always incorrectly reported as a 'natural death'. In the period 1986-1989 the rate of accu-

---

19   See Philipsen et al. 1994 for these last data, based on the same research.

20   See Muller 1996 for these data, based on the same research. According to Melief (1991) the nurses in his research in Utrecht (see note 1 above) often complained of poor communication and lack of coordination with doctors.

21   It was as of 1990 apparently much more common for hospital nurses to administer lethal drugs. Data from Van der Wal's research show a frequency of 21% administration (usually of morphine) by nurses, of which 16% without the specialist being (continuously) present; 28% of all specialists, but less than 10% of GPs and nursing-home doctors, considered it appropriate for nurses to do this (see Muller 1996: 85-86, 88).

rate reporting, according to the doctors interviewed, had risen to almost 30%.[22] By comparing the reporting rates stated by doctors with the number of cases known to the prosecutorial authorities, Van der Wal was able to show that reporting rates based on the number of cases doctors claim to have reported are probably highly inflated. They seem to be about double the rate of actual reporting, which was only about 13% in his research on GPs (this had risen from 8% in 1986 to 18% in 1989).[23]

There was a strong correlation between reporting a death as 'natural' and failure to comply with the various 'requirements of careful practice' such as consultation, written requests, and proper record-keeping. And when cases were reported, the facts tended to be presented in a way that, by comparison with the descriptions given to the researchers, made criminal investigation less likely (the suffering worse, the first initiative more often by the patient, the execution more in conformity with the procedural and medical-technical norms, etc.).

The reasons given for not reporting mostly had to do with the illegality of euthanasia: the burden for the doctor or the family of a criminal investigation played a major role in at least three-quarters of all cases (fear of prosecution in about a third). Half of all doctors gave as an important reason their opinion that euthanasia is a matter between doctor and patient.

Finally, Van der Wal's survey casts some quantitative light on the question, how often and under what circumstances GPs terminate life without an (explicit) request from the patient.[24] Nine percent of the respondents had done so one or more times (generally once or twice). Extrapolation leads to a national rate of about 100 cases per year by GPs (0.2% of all deaths in their practice). In 83% of these cases, it was no longer possible to communicate with the patient. In 28% the doctor thought he was carrying out the wishes of the patient. In half of the remaining cases, active termination of life took place at the

---

22 The rate of accurate reporting by GPs varied considerably between the different regions of the country (from 11% in some provinces to 35% in others); it seemed to be highest in the judicial district (Alkmaar) where the prosecutor's office had, since late 1985, had a clear policy of not prosecuting cases that met the emerging legal criteria (Van der Wal 1992: 107; see chapter 2.3.1 for this precursor of the current reporting procedure). The 1995 research confirmed the geographic variability in reporting: from 10% below the national rate to 20% above it (1996: 111).

23 1992: 106-107. A similar comparison done on the results of the 1990 research led Van der Wal to a reporting rate of 12% rather than the 28% that the doctors had claimed.

24 See Muller 1996 for these data.

urgent request of the patient's partner or family. In practically all cases, the doctor believed the patient to be suffering unbearably.[25]

EUTHANASIA AND ASSISTANCE WITH SUICIDE BY NURSING-HOME DOCTORS[26]

The survey of nursing-home doctors covered all of the more than 700 doctors registered as such.[27] Seventy-eight percent of these doctors reported discussing euthanasia or assistance with suicide with at least one patient per year in the period 1986-1990: 66% with 1-5 patients, 12% with more than that (2% with 21 or more patients per year).

Dutch nursing-home doctors received more than 300 explicit requests per year in the period 1986-1990, of which some 15% were for assistance with suicide. About two-fifths of the doctors had not had a single such request. About 7% of all requests for euthanasia and 22% of those for assistance with suicide were honored. The frequency of euthanasia and assistance with suicide in nursing homes seemed to have been stable over the preceding 5 years, amounting to roughly 0.1% of all deaths in nursing homes or about 25 cases per year. Twelve percent of all nursing-home doctors had performed euthanasia or assistance with suicide at least once.

As far as conformity with the 'requirements of careful practice' is concerned the picture was very similar to that for GPs: the substantive requirements seemed on the whole to be met, the procedural requirements often were not (41% full compliance). In more than half of all cases, no written request was obtained. Consultation, although common practice (85%), was more often than not with another doctor in the same nursing home or an otherwise not entirely independent colleague. The rate of accurate reporting was surprisingly high: after 1986 this had risen to over 60%. But the correlation between procedural lapses and non-reporting was strong.

Nurses were always involved in the care of nursing-home patients, and the doctors reported discussing the situation with them in all but 5% of the cases. Nurses were almost always present when the lethal drugs are administered (90%) but almost never carried out the euthanasia themselves.

---

25   Van der Wal (1992: 128) describes these situations as follows: "The patient – a very sick and dying (cancer) patient who is no longer able to express his wishes – is apparently suffering unbearably and hopelessly, and the family often cannot deal with the situation any longer; sometimes the nurses cannot cope either. The GP feels up against a wall; he sees no other way to put an end to the suffering than to end the patient's life."

26   See Muller 1996 (reporting the findings of Van der Wal and others).

27   The response-rate was 86%.

Five percent of the nursing-home doctors had at some point in their career terminated the life of a patient without an explicit request, usually once or twice.[28] Extrapolated, this amounts to some 10 cases per year (0.07% of the deaths in the practice of nursing-home doctors). In well over half of these cases the patient was suffering severely, and the patient was non-responsive in more than half. The doctor rarely knew the patient's wishes and in such cases often acted at the urgent request of the family.

5.3   Two major national surveys of MBSL

Van der Wal's results are important as the first reliable national quantitative data on the frequency and characteristics of euthanasia and assistance with suicide. His basic findings are confirmed in two national surveys carried out on behalf of the Government in 1990 and 1995. The three studies share some important shortcomings: the limitations of survey data as far as both the reliability of the answers and their interpretation is concerned (e.g., what is a 'request' in practice?), the one-sidedness of data derived only from doctors,[29] and the absence of data on the concrete context in which decisions are made (among other things, on organisational and normative features of the setting such as institutional policy – see section 5.4.2 below). Nevertheless, taken together they afford a wealth of information that is unique in the world.

In 1990 the Dutch Government commissioned the first major study of euthanasia practice, the results of which were published in English in 1992.[30] In 1995 a follow-up study was commissioned and its results were published in 1996.[31] The two studies covered not only euthanasia and assistance with suicide but also other medical behavior that shortens life.

The 1990 research was based on three different sources of information: interviews with a national sample of doctors; a sample of registered deaths; and a study of deaths in the practices of a national sample of doctors. The 1995 research was based on four sources:

---

28   A disturbing note in these findings concerns the doctor who reported 30 cases during his career and the doctor (possibly the same one) who reported 18 cases from 1986-1990 (Muller 1996: 95).

29   Concern with this state of affairs has recently induced the Association for Voluntary Euthanasia (NVVE) to carry out its own research on euthanasia practice from the patient's perspective. See section 5.4.1 below. See also The 1997 on the experience of nurses.

30   Van der Maas, Van Delden & Pijnenborg 1992 – in this chapter referred to simply as '1992'. The Dutch version was published in 1991.

31   Van der Wal & Van der Maas 1996 – in this chapter referred to simply as '1996'. Some of the most important findings of this research are published in English in Van der Maas et al. 1996, and Van der Wal et al. 1996.

interviews with a national sample of doctors (similar to 1990 but adding specific samples of pediatricians and psychiatrists); a sample of registered deaths (with a specific study of infant mortality); a study of reported cases (interviews with those involved, study of the dossiers, and study of the prosecutorial decision-making); and interviews with a variety of professional participants in the regulatory process. The research was carried out in both cases with admirable care and thoroughness.

'MEDICAL BEHAVIOR THAT SHORTENS LIFE' (MBSL)

One of the most important contributions the researchers have made to the political discussion concerning euthanasia has been to study it in the context of other kinds of what they call "medical decisions concerning the end of life" (MDEL), which as they operationalize it can be defined as behavior by a doctor that he knows will probably shorten the patient's life and that in fact does result in death.[32] For reasons we have seen in chapter 3.1.2, the term 'medical behavior that shortens life' (MBSL) is more satisfactory. The concept MBSL includes, apart from euthanasia and assistance with suicide: not initiating or terminating life-prolonging treatment, with or without the request of the patient (abstinence); administering, with or without a request, pain or symptom relieving drugs in doses known to be likely to cause death (pain relief); and termination of life without an explicit request.

THE INTENT OF THE DOCTOR

The researchers distinguish three levels of intentionality in the case of MBSL: the doctor may act with the "express purpose" of shortening life (hereafter referred to as 'express purpose'); he may act "partly with the purpose" of shortening life, that is, this is a subsidiary purpose associated with a primary intent to accomplish some other goal (e.g. relieving pain) (hereafter referred to as 'subsidiary purpose'); and he may act not with the purpose of shortening the patient's life but "taking into account the probability" that what he does for another reason (pain relief) will have that effect (hereafter referred to as 'accepting risk'). In the experience of the researchers, the first and third categories (well-

---

32   Van der Maas and his colleagues have on a number of occasions objected to such an interpretation of their concept MDEL and to our presentation of their results in terms of our concept MBSL. Their argument is that a MDEL is not, as they conceive it, necessarily a cause of death. As far as their definition of the term is concerned, of course they are right. What interests us, however, is its operationalization in their research. With two exceptions, a MDEL is in all their quantitative data a cause of death. The two exceptions are NTBR practice and refusals to perform euthanasia, both of which played only a marginal role in their 1990 research and can easily be defined in terms of the concept MBSL. Since it fits their quantitative data, we feel entitled to use the concept MBSL in presenting their results.

known from discussions about the 'doctrine of double effect', according to which the death is intentional in the former but not in the latter case, see chapter 4.1.2) are, in the case of pain relief, not sufficient to describe the range of intentionality actually encountered in research: "there were occasions when, in the opinion of the physician, neither description did justice to his intention".[33]

Although their analysis of the doctor's intent would seem equally applicable to abstinence and to pain relief, the researchers distinguish in practice between the two.[34] The doctor's intent in the case of abstinence from (further) life-prolonging treatment is divided into only the two extreme categories of 'accepting risk' and 'express purpose' and in both cases the death is treated as due to abstention. Deaths due to pain relief are, if the doctor's intent falls in the categories of 'accepting risk' and 'subsidiary purpose', treated as a by-product of pain relief. But pain relief administered with the 'express purpose' to shorten life, if done on request, is considered euthanasia, and if done without an explicit request from the patient, is considered part of a 'grey area' between pain relief and termination of life without an explicit request.[35]

---

33   1992: 21; see also 1996: 41. Benjaminsen (1988) reported earlier that doctors are, despite general agreement on the definition of 'euthanasia', vague and confused about its precise contours, in particular about the dividing line between euthanasia and death as a foreseen but not as such intended consequence of administering pain killers and about the fact that not initiating or terminating futile medical treatment does not constitute 'euthanasia'. The boundaries between these categories apparently do not correspond very well to the practical experience of many medical professionals. Melief notes (1991: 103-104) that the boundary between a natural death, hastened by pain killers, and euthanasia is a difficult one, so that euthanasia statistics will never be entirely reliable.

34   No explanation is given for this different treatment. It is apparently based on the subjective experience of doctors. One can surmise that such a difference in experience is based on the fact that euthanasia and pain relief both involve administration of a drug (often the same drug: morphine), whereas abstention involves a variety of behavior that mostly does not 'look like' administration of a euthanaticum. The moral or legal relevance of such subjective experiences seems dubious, and as Quill (1996), for example, shows, in practice they can be very relative.

35   1996: 92-93. This 'grey area' also includes cases that the doctor himself characterized as termination of life without an explicit request but where he also reported that he had not had the 'express purpose' to shorten life. The whole of the 'grey area' amounted to 2.0% of all deaths in 1990 and 1995 and is included by Van der Wal and Van der Maas in the data given for pain relief.

5.3.1 Euthanasia and other MBSL: frequencies, circumstances and characteristics[36]

The 1990 and 1995 studies offer a wealth of information concerning the frequency, circumstances and characteristics of various MBSL. Table 5.2 summarizes the frequencies of the various sorts of MBSL.

Table 5.2 Estimates of frequencies of MBSL, 1990 and 1995 (percentages of all deaths)

	1990		1995	
	%	N	%	N
euthanasia:				
– death on request	1.8	2300	2.4	3200
– assistance with suicide	0.3	400	0.3	400
termination of life without an explicit request	0.8	1000	0.7	900
death due to pain relief	17.5	22500	18.5	25100
– accepting risk	14.0	18000	15.5	21000
– subsidiary purpose	3.5	4500	3	4100
death due to abstinence	17.5	22500	20	27100
– accepting risk	9	11500	7	9500
– express purpose	8.5	11000	13	17600
total MBSL	38	48700	42	56700
total deaths in the Netherlands	100	128800	100	135500

Source: Table received from prof. Van der Maas and based on an integration of data from: Van der Maas et al. 1991, 1992, 1996; Van der Wal et al. 1996; Van der Wal & Van der Maas 1996; CBS 1996. The table will appear in G. van der Wal, *Euthanasie in Nederland* (forthcoming, Houten: Bohn, Stafleu & Van Loghum).

In 1995, almost 60,000 deaths per year resulted from a decision of a doctor that the doctor knew would probably shorten the patient's life; as in 1990, this is about two-fifths of all deaths. When we exclude cases of sudden and unexpected death in which there is no possibility of any such medical intervention,[37] a MBSL is the immediate cause of death in more than half of all deaths. In short, the precise time at which a patient's death occurs is

---

36   Unless otherwise indicated, Van der Maas, Van Delden & Pijnenborg 1992 and Van der Wal & Van der Maas 1996 are the source of all quantitative data in this section.

37   This is estimated at about a third of all deaths (1992: 194).

often advanced by something a doctor does with the foresight that it will probably have such an effect. The shortening of life involved, as estimated by the doctors themselves, ranges from hours to weeks or even months, but is usually quite limited (see table 5.11). Apart from the modest role of euthanasia and assistance with suicide in the total – about 5% of all MBSL – the general picture seems to be the same as estimates with regard to 'physician-negotiated death' in the United States and Australia.[38]

The overall rate of MBSL increased between 1990 and 1995, confirming the prediction made in the report of the 1990 research. Van der Wal and Van der Maas expect a further increase over the coming years and for the same reasons: the increasing proportion of elderly persons in the population, the increasing average age at death, the increasing importance of cancer as a cause of death, and the increasing possibilities of life-prolonging technology.[39]

Relative to death due to pain relief or to abstention, euthanasia and assistance with suicide are infrequent. Nevertheless, the frequency of death due to euthanasia increased significantly in both absolute and relative terms from 1990 to 1995 (assistance with suicide remained unchanged). This cannot be entirely attributed either to the increased total number of deaths per year nor to the increasing role of cancer as a cause of death. Van der Wal and Van der Maas suspect that part of the explanation lies in the increased willingness of doctors to ascribe to themselves a 'heavier' intent when administering lethal doses of pain relief.[40] But as table 5.3 shows, the number of *requests* for euthanasia and assistance with suicide also increased substantially in this period; and the rate of requests honored increased from 30% in 1990 to 37% in 1995.

However rare they may be as a cause of death, as table 5.3 shows, euthanasia and assistance with suicide have become a rather 'normal' part of Dutch medical practice. There are currently almost 10,000 concrete requests per year for euthanasia (including assistance with suicide), of which about 6000 are not carried out, half of these because the doctor declines and most of the rest because the patient dies before the request can be carried out.[41] The number of requests 'in general terms' increased 37% and the number of concrete requests 9% between 1990 and 1995. Van der Wal and Van der Maas see cultural changes, with younger generations increasingly inclined to request euthanasia or assistance with suicide, as the basic cause of this increase in the frequency of requests.[42]

---

38   See chapter 1, note 23.
39   1996: 93.
40   1996: 94.
41   1996: 61.
42   1996: 93.

Table 5.3 Euthanasia experience of different sorts of doctor, 1990/1995
(percentages of all doctor per category)

	GP	nursing-home doctor	specialist	all doctors
communication concerning euthanasia and assistance with suicide				
ever discussed with patient	98/99	85/85	89/90	95/96
ever a concrete request	80/85	57/62	71/64	76/77
estimated number of requests per year (N)				
requests in general terms	15700/26900	450/300	8950/7200	25100/34500
concrete requests	5200/6400	230/300	3470/3000	8900/9700
euthanasia practice				
ever carried out	62/63	12/21	44/37	54/53
(last 24 months)	(28/38)	(6/3)	(20/16)	(24/29)
never carried out/willing	28/28	60/64	40/43	34/35
unwilling/would refer	6/7	26/10	9/15	8/9
unwilling	3/2	2/5	8/4	4/3
ever refused (1990)[1]	44	46	46	44
(last 24 months)	(30)	(29)	(29)	(30)

1. Comparable data not available for 1995.
Source: interview study, 1992: 39-40; 1996: 51-52.

Almost all doctors have discussed euthanasia or assistance with suicide with a patient, most doctors have been confronted with a concrete request, more than half of all doctors have honored such a request, and almost half have refused to do so at some time. About 90% of Dutch doctors have either carried out euthanasia or would be willing to do so, and most of the rest say they would refer a patient who requests it to another doctor. These figures remained essentially unchanged from 1990 to 1995.[43]

From the 1995 research[44] it appears that roughly a third of all requests were refused by the doctor. In three-quarters of these cases of refusal, the request was emphatic, and in a third of the cases it was in writing (in 1990: a fifth). The most important reasons mentioned by doctors for their refusal were the existence of alternatives (including pain relief), the doctor's judgment that the patient's suffering was not unbearable, and doubts about the patient's competence (each of these was mentioned in about a third of the cases); doubts concerning the well-consideredness of the request (mentioned in about a quarter of the cases); and concerns that the request was made under pressure from family or close friends or was otherwise not voluntary (mentioned in about a tenth of the cases). A handful of doctors mentioned fear of legal consequences. In only 4% of the cases of refusal (in 1990: 19%) did the doctor say he had principled objections to euthanasia or assistance with suicide in general.

While looked at in the aggregate euthanasia may have become a normal part of Dutch medical practice, it appears from table 5.3 that there are important differences in the euthanasia experience of the three relevant categories of Dutch doctors: GPs, nursing-

------

43   According to Melief (1991), opponents of euthanasia seem to be distinguishable into a group of ideological opponents (who deny that there is a serious problem of untreatable suffering) and opponents who acknowledge that some patients earnestly desire euthanasia and that there are no real medical alternatives but are themselves not willing to perform it. Table 5.3 suggests that the former group amounts to less than 5% of all Dutch doctors, the latter group to less than 10%.

70% of all doctors say that their attitude toward euthanasia has not changed over the last 5 years, and three-fifths of the rest have become more permissive; 80% have not changed with regard to assistance with suicide, and two-thirds of the rest have become more permissive; 90% have not changed with regard to termination of life without an explicit request, and the rest are equally divided between more permissive and more restrictive. (Interestingly, such changes in opinion are far more pronounced in the case of prosecutors, and strongly in the direction of more permissiveness.) (1996: 175)

Less than a third of all doctors consider assistance with suicide acceptable in the case of very old people who are 'tired of living'. As in the case of psychiatric patients (see note 100), doctors are less permissive in this regard than prosecutors (1996: 174).

44   1996: 60-63.

home doctors and specialists (see the *Intermezzo* on these categories). Across the board, GPs have the most experience with euthanasia and assistance with suicide: in 1995 they received 66% of all requests and performed 74% of all euthanasia and 98% of all assistance with suicide. They also express the greatest willingness to honor the requests of their patients. Specialists exhibit a similar pattern at a slightly lower level (31% of all requests, 26% of all euthanasia, 2% of all assistance with suicide). The impression that was generally held before the study and confirmed in Van der Wal's earlier research – that euthanasia plays a relatively small role in the practice of nursing-home doctors – is plainly correct: they receive only 3% of all requests and almost never agree to carry it out.[45]

The differences between the different categories of doctors become more complicated and interesting if we look at the frequency of MBSL in their practice. Table 5.4 gives the key data in this respect. The bottom line of table 5.4 seems to give the opposite impression from that of table 5.3: the total frequency of MBSL is lowest in the case of GPs and highest in that of nursing-home doctors. The reason is simple: nursing-home doctors perform far less euthanasia than GPs but they cause death by administering pain relief rather more frequently than GPs and the rate at which they cause death by stopping or

Table 5.4 Frequencies of MBSL per category of doctor, 1990/1995 (percentages of all deaths per category)

	GP	nursing-home doctor	specialist	all docs.
euthanasia (including termination of life without an explicit request[1])	4/5	0/1	3/3	3/3
death due to pain relief	17/18	25/27	19/17	19/19
– accepting risk	13/15	21/25	15/14	15/16
– subsidiary purpose	4/3	4/2	4/3	4/3
death due to abstinence	13/11	31/35	19/24	18/20
– accepting risk	7/5	17/12	9/7	9/7
– express purpose	8/6	14/23	10/17	9/13
total MBSL	34/34	56/64	40/45	39/43

1. This aggregation of two very different categories of MBSL is an unfortunate feature of the way in which the data from the registered-death study are presented.

Source: registered-death study, 1996: 108.

_____

45   See table 5.3 and 1996: 52.

not initiating treatment is almost twice that of GPs. We see here the first indication that differences in the rate of 'euthanasia' may reflect not so much real difference in substance as a different characterization of what is taking place.[46]

NTBR PRACTICE[47]

If we look at prospective decisions to abstain from treatment (NTBR or DNR decisions, from the inscriptions 'Not To Be Reanimated' or 'Do Not Reanimate' on the patient's chart[48]), we seem to see differences between different sorts of doctors similar to those in the case of euthanasia. Such a decision involves an instruction (generally in writing), addressed to the nursing personnel or to other doctors, not to intervene in the case of a specified sort of life-threatening situation (such as cardiac arrest). A NTBR decision does not necessarily result in the death of the patient: the life-threatening situation may not

Table 5.5 NTBR practice of different categories of doctor, 1990
(percentages of all doctors per category)

	GP	nursing home doctor	specialist
never reanimate/resuscitate	4	40	–
ever made a NTBR decision (last year)	21 (15)	40 (33)	100 (96)
in principle prepared	69	18	–
would never make such a decision	6	2	–
total NTBR	3000	3100	91000

Source: interview study, 1992: 91.

---

46   Before reaching such a conclusion one would have to take account of differences in the patient populations (the average age at death in a nursing home is high, and euthanasia is rare above age 75; the frequency of death due to cancer, with which euthanasia is strongly associated, is lower in nursing homes than in the case of GPs; about half of the population of nursing homes is not competent to make a request for euthanasia) (Van der Wal 1993: 448). On the other hand, nursing homes are known to have relatively restrictive internal policies with respect to euthanasia (see section 5.4.2 below).

47   NTBR practice was only covered in the 1990 research.

48   Strictly speaking, reanimation covers only cardiopulmonary treatment if the patient's heart or breathing stops. But prospective decisions not to administer antibiotics in the case of pneumonia, for example, are also an important sort of MBSL. It is not entirely clear if all anticipatory decisions to abstain or only the two sorts mentioned in the text were covered in the 1990 research (see 1992: 17, 75, 118-119, 148).

materialize, the patient may not die from it, or intervention may take place despite the instruction. Nevertheless, as table 5.5 shows, the sheer size of NTBR practice makes it important to include it in any discussion of medical decisions that affect the moment of death.

Two things, in particular, attract attention: First, 40% of all nursing-home doctors said, when asked about their NTBR practice, that the question is not applicable to them because in their institution reanimation/resuscitation *never* takes place (presumably this means: in the case of otherwise dying patients). Second, more than 90,000 NTBR decisions were taken in hospitals in 1990; this amounts to about 6% of all admissions. In about 60% of all deaths for which a specialist was the responsible doctor, a NTBR decision had been taken.[49]

THE 'REQUIREMENTS OF CAREFUL PRACTICE'

Essentially all doctors were by 1990 aware of the substantive conditions and procedural safeguards applicable to euthanasia.[50]

The substantive conditions (voluntariness of the request, unbearable and hopeless suffering) were regarded as (very) important in both 1990 and 1995 by over 95% of all doctors, as was the technical quality of the method used, and over 90% considered informing the patient with regard to the diagnosis, prognosis and possible treatment (very) important. About 80% regarded an incurable disease as (very) important, two-thirds to three-quarters the absence of a treatment alternative, and somewhat over half thought the patient must be in the 'terminal phase' (as we have seen in chapter 3.1.3, none of these is in fact a legal requirement).

---

49 1992: 187. A recent publication of further findings of the 1995 research (Van der Heide et al. 1997) deals with decisions not (artificially) to feed or hydrate a patient (compare chapter 3.1.2 note 11 and 3.4.4 on 'letting oneself die' [*versterven*]). It seems that about 8% of all deaths in the Netherlands are preceded by such a decision (nursing homes: 23%; GPs and specialists: 4%). About two-thirds of the patients concerned were 80 or older and three-quarters were partly or wholly incompetent. The decision to abstain was discussed with the family in 82% of the cases (nursing-hime doctors: 89%).

50 1992: 95-96. Melief concluded in 1991 (see note 1 above) that legal knowledge concerning euthanasia was gradually penetrating to the shop-floor of medical practice. By contrast with the situation less than a decade earlier (see chapter 2.2), 'euthanasia' was used by medical personnel in the technical sense introduced by the State Commission (killing on request; assistance with suicide). The criteria for euthanasia as formulated by doctors corresponded closely to those that had emerged in the national political and legal discussion (explicit request, unbearable suffering, lack of alternatives) except that doctors tended to regard a 'terminal illness' as required.

Doctors' opinions concerning the importance of the procedural requirements surrounding euthanasia were less congruent with legal expectations as formulated in the
'requirements of careful practice'. Both consultation with a colleague and keeping a written record were regarded as (very) important by three-quarters of the doctors in 1995,
up from just above and rather below two-thirds, respectively, in 1990. Informing the relatives was regarded as (very) important by three-quarters of the doctors in both years.
Including nursing personnel in the decision-making was deemed (very) important by
rather less than half of all doctors.[51] Almost half of all doctors (almost three-quarters of
all nursing-home doctors) were of the opinion that if the patient is capable of carrying it
out, assistance with suicide is preferable to euthanasia.[52] Opinions concerning the
reporting procedure in effect since 1991 are discussed in section 5.3.5 below: in 1995,
about two-thirds of the doctors were generally positive but most doctors would have
preferred a non-criminal system of control.

The question remains to what extent doctors are actually conforming with the 'requirements of careful practice'. In general, as table 5.6 shows, the answer is that the level of
conformity is rather high in the case of euthanasia but that comparable procedural care
is far more problematic in the case of the other forms of MBSL.[53]

Euthanasia and assistance with suicide require by definition an explicit request from the
patient; the doctor considered this request 'entirely that of the patient himself' in almost
all cases.[54] The interview data give a higher rate of written requests than the registered
death data on table 5.6: 43% in 1990, 70% in 1995.[55]

---

51   See 1996: 158-159.

52   1996: 174.

53   There is some sketchy data from 1990 on two other related situations: refusals of euthanasia
     and NTBR decisions. In the case of refusals, there was discussion with another doctor in 45%,
     with nursing staff in 18%, with the patient's partner in 16% and with other family members
     in 15% (1992: 53). NTBR decisions were discussed with the patient by specialists in 30% of
     the cases in which this would have been possible, by nursing-home doctors in 17% of these
     cases. A colleague was consulted in about three-quarters of all cases of a NTBR decision
     (1992: 92-93).

54   1992: 57 (1990: 99%; 1995: 98%). Hendin (1997: 52) refers to a 'finding' of the 1990 research
     to the effect that "the doctor was often the person who first raised the subject". There is no
     such finding in the report. What there is, is the *opinion* of about half of all doctors (1990: 54%;
     1995: 56%) that "There are certain situations in which it is appropriate for the doctor to intro-
     duce the possibility of euthanasia." (1996: 174) The later somewhat less irresponsible claim by
     Hendin et al. (1997: 1721) that these Dutch doctors find it appropriate to "suggest" euthana-
     sia does not do justice to the phrasing of the question put to them, which had to do with being
     sure that the subject was explicitly discussed, not influencing the patient's decision.

55   1996: 57.

Table 5.6 Procedural safeguards in the case of various MBSL, 1990/1995 (percentages of deaths per cause of death)

cause of death	discussion with				written	
	patient	family	other doctor	nursing staff	record[1]	request
euthanasia (incl. assistance with suicide)	[100]	86/70[2]	84/83[2]	39/33	60/85	35/59
termination of life without an explicit request	46/37	84/70	69/59	64/66	[3]	1/–
death due to pain relief						
– accepting risk	30/33[4]	44/47	34/30	34/29	[3]	1/4
– subsidiary purpose	53/52[4]	69/65	51/36	57/34		6/11
death due to abstinence						
- accepting risk	24/29[5]	55/57	41/41	47/42	[3]	2/4
- express purpose	36/37[5]	77/73	55/58	64/51		2/5

1. Interview data.
2. The interview data for consultation with a colleague and with the family are, respectively, 84/92 and 94/93.
3. Not available.
4. There was a specific request from the patient in 14%/14% (accepting risk) and 29%/36% (subsidiary purpose).
5. There was a specific request from the patient in 12%/15% (accepting risk) and 23%/21% (express purpose).
Source: registered death study (except where noted), 1992: 63; 1996: 57-58, 60-61, 70-71, 80-81, 87-88; CBS 1996: 46-47.

In the case of other MBSL, involvement of the patient is not effectively guaranteed. This applies especially to the case of decisions not to initiate or not to continue treatment (except when at the request of the patient): it appears that in 22% of these cases the doctor considered the patient 'entirely' capable of deciding for him- or herself and in another 21% the patient was at least partly capable, but the decision was in fact only discussed with the patient in 13% of these cases (in 18% of the cases, the patient had at some earlier point indicated his wishes).[56] Specialists and nursing-home doctors seldom discuss a proposed NTBR decision with a patient: even in cases in which the patient (according to the doctor) was fully capable of making a decision, they did not discuss the matter with the patient a third of the time.[57]

---

56   Interview study, 1992: 88. The 1995 data are presented in a way that is not entirely comparable (see 1996: 87).
57   Interview study, 1992: 92; see also 1991: 74-75. No NTBR data are available for 1995.

The family is usually included in discussions concerning euthanasia and termination of life without an explicit request, far less so in the case of the other MBSL. A colleague is usually consulted in the case of euthanasia, less than half the time in the case of other MBSL.

Discussion with nursing staff took place in about a third of all cases of euthanasia, which is about the same as for pain relief and rather lower than for abstinence. In the case of termination of life without an explicit request, such discussion is far more common.[58] Virtually across the board, the frequency of discussion with nursing staff declined between 1990 and 1995.[59] From recent qualitative research it appears that the communication between doctors and nurses concerning euthanasia is marked by tensions and misunderstandings.[60]

Written requests and record-keeping are rare except in the case of euthanasia, where the situation has improved considerably since 1990.[61] Reporting of euthanasia, and especially of termination of life without an explicit request is, as we will see in section 5.3.5, still very problematic.

CONSULTATION[62]

Table 5.6 gives the findings from the registered-deaths studies of the frequency with which the doctor discusses a MBSL with another doctor before carrying it out. More detailed (and slightly different) information, in which formal consultation is distinguished from mere discussion, is available for 1995 from the interview study. In 92% of the cases of euthanasia (including assistance with suicide), the doctor said he had discussed the case with a colleague and in 79% there had been formal consultation; formal consultation was far more common in reported (99%) than in non-reported cases (18%), and in a third of the latter there was no discussion at all with another doctor. In the case of termination of life without an explicit request, there was discussion in 43%, of which only 3% was formal consultation.

58　The differences in frequencies probably reflect primarily the influence of the place where patients die: euthanasia is largely an affair of GPs, where nursing staff is usually less closely involved in treatment.

59　Compare section 5.2 for the situation in the late 1980s.

60　See Pool 1996 and The 1997 (both based on observation research in large Dutch hospitals).

61　The same applies to refusals of euthanasia: there were written requests in 19% of these cases in 1990, 34% in 1995 (1996: 61).

62　See 1996: 99-109.

The consulted doctor is seldom entirely independent. In the case of GPs, only 19% were entirely independent; 70% were members of the same local (substitution) group, 5% colleagues in a joint practice, 5% involved in the treatment of the patient. In the case of specialists, only 5% were entirely independent; 48% were colleagues in the same institution, 30% colleagues in a joint practice, 4% involved in the treatment of the patient and 3% personal friends. The consulted doctor usually (75%) did not know the patient beforehand, and if he did, this was mostly from having substituted for the patient's regular GP (16%) or, in the case of specialists, from having been involved in the patient's treatment (13%).

Forty-one percent of the doctors interviewed had at some time been asked to function as consultant. Asked about the last occasion on which they had done so, the consultants gave the following answers:

Table 5.7 Activities of consulted doctors, 1995 (percentages of last cases)

	GP	specialist	total
talk with patient	89	72	86
study dossier	64	85	69
talk with responsible GP	64	67	65
talk with family/friends	48	37	46
physical examination	36	33	35
talk with another doctor	13	11	12
written report	89	91	89

Source: interview study, 1996: 104.

As table 5.7 shows, according to the consultant he almost always talked with or examined the patient and talked to the responsible doctor or studied the dossier. About 90% of the time he made a written report of his findings.

The consulting doctor was very rarely (4%) still in doubt as to his own position when he requested consultation, and the consultant never disagreed.[63] However, these results concern cases in which euthanasia was carried out. Asked if they had ever been advised not to carry out euthanasia, a small number (7%) of the respondents said that they had; three-fourths of them had followed the advice. Consulted doctors report disagreeing with the proposed euthanasia almost a fifth of the time (their doubts concerned the patient's request, the suffering and the existence of alternatives); and according to them their judgment is followed over 90% of the time.

---

63   Nevertheless, doctors (especially specialists) report their judgment having been influenced by the consultant in about two-fifths of all cases.

Although data on the frequency and characteristics of consultation are not available from the 1990 study, such data are available for GPs from Van der Wal's study of euthanasia and assistance with suicide.[64] Comparison of those findings with the findings of the 1995 research confirms that the rate of consultation did not substantially increase between 1990 and 1995.[65] However, Van der Wal and Van der Maas conclude, consultation had become considerably more professional: the rate of written reports had increased from 31% to 89%, the rates both of personal examination of the patient and of a reasonable degree of independence (consultant not a member of a joint practice, involved in the treatment, or a resident) had increased from 54% to 91%.

CARRYING OUT EUTHANASIA

Melief[66] observed of euthanasia practice in the late 1980s, that three ways of carrying out euthanasia could be distinguished: a 'quick' method involving a combination of intravenously administered drugs from which the patient dies within a half hour, a 'slow' method involving very high doses of morphine from which the patient dies within several hours to a couple of days, and a method by which the patient himself administers the lethal drug (sometimes followed by a second euthanaticum administered by the doctor). There was some verbal preference for the latter method, but in practice it was rarely used.[67] The 'quick' method was used in institutions with an established procedure for euthanasia and, occasionally, by GPs; such cases were virtually always reported as 'non-natural' deaths. The 'slow' method was used in institutions without an established procedure and, in most cases, by GPs; death was generally reported as 'natural'. The proponents of the 'quick' method regarded it as medically irresponsible to use morphine as a euthanaticum: to do so creates confusion between relieving pain and euthanasia; the process of dying is difficult to control (in one of the cases described, the patient actually reawakened after the 'lethal' dose); and, because the method takes so long, the family cannot all be present together. Proponents of the 'slow' method regarded the gradualness of the process as an advantage, and they found such a death more 'natural' because less controlled.

It appears from the interview studies that the way in which euthanasia is carried out became rather more professional between 1990 and 1995.[68] The most appropriate euthanaticum, a muscle relaxant, was used alone or in combination with another drug (such

64   Philipsen, Van der Wal & Van Eijk 1994 (see section 5.2).
65   1996: 108-109.
66   See note 1 above on Melief's research.
67   In only one of the cases described did death take place in this way; in several other cases, euthanatica had been made available to the patient but were ultimately not used.
68   1996: 58-59.

as morphine) in 90% of all cases in 1995, whereas in 1990 this had been only 53%. Morphine, generally not considered an appropriate euthanaticum, was used alone or in combination with other drugs (other than muscle relaxants) 8% of the time in 1995, down from 24% in 1990. In 1990, assistance with suicide was usually carried out with sedatives (72%) or morphine (12%) alone; in 1995 these accounted for only 47% and in the other 53% morphine combined with another drug was used. The time between administration and death (in the case of euthanasia) declined markedly: in 1990 67% died within an hour, 27% more within a day and the remaining 7% within a week; in 1995 these figures were 85%, 11% and 3%.

The level of acceptance of administration of a euthanaticum by a nurse under instructions from the responsible doctor may be declining. Only 10% of Dutch doctors (7% of GPs and 17% of specialists) now consider this legitimate.[69] Van der Wal's research (see section 5.2) gives as of 1990 a frequency of actual administration by a nurse of 4% for GPs and 21% for specialists.

There are usually other persons than the doctor present when euthanasia is carried out. According to Van der Wal's research, a GP is alone in only 3% of the cases. Most frequently present together with the doctor are the patient's partner (78%), children (62%) and other family or intimate friends. A visiting nurse or other professional is much less often present (13% and 17%).[70]

CHARACTERISTICS OF PERSONS WHO DIE AS A RESULT OF A MBSL

In the literature concerning euthanasia there has been considerable controversy concerning the medical possibilities of treating pain but it seems now to be widely accepted that in some residual category (often estimated at about 5%) pain cannot effectively be treated. As Van der Wal had found earlier (see section 5.2), pain is not the main reason people request euthanasia. It was considered by the doctor one of the reasons for the patient's request in 32% of the cases in 1995 (in 1990 this was 48%) and in no case was pain the only reason. The pointlessness of the pain (44%) and the prospect of more or worsening pain (47%) were more important, as was the wish to avoid inhuman deterioration (*ontluistering*) (56%, essentially the same as in 1990).[71]

The following tables give some basic characteristics of persons who die as a result of a MBSL. The data given are for 1995 but, except where noted, do not differ significantly from those of 1990; they are based on the study of registered deaths. (The total number

---

69   1996: 172.
70   1992: 97-98.
71   1996: 57.

of cases of assistance with suicide is too small to warrant separate analysis; they have been included under euthanasia on tables 5.8 through 5.11.)

Table 5.8 Persons whose death results from a MBSL: Age, 1995
(percentages of all deaths per MBSL)

	euthanasia/assistance with suicide	termination of life without an explicit request	pain relief	abstinence	all deaths
0-49	10	18	6	4	8
50-64	27	16	16	10	12
65-79	41	31	38	31	36
≥80	20	36	40	55	44

Source: registered deaths study, 1996: 54, 68, 79, 85.

Age at death for persons who die from euthanasia is notably younger than for persons generally (some 37% below age 65, as against 20%), and relatively few persons above 80 die from euthanasia (20% as against 44%); the same is true, albeit to a lesser degree, for termination of life without an explicit request. Age at death due to pain relief is about the same as that for persons generally. And death due to abstinence is relatively frequent among the very elderly.

Table 5.9 Persons whose death results from a MBSL: Sex, 1995
(percentages of all deaths per MBSL)

	euthanasia/assistance with suicide	termination of life without an explicit request	pain relief	abstinence	all deaths
M	45	49	50	42	50
F	55	51	50	58	50

Source: registered deaths study, 1996: 54, 68, 79, 85.

Women died as a result of euthanasia slightly more often than men in 1995. Since the results of the 1990 research were precisely the other way around (men: 58%), and the interview study and the study of reported cases also give the opposite result, Van der Wal and Van der Maas conclude that this finding should be regarded as accidental.[72] Deaths due to abstinence involve women rather more often than men (the difference is some-

---

72 1996: 55.

what greater than it was in 1990: 54% women); as Van der Wal and Van der Maas note[73] this may be due to the fact that in the highest age-category (where most of this MBSL occurs) there are far more women than men.

Table 5.10 Persons whose death results from a MBSL: Disease, 1995 (percentages of all deaths per MBSL)

	euthanasia/ assistance with suicide	termination of life without an explicit request	pain relief	abstinence	all deaths
cancer	80	40	54	24	27
heart/circulatory disorders	3	5	12	16	29
nervous system (incl. strokes)	4	22	8	18	11
pulmonary	2	7	7	12	9
other	11	26	19	30	24

Source: registered deaths study, 1996: 54, 68, 79, 85.

Cancer is by far the most common disease from which patients who die from euthanasia suffer; euthanasia is, on the other hand, uncommon among those suffering from the other major cause of death: heart and circulatory disorders. Cancer also plays a major, if apparently diminishing, role in the case of termination of life without an explicit request (in 1990 this percentage had been over 60%); diseases of the nervous system are the second most frequently associated with termination of life without an explicit request (but this may be accidental, since in 1990 the comparable figure was only 2% and in the interview study it was 9%).[74] Cancer is the most frequent disease of those who die from pain relief, with heart and circulatory disorders second in importance. By contrast with the other MBSL, cancer is far less common among those who died due to abstinence: the distribution of diseases here approximates that of all deaths.

---

73 1996: 85.
74 1996: 67-68.

Table 5.11 *Persons whose death results from a MBSL: Estimated shortening of life, 1995 (percentages of all deaths per MBSL)*

	euthanasia/ assistance with suicide	termination of life without an explicit request	pain relief	abstinence
unknown	–	–	15	7
none or <24 hours	17	33	64	42
1-7 days	42	58	16	28
1-4 weeks	32	3	4	15
>1 month	9	6	1	7

Source: registered deaths study, 1996: 54, 68, 79, 85.

The extent to which life was shortened by various MBSL, as estimated by the doctor concerned, is relatively great for euthanasia (and seems to be even greater for assistance with suicide), but nevertheless in 90% of the cases is a month or less. The estimated shortening in the case of termination without an explicit request is much less: in 90% of the cases a week or less. The estimated shortening of life due to pain relief is the least of all MBSL: in almost two-thirds of the cases it was a day or less (in a case of 'subsidiary purpose' there were about twice as many cases in which the shortening fell in the range 1-7 days). Shortening of life due to abstinence is usually a week or less; however, it is rather less if the intent is to 'accept the risk' of death than if there is a 'subsidiary purpose' to bring about death – in the former case, the estimated shortening was a day or less 53% of the time, whereas all the longer estimates were several percent higher in the latter case.

Finally, the research produced data on the treatment situation of the patient for cases of euthanasia (together with assistance with suicide) and termination of life without an explicit request. At the time the decision to carry out euthanasia is made, current treatment is only palliative almost 90% of the time; in another 10% it is aimed at prolonging life but not at cure. In about 80% of the cases there are no longer any treatment alternatives; in almost all of the remaining cases the patient does not want further treatment. In the case of termination of life without an explicit request, there are no treatment alternatives more than 80% of the time; in about 75% of the cases pain relief in the form of morphine or the like was being given but in about half the cases it was not effective.[75]

---

75   1996: 56, 69.

5.3.2   Termination of life without an explicit request[76]

From table 5.2 it appears that slightly less than 1% of all deaths are due to the doctor having terminated the life of the patient without the latter explicitly requesting this (the
researchers estimate a total of 1000 deaths in 1990 and 900 in 1995, but the difference is
not statistically significant).[77]

Table 5.12 gives some further information on the frequency of this category of MBSL in
the practice of Dutch doctors.

Table 5.12 Termination of life without an explicit request, 1990 and 1995
(percentages of doctors interviewed)

	1990	1995
ever performed	27	23
(performed in 1994/1995)	(10)	(11)
never performed/conceivably willing	32	32
unwilling	41	45

Source: interview study, 1996: 65.

The researchers and the Government regard this category as highly troublesome and
they consider it an important objective of policy to reduce its incidence.[78] However, as
we have seen in chapter 3.3.4, the category is quite heterogeneous. Not all of its compo-
nent parts are necessarily legally problematic. Included in the category are:[79]

– a very small number of severely defective newborn babies;[80]
– a very small number of coma patients;[81]

---

76   Except where otherwise noted, this section is based on 1996: 64-74.
77   Of the 1000 cases in 1990, 710 were by specialists, 270 by GPs and 50 by nursing-home doc-
     tors (Muller: 97). The latter two figures are several times higher than the estimates of 100 and
     10 found in the research of Van der Wal and his colleagues in the late 1980s (see section 5.2).
     See Van der Wal 1992: 127-128 for possible explanations of these differences.
78   See 1996: 236; 'Standpunt van het Kabinet naar aanleiding van de evaluatie van de meldings-
     procedure euthanasie [Position of the Cabinet with regard to the evaluation of the reporting
     procedure for euthanasia],' January 1997.
79   Since the numbers are very small, no significance can be attributed to small differences
     between, for example, 1990 and 1995 or between GPs and specialists; the data given below are
     for 1995 and except where otherwise stated, are for GPs and specialists together.
80   Some 15 per year: see section 5.3.3.
81   A fraction of some 100 long-term coma cases per year: see section 5.4.4.

– a very small number of cases of inhabitants of institutions for the mentally handicapped;[82]
– a small number of cases of dementia;[83]
– a relatively large number of very sick or dying (cancer) patients who are no longer able to make their will known, and who are clearly suffering severely.[84]

Not only are patients of very different sorts involved, the nature of the treatment situation and the degree of involvement of the patient or a surrogate can be very different. Thus 'termination of life without an explicit request' includes:

– an unknown number of cases of 'help in dying' (*stervenshulp*), in which a MBSL (usually abstaining from further treatment) has already been taken, and a lethal drug is administered to speed up the final throes of dying;[85]
– a large number of cases – about half of the entire category – in which there had been some discussion with the patient (who, however, often was not fully competent) or the patient had expressed a general wish for euthanasia at some earlier time;
– a number of cases in which the parent or some other (legal) representative of the patient requested, or agreed to, the termination of life.

The most frequent reasons given by the doctors concerned for having terminated the patient's life in the absence of a request was that all further treatment had become pointless (67%) and that there was no prospect of improvement (44%). Other reasons – each given by about a third of the doctors – were the presumed will of the patient, the limited quality of life, the wish not to prolong the dying process any further, and the fact that the family/friends could not bear the situation any longer.

In about four-fifths of the cases, the patient was not (fully) competent, and in almost all cases this is the reason the doctor did not discuss the matter with the patient (the

---

82 On the order of 1 per year: see section 5.4.4.

83 Apparently on the order of 30-130 cases per year: in 1990, the reason there had been no discussion with the patient was dementia in 3% of all cases of termination of life without a request; in 1995 this was 14% (1996: 70).

84 See 1992: 194; cf. 1996: 70.

85 This situation apparently accounts for only a very small number of cases of termination of life without an explicit request, although the data are not unambiguous on this point (as an important reason for active termination of life, "treatment was stopped but the patient did not die" was mentioned by the doctor in 2% of all cases of termination of life without an explicit request, see 1996: 72). In the case of newborn babies, the situation is relatively common (though the numbers are very small), but it is included there in the category of 'natural death' – thus not in that of termination of life without an explicit request (see section 5.3.3).

researchers came across two cases in which the doctor terminated the life of a competent patient without discussing the matter, but the reasons for this could not be ascertained).

In rather more than half of the cases of termination of life without an explicit request (GPs: 11%; specialists: 90%), the doctor discussed the case with another doctor; the same applies to discussion with nursing personnel (GPs: 37%; specialists: 72%). In over two-thirds of the cases there was discussion with family/friends. Only among GPs were there some doctors (18%) who had discussed the case with none of these.

The researchers consider that in most respects most of these cases resemble death due to administration of pain relief more than they do euthanasia.[86] The shortening of life is estimated by the doctors in a third of the cases as less than a day and in less than 10% as more than a week – notably less than in the case of euthanasia. In 65% of the cases only morphine or the like was used, and in only 8% were muscle relaxants used, whereas in the case of euthanasia muscle relaxants are now used 90% of the time. The time-span from the beginning of termination of life to the moment of death is more than a day in a third of the cases, which is considerably longer than in the case of euthanasia.

A small number of these cases (apparently 6% or less) are of quite a different nature, involving patients with a life expectancy of more than a month who appear to be suffering greatly, whose suffering cannot be relieved in any other way, and who are not capable of making their wishes known.[87]

These cases are essentially never reported to the authorities as such, but always as a 'natural death'. The most commonly cited reason for this (mentioned as relevant in the most recent case of this MBSL by 44% of the doctors) is that the doctor considers the death a 'natural' one. Saving himself or the relatives the burden of a criminal investigation was mentioned as relevant in roughly a third of such cases, failure to meet all of the 'requirements of careful practice' in 15%, and fear of prosecution in only 9%.[88]

---

86   In fact, they recharacterized about half the cases initially reported to them as termination of life without an explicit request as deaths due to pain relief, because the doctor concerned indicated that hastening the moment of death was not the 'express purpose' of the MBSL (1996: 90-93).

87   1996: 68, 74.

88   1996: 119.

5.3.3   Severely defective newborn babies (and late abortion)[89]

There were approximately 190,000 live births in the Netherlands in 1995 and 1041 deaths within the first year of life; the Netherlands thereby has one of the lowest rates of infant mortality in the world. A MBSL was involved in some 62% of these deaths.

Table 5.13 Frequency of various MBSL as cause of death of newborn babies, 1995 (percentages of all deaths of babies under 1 year)

no MBSL –	
– baby died suddenly	24
– treatment continued to moment of death	14
life-prolonging treatment stopped or not initiated, accepting likelihood or certainty of death, and –	
– no drugs administered	8
– intensification of pain relief	6
– drug administered with express purpose to hasten death	1
life-prolonging treatment stopped or not initiated with the express purpose of hastening death, and –	
– no drugs administered	17
– intensification of pain relief	17
– drug administered with express purpose to hasten death	7
no life-prolonging treatment stopped or not initiated, and –	
– intensification of pain relief	4
– drug administered with express purpose to hasten death	1
total	100

Source: registered deaths study, 1996: 188.

In chapter 3.3 we discussed authoritative reports of two organs of the medical profession that recently considered the substantive and procedural requirements that should apply to MBSL in the case of severely defective newborn babies. The data from the 1995 survey indicate that the recommendations of the Dutch Association of Pediatricians (NVK)

---

89   Unless otherwise indicated, this section is based on 1996: 181-201; the data derive from interviews with a sample (N=66) of pediatricians and a questionnaire sent to all of the doctors responsible for infants younger than 1 year who died in the period August-November 1995, with the exception of a small number whose death was clearly sudden and unexpected (response: 88%).

and the Medical Association's Commission on the Acceptability of Termination of Life (CAL) are being widely followed in practice.

Abstention from (further) life-prolonging treatment is directly associated with the death of more than half of these babies (57%). In these cases, death is either an expected result (16%) or the express purpose (41%) of the abstention. Abstention was frequently (23%) accompanied by intensification of pain relief with hastening of death as an accepted consequence; it was also regularly (8%) accompanied by administration of a drug with the express purpose of hastening death. In almost 80% of all cases of death following abstention, the reason for abstaining was that further treatment was considered futile; in almost 20% the reason was that the expected quality of life did not justify further treatment.[90]

Five percent of all deaths were not immediately preceded by stopping or not initiating a life-prolonging treatment. Of these, 4% involved pain relief and 1% (about 15 cases per year) use of a euthanaticum. In about half of the latter cases the 'priority principle' (see chapter 3.3.1) was not entirely irrelevant, since life-prolonging treatment had been stopped or not initiated at some earlier stage.[91] Only these 1% are considered by the researchers 'active termination of life'.[92]

The experience of individual pediatricians with MBSL is shown on table 5.14.

The data support the assertion of the report of the NVK that abstention is almost universally subscribed to by Dutch pediatricians, both if further treatment would be futile and if it is not justifiable in the light of the baby's expected quality of life ('life worth living' – see chapter 3.3.2), and that 'active termination of life' is considered acceptable by many doctors, whose position is respected by those who disagree. Most of the group that would not be willing actively to terminate life would in principle be willing to cooperate in referring the baby to another doctor if the parents request this.[93]

---

90 The researchers note that in a substantial number of cases both reasons are important, so that definitive classification in these two categories is not possible.

91 1996: 189-190. The national estimates resulting from the 1995 research are very close to those of the Dutch Association of Pediatricians. Retrospective research in 4 of the 10 neonatal intensive care units in the Nederlands led the NVK to the estimate that "several hundred" babies per year die as a result of a decision to abstain from (further) life-prolonging treatment; in two-thirds of these cases, the basis for the decision is the lack of chance of survival, in the other cases the poor prognosis as to the quality of life. Termination of life with drugs (including cases in which the 'priority principle' was applied) was estimated at about 10 cases per year (NVK 1992: 19-20).

92 1996: 189.

93 1996: 187.

Table 5.14 Experience of pediatricians with MBSL, 1995 (percentages of pediatricians)

sort of MBSL/reason	neonatology/ intensive care	other pediatricians
stopping treatment/no chance of success [kansloos]	100	68
stopping treatment/pointless [zinloos]	97	40
non-initiation of treatment/no chance of success	67	66
non-initiation of treatment/pointless	55	30
active termination of life (lethal drug)	45	31
never actively terminated life/would consider	29	49
never actively terminated life/not willing	26	20

Source: interview study, 1996:187.

On the whole, the 'requirements of careful practice' seem to be fairly well adhered to when a decision is made to abstain from (further) treatment. The parents were usually (77-98% of the cases, depending on the exact circumstances) involved in the decision-making (about a third of the time the MBSL was at the parents' request); when consulted, the decision taken always had their approval.[94] Over 90% of the doctors consider the agreement of the parents a (very) important 'requirement of careful practice' in the case of abstinence based on 'quality-of-life' considerations and 100% in the case of 'active termination of life'; a half to three-quarters consider a request by the parents important in such cases; but two-thirds reject the view that parents 'have the right to decide on the life or death of their very sick child'.

The case was discussed with colleagues about 90% of the time (either because a team decision was involved or because the responsible doctor sought a second opinion), and they essentially always agreed with the decision taken. How often nurses were involved in the decision-making is not entirely clear,[95] but this seems to occur about half the time or more (which is about the same as for MBSL generally – see table 5.6).

In almost all cases of 'active termination of life' the death was reported as a 'natural death'. The reasons given for this were most frequently the wish to spare the parents or the doctor himself a criminal investigation. In about a third of the cases the doctor con-

---

94 Lack of involvement of the parents was usually explained by the doctors as due either to the fact that the situation was so obvious that there was no need for discussion or to the fact that in the circumstances there was no time for it.

95 The estimates vary from 41% to 93% depending on the sort of MBSL and the source of data. There may well be considerable variation in what different doctors consider 'discussing a case' with nurses.

sidered that the death of the child actually was a 'natural death'. And in a substantial number of cases (about a fifth) the doctor's position was that the matter was a private one between parents and doctor. There have been two prosecutions of cases reported by the doctors concerned, both of which resulted in acquittal (see chapter 2.4, 3.3.2 and appendix II-3).

Essentially all pediatricians consider some form of control over 'active termination of life' important, although a small minority does not consider this necessary in every case. But most of them regard the present system of control based on the criminal law as an obstacle to openness and effective control. On the whole, they would prefer a system in which initial control was in the hands of the profession or of a medical-ethical committee. Over 80% of the pediatricians were of the view that such control should also obtain in some or all cases of abstention.

As noted in chapter 3.3.2, the problem of late-term abortion where the foetus is discovered to be suffering from very serious defects is very similar to that of termination of life. Research in one Dutch province (North-Holland, 1990-1994)[96] reveals that more than half of all gynecologists have performed such an abortion and that the practice exists in almost three-quarters of all hospitals. The total number of cases averages 21 per year (6% of all live or stillbirths involving similar severe defects; about one in ten thousand births). In most of these cases the defect would quickly have been fatal even with extra-uterine life-prolonging treatment.[97] In a few cases life-prolonging extra-uterine treatment would have been possible but would have led to a 'life not worth living'; in a few cases legitimate life-prolonging treatment might have been possible; and in one case the child might have survived without life-prolonging treatment, but the defect was so serious that it would have been legitimate to consider 'active termination' of the baby's life had no abortion taken place. The 'requirements of careful practice' proposed by the Association for Obstetrics and Gynecology (NVOG) were almost always followed, except that in 88% of all cases the death of the foetus was reported as a 'natural death'. More than half of all respondents and two-thirds of those who had performed such an abortion were of the opinion that the death in such a case is a 'natural' one.[98] So far as is known, there have been no prosecutions.

---

96   Van der Wal, Bosma & Hosman-Benjaminse 1996; Bosma, Van der Wal & Hosman-Benjaminse 1996.
97   These were therefore presumably legal abortions: see chapter 3.3.2.
98   The NVOG report, which takes an opposite position except when the foetus is not considered capable of life, was only published in 1994.

5.3.4 Psychiatric patients and patients with a psychiatric disorder[99]

Each year Dutch psychiatrists are confronted by about 320 patients, under treatment for a psychiatric disorder, who make explicit and repeated requests for assistance with suicide. Two to five of these requests are honored, of which at least half concern patients who suffer not only from a psychiatric but also from a serious somatic disorder. Table 5.15 gives the views of Dutch psychiatrists concerning such requests and their experience in dealing with them.[100]

Table 5.15 Assistance with suicide in psychiatric practice, 1995 (percentages of psychiatrists)

ever received an explicit and repeated request	37
ever honored a request	2
never honored a request, in principle willing	44
never honored a request, personally unwilling, considers assistance in principle acceptable	19
considers such assistance never acceptable	31
no opinion	5

Source: questionnaire, 1996: 204-205.

In short: most Dutch psychiatrists accept the idea of giving assistance with suicide to a psychiatric patient, but their actual practice is extremely cautious.

The psychiatrists were asked to describe the last case in which a request had been made for assistance with suicide (N = 202). The patients who made such requests were preponderantly women (63%), and rather young relative to the general population of those who request euthanasia (64% younger than 50). More than half were ambulatory at the time of the request, although many of these had been institutionalized (often involuntarily) at some earlier time. The patient's request reflected a lasting desire for death in 70% of the cases and was considered voluntary in 86%; in a third of the cases the psychiatrist considered the patient entirely competent and in a fifth entirely non-competent. The most important reasons for the request were the unbearability of mental suffering and/or the lack of any prospect of improvement (each in more than half of all cases); not wanting to be a burden (any more) (a third); pain or other somatic suffering (a fifth); and wanting to avoid deterioration and loss of dignity (a tenth).

---

99   This section is based, unless stated otherwise, on 1996: 202-217; see also Groenewoud et al. 1997. The data derive from a written questionnaire sent to a sample of half of all Dutch psychiatrists, with a response rate of 84%.

100 By way of comparison: about half of all doctors consider assistance with suicide in the case of psychiatric patients acceptable. Prosecutors are rather more permissive in this respect than doctors (1996: 174).

The request was seriously considered in a fifth of all cases, in practically all of which the psychiatrist consulted another doctor, usually another psychiatrist (in two-fifths of these cases the patient's GP was consulted). Consultation concerned in particular whether the request was well-considered, whether it was based on a treatable psychiatric disorder, and whether (counter)transference was involved (each of these in roughly half of all cases).

The reasons given for not honoring these most recent requests are shown on table 5.16.

Table 5.16 *Reasons for refusing a request for assistance with suicide by a psychiatric patient (percentages of most recent requests)*

	honoring request not considered	honoring request considered
treatable psychiatric disorder	67	37
opposed in principle	37	8
suffering not unbearable or without prospect of improvement	35	21
wish for death not lasting	25	13
request not well considered	25	13
negative advice of consulted doctor	–	26
decision not yet definitive	–	13
patient no longer wished to die	–	8
other	17	11

Source: questionnaire, 1996: 209.

Factors mentioned as relevant for the decision-making were the nature of the disorder and the nature and duration of the preceding treatment (both by about 90%), the nature and duration of treatment alternatives (by about two-thirds), the views of family/intimates, the age of the patient and the threat of violent suicide (all by about a third).

About 25% of the patients had died in the meantime: in 2% the psychiatrist gave assistance with suicide, in 3% another doctor did so, in 16% the patient had committed suicide without medical assistance, and in 5% the patient had died a natural death. Of the remaining three-quarters, the situation of 11% was unknown, 35% no longer wished to die, 10% were no longer so insistent, and 18% persisted in their request for assistance with suicide.

Ninety percent or more of psychiatrists who consider assistance with suicide in principle acceptable regard as (very) important the requirements that the request be voluntary and well-considered, the wish for death a lasting one, the suffering unbearable and hopeless, and a real treatment alternative non-existent. Only half consider a written request (very) important, compared with 75% of doctors generally.[101] More than ninety percent consider consultation with a second psychiatrist (very) important, and more than half that two or more should be consulted. Three-quarters consider that the second psychiatrist should not be in the same institution or practice.

Psychiatrists are frequently consulted by other doctors in connection with a request for euthanasia or assistance with suicide. Eleven percent of the respondents had been consulted by another psychiatrist (mostly in connection with a request based on a psychiatric disorder); the patient's request was honored in less than a tenth of these cases. Thirty percent of the psychiatrists had been consulted by a non-psychiatrist (mostly in connection with a request based on a somatic disorder); in more than a third of these cases, the patient's request was honored. A fifth of the psychiatrists think a psychiatrist should always be consulted if a request for euthanasia or assistance with suicide is being seriously considered in a case of somatic suffering, but four-fifths think the responsible doctor should determine whether such consultation is necessary.

Almost all psychiatrists think it important that the responsible doctor's judgment be checked before assistance with suicide takes place, and about two-thirds think there should also be control afterwards. On the whole, they would prefer control in advance to be carried out by colleagues or by local or regional professional committees; almost fifty percent mention consultation in this connection. Almost two-fifths considers the Medical Inspectorate an appropriate body to carry out such control. As far as control afterwards is concerned, there is less outspoken preference for collegial control, and the most commonly mentioned form is control by the Inspectorate. About two-fifths of the psychiatrists – double the proportion among doctors generally – considers control by the prosecutorial authorities appropriate.

In about 5 of the 12 most recent cases in which, according to the psychiatrists, they had given assistance with suicide, the death was accurately reported; in 3 of the remaining cases it was reported as a 'natural death' as a result of assistance with suicide. Non-reporting was for the usual sorts of reasons. With the exception of the *Chabot* case (see chapter 2.4, 3.5, appendix II-2), the reported cases were not prosecuted, either because somatic suffering was also involved or because the non-somatic suffering had its origin in a somatic condition for which no further treatment was possible.[102]

---

101 This may reflect the concern expressed by the NVP (1997: § 3.2; but compare CAL 4: 31) that a written request may make a patient feel he or she is 'committed' to carry out the suicide.
102 1996: 146.

5.3.5 *The control system and its operation in practice*

As we have seen in chapter 3, legal control over euthanasia and termination of life without an explicit request is at present largely limited to criminal prosecutions, with an occasional medical disciplinary proceeding in the margins. The system of control begins when the responsible doctor reports a 'non-natural' death to the coroner who passes the case along to the local prosecutor. The prosecutor investigates the case and makes a prosecutorial recommendation which is passed upward in the prosecutorial hierarchy, receiving additional assessments on the way, and ultimately reaches the national Committee of Procurators-General (PGs), the highest prosecutorial authority in the country. Since 1982 all final decisions on whether or not to prosecute have been made by the PGs.[103]

SELF-REPORTING BY DOCTORS

The control system is based on self-reporting. There is essentially no proactive control, and most prosecutions have been the result of self-reports. In a very small number of cases, the Inspector learns of a case that the doctor concerned did not report and turns this over to the prosecuting authorities, or the prosecuting authorities learn of the case in some other, more or less accidental, way;[104] these cases always concern situations more serious than departure from the established procedural 'requirements of careful practice' governing euthanasia and termination of life without an explicit request. It is hard to see how more effective control with criminal law could be designed, since law-enforcement officials can hardly be present at every deathbed, and so long as control is based ultimately on self-reporting, a doctor who wants to conceal what he has done would have to be extraordinarily careless to give them reason to doubt his report of a 'natural death' (see further chapter 6.2.3).

The system of self-reporting is, as we have seen in chapter 3, only applicable if the death is not a 'natural' one. The first difficulty with the system of control resides, therefore, in the possibility that the doctor considers a death 'natural' that, legally speaking, should have been reported. The available empirical data show that these difficulties have reper-

---

103 1996: 138; see chapter 2.2, 3.2.

104 The *Schat* case (see chapter 3 note 57) seems to be an example: according to newspaper accounts of the case (see e.g. *Het Parool*, 22 March 1997) the doctor involved had very strained relations with the local medical community and with the director of the residential home where his patient lived; the latter found the patient's death suspicious and reported the doctor to the authorities (compare also the *Postma* case, discussed in chapter 2.2). In other cases that have come to the attention of the authorities (usually involving nurses), the persons concerned killed several patients and in other ways called attention to what they were doing.

cussions in practice: as we have seen in section 5.3.2, in almost half of all cases of termination of life without an explicit request the doctor reported the death as a 'natural' one because that is what he considered it to be (see further chapter 6.2.2).

Once the doctor considers a death not 'natural', the question remains whether he will report it as such. As we have seen in section 5.2, Van der Wal's research covering the period 1986-1990 came to the conclusion that in about 70% of all cases the death had been incorrectly reported as a 'natural death'. The rate of reporting was, however, increasing fast: it was essentially zero before 1986 and for cases in 1989 it was about a third. On the basis of the research carried out in 1990 and 1995, Van der Wal and Van der Maas conclude that the reporting rate in 1990 was 18% and that by 1995 it had risen to 41%;[105] the biggest increase had taken place in 1991 and 1992, and by 1995 the rate of reporting appeared to them to have stabilized.[106]

In short, after 5 years of a formally instituted reporting procedure and despite the fact that a doctor who conforms to the substantive and procedural requirements does not face any significant risk of prosecution, about 60% of all cases of euthanasia were still being reported by doctors to the authorities as a 'natural death'. In the 1995 research it also appeared that half of the doctors who had reported their most recent case had failed to report on at least one occasion in the past (usually, however, this was before the formal reporting pro-

---

105 This frequency applies only to euthanasia and assistance with suicide; if the 900 cases of termination of life without an explicit request are added to the total of cases that doctors are required to report, the overall rate of reporting in 1995 was 32%.
106 1996: 110-111.

cedure went into effect in June 1994); and of the half who claimed always to have reported, one out of five could imagine circumstances in which he would not do so.[107]

The reporting system is a weak control instrument not only because of the fact that a majority of cases that doctors themselves consider 'euthanasia' are not reported, but perhaps even more importantly because of the characteristics of the cases they choose not to report. Van der Wal showed on the basis of his research on the euthanasia practice of GPs (see section 5.2) what one might have expected: problematic cases are much less likely to be reported, and in their reporting doctors make cases appear legally more clear-cut than they actually are. The 1996 research confirms this finding. While there is little or no difference between reported and not-reported cases as far as the situation of the patient and the substantive requirements are concerned, there is a substantial difference with respect to the procedural requirements. Consultation took place in 94% of the reported cases and 11% of the not-reported cases; there was written record-keeping in 97% of the former and 57% of the latter.[108]

What reasons do doctors give for not reporting? To begin with, three-quarters of the doctors interviewed in 1995 claim they always report (which can hardly be true – presumably they mean 'in principle'); in 1990 this was only a quarter. Reasons having to do

---

107 1996: 110-114. Anecdotal evidence suggests that a highly conscientious doctor who is in principle strongly in favor of reporting can sometimes have understandable reasons for not doing so. In an informal gathering, for example, a GP known for his strict adherence to the reporting procedure described a case which he had not reported. At the time he was in the midst of a criminal investigation of another case, regarded by the prosecutorial authorities as a possible test case with respect to a requirement that the then Minister of Justice insisted upon – that the patient be in the 'terminal phase' – and this put a considerable burden on himself, his practice and his family. He was called upon as a consultant by another doctor in the case of a cancer patient who had requested euthanasia should the pain become too much to bear. He had examined the patient and had come to the same conclusion as his colleague, that the patient's request could be honored. Some time later, the patient's condition took a sudden turn for the worse. The patient decided that the time had come and became quite insistent and desperate. But the colleague who had agreed to the euthanasia was seriously ill. The consultant was contacted by the hospital to which the patient had in the meantime been admitted and urged to come and carry out the euthanasia. Having satisfied himself that the situation was a real emergency, he did so. He did not report the case since it involved a formal violation of the requirements of a doctor-patient relationship and of consultation by the doctor who carries out the euthanasia (see table 5.18 for the attention that the prosecutorial authorities give to such cases). He did not think he could bear the strain of two test cases simultaneously.

108 1996: 114-117.

with the fact that the reporting procedure is part of a (potential) criminal investigation that can be unpleasant for both the doctor and the family of the deceased are cited in a third to a half of all not reported cases. Fear of prosecution is mentioned in a third, as is the fact that not all of the 'requirements of careful practice' had been complied with. In 1990, a fifth of all doctors said that they would not report a case of euthanasia under any circumstances; by 1995 this had apparently declined to a very small number, who consider euthanasia as a matter of principle a matter between doctor and patient.[109]

In 1990, most doctors said that they considered it important that cases of euthanasia be subject to some kind of external control; most of them had a preference for control outside the criminal law. In 1995, the formal reporting procedure having in the meantime come into effect, most doctors had a generally favorable opinion of it: a large majority thought the procedure promotes conformity with the 'requirements of careful practice' and makes doctors accountable. But only a small proportion considers control in the context of the criminal law desirable, the large majority having a preference for control by the profession itself or by a committee outside the framework of the criminal law.[110]

The reporting rate in the case of termination of life without a request is negligible: in 1990 there were two reported cases (out of an estimated 1000) and in 1995 three (out of 900), all of which concerned severely defective newborn babies.[111] Almost half of the doctors involved stated that they would never consider reporting such a case (perhaps these are the same doctors who consider such a death a 'natural' one); the other reasons given for not reporting had largely to do with the criminal law framework of the reporting requirement. The most frequently mentioned considerations that would make them more willing to report concern clarification of the legal situation and the availability of a medical protocol for such cases.[112]

---

109 1992: 97-99; 1996: 118-121. Due to differences in the wording of the questions in the two studies, and the fact that N is very small in the 1995 research, only a rough and impressionistic summary is given here.

110 See 1992: 97-98; 1996: 159-165. Compare section 5.3.3 on the views of pediatricians and 5.3.4 on those of psychiatrists. A third of the coroners and half of the prosecuting attorneys interviewed in 1995 were of the view that control should continue to be in the hands of the criminal law authorities: about half of both groups favored professional control or a committee outside the framework of the criminal law.

111 1996: 112. Included in the 120 cases discussed by the PGs in the period 1991-1995 were 11 without an explicit request, of which 8 concerned newborn babies and 5 (sub)comatose patients (see table 5.18).

112 1996: 118-121.

THE ROLE OF THE CORONER[113]

In practically all cases that the responsible doctor reported as a non-natural death the report was made, as it is supposed to be, to the coroner. In about two-thirds of these cases, the doctor had already had contact with the coroner before carrying out the euthanasia or assistance with suicide. Usually the doctor concerned had already reached a decision and contacted the coroner simply to inform him of the impending death. But some doctors also contacted the coroner for information concerning the reporting procedure and the 'requirements of careful practice'. Only very rarely did a doctor seek approval of his decision, but in a tenth of all cases, according to the doctor, the coroner explicitly indicated his agreement, and in another 23% he did so implicitly.

When responding to a doctor's report of a non-natural death due to euthanasia, assistance with suicide or termination of life without an explicit request, the coroner almost always examines the corpse and he usually (over 90% of the time) does this within three hours of death. He examines the report submitted by the doctor (78%) and if necessary helps him with it, checks whether the 'requirements of careful practice' have been followed (74%), and usually speaks to the doctor and the family of the deceased. In his written report to the local prosecutor, a coroner usually (73%) includes his own judgment as to whether the doctor had complied with the 'requirements of careful practice'. According to prosecutors, the coroner's judgment influences their own judgment of a case more than half the time.

About half of the doctors, two-thirds of the prosecutors and three-quarters of the coroners interviewed regard it as part of the task of the coroner to render his own judgment on the question whether the 'requirements of careful practice' have been followed. Substantial majorities, especially of prosecutors (86%), think the role of the coroner in the procedure for legal control of euthanasia, assistance with suicide, and termination of life without an explicit request should remain as it is. Two-fifths of the coroners thought they should have a more prominent role in the reporting procedure, but this view was shared by only about half as many doctors and prosecutors.

As we have seen in the *Intermezzo*, the independence of the coroner is a point of current concern. The 1995 research shows that there is reason for this. Some 69% of the coroners to whom doctors reported cases of euthanasia were their colleagues or fellow members of a substitution-group. Thirty-seven percent of the GP-coroners thought their independence was to some extent compromised by their relationship to the reporting doctor.

---

113 See 1996: 123-130. On the office of coroner, see the *Intermezzo*.

PROSECUTORIAL DECISION-MAKING[114]

Table 5.17 shows the numbers of cases of euthanasia and termination of life without an explicit request reported to coroners and, via them, to the prosecutorial authorities and dealt with by the Committee of Procurators-General. The whole procedure is very time-consuming, which is widely supposed to be one of the biggest objections that doctors have to reporting. In cases not further discussed by the PGs the average time elapsed between reporting and a final prosecutorial decision is three and a half months; the longest 10% take six months or more.[115]

Table 5.17 *Cases of euthanasia and termination of life without an explicit request brought to the attention of the prosecutorial authorities, 1981-1995*

	reported	discussed by PGs	decision not to prosecute after further investigation	indictment
1981-1985	71		1	8
1986	84		1	2
1987	126		1	3
1988	184		1	2
1989	338		2	1
1990	486		–	–
1991	866	14	–	1
1992	1201	17	2	2
1993	1304	26	11	4
1994	1487	27	6[1]	5[1]
1995	1466	36[2]	3[3]	1[3]

1. In 3 additional cases the criminal investigation was not yet complete.
2. Two of these cases were settled with payment of a fine for falsely submitting a certificate of natural death.
3. In 4 additional cases the criminal investigation was not yet complete.
Source: 1996: 137.

The 1995 research included a study of the decision-making in the Committee of PGs. The dossiers forwarded by local prosecutors to the PGs almost always included written reports by the responsible doctor and by the coroner. Ninety-three percent of the

---

114 The following discussion is based on 1996: 136-151.
115 1996: 132-134. Such differences are largely the result of variation between the different local prosecutors' offices in the amount of time that elapses between a report and the forwarding of the case to the PGs: the average per local office ranges from 8 to 108 days (overall average: 33 days).

dossiers included a written request by the deceased (40% included a personal, usually handwritten, request; 33% a preprinted request distributed by the NVVE; 11% a pre-printed request based on that of the NVVE; 21% other written requests[116]). Seventy-eight percent included a written report of one or more consulted doctors.

The results of the consideration of these reported cases by the Committee of PGs are shown on table 5.18.

The researchers discuss in some detail the disposition by the PGs of the 120 cases fully considered by them. In most cases, specific features of the individual case were determinative of the outcome. A few matters of a more general nature deserve mention:[117]

–   *termination of life without an explicit request:* The decisions not to prosecute in 2 of the 5 cases of (sub)comatose patients were based on the consideration that the doctor's behavior hardly differed from ceasing a 'medically futile' treatment.
    Until the prosecutions in the *Prins* and *Kadijk* cases were ordered by the Minister to secure legal clarification (see chapter 3.3.2), the PGs had decided not to prosecute a number of cases of active termination of life of severely defective newborn babies, for essentially the same reasons as emerged from these two prosecutions.
–   *terminal phase:* In 1993, responding to questions in Parliament, the then Minister of Justice (a Christian Democrat) took the position that the 'terminal phase' is an essential condition of the justification of euthanasia, and in the Committee of PGs he insisted on prosecution despite the position of some of the PGs that no such condition could be inferred from the case law and their worry that the willingness of doctors to report might thereby be undermined. After the decision of the Supreme Court in the *Chabot* case, the Committee of PGs, with a new liberal (D66) Minister present, decided not to prosecute most of the pending cases.
–   *unbearable and hopeless suffering:* In 1995 the Committee of PGs, concerned that doctors appeared to them increasingly to be leaving the question whether the patient's suffering was 'unbearable and hopeless' to the subjective judgment of the patient, proposed to the Minister to separate the two elements and try to come to some objective criteria for each of them. She rejected the proposal on the ground that the two elements had always been used conjointly in the case law, that the unbearability of suffering is in its nature subjective and therefore needs to be considered in conjunction with the more objective question of the prospects of improvement, and that the tightening of prosecutorial policy implied by the PGs' proposal would lead to uncertainty in the medical world and was in conflict with the position of the Government that no changes should be made in the reporting pro-

---

116 1996: 133. Some dossiers apparently included more than one request.
117 1996: 138-148.

Table 5.18 Prosecutorial decisions, 1991-1995

total number of reported cases	6324
full consideration by PGs	120
full consideration because of doubt concerning[1] –	
– 'terminal phase'	38%
– the request	25%
· (no request)	(11%)[2]
· (too old or unwritten)	(8%)
· (voluntary, well-considered, lasting)	(7%)
– the consultation	24%
· (none or insufficient)	(13%)
· (consulted doctor not independent)	(9%)
· (performance by consulted doctor)	(3%)
– the unbearability and lack of prospect of improvement	23%
· (alternatives rejected)	(9%)
· (other)	(13%)
– the performance	13%
· (doctor not present during (all of) execution)	(7%)
· (inappropriate method)	(4%)
· (carried out by non-doctor)	(2%)
– the necessity	5%
· (no treatment relationship)	(3%)
· (drugs only used some weeks after being given)	(2%)
– primarily non-somatic suffering	5%
– false report of natural death	4%
– incorrect medical record-keeping	3%
– other	4%
outcome	
- initial decision not to prosecute	6292
- further investigation followed by decision not to prosecute	21[3]
- indictment	11[4]

1. More than one reason possible.
2. Eight newborn babies and 5 (sub)comatose patients.
3. 22 doctors.
4. 13 doctors.
Source: 1996: 138-139

cedure until the results of the 1995 research were available. She insisted that the PGs apply the prosecutorial policy that she (together with the Minister of Health) had reported to Parliament in a letter of 16 September 1994 (see chapter 2.4). She urged the PGs in such cases to secure the advice of the Medical Inspector, which in case of doubt should weigh very heavily. It seems that the tension between the PGs and the Minister primarily concerned the situation of patients who refuse all (further) treatment.

–   *consultation:* Cases in which the requirement of consultation had not been met, or in which the consultant had actually carried out the euthanasia, were turned over to the Medical Inspector (with or without the advice to bring a disciplinary proceeding). A further criminal investigation was ordered only in cases in which there was also doubt as to whether other 'requirements of careful practice' had been met.

–   *the execution of euthanasia:* Cases in which the doctor, having prescribed the means for suicide, was not present when it was carried out, and in which not the doctor but a family member or a nurse carried out the euthanasia, were not prosecuted[118] but (in some cases) turned over to the Medical Inspector to bring a disciplinary proceeding.

–   *doctor responsible for treatment:* In several cases there was discussion about the requirement that the doctor have a treatment relationship with the patient and concerns were expressed about the phenomenon of 'travelling euthanasia doctors'.[119] Further criminal investigation was ordered in three such cases, but principally because of problems with other 'requirements of careful practice'. One case was turned over to the Medical Inspector.

–   *non-somatic suffering:* Apart from the *Chabot* case, several cases of primarily non-somatic suffering were not prosecuted because somatic suffering seemed also to be involved or the non-somatic suffering was the result of a somatic condition for which no further treatment was possible.

Either before or following a further criminal investigation, most of the 120 cases discussed by the Committee of PGs resulted in a decision not to prosecute. Indictments were ultimately brought against 13 doctors. According to the researchers, such cases either involved flagrant violation of the applicable legal requirements or were seen by the prosecutorial authorities (in particular, the Minister of Justice) as appropriate test cases. A small number of cases (20) were turned over to the Medical Inspector to discuss with the doctor concerned or to initiate medical disciplinary proceedings; one doctor was invited to the prosecutor's office to discuss two cases and another doctor was offered the possibility of avoiding prosecution by paying a fine for two violations.

---

118   See however chapter 3.1.3, note 67, for an example of a prosecution of a nurse in such a case.
119   See chapter 3.1.3, note 41.

OUTCOMES OF CRIMINAL PROSECUTIONS

Because a year or more can elapse between indictment and final judicial decision, the available data on the outcomes of criminal prosecutions cannot be directly related to the data discussed above on prosecutorial decisions. Nevertheless, table 5.19 gives a general impression of the ultimate fate of criminal prosecutions for euthanasia and assistance with suicide (articles 293 and 294) and termination of life without an explicit request (murder or manslaughter, articles 289 and 287).

Table 5.19 Final judicial disposition of prosecutions for euthanasia and termination of life without an explicit request, 1981-1995

charges dismissed	2
acquittal/facts proved not punishable	7
acquittal/facts not proved	2
guilty, no sanction	3
guilty, suspended sentence	6
total	20

Source: 1996: 137

THE ROLE OF MEDICAL DISCIPLINARY LAW

So far as we have been able to ascertain from the Medical Inspectorate, there have been only a handful of medical disciplinary proceedings concerning euthanasia and assistance with suicide and we know of none concerning termination of life without an explicit request. Recently there have been a small number of complaints to the Inspectorate (fewer than 10 per year) concerning abstention from or continuance of artificial feeding and hydration, but apparently none has led to a disciplinary proceeding; the complaints usually originate in poor communication between the family and those responsible for treatment (*NRC Handelsblad*, 30 September 1997). The Inspectorate and the prosecutorial authorities coordinate their handling of MBSL cases, with temporal priority being given to criminal prosecution.[120] As we have seen, of the 120 cases discussed by the PGs in the period 1991-1995 (see table 5.18), 20 were referred to the Medical Inspectorate for further disposition.

OVERALL ASSESSMENT OF THE REPORTING PROCEDURE

Despite all the evidence that the reporting procedure, at least to date, is a bit of a paper tiger, in the sense that only a minority of cases (and these the least problematic ones) are reported, and that little serious enforcement is undertaken in reported cases that do not

---

120 The *Chabot* case (see appendix II-2) is an example of this, disciplinary proceedings having been postponed until after the criminal prosecution was complete.

meet the legal criteria, Van der Wal and Van der Maas conclude that in the brief period of its existence, the reporting procedure has led to increased public accountability by doctors, careful control of reported cases, and better adherence to the 'requirements of careful practice', in particular a more professional consultation practice and better record-keeping.[121] Except for the fact that, as we have seen, doctors themselves voice the same judgment, there seems to be little concrete evidence for such optimism. On the other hand, it does seem likely that the publicity surrounding the reporting procedure, the growing awareness among patients and their families of the legal requirements, and the fact that most doctors are now aware of the duty to report and of the substantive and procedural requirements applicable to euthanasia, will have been at least partly responsible for the increasing conformity even among those who do not keep to all of the requirements all of the time and do not report euthanasia as such.

5.4   Other recent research

In addition to the national surveys whose results have been presented and discussed in sections 5.2 and 5.3, there have been a number of studies directed to specific aspects of MBSL practice and its control. We present the results briefly in this section.

5.4.1 Communication between doctor and patient

The patient's point of view is entirely missing from the national research discussed in the previous section, and there are therefore no systematic and representative data available on the experiences of patients who seek euthanasia (or, for that matter, those who seek to reassure themselves that they will not be subjected to 'non-voluntary euthanasia'). There is considerable incidental and anecdotal indication that the communication between doctors and patients concerning MBSL sometimes leaves a great deal to be desired, but how common this is and what the reasons for it are, is largely unknown.[122]

---

121 1996: 230-232. Earlier, Van der Wal had concluded from his research on GPs (see section 5.2) that the reporting procedure cannot be effective so long as euthanasia remains a criminal offence (1992: 121).

122 Some systematic data are available with respect to doctor-patient communication in general. See Verkruisen (1993), for example, with regard to the frequency with which communication problems account for patient dissatisfaction with medical care.
On communication concerning euthanasia, see Melief (1991), who on the basis of his study of the care for terminal patients in Utrecht (see note 1 above) observes that some doctors opposed to euthanasia on principle report few or no 'real' requests because they are simply unreceptive to this sort of communication from patients. See Pool (1996), an observation study of euthanasia in a hospital in the urban area of the western part of the Netherlands, for support of the view, often voiced by doctors, that requests for euthanasia are not always unambiguous.

A recent study sheds some light on the subject and suggests that the impression GPs have given to quantitative researchers of their openness to euthanasia requests may not always correspond with their actual behavior. The Dutch Association for Voluntary Euthanasia (NVVE) commissioned research into the experiences of patients who had raised the subject of euthanasia with their GP (Van Overbeek 1996). Because of the limited scope of the study generalization of its results would be irresponsible; and because of its sources of data, it is reasonable to assume that the results paint an unduly negative picture.[123] However, this does not diminish the fact that although their frequency cannot be estimated on the basis of such research, the situations described apparently do occur in practice.

The study covers both the situation of patients who seek to discuss their wish for euthanasia 'in general terms' with their GP and that of patients who concretely request it. On the whole, GPs respond positively to a patient's expression of a wish for euthanasia at some time in the future. The discussion is usually not very concrete – sometimes the GP simply receives the patient's written 'request for euthanasia'[124] without comment – and patients come away from it with the idea that they have taken care of the matter and that the GP will honor their request should the time come. In fact, in the GP's view (as patients later discover), he has done nothing more than give the rather noncommittal reaction that if the occasion should arise, he is prepared to entertain such a request. In the minority of cases where the GP reacts negatively, some patients (especially if they have a good relationship with the GP) accept the doctor's position; others seek out a GP who does not reject euthanasia on principle, and those suffering from a terminal illness are usually successful in this (but patients considering euthanasia for non-somatic reasons usually cannot find a GP who would be willing).

When a patient considers that the time has arrived for carrying out his or her earlier decision, a concrete request is made to the GP (sometimes this is rather vague, consisting

---

123 The findings are based on information from: (1) 29 persons who responded to a request in the NVVE's magazine for participation in the research (as well as, where possible, their GP and close relatives); and (2) 30 persons selected from among those who contacted a special telephone number set up to collect the experiences of surviving relatives of persons who died without their request for euthanasia having been carried out.

124 The NVVE distributes a printed advance directive requesting euthanasia [*euthanasieverklaring*] that patients are advised to give to their GP or other doctor responsible for their treatment. It requests euthanasia in case of unbearable suffering or of a situation that offers no hope of "recovery to a state that I regard as reasonable and dignified" (specifically including coma of more than a specified number of months, dependency on artificial breathing, and severe diminution of mental powers). The legal status of such an advance directive is dubious (see chapter 3.1.3).

of expressions such as 'I've had enough', without an explicit reference to euthanasia). In the cases studied, the doctor's response at this point is usually either evasive or negative. Patients and their family and close friends often interpret this as a failure of the doctor to live up to his earlier 'commitment'.

The GPs involved were reluctant actually to carry out euthanasia and employed a number of strategies to keep from having to do so: postponement (the patient is told that the situation is not yet serious enough); avoidance (the doctor has as little contact as possible with the patient after the latter makes a concrete request); or denial (the doctor does not react to the request). In effect, they play it safe, hoping that it will ultimately not be necessary to accede to the patient's request, and being willing to do so, if at all, only in the final stage of a terminal sickness. The researchers believe that this strategy is a result of the uncertainties and dangers of the current legal regime, as perceived by doctors. These findings suggest that, far from being a danger to the poor and powerless, euthanasia may to some extent be a privilege of the younger, better-educated patient from a privileged social background and with an assertive personality who manages to overcome the resistance of his doctor.

5.4.2   The euthanasia policy of hospitals and nursing homes

Blad (1990) gives an overview of the internal policy of Dutch hospitals and nursing homes, based on a national survey in 1989 of all such institutions.[125] Five years later, Haverkate and Van der Wal (1996) conducted a similar national survey, with a better response and slightly different results.[126] The picture, very globally, is shown on table 5.20.

In 1989 42% of Dutch hospitals and 29% of Dutch nursing homes had a permissive policy; in 1994 this had risen to 77% and 57%, respectively. Prohibitive policies had considerably declined, especially unwritten prohibitive policies. Written policies of hospitals were in 1994 almost always permissive, while this was less frequently true of nursing homes.

---

125 The response in both categories was about two-thirds. About a fifth of the hospitals that responded and less than a tenth of the nursing homes refused to cooperate in the research (1990: 32-34).

126 The response was 86%. This research also covered institutions for the mentally disabled, only 15% of which had a written policy on euthanasia, which in almost three-quarters of the cases was prohibitive. In addition to euthanasia, data were collected on institutional guidelines for other MBSL. Over three-quarters of hospitals and nursing homes have no such guideline with respect to any other MBSL. In the case of NTBR decisions, 54% of the hospitals do have guidelines either at the institutional or at the ward level (see Blijham & Van Delden, 1996, for the NTBR guidelines of one academic hospital).

*Table 5.20 Euthanasia policies of hospitals and nursing homes in 1989 and 1994
(percentages of institutions)*

| | hospitals | | nursing homes | |
	1989	1994[1]	1989	1994[1]
no policy	14	18	8	9
verbal policy/permissive[2]	8	12	9	8
written policy/permissive	34	65	20	49
verbal policy/prohibitive[3]	16	(1)	23	(11)
written policy/prohibitive	5	4	30	23
policy in preparation (1989)[4]	23		10	
total	100	100	100	100
policy in preparation (1994)[5]		9		12
N	96	117	186	270

1. The 1994 research distinguishes between `tolerant' and `permissive' policies, but these categories are collapsed here.
2. In the 1994 research the categories `no policy' and `verbal policy' were not distinguished in reporting the content of the policy: the percentages here are those given for the situation of `no written policy' in which the institution leaves the decision up to the doctor.
3. No data available for 1994; the percentage given between parentheses is derived from adding the other percentages and subtracting the sum from 100.
4. In 1989 in 31 of 40 such cases the policy was available in draft; the proposed policy was permissive in all but one case.
5. Included in the categories `no policy' and `verbal policy'.
Source: Blad 1990: 31-35; Haverkate & Van der Wal 1996: 437.

In both 1989 and 1994 the religious affiliation of a hospital appeared to have relatively little influence on its euthanasia policy. In the case of nursing homes the influence was stronger: in 1994 it was cited as the major reason for a prohibitive policy by half of such institutions. Small hospitals and nursing homes more often had prohibitive policies. Regional location seemed to have no influence.[127]

The difference in policy between hospitals and nursing homes seems largely explainable on practical grounds. Many inhabitants of nursing homes are not considered competent to make a request (a quarter of the nursing homes with a prohibitive policy gave this reason in 1994). A number of nursing homes refer explicitly to the internal problems that a permissive policy on euthanasia would entail: the policy itself might be unsettling to

127 Blad 1990: 177-182; Haverkate & Van der Wal 1996: 437-438.

some patients, and because privacy and secrecy are impossible to guarantee in such institutions, a case of euthanasia would become generally known and lead to fear and insecurity among the other patients.[128]

It would be wrong to exaggerate the difference between institutions with a permissive and a prohibitive policy, for many of the latter exhibit in one way or another a certain degree of acceptance of euthanasia.[129] Most non-permissive institutions, in particular nursing homes, would cooperate in transferring a patient who desires euthanasia to an institution with a permissive policy. They also would cooperate with a patient's GP to have the patient transferred home for euthanasia.[130]

One of the most striking features of Blad's data on hospital and nursing-home euthanasia policy is what it tells us about the capacity of medical institutions to receive and transmit this sort of legal information. The influence of the State Commission's Report and of the guidelines of the Medical Association is obvious in the definitions of euthanasia used (and the exclusion from that term of deaths due to abstinence and pain relief), in the limited categories of patients for whom euthanasia is available, and in the procedural requirements in case it is applied. In general, one can say that the national, legal norms as these have been emerging over the past few years are clearly reflected in the euthanasia policies of permissive institutions.[131]

The surveys of institutional policy are significant contributions to our understanding of the transmission to the 'shop floor' of medical practice of legal requirements concerning

---

128 Blad 1990: 120-121.
129 Several non-permissive institutions referred in the 1989 study explicitly to the fact that the doctor-patient relationship can lead to a conflict of duties, and they accept the idea that a doctor, in such a situation, may feel 'forced' to accede to a patient's request despite the policy of the institution; the doctor does this, however, entirely on his own authority (Blad 1990: 108, 168-169). One non-permissive hospital acknowledged the fact that it does not know what the euthanasia policy of its specialists is (*id.*, 107) and several indicated that their policy only applies to their own staff, not to external doctors who have patients there (*id.*, 167-168). One hospital noted that although its policy is not permissive, euthanasia does in fact occur (*id.*, 108).
130 Blad 1990: 109-111, 161-167, 186. It is interesting to note that the permissive policies generally exclude employment sanctions and promise assistance in case of legal difficulties, if a case of euthanasia falls within the institution's policy (Blad 1990: 46, 99); at least some prohibitive institutions would regard violation of institutional policy as ground for dismissal (Benjaminsen 1988).
131 Several institutions indicated that their policies had been adopted under pressure from or in cooperation with the local prosecutor or medical inspector (Blad 1990: 45, 89-93; compare Benjaminsen 1988).

euthanasia, but from that point of view they also have some serious limitations. The most important of these is that they only inform us about institutional policy which – however important it may be – is certainly not the same thing as actual practice. Haverkate and Van der Wal asked whether the institutions took active steps to make their policy known to their staff: about 90% of the hospitals and nursing homes with a written policy did this (only 4% of the hospitals and 30% of the nursing homes made their policies known to patients unless requested). But as the authors note, their information comes from self-reports of institutional managers, from which one cannot infer that institutional policy is known on the work floor, let alone that it is actually implemented there.[132]

Residential homes (see the *Intermezzo*) have not been studied on a national basis. Research in Utrecht in the late 1980s[133] indicates that residential homes tend to have no policy on euthanasia, except that their own staff may not participate. It is difficult for these institutions to exercise as much control over the situation as they would like because residents have their own GPs: each home must therefore deal with a large number of different, entirely independent GPs. In general, the relationship between GPs and residential homes seems to be a difficult one, at least from the point of view of the homes, and they are quite dissatisfied with the lack of consultation concerning euthanasia. Some residential homes were considering adopting a policy on euthanasia in an effort to improve the communication with GPs: they expected that openness on their part concerning their policy would stimulate more openness on the part of the doctors.

5.4.3   The role of pharmacists

In 1994 a national mail survey of the role of pharmacists (in both public and hospital pharmacies) in euthanasia and assistance with suicide was carried out by Lau and a number of colleagues.[134] Over 90% of all pharmacists consider euthanasia and assistance with suicide legitimate, consider it appropriate for a pharmacist to furnish the euthanaticum, and would themselves do so. About 80% of all pharmacists have had at least one request. About 95% of all requests – some 1690 per year – are in fact fulfilled. About 10% of all pharmacists have at some time refused a request, often because the doctor had not followed the guidelines of the pharmacists' professional association (KNMP) (see chapter 3.1.3). Most pharmacists agree with these guidelines and they are generally fol-

---

132 1996: 438-439. Benjaminsen's research in Utrecht (1988) suggests that an institution's euthanasia policy is indeed not always known to all of its staff members.

133 Benjaminsen 1988; see note 1 concerning this research.

134 Lau et al. 1996; n.d. The response was about 50% which means that the extrapolations to national frequencies must be approached with some reserve.

lowed in practice, although the arguably most important requirement – a written request by the doctor – was not followed in a quarter of all cases (and was not fully adequate in another quarter). Roughly a fifth of the pharmacists reported having at least once received a 'suspicious' prescription from a doctor; usually they sought further explanation from the doctor concerned, but in a large minority of the cases they simply went ahead and dispensed the drugs requested.

5.4.4 Institutionalized, mentally handicapped patients

Van Thiel, Huibers and De Haan studied MBSL in the case of institutionalized mentally handicapped patients, basing their approach on that of the national research of 1995.[135] Extrapolation from the doctors contacted to all doctors gives the following estimated frequencies of MBSL as a percentage of all deaths of such patients in 1995: abstinence 34%, pain relief 10%, no MBSL 56%. In most cases, the doctor states his intention as having been 'accepting the risk' that the patient would die (pain relief: 100%; abstinence: 75% – almost all the rest being cases of 'subsidiary purpose'). Nevertheless, in most cases the doctor considered the patient's death 'at that time desireable', and in a number of cases it was 'the most important consideration'. A handful of patients were considered competent, and in those cases there was always some kind of request. In most cases, the responsible doctor discussed his decision with colleagues, with others in the institution, and with representatives of the patient, and consensus was almost always reached.

There was fewer than one case per year of termination of life without an explicit request; these involved very sick patients who in most cases were within a week or so of death and with whom communication was no longer possible. In most of these cases there were representatives of the patient available and the decision was reached together with them. All of these cases were reported as a 'natural death', apparently because the doctors concerned considered the chances of prosecution considerable.

5.5   Summary and conclusions

In societies with modern health-care systems, the precise time at which many people die is determined by something their doctor does or does not do, referred to in this book as 'medical behavior that shortens life'. In the Netherlands these MBSL were the immediate

---

135 Van Thiel, Huibers & de Haan 1997; see also Van Thiel et al. 1997 for a summary of the results in English, including most of the data included here. The study was based on a random sample of about half of all doctors who work in such institutions (response 88%), and it covered some 859 deaths over a period of 4.7 years. Because the absolute numbers are very small, most of the findings are of doubtful significance and are therefore not presented here.

cause of death in almost 60,000 deaths in 1995, or about two-fifths of all deaths and more than half of those which were not sudden and unexpected. These frequencies are apparently not unusual when compared with those for other countries.

Quantitatively speaking, the most important MBSL are decisions not to engage in (further) life-prolonging treatment (27,100 deaths, about 20% of all deaths) and to administer pain relief in doses known to be likely to hasten death (25,100 deaths, about 19% of all deaths). Both have risen significantly between 1990 and 1995, the frequency of death due to abstention particularly so. Euthanasia accounts for 2.4% of all deaths (3200 deaths), up from 1.8% five years earlier. The frequency of assistance with suicide has remained unchanged at 0.3% (400 deaths). And the frequency of termination of life without an explicit request has remained essentially the same at 0.7% (900 deaths).

Although their frequency is relatively low, euthanasia and assistance with suicide have become essentially normal procedures in Dutch medicine. Dutch doctors receive some 34,500 requests 'in general terms' per year, and 96% of them have at some time discussed euthanasia or assistance with suicide with a patient. They receive about 9700 concrete requests per year, and 77% of them have at some time had such a request. About a third of all requests are refused (in about an equal number of cases the patient dies before the request can be carried out). Twelve percent are in principle unwilling to perform euthanasia and most of these would refer a patient requesting it to another doctor. Slightly over half of all doctors have honored a request at some time, and about a third of them did so during the two years preceding the research in 1995.

The conditions under which euthanasia by a doctor is legally justifiable (voluntary, competent and explicit request; unbearable and hopeless suffering) enjoy overwhelming support from Dutch doctors and are generally complied with. The most important 'requirements of careful practice' (consultation with another doctor and keeping a written record) are considered very important by most doctors, and most of them say they abide by these requirements (albeit not always to the letter). The professionalism with which euthanasia decisions are taken and carried out seems to be increasing. The least satisfactory part of the picture concerns reporting: in 1990 the rate was 18% and by 1995 it had risen to 41%. More troubling yet are the indications that the cases that doctors report are on the whole those in which everything was done 'according to the book' and that cases where the requirements were not correctly followed are on the whole not reported. Furthermore, doctors tend to describe what happened in rather self-serving terms.

Termination of life without an explicit request is a very heterogeneous category, and, as we have seen in chapter 3.3, many of its sub-categories (comatose patients, severely defective newborn babies, 'help in dying') are not legally as problematic as is often supposed. On the whole, the procedural requirements seem in these cases to be working well. Nevertheless, because of the high level of uncertainty surrounding prosecution policy in the case of termination of life without an explicit request, the reporting rate is essentially nil, with as a result that external control is minimal.

As far as substantive and procedural regularity is concerned, the picture is far more troubling in the case of deaths due to abstention or to pain relief than in that of euthanasia or termination of life without an explicit request. Even when this could perfectly well be done, the patient's informed consent is often not secured, and consultation takes place in fewer than half of all cases. Discussion with the patient's family is also far less frequent. Since these sorts of MBSL, by contrast with euthanasia, are considered to fall within the legal category 'normal medical practice', reporting is not required at all. It does not seem likely that these facts are in themselves cause for any great alarm, but the absence of any legally organized external control does seem a matter for concern. Invocation of what often seems rather a mantra – 'normal medical practice' – does little to relieve such concern. There are indications that within the medical profession itself this situation is increasingly regarded as troublesome.[136]

Absence of control over abstinence and pain relief is a matter of concern in its own right, but it also makes investment of energy in the control of euthanasia and termination of life without an explicit request largely futile. This is because the boundaries of the different categories of MBSL are highly permeable. A case to which the procedural guarantees surrounding euthanasia or termination of life without an explicit request ought to be applicable can often be described as one of abstinence or of pain relief – as 'normal medical practice' – and thus escape the 'requirements of careful practice' altogether. A doctor who prefers not to perform 'euthanasia', whether for ethical reasons, or to avoid the paperwork and headaches supposed to accompany the special reporting procedure for euthanasia, or for some less honorable motive, has little reason to do so. In most cases the same result, the earlier death of the patient, can be accomplished under another name.

The problem is not just that a doctor can describe the same sort of behavior in different terms, but that he can choose different ways of accomplishing the same result. In effect, he 'constructs' the patient's death. By this we mean: he behaves in a way that permits a certain description. It is probably safe to assume that in many cases doctors are not consciously aware of their construction of a case as one of abstinence or pain relief rather than euthanasia or termination of life without an explicit request. Thus, Quill observes

---

136 As we saw in section 5.3.3, for example, most pediatricians are of the view that some kind of formalized control should obtain for at least some decisions to abstain in the case of severely defective newborn babies. Hospitals increasingly have internal policies covering NTBR decisions and abstinence. And the problem of unregulated pain relief has attracted attention not only in the United States (see Preston 1994) but also in the Netherlands (see Zwaveling 1994).

of American practice, where anything called 'euthanasia' is taboo but abstinence and pain relief are perfectly acceptable:

> The difference between terminal sedation and euthanasia … is paper thin, requiring a highly intellectualized analysis and presentation of the physician's intentions. In both circumstances, the patient inevitably dies as a result of the treatment. With terminal sedation, the wished-for death must be foreseen but not intended if it is to remain under the protective umbrella of the 'double effect'. The potential for self-deception in such justifications is substantial.[137]

The constructibility of the distinction between 'intentional termination' (euthanasia and termination of life without an explicit request) and pain relief is illustrated by a number of things we have seen in the course of this chapter. There is, for example, the fact that nursing-home doctors, while rarely performing 'euthanasia', have the highest rates of death due to pain relief. The inability of many doctors to describe their intention and their actual behavior in a way consistent with the definitions used in the research (and in current law) forced the researchers to allocate 2% of all deaths – almost two-thirds as many as euthanasia itself – to a 'grey area' between termination of life without an explicit request on the one side and pain relief on the other. And one explanation Van der Wal and Van der Maas themselves give for the increased rate of euthanasia between 1990 and 1995 is the increased willingness of doctors to ascribe a 'heavier' intent to their behavior.

The line between euthanasia and termination of life without an explicit request on the one hand, and death due to non-treatment on the other, is also highly constructible. As we have seen, 13% of all deaths in 1995 were due to abstention whereby the death of the patient was the doctor's *express purpose;* frequently, this was with the consent or at the specific request of the patient. If there is any difference from euthanasia or termination of life without an explicit request here, it lies not in the question *why* the doctor does what he does nor in the *result* but only in the *technique* used (something largely determined not by substantive or regulatory considerations having to do with the control of medical power, but only by the fairly arbitrary question, what the patient's specific medical problem happens to be). The arbitrariness of the distinction – the essential constructibility of 'abstention' – is reflected in the fact that in two of five reported cases of termination of life without an explicit request in the case of coma patients the PGs decided not to prosecute because the doctors' behavior hardly differed from ceasing a futile treatment.[138]

---

137 Quill 1996: 210-211.
138 In the case of adult patients who want to die, Quill (1996: 90, 146, 151, 193, 209) has described the essential arbitrariness and constructibility of the distinction between 'killing' and 'letting die' with quiet and persuasive eloquence.

Finally, the problem of constructibility reflects itself in the profound confusion sur-rounding the concept of a 'natural death' which is, as we have seen in chapter 3.2, the foundation of the reporting procedure on which the control of euthanasia and termina-tion of life without an explicit request is based. There are a variety of indications in the data that doctors find it difficult to decide whether a case is a (non-reportable) one of pain relief or of abstinence (possibly with some 'help in dying'), on the one hand, or a (reportable) one of euthanasia or termination of life without an explicit request on the other hand. In close to half of all cases of termination of life without an explicit request, the doctor's reason for not reporting the case was that he considered the patient's death a 'natural' one.

The researchers in 1995, while not themselves concerned with the question whether a death is 'natural' nor whether it must be reported, do contribute to the confusion by the way they treat life-shortening behavior in the case of severely defective newborn babies. Only when administration of a lethal drug is not preceded by abstinence, not in the far more frequent case of abstinence followed by such administration, do they consider this a case of 'active termination of life' (see table 5.13). If the same approach were applied to the whole category of termination of life without an explicit request, a considerable part of it would have to be recategorized as abstention (which may help explain why doctors themselves regard half of the category as natural deaths).

The constructibility of a case of MBSL is primarily a result of the central role that the subjective intention of the doctor and the manipulable distinction between action and omission play in the current regulatory regime (see chapter 4.1). The exigencies of prac-tice in the case of terminal patients make refined distinctions between different sorts of intent highly remote from the practical business of effective regulation. The medical decisions involved follow closely upon one another, and the whole decision-making process is situationally highly determined. In such circumstances, isolating one moment as that at which the doctor's 'intention' changed from 'relieving pain' to 'killing' – with as a consequence that entirely different legal controls come into play – is inevitably an arbi-trary enterprise. Similarly, whether a case is presented as one of 'active' intervention or of 'passive' non-treatment is in many cases quite arbitrary.

In short, one can hardly blame doctors for constructing cases of MBSL in a way that is most convenient for them since the legal instruments with which they are supposed to work are unusable. A legal control regime confined to euthanasia – a regime in which euthanasia is distinguished from 'normal medical practice' in terms of a subjective 'intention' and an 'active' intervention to cause the death of the patient – cannot offer effective legal protection against the abuse of medical power. Its real function can never be more than symbolic.

The practical result of the constructibility of many cases of MBSL is simple: strict formal control of euthanasia and termination of life without an explicit request, and little or no control of other MBSL, makes effective legal protection of patients impossible and manifests itself primarily in the sort of skewed medical statistics we have seen in comparing the rates of different MBSL in the practice of different sorts of doctors. It seems quite clear, for example, that the constructibility of euthanasia accounts, at least in part, for the relatively low rate of euthanasia in nursing homes: doctors act to shorten life for the same reasons but in slightly different ways. The constructibility of euthanasia also means that all comparisons of 'euthanasia' rates over time and between jurisdictions are founded on quicksand: the relatively high rate in the Netherlands in the last few years, compared with a presumably very low rate in other countries with which the Netherlands are (often unfavourably) compared, probably reflects the willingness of the Dutch and the reluctance of other cultures to call a spade a spade more than it does any real difference in rates of behavior.

We can conclude from the empirical evidence discussed in this chapter that the two fundamental problems confronting the present system of legal control over euthanasia and termination of life without an explicit request are the conceptual categories employed (a fatal weakness of legal control both in the Netherlands and *a fortiori* elsewhere) and the intrinsic ineffectiveness of control based on self-reporting. In chapter 6 we address these problems directly and consider the question whether anything can be done to remedy them.

6 Euthanasia and Other Medical Behavior that Shortens Life as a Problem of Regulation

It is generally assumed – not in the least, as we have seen in chapter 5.3.5, among doctors themselves – that effective control of euthanasia is important and that at least some of this control must take the form of *legal* control. That assumption is the point of departure in this chapter.

Legal control is of course not the only possible, nor necessarily the most effective, form of control over the behavior of doctors (or anyone else). We can safely assume that doctors generally experience far more and more pressing social control from their professional surroundings than from the law and that this applies as much to euthanasia as to other aspects of their practice.[1] We can also safely assume that this professional control is sufficient – especially when taken together with general social norms and control – to ensure that the behavior of most doctors is socially acceptable most of the time.

Nevertheless, it is hardly a conceivable outcome of the public euthanasia debate that the question how and when euthanasia is performed is regarded as a matter of public indifference and therefore as not demanding any special legal regulation. Questions of life and death are nowhere regarded as belonging entirely to the private sphere, and this is all the more so when the power of the medical profession is involved as well. Euthanasia seems inevitably a matter of *politics* and control over euthanasia inevitably a matter of *law*. But as we will argue in this chapter, it does not follow that the most effective form of legal control takes the form of criminal prohibitions and prosecutions. Legal control, we will argue, can best confine itself, within wide margins, to supporting, strengthening and structuring professional control.

6.1 Criteria for a control system

To raise the question, whether there is effective legal control of the behavior of doctors in the case of euthanasia and related MBSL, does not imply that one supposes that what they are actually doing is cause for alarm. Nor does it imply a fundamental distrust of doctors. Both the available literature and extensive discussions over several years with

---

1   For important contributions to the medical-sociological literature that generally support this proposition, see Anspach 1993; Freidson 1975; Sudnow 1976; Zussman 1992.

doctors, defence lawyers, prosecutors and others convince us that the euthanasia practice of Dutch doctors is on the whole careful and responsible, that most of them perform it rarely, with reluctance and as a last resort. The fear that they would come over time to regard it as 'routine' does not seem to have materialized. Nor is there any substantial evidence that Dutch doctors perform what amounts in substance to euthanasia more frequently than their colleagues do elsewhere. If there is a difference between the behavior of doctors in the Netherlands and in other countries, it lies in the fact that Dutch doctors have been willing to take public responsibility for what they are doing, to submit it to public scrutiny and debate and, ultimately, control. In this they have generally had the support both of the public generally and of the legal and political elite.

Nevertheless, we assume that the adequacy of legal control of medical power over matters of life and death is a serious matter in itself, regardless of whether that power is currently being abused. Furthermore, while there is no evidence of serious abuse, there is plenty of evidence that significant numbers of doctors do not take the procedural and reporting requirements as seriously as they should, something that is a certainly a matter of legitimate public concern. As we have seen in earlier chapters, the Dutch public debate on euthanasia is in fact largely focussed at present on improvement of the control regime.

6.1.1   What are the objectives of legal control?

Before we can assess the effectiveness of a regulatory regime it is essential to identify the objectives legal control of MBSL is supposed to accomplish. If an excuse is needed for laboring the rather obvious, it is that no one else seems to have done so.

To impose some order on the matter, we distinguish between primary and derivative objectives of regulation.

The *primary objectives* of legal regulation are to protect the life and the autonomy of the patient.

1   *Protecting the patient's life.* Doctors are subject to the same weaknesses that afflict all other human beings. Especially when their behavior touches matters of life or death, the interests of the patient require effective protection against these human weaknesses. The greatest threat to the patient's life undoubtedly derives from mundane faults such as sloppiness, corner-cutting, authoritarianism, and lack of the moral fibre required to resist undue influence and improper motives (including such things as the pressure of governments bent on budget-cutting).

2   *Protecting the patient's autonomy.* Not only life but also individual autonomy is an important legal value.[2] In particular because dying or very ill or unhappy people are often not in a good position to defend their own interests, and because the patients for whom a MBSL may be relevant often suffer from diminished competence, they require effective protection of their autonomy against the paternalistic power of doctors who think they know better than their patients what the latter's interests are. The need for protection is not less, and perhaps even greater, when the doctor acts with honorable motives.

Medical paternalism can take the form both of putting a patient out of his misery without involving him fully in the decision-making, and of denying the patient euthanasia or another MBSL either because the doctor does not consider it in the patient's interest or because he imposes on the patient some personal view of his own, for example the view that no one can ever really desire his own death.

3   *Providing legal facilities for the exercise of autonomy.* It is not enough that the law protect the patient's autonomy from medical paternalism. The patient's ability to exercise his autonomy depends in practice on a number of conditions being met. The doctor must be required to ensure that the patient is fully informed with respect to his condition, the possibilities of treatment, and alternatives to euthanasia or another MBSL. Doctors who have conscientious or other objections to euthanasia or another MBSL must be required to inform the patient of this at a time when the patient can still make other arrangements and to assist the patient to find a doctor who is willing. Finally, the law itself must offer adequate facilities, especially for the indirect exercise of autonomy: advance directives, legal representation, surrogate decision-making, etc. And there must be provision for the effective implementation of such facilities.

4   *Permitting doctors, within legal margins set as wide as possible, to let their behavior be guided by the principles of medical ethics.* In the history of Western medicine, a great deal of thought has been addressed to the principles of medical ethics. Among these the ideal of selfless devotion to the relief of suffering and indignity is central. Surrounding this are derivative principles such as the confidentiality of the doctor-patient relationship. And because medicine is an imperfect science, principles guiding practice under circumstances of uncertainty – *primum non nocere* and *in dubio abstine*[3] – are of great practical importance.

---

2   We do not propose to defend the legal value of individual autonomy here against those few who – usually on religious grounds – deny its importance. It suffices to note that most people in modern societies disagree with them. See chapter 4.2.1 for discussion of the principle of autonomy; chapter 5.1 for public opinion concerning its importance.

3   'Above all, do no harm.' 'When in doubt, abstain.'

Medical ethics could perhaps be formulated as a set of black-letter rules but these would have little connection with reality: they would afford the doctor no guidance in the hard cases he confronts, nor anyone else a firm basis for assessing medical behavior after it has taken place. The medical ethics that lives in medical practice is essentially *casuistic*: it exemplifies the art of moral judgment in which the specific features of the case at hand, not black-letter rules, are the starting point.

Provision for the primary objectives of legal regulation brings with it a number of derivative matters that also require attention. The most important *derivative objectives* of a regulatory regime are:

5   *Affording doctors a secure legal position.* The legal norms applicable to MBSL must be clear enough that doctors can rely on them safely. And they must also offer adequate protection against the risks of false accusations, blackmail and the like. An adequate regulatory regime requires in this latter connection a variety of prophylactic rules to mitigate the risks: simple things like a strong requirement that the patient's request be written (or tape-recorded), and an absolute prohibition on accepting bequests from a former patient who died from a MBSL.[4]

6   *Affording others involved in a case of MBSL a secure legal position.* The position of nurses, for which most of the proposals for legislative change to date do not make adequate provision (see chapter 3.1.3), is a special matter of concern. In the case of assistance with suicide, there is still too little clarity concerning the differences between giving information and advice, and rendering comfort and support, on the one hand, and forbidden 'assistance' on the other. There is still far too much uncertainty surrounding the legal position of surrogate decision-makers, in particular the parents of severely defective newborn babies (see chapter 3.3.2). Family, intimate friends, nurses, fellow inhabitants of an institution, and the like have their own interests that deserve explicit legal respect.[5]

---

4   Experience teaches that doctors can be terrifyingly naive about the risks they run when they perform euthanasia without a written request (or other clear and independent evidence of the dead person's wishes) or allow a patient to leave them something in his will. (Information from G. Verkruisen, an expert in the field of medical law, based on his experience advising and representing doctors.)

5   See e.g. KNMG 1995: 18-22. In taking a NTBR decision or in deciding to cease treatment, for example, the religious convictions of the family and even their practical concerns on matters such as timing (e.g., to enable members of a far-flung family to assemble) should be given some – not determinative – weight. Put another way, a doctor should not be considered free simply to ignore this aspect of the situation.

7   *Quality control of MBSL practice.* A regulatory regime must include measures to ensure the required expertise (for example, with regard to diagnosis, treatment possibilities, alternatives, and execution); it must allocate responsibility for decision-making (making clear whether this is individual or collective, what the role is of the consultant, etc.); it must insist on professionalism in the relationship with the patient,[6] in the way the termination of life is carried out, etc. One serious objection to the current predominant role of criminal law in the control of euthanasia is that it stands in the way of the intercollegial openness and feedback required to maintain high quality standards.[7]

8   *Control of the availability of dangerous drugs.* The risk of abuse of euthanatica can probably be exaggerated, but the problem is a serious one that has received relatively little explicit attention.[8] Objections sometimes raised to assistance with suicide outside the presence of the doctor are to some extent based on a concern to prevent euthanatica from falling into the 'wrong' hands.

9   *Clarifying the private law consequences of MBSL.* Legal development has so far confined itself almost exclusively[9] to the criminal and disciplinary aspects of the problem. The civil liability of doctors (for example, for ignoring an advance directive, for taking a NTBR decision without informing the patient, for abstaining without informing the family of a non-competent patient) and the social insurance consequences (e.g. the question whether a health insurance fund remains responsible for hospital care after euthanasia or abstinence have been refused by an institution) remain to be explored.

The present regulatory regime is more or less defective on many of the above points. But political attention, and the research of 1990 and 1995, have been almost exclusively addressed to protecting the life of the patient, and in discussing the question of legal control in the rest of this chapter we will therefore limit ourselves largely to that objective of control.

----

6   See, for example, the criticism by the Medical Disciplinary Tribunal of the doctor's alleged failure to maintain professional distance from his patient in the *Chabot* case (appendix II-2).

7   See Bosma & Van der Wal 1997. See further section 6.3.2.

8   See, however, KNMP 1994, discussed in chapter 3.1.3.

9   Civil cases with regard to abstinence (e.g. the *Stinissen* case, discussed in chapter 2.4; cases involving temporary custodial measures for children when their parents refuse medical care for them) are the only obvious exceptions to this generalization. See also the civil commitment case referred to in chapter 3.1.2 note 10.

6.1.2   What should we expect of a regulatory regime?

That a regulatory regime makes provision for the various objectives discussed above is not sufficient. It must also be reasonably effective. To that end it must be well-adapted to the needs of the sort of practice it regulates and enjoy the support of those being regulated. Finally, it should inspire public confidence.

REASONABLY EFFECTIVE CONTROL

Control over power is a practical project and must be judged according to practical criteria. The best is often the enemy of the good. One is often better off with a reasonably effective second-best sort of regulation than with one whose requirements, if enforceable, would be ideal, but which is in practice ineffective.

The most common objection to any given proposal for control over MBSL – that it will not be able to 'catch' some offenders – is undoubtedly true. But the same objection applies to all of the alternatives. The interesting question is whether we have reason to believe that a particular alternative is *better* than the rest: likely to achieve more control without 'costing' disproportionately much more than the others. Incidental failures are in general not a significant argument against a legal institution.[10]

In the assessment of a regulatory regime for MBSL, what is particularly needed is some realism concerning the regulatory capacities of criminal law. The participants on both sides of the public debate over legalization of euthanasia often seem extraordinarily naive about this, assuming, for example, that the doctor who abuses his medical power and kills a patient 'like a real criminal', will generally get caught and punished by the criminal law authorities. Even when confronted with the evidence that this assumption is groundless, that the criminal law authorities have almost no chance of finding out about such crimes (see section 6.2.3), people tend to hold to their faith in the criminal law as the only form of control that is 'good enough' if a really fundamental value is at stake. Nevertheless, one will not get far in considering the possibilities of effective regulation of MBSL if one is not prepared seriously to entertain the possibility that the whole apparatus of the criminal law – prohibitions, investigations, prosecutions and punishments – may sometimes be an extraordinarily *ineffective* way of trying to protect a fundamental value.

ADAPTATION TO THE DEMANDS OF THE BEHAVIORAL SITUATION

In the second place, a regulatory regime should be adapted to the needs of the situation to be regulated. Where this is as extraordinarily complex and variegated as in the case of

---

10 Compare Battin (1994), cited in chapter 1, note 13.

MBSL and where societal and professional insight and opinion and the technological, economic and organizational context of behavior are all changing fast and fundamentally – in such circumstances it would be folly to act as if one were drafting a tax code or a law of inheritance and try to lay down a lot of hard and fast rules to govern all imaginable future situations. A regulatory regime that is well-adapted to the situation of MBSL must be capable of recognizing and reacting appropriately to a vast array of situations that differ gradually, subtly, but often quite profoundly from each other. And it must be able to adjust flexibly to changing moral and practical conditions. It must therefore seek as far as possible to assess each individual case in a *casuistic* manner: not with black-letter rules fixed in advance, but in light of its specific circumstances.

The way in which Dutch judges and prosecutors have dealt with the cases that have been presented to them over the past 20 years should be, in this respect, a model for any future system of control. Working with ill-adapted and apparently inflexible[11] legal instruments, they have had the good sense not to follow the path of least legal resistance by disposing of the cases presented to them simply by forcing them onto the positivistic Procrustes bed of the Criminal Code. They have managed to remain open to moral and practical differences and to respond to the demands of the concrete situations in which the doctors concerned have found themselves. In particular, they have left as much room as possible for medical professionals to apply the norms of medical ethics and the medical standard to unique situations. Only where a behavioral requirement can be simply and clearly defined and admits of no exceptions – as in the case of the requirement of accurate reporting – have they drawn a clear line and refused to allow themselves to be talked out of it.[12]

---

11 This generalization applies only to the definitions of offences in the Criminal Code. Other relevant aspects of Dutch law are extraordinarily flexible, such as, for example, the discretion allowed prosecutors not to prosecute (article 167, Code of Criminal Procedure), the wide range of sentencing discretion (with minima of 1 day or 5 guilders), the judicial discretion partly or wholly to suspend a sentence and to find a defendant guilty but not impose punishment (Criminal Code articles 9a, 10, 14a, 23). As we have seen in chapters 2, 3, and 5, extensive use has been made of all these forms of discretion in applying the criminal law to MBSL. In effect, the applicable substantive law is partly a matter of the contours of the defence of justification and partly to be found in the way in which these various forms of discretion have been exercised.

12 Even the fact that this clear line, because of the criminal law context of the current regulatory regime, raises problems of self-incrimination, has not caused them to waver. See chapter 3.2.

ACTIVE SUPPORT FROM THE MEDICAL PROFESSION

There have been politicians (former Minister of Justice Hirsch Ballin sometimes seemed an example) and prosecutors who, in their public utterances concerning the legal control of euthanasia, seem to have got Theodore Roosevelt's adage the wrong way around: they talk loud and act as if they have a big stick. They may be fooling themselves and perhaps they fool the general public. But in fact they have hardly any stick at all.

The *sine qua non* of adaptation to the situation to be regulated is, in the case of medical behavior, the ability of a regulatory regime to secure the active support of medical professionals. This is a fact of which Dutch prosecutors and judges have been quite aware.[13] The nature and sheer size of the regulatory problem are such that no system of legal control that tries to rely on its own resources has any chance of success: the law simply does not possess instruments capable of working on the shop-floor of medical practice without the active support of doctors and others (such as nurses) who are actually present there. The vast preponderance of all control that actually takes place will have in the nature of things to be effectuated by medical professionals themselves. And they can only be expected to do this if the regulatory regime has earned their confidence and respect.[14]

The verbal support for legal control by the leaders of the medical profession – apparently intended for public and political consumption – is not enough. However important the role of the Medical Association has been in the development of euthanasia law and practice, the Association has always wanted to seem politically 'responsible'. The result is that its public positions are demonstrably different from the opinions of Dutch doctors and even farther removed from actual medical practice. The Medical Association has for years taken the position, for example, that every case of euthanasia must be reported as such. In fact, as we have seen in chapter 5.2 and 5.3.5, most cases are not reported and even doctors who usually report do not do so always; a significant (if declining) number of doctors rejects as a matter of principle reporting to the criminal law authorities. The

---

13 There are a number of indications of such awareness. For example, from a fairly early date local prosecutors discussed prosecution policy with local representatives of the medical profession (see chapter 2.3.1, 2.4) and gave assistance to hospitals which were drawing up internal policy guidelines (see chapter 5.4.2 note 131); since the early 1980s there have been periodic meetings at the national level between prosecutorial authorities and the KNMG (letter of Meijers to JG, 4 June 1997). Another indication lies in the great deference paid to the medical profession in judicial decisions and the possibility that the KNMG's change of position in 1984 caused the Supreme Court to change its mind about how to dispose of the *Schoonheim* case (see chapter 2, note 60).

14 This line of thought is worked out as part of a general theory of legal effectiveness in Griffiths 1996.

active support that an effective system of control requires is, in short, not lip service from the leaders of the profession but support founded in the relationships and interactions that make up the daily routine of medical practice. The requirements to be followed by doctors must be congruent with their moral and practical experience, and the institutions with which they are expected to deal must inspire confidence.

Moral: Better a 'weak' form of regulatory control that commands the active support of doctors than a 'tough' one which is all bark and no bite.

PUBLIC CONFIDENCE

A final requisite is public confidence in the regulatory regime. To paraphrase the adage about justice: 'control must not only be done, it must manifestly and distinctly be seen to be done'. It must be clear to everyone what the requirements are and that there is an effective means for enforcing them, and that such enforcement is in fact taking place. Openness and 'transparency' (a term frequently used in circles of the Medical Association) must characterize not only the behavior of doctors but also the control system. Taking euthanasia out of the realm of taboo and exposing it to the light of day is a necessary first step, for no one can ultimately have confidence in a system that forbids but in fact tolerates a great deal of behavior that cannot be talked about in public.[15] The openness of the Dutch situation and a vast number of publications in every sort of medium have helped maintain public confidence in what doctors are doing and how the authorities are dealing with it. But up to now, the only provision for systematic information about euthanasia practice and the enforcement of requirements applicable to it has been the national research projects discussed in chapter 5. A good regulatory regime would itself make provision for regular and thoroughgoing public insight into what is going on.

6.2   Criminal law is the problem, not the solution

As we have seen earlier in this book (chapters 2 and 3), Dutch criminal law and those responsible for enforcing and applying it have over the past 20 years served the development of the law concerning euthanasia well. They have proven themselves creative and flexible enough to allow the law (despite stagnation on the legislative front) to adapt to

---

15   Until as late as the 1980s (see the brief of Advocate-General Remmelink in the *Schoonheim* case, appendix II-1, note 11), it was apparently possible to believe that a politically passive public would be satisfied with a control system in which honorable doctors and honorable prosecutors ignored the rules of the criminal law and discretely did what was reasonable. Those days are behind us (see the *Prologue*).

the changing circumstances of medical practice and to developments in societal values concerning personal autonomy in the dying process.

The fundamental structure of the current regulatory regime, shared also by most proposals for legislative liberalization, consists of a criminal prohibition and a justification that has developed into a general exception subject to certain conditions and a duty to report; all of this is principally enforced, as far as legal control is concerned, by the possibility of criminal prosecution for one or another serious offence against the person.

The national research carried out in 1995 was pursuant to a mandate that specifically concerned the evaluation of the reporting procedure. Although the regular spectacle of doctors reporting and the occasional spectacle of a prosecution has undoubtedly contributed to public confidence (as the procedure has undoubtedly also contributed to improving doctors' knowledge of the requirements applicable to euthanasia and the care that they bring to its performance) it nevertheless seems fair to describe the results of that research (taken together with the earlier research of 1990), as far as the effectiveness of control is concerned, as pretty devastating (see chapter 5.3.5). This conclusion forms the point of departure for the argument in this chapter. The line of argument is straightforward: the present control-regime does not offer effective control; its ineffectiveness is not an accidental and reparable defect but rather an inherent shortcoming of control in the context of criminal law; there is an available alternative that offers more prospect of effective control, namely non-criminal regulation in the context of the 'medical exception'; the 'medical exception' does not mean 'turning the whole question over to doctors', as is sometimes supposed, but rather *organizing legal control in a different and more effective way*.

6.2.1   The regulatory situation recapitulated

Let us begin by briefly recapitulating the relevant data (see chapter 5.3.5) concerning the present control regime. Currently about 1500 cases per year of euthanasia and termination of life without an explicit request are reported by the doctor concerned in accordance with the reporting procedure. This amounts to about 40% of all cases of euthanasia, and it is in particular the more problematic cases that are not reported; essentially none of the cases of termination of life without an explicit request are reported. The cases that do get reported are assessed by the prosecutorial authorities, who practically always decide not to prosecute. Fewer than 5 cases per year are prosecuted, of which about half are 'test cases' brought at the request of the Minister of Justice in order to clarify the conditions under which euthanasia or termination of life are justifiable. Since 1981 there have been some 20 final judgments: in 9 the doctor was found guilty (in 3 no punishment was imposed and in 6 the doctor received a suspended sentence).[16] Such a control regime seems on its face to deserve being described as all bark and no bite.

---

16   In a handful of cases, a fine was imposed for falsely reporting the death as a 'natural death'.

The situation is, however, worse than it first appears. The present control regime actually covers only a small part of the total problem. If we leave sudden deaths in which no doctor is involved aside, about half of all death in the Netherlands – more accurately, the time at which they occur – is the result of a doctor's behavior whose expected result was the death of the patient (almost 60,000 deaths in 1995). Of these, the largest categories by far are death due to abstaining from a life-prolonging treatment (20% of all deaths) and death due to pain relief (18.5% of all deaths). Euthanasia and assistance with suicide are responsible for less than 3% of all deaths and termination of life without an explicit request for less than 1% (see table 5.2).

Despite such numbers, despite the fact that many cases of abstinence or of pain relief are in all practical, moral and legal respects essentially indistinguishable from euthanasia or termination of life without an explicit request, despite the fact, as we have seen in chapter 5.5, that a doctor is usually in a position to 'construct' a case either as one of euthanasia or termination of life without an explicit request, or as one of abstinence or pain relief, and despite the fact that the decision-making and performance of euthanasia are already far better regulated than in the case of the other MBSL, it is euthanasia and termination of life that receive practically all attention from both the critics and the supporters of the Dutch situation. But euthanasia and termination of life are not where the real problems of regulation are to be found, and regulating them in isolation from the rest of MBSL is like trying to make a balloon smaller by squeezing it on one end.

6.2.2   The intrinsic unsuitability of criminal law

There are two basic reasons why the criminal law is an ineffective instrument for the maintenance of societal norms concerning euthanasia and termination of life without an explicit request, one intrinsic, the other practical. In this section we argue that the conceptual apparatus of the criminal law is ill adapted to the situation of MBSL. In the next section we argue that the risk that a doctor who violates the requirements will be caught is so small and the ability (both quantitative and qualitative) of the prosecutorial authorities to process the cases that come to their attention so limited that criminal enforcement will necessarily never amount to anything more than a symbolic threat.

CONCEPTUAL INCONGRUITY

The intrinsic unsuitability of the criminal law derives from the fact that the criminal law makes use of a number of concepts that are conceptually incongruent with those used on the shop floor of medical practice. The concepts of causality, intentionality and omission are central to the analysis of criminal responsibility. But the meanings given to these concepts in the criminal law do not correspond to the meanings that comparable concepts have in the world of medical practice.[17]

The concept of *causality* would appear to be the (implicit) basis of the distinction the law makes in cases of MBSL between a 'natural death' and a 'not natural death', a distinction that, as we have seen in chapter 3.2, is fundamental to the reporting procedure. From the point of view of normal criminal law doctrine, however, a death is attributable to the behavior of a doctor and not to the pre-existing disorder of the patient if the doctor hastens the moment of death, even if only by minutes. In such a case, the death must legally be considered 'not natural'. Doctors, on the other hand, are inclined to think of causality in terms of the dominant factor in the death of the patient, and they do not understand the legal position at all. This is apparent, among other things, from the fact that many doctors report a death as 'natural' even when they themselves regard it as involving termination of life, and when asked say that they did so because they regarded the death as a 'natural' one. The Remmelink Commission, in its advice to the Government based on the 1990 research, also argued that what it called 'help in dying' (*stervenshulp*) – when the patient's vital functions have begun irreversibly to fail and the doctor administers a drug to shorten the process – could be regarded as 'normal medical practice' leading to a 'natural death'. This position goes a long way in the direction of the medical idea of causality, but from the point of view of the criminal law's conception of causality it is hard to see how 'help in dying' can be distinguished from the case of the doctor who hastens the death of the patient not by minutes but by hours, days or even weeks or, for that matter, from the case in which the doctor does so by administering pain relief or by abstaining from treatment. The job cannot be done: making such distinctions does too much violence to the logic of a criminal law analysis of the situation. The foundation of the reporting procedure rests, thus, in the conceptual quicksand that lies between the meaning of causality in the legal and the medical worlds.[18]

The concept of *intentionality* is the basis for the distinction between euthanasia and termination of life without an explicit request, on the one hand, and death due to pain relief on the other.[19] The criminal law works with an objective conception of intentionality: a

---

17 The discussion here is a general one of the fundamental legal approach to accountability common to Dutch and Anglo-American criminal law; it should not be mistaken for an exercise in positive doctrinal exegesis.

18 See chapter 3.2, note 84, on the legal concept of a 'natural death', which is a sort of uneasy compromise between the normal legal conception of causality and the medical conception.

19 The analysis here is equally applicable to the case of abstinence, which, as we have seen in chapter 5.3.1, is often done with the express purpose of causing the death of the patient. The doctrine of double intent could be used in this case, too, but it is generally not considered necessary to do so because the doctrine of omissions is available.

person is taken to intend the natural and probable consequences of his act. In this normal legal sense, the doctor intends the death of the patient in every case of medical behavior that shortens life.[20] To escape from that conclusion and to be able to define the difference between death due to euthanasia and to pain relief in terms of the doctor's intent, practically all participants in the public debate about euthanasia make use of the 'doctrine of double effect' (see chapter 4.1.2): if the doctor's intention is to relieve pain, even if he knows to a virtual certainty that this entails shortening the patient's life, then the case is regarded as one of pain relief and not of taking life. In practice, current legal regulation is also founded on this distinction.

In the reports of the 1990 and 1995 research, the subjective intentionality involved in the 'doctrine of double effect' is subjected to what seems to a lawyer like a *reductio ad absurdum*. Not just two but three levels of subjective intent are distinguished: the doctor administers pain relief *accepting the risk* that the life of the patient will be shortened; the doctor does so with the *subsidiary purpose* of shortening the patient's life; the doctor does so with the *express purpose* of shortening the patient's life. Only the last case is considered euthanasia or termination of life without an explicit request. We are told by the researchers that such refinements of the idea of intent correspond to the subjective experience of doctors,[21] and perhaps that is so, although doctors who write on the subject often give the opposite impression and themselves emphasize how impossible such distinctions are in practice.[22] However that may be, such an approach to intentionality is quite at odds with the normal approach to criminal liability and renders legal control essentially impossible. The doctor who does not want to subject his behavior to scrutiny by the prosecutorial authorities and the courts has only to describe his intention in the required way. He does not have to do so wilfully – no one is accusing all the doctors who do this of lying – for people generally describe their behavior in a socially desirable way without even thinking about it.

The research of 1990 and 1995 affords many different indications that the subjective distinction between euthanasia and termination of life on the one hand and 'normal medical practice' on the other makes serious enforcement of the requirements applicable to euthanasia impossible. To cite but one: the researchers estimate the 'grey area' between termination of life without an explicit request and pain relief at about 2% of all deaths (2700): these are, for example, cases that fall into the third category of intentionality – express purpose – but were reported by the doctor to the researchers as 'pain relief'. In

---

20 For the same conclusion, see: Wöretshofer 1992: 153; Blad 1996: 413-414. As we have seen in chapter 3, the CAL likewise came ultimately to the conclusion that not the intent of the doctor but the (expected) results of his behavior are what is relevant.

21 Van der Wal & Van der Maas 1996: 41; compare Van der Maas et al. 1992: 21.

22 See Quill 1996; Preston 1994; Zwaveling 1994.

presenting the results, the researchers count all of these as cases of pain relief. In fact, of course, the situation is far worse, since only cases in which the doctor was conscious that his intention was to cause the death of the patient are included. If we take into account cases in which the doctor, without being aware that he is doing so, conveniently regards his intent as in one of the first two categories, the number, while unknown, is presumably far greater.

In short, the 'doctrine of double effect' is not only philosophically untenable, as we saw in chapter 4.1.2, it calls for distinctions that simply cannot be made in actual criminal prosecution practice, and by defining intent subjectively it makes enforcement essentially impossible.

Finally, in our survey of criminal law anomalies in the current regulatory regime, there is the use of the idea of an *omission* to distinguish between euthanasia and other 'active' termination of life on the one hand, and abstinence on the other (see chapter 4.1.1 for a philosophical discussion of acts and omissions). In about two of every three cases of abstinence, the doctor's express purpose is to hasten the moment of death (see table 5.2), and the difference between abstinence and euthanasia can be marginal in other ways as well.[23] But because abstinence is regarded as an omission, it is thought, unlike 'active' termination of life, not to involve violation of the various prohibitions of intentional killing (euthanasia, murder and the like). The normal analysis of criminal liability for omissions would seem, however, to require quite a different conclusion. The doctor has a general duty of care toward a patient for whom he is responsible,[24] and under such circumstances refraining from life-prolonging treatment is no longer the sort of omission to which criminal liability does not attach. Furthermore, abstinence consists in practice of a collection of active behavior (things like giving the nurses the appropriate instructions). In short, the circumstances of medical practice are totally different from those contemplated by classic examples of omissions often invoked in discussions of the subject (man sees baby drowning in ditch and walks by). From the point of view of criminal liability, we are talking about some 14,000 cases of 'intentionally' causing death without the patient's request per year.[25] Whether or not in any individual case such medical behavior is justifiable is another question, but it seems clear that the concept of omission will not help us to decide that question.

------

23   Compare Quill 1996: 90, 212-213.
24   Article 255 of the Criminal Code (see appendix I-1) specifically prohibits intentionally placing or keeping in a helpless condition a person for whose support, nursing or care one is legally or contractually responsible.
25   27,500 cases of death due to abstinence, of which about two-thirds with the express purpose of hastening the death of the patient, of which in only 21% the abstinence was at the explicit request of the patient.

The fact that the distinction in criminal law between acts and omissions does not lend itself to application in the case of medical practice is manifest, for example, in the fact that in 2 of the 5 cases of 'active' termination of life of coma patients that the Committee of Procurators-General dealt with in recent years (chapter 5.3.5), the Committee decided not to prosecute because what the doctor had done did not differ significantly from abstaining from (further) medically futile treatment.

Conclusion: At three crucial points the normal criminal law analysis of criminal responsibility is radically incongruent with the way in which the current control regime seeks to regulate medical behavior that shortens life. The 'constructibility' of euthanasia and termination of life without an explicit request, which we have considered in chapter 5.5, is the result of the attempt to use alien conceptualizations of behavior for purposes of legal control, and dooms the effort to enforce societal norms with criminal prohibitions to ineffectiveness.

SYSTEM RESISTANCE TO INAPPROPRIATE USE

Another intrinsic problem with the use of criminal law to enforce societal norms concerning medical behavior that shortens life should be mentioned. The criminal law system itself resists the use of offences such as 'murder', 'manslaughter' and 'euthanasia' to deal with behavior that may or may not be reproachable, but for which such characterizations (and the punishments that would normally be imposed) are deemed quite inappropriate. The extraordinarily mild punishments meted out in cases in which doctors have been convicted of crimes like 'murder' or 'euthanasia' (see table 5.19) speak volumes: they are the sorts of penalties one would expect for procedural corner-cutting or errors of judgment, but hardly for the homicides for which the doctors were formally convicted. The virtual apology that the Court of Appeals in the *Kadijk* case (appendix II-3) felt called upon to offer the GP it had just acquitted, for the fact he had had to stand trial at all for the 'murder' of a severely defective, dying baby, is likewise revealing. In short, one can predict with some confidence that the criminal law system will not allow itself to be used except in an incidental and symbolic way for the prosecution and punishment of doctors for serious offences against the person when what they really are accused of is not keeping proper records or not properly consulting a colleague. In fact, shortly after euthanasia was held justifiable when performed according to the 'requirements of careful practice', the courts began to hold that doctors could also be acquitted despite failure to conform to those requirements. Both the case-law and prosecution policy make clear that as far as the 'procedural' requirements are concerned, it is not the criminal law but medical disciplinary law that is primarily responsible for enforcement.

The lesson seems to have been lost on many proponents of various forms of legislative liberalization. Even the most recent draft bill of the Dutch Association for Voluntary Euthanasia (appendix I-C-3) integrally incorporates the 'requirements of careful prac-

tice' in a revised version of article 293 of the Criminal Code, thereby making them conditions of a successful defence by a doctor charged with euthanasia. This would set the
clock back about 10 years and virtually ensure that the requirements – which in themselves are of great importance – remain a dead, or at least a moribund, letter. If criminal
enforcement of the procedural requirements is politically inescapable, then at the very
least this should be by means of a specific provision with punishments adapted to the
nature and seriousness of the offence.[26] At present, only the prohibition of a false certificate of natural death is specifically provided for in this way and, in contrast to the other
'procedural' requirements, this one seems in fact to attract systematic enforcement
whenever a violation happens to come to the attention of the prosecutorial authorities.

6.2.3   The impossibility of enforcing criminal prohibitions

Even if the conceptual apparatus and the specific criminal offences deployed for the regulation of MBSL were tailored to the nature of the medical situation, enforcement of the
societal norms involved by means of criminal prosecutions would remain essentially an
exercise in self-deception because of the absence of any real chance that offending doctors could be caught. Criminal enforcement is entirely dependent on self-reporting by
doctors, except in an occasional case in which the doctor is guilty of more or less gross
violation of the requirements and makes no effort to avoid being caught but falls as a
ripe fruit into the lap of the prosecution. Practically all prosecutions for euthanasia or
termination of life without an explicit request have originated with a self-report by the
doctor concerned.[27] Such an enforcement system is by its very nature ineffective; one
could as well enforce speed limits by asking drivers to report whether they have obeyed
the law or not. The reporting procedure suffers, as an enforcement regime, from a fundamental paradox: if cases that involve a departure from the requirements are prosecuted, doctors will not report, and the procedure will be ineffective; if there is no such risk
of prosecution, doctors will report, but the procedure is ineffective in that case, too.

The ineffectiveness of criminal enforcement is clearly reflected in the research findings
discussed in chapter 5. In general, doctors only report cases in which they closely adhered
to the applicable legal requirements. In cases where, for good reasons or for bad, they devi-
ated from the requirements – and in essentially all cases of termination of life without an
explicit request – doctors do not report. What we have is an enforcement system almost all
of whose attention is devoted to unproblematic cases. Van der Wal (1993) concludes on

---

26   See for examples of this approach the Wessel-Tuinstra bill of 1984-1986 (appendix I-C-2);
     Kelk 1997.
27   The same seems to be true in the United States. The prosecution of Quill took place after he
     'reported' what he had done in a famous article in the *New England Journal of Medicine*
     (1991). Kevorkian, too, has taken no pains to conceal what he does.

this ground alone that the current effort to secure effective regulation of euthanasia decision-making via self-reporting and criminal sanctions is doomed to failure.

Let us nevertheless suspend disbelief for a moment and suppose that the improved rate of reporting to which Government policy is currently addressed (see section 6.2.5) were to materialize, so that a significant number of cases in which there has been some deviation from the requirements came to the attention of the prosecutorial authorities. Could we then regard criminal enforcement as effective? No, because the prosecutorial authorities completely lack the capacity and the expertise required to deal with the number and complexity of cases that would be involved. At the moment, some 1500 cases per year are reported and (after initial assessments at the local and regional level) are disposed of by the Committee of Procurators-General. The PGs actually discuss about 20 cases per year, which result in fewer than 3 indictments. Considering among other things the serious complaints over the long delays already entailed by this procedure, it would seem out of the question that the system could deal with a far larger input.

But really effective enforcement would involve at a minimum an annual input approaching 5 times the current size (1500 euthanasia cases currently reported, 2250 currently unreported cases, 900 cases of termination of life without an explicit request, and 2700 cases in the 'grey area' between termination of life and pain relief). Included in this gigantic increase will be a large number of cases in which there has been some deviation from the requirements or which – as in the case of termination of life without an explicit request – are otherwise controversial. These problem cases of course take much more time to process than 'textbook' cases of euthanasia. And assessing them requires far more medical expertise for, as Van der Wal has shown (see chapter 5.2), doctors regularly exhibit the human failing of describing what they have done in a way that makes it look better than it actually was. To pierce through such disingenuousness (or deliberate concealment) requires medical training. It does not require much imagination to reach the conclusion that such a 'full-enforcement' scenario is about as realistic as the Great Rock-Candy Mountain.

All this is deadly enough for the current system of criminal enforcement. But the situation is actually far worse. The current rather low reporting rate is based on cases that the doctor interviewed by the researchers himself describes as 'euthanasia' or 'termination of life without an explicit request'. But as we have seen in chapter 5.5, euthanasia and termination of life without an explicit request are constructible. In the nature of things, cases involving a socially convenient 'definition of the situation' of which the doctor himself is unaware – 'pain relief' instead of 'termination of life', for example – are not reported as euthanasia or termination of life without an explicit request. If the ambiguous area between cases of termination of life, on the one hand, and largely similar cases of pain relief and abstention on the other, were included in the reporting statistics, the rate of reporting, and hence of apparent control, would drop dramatically.

In short, an effective system of control would have to include 'normal medical practice' that intentionally causes death. Including what are currently deemed 'natural deaths' due to MBSL in the control regime now applicable only to 'non-natural deaths' would mean we are talking about some 60,000 cases per year that would have to be examined. There is nobody who seriously thinks that the criminal law apparatus could even begin to handle numbers of that magnitude. In other words, effective control of this sort of medical practice within the context of criminal enforcement is impossible. The only thing the criminal law, with some difficulty, can do is to dispose of a fairly small number of relatively unproblematic cases after an examination that is usually rather superficial.[28]

6.2.4   Control in the context of criminal enforcement offers the doctor insufficient legal security

So far the discussion has been limited to the defectiveness of criminal enforcement from the point of view of effective control. But there is another reason why the criminal law is not a suitable instrument of control over medical behavior that shortens life. That is that in this context it is an unpredictable, politically manipulable instrument offering doctors too little legal security (which means, among other things, that other objectives of a regulatory regime, such as protecting the autonomy of the patient and enabling doctors to let their behavior be guided by the goals of medical ethics, are endangered).

Unpredictable and manipulable? Unpredictable, because the risk of criminal liability could not be known in advance with a reasonable degree of certainty in a large number of the almost 7500 cases per year that as we have just seen would at a minimum have to be disposed of by an effective system of control.[29] The law concerning MBSL is in a state of fairly rapid development and – even if the legislative stalemate we described in chapter 2 continues – it will remain so during the coming decades. The probable outcome of the process of change can be predicted in general terms with fair assurance in many areas, but many more criminal prosecutions will be required before the dust settles and a reasonably clear legal situation has been realized. The legal position of a doctor who performs anything other than a 'textbook' euthanasia will therefore over the coming years remain dependent on the outcome of prosecutorial decisions.

---

28   Former chief prosecutor Josephus Jitta argues that the Law on the Disposal of Corpses makes the possibilities of enforcement with criminal law very limited, and that only a national corps of forensically-trained coroners, required to certify the cause of death *in every case* (i.e. at present some 130,000 per year), would change this situation appreciably; he himself is doubtful whether the costs (to the state and in terms of the imposition on the relatives of the deceased) are worth it. Letter of Josephus Jitta to JG, 27 May 1997.

29   That is: 900 cases of termination of life without an explicit request + some proportion of 2700 cases in the 'grey area' + some proportion of the 2250 cases that are currently not reported.

It is precisely these prosecutorial decisions in unsettled areas of the law concerning euthanasia and termination of life without an explicit request that lend themselves to political manipulation. Prosecutorial decision-making is centralized, as we have seen, at the national level (Committee of Procurators-General) where the political intervention of the Minister of Justice has on several occasions been direct and unabashed; and the Minister takes the position that her authority extends all the way down to specific instructions in individual cases. The way is thus open to prosecutorial decisions based not on professional but on political considerations. In fact, as we have seen in chapter 5.3.5, crucial prosecutorial decisions have been taken rather haphazardly, based on the idiosyncratic personal views of a Minister or on his or her wish to make a political gesture to a particular political group. The previous (Christian Democratic) Minister of Justice seems to have been looking for suitable test cases in which he hoped that his opinion that euthanasia should be limited to the 'terminal phase' would be adopted by the courts (he got his come-uppance in the *Chabot* case – see appendix II-2). The current (left-liberal D66) Minister seems to be doing the opposite: looking for cases in which the courts will *expand* the possibilities for legal life-shortening practice. Prior to the prosecutions in the *Kadijk* case (appendix II-3) and a companion case, she announced (together with the Minister of Health) that she did not regard the behavior of the doctors involved as blameworthy and that prosecutions were being brought simply for the sake of clarification of the law.[30] In the case of both the former and the present Minister one could argue that prosecutorial discretion is being abused – the courts manipulated and individual doctors sacrificed – for essentially political ends.

Lawyers often shrug this sort of thing off. They are inclined to think in formal terms about the problem of legal security. Their answer to the above argument would be that there is really no problem, since doctors can count on protection from independent judges. That is true and of course it is important. But it is not enough. The doctor of whom we expect that he respect the autonomy of his patient, that he be guided by principles of medical ethics that require him to prevent suffering and to protect human dignity, and that in the interests of effective control he be frank and open about what he has done, needs not just *formal* but *substantial* legal security. The prospect of ultimately being vindicated by the Supreme Court is not enough: the doctor needs assurance that he will *not be prosecuted*. A criminal prosecution – even for the doctor who is confident of being acquitted – is a long and exhausting experience, and it can in many ways also be a very expensive one. With such a prospect, the doctor who regards himself as running any risk will not be likely to report a case of 'non-natural death'.[31] Only highly principled

---

30   See Sorgdrager & Borst-Eilers 1995; cf. also *Nederlands Juristenblad* 70: 36 (1995).

31   Compare Van der Wal & Van der Maas 1996: 237. It appears, for instance, from the judgment in the *Kadijk* case (see appendix II-3) that the doctor's behavior in that case, and perhaps his decision to report what he had done, were influenced by an assurance he (wrongly) believed to have received from the local prosecution office, to the effect that he would not be prosecuted.

and legally naive doctors do such a thing and they often have regrets later on. And for a doctor who is the least bit worried, for whatever reason, the alternative to reporting is so easy: either simply file a false report of a 'natural death' that the authorities will never find out about, or construct the case as one of abstinence or pain relief. Getting indignant about this sort of all-too-human behavior is irrelevant – as Holmes would have said, it is like shaking one's fist at the weather – since it is with how normal people normally behave and not with how it would be morally desireable for them to behave that a control regime must take account.

The rate of reporting seems in fact to be highly sensitive to doctors' perceptions of the risk of prosecution. When, in the 1980s, the local prosecutorial office in Alkmaar began its experiment with a formalized reporting procedure, assuring doctors in advance that if they had met the the 'requirements of careful practice' they need not fear prosecution, the rate of reporting there rose to a level only many years later achieved in the rest of the country.[32] The substantial increase in the rate of reporting between 1990 and 1995 seems to be largely thanks to the fact that prosecutorial practice in these years gave doctors a sense of legal security, and the insistence of the former Minister of Justice on prosecuting cases in which the 'terminal phase' was at issue, as well as some later prosecutorial decisions, is widely believed to have undermined confidence in the reporting procedure and hence the willingness of doctors to report. Similarly, the fact that the former Minister of Justice announced that all cases of termination of life without an explicit request would be prosecuted presumably helps account for the fact that virtually no such cases are reported.[33]

6.2.5   Can tinkering with the reporting procedure improve the effectiveness of criminal enforcement?

Especially in light of the results of the national research of 1995, which had specifically been commissioned to evaluate the reporting procedure, a general consensus has emerged in the Netherlands that the low reporting rate is the Achilles heel of the system of control over euthanasia and termination of life without an explicit request.

It is curious in this regard that a simple, fundamental question receives hardly any attention in the public discussion: Why *would* a doctor report? It can be revealing to confront the essentially moralistic terms of public and political debate with the acidic question of the 'rational actor' approach to behavior. Not: Is it morally or legally required? but: What's in it for him? Bosma and Van der Wal have inventoried some of the costs and benefits to the doctor considering reporting. Doctors are keenly aware of the costs, both

32   See chapter 2.3.1.
33   Compare Van der Wal & Van der Maas 1996: 237.

those to themselves and those to the family of the deceased. These revolve around two matters: the bureaucratic hassle and unpleasantness of the procedure itself (filling out forms; having the coroner visit the scene shortly after death; etc.), and the risk that reporting will attract prosecutorial attention (confrontation with police and prosecutors; a fairly long period of uncertainty; the risk of actual investigation or prosecution with the attendant costs in time, money, and emotional strain).

The concrete benefits for the doctor are harder to specify. Reporting frees the doctor from the (minuscule) risk of prosecution for filing a false certificate of natural death, but since the sanction if caught is a modest fine, this benefit is at best a small one. Reporting frees the doctor from the risk of being subjected to blackmail and the like. Knowing in advance that he will report frees him from having to keep everything secret (which can be a practical nuisance, complicate the relationship with other doctors and with the family, and be emotionally unpleasant). Reporting is said by some doctors to fulfill an important emotional function: formally 'confessing' what they have done and receiving legal 'absolution' helps them come to terms with having killed a fellow human being. And finally, to the limited extent that failure to report is under present circumstances frowned upon by one's colleagues, reporting saves one from possible exposure to informal intercollegial sanctions. In fact, however, most doctors do not mention such practical matters but give idealistic motives for reporting; it is for *not* reporting that they refer to practical considerations.[34]

However complex the decision to report may be, however, proposals for change in the reporting procedure assume that the key factor leading to decisions not to report is that doctors do not like having their behavior judged by lawyers and do not want to run the perceived risk of prosecution. The Government recently proposed to deal with these problems by creating a buffer between the reporting doctor and the prosecutorial authorities.[35] Assessment committees in which "medical, legal and ethical expertise" is represented will be appointed by the Ministers of Justice and of Health. It would be prosecutorial policy only to deviate from the advice of such a committee under exceptional circumstances.[36] Protected by such a buffer, according to the Government's line of thought, doctors will be more inclined to report.[37]

---

34 See Van der Wal & Van der Maas 1996: 118-121; Van der Wal et al. 1996: 1707-1708.

35 See Bosma & Van der Wal, 1997, for an exploration of the possibilities of such a buffer.

36 The constitutional position of the prosecutorial authorities – according to their professional ideology, supported by general legal opinion – makes complete delegation of the decision whether to prosecute impossible.

37 'Standpunt van het Kabinet naar aanleiding van de evaluatie van de meldingsprocedure euthanasie [Position of the Government with regard to the evaluation of the reporting procedure for euthanasia],' January 1997. See also the draft of a new Order in Council pursuant to the Law on the Disposal of Corpses, and a draft Ministerial Decree setting up the committees, prepared in the Spring of 1997 for submission to the Council of State.

There are to be five regional committees for cases of euthanasia and assistance with suicide. These committees will have substantial caseloads and will therefore have to go about their work in a rather routine way. Actually, that is what the Government expects of them. The Minister of Health was emphatic about this when she presented the Government's proposal at a recent congress organized by the Medical Association: appropriate steps will be taken to ensure that the decisions of the various committees are uniform. They will be bound by the applicable legal norms, and they will report to the Committee of Procurators-General, which (subject to the approval of the Minister of Justice) will make the final prosecutorial decisions. The committee that advises things of which the Committee of Procurators-General does not approve will be called to task or ignored.

Should we expect doctors to have more confidence in such a procedure than in one in which the same legal norms are applied directly by the prosecutorial officials? Doctors are legal innocents and they may at first feel some sense of added security because 'some of us' are in the committee that first assesses what they did. But they are not so innocent that they will not soon enough notice that the grounds on which and the frequency with which they are prosecuted have not changed.[38] Any additional reporting will be limited to non-problematic cases in which the doctor is satisfied that he runs no risk of prosecution. In short, the added value of such assessment committees, in terms of an increased rate of reporting, seems doubtful.[39]

The bureaucratic guidelines and other measures required to secure the desired uniformity are pregnant with the risk of turning the current flexible and adaptive legal norms into a set of calcified rules. It is hard to imagine assessment committees that conform to the Government's vision approaching their task in the same casuistic way that the prosecutorial authorities and the courts have manifested. A step-by-step, casuistic approach

---

38 There are those who suggest that the committees may be rather more critical than the prosecutorial authorities have been and that the Committee of Procurators-General will find it embarassing to ignore an advice to prosecute. If this prediction proves well-founded, the frequency of prosecution will increase as a result of the proposed change in the reporting procedure, and the reporting frequency will presumably decline.

39 The Government proposes to deal with the risk that adding a whole new decision-making circuit to the current procedure will increase the time a doctor has to wait before hearing whether he will be prosecuted or not, by imposing a limit of 6 weeks (subject to an extension of another 6 weeks) on the deliberations of the committees. Six weeks corresponds roughly to the average time now required by local prosecutors' offices to forward a case to the PGs (see chapter 5.3.5). It remains to be seen whether the committees will in fact meet the deadline. Also remaining to be seen is how long the PGs will take in acting on cases received from the committees.

has been serving the cause of careful legal development well. It will be a great loss if bureaucratic guidelines and procedures take the place of a complex mix of judicial, prosecutorial, professional and public consideration of the problems involved. In short, assessment committees answerable to the prosecutorial authorities seem likely to solve nothing and they probably bring new dangers.

In the Government's original conception, there was to be a single national committee for termination of life without an explicit request. Such a committee would have had to have instructions telling it how to deal, for example, with the problems of severely defective newborn babies and coma patients, two areas in which, as we have seen in chapter 3.3, the legal norms of the future have become reasonably clear. It would also have had to be instructed on how to handle cases involving 'help in dying', where a reasonable prediction can perhaps be made about what the legal requirements will be, but which is still highly controversial. And, if it was also to be responsible for cases in which the patient's competence is in question (see below), it would have needed instructions on the complicated and controversial issues surrounding euthanasia requests by somatic patients whose competence is in question and by psychiatric patients, and the perhaps even more intractable problems of the advance directives of patients suffering from dementia. Finally, instructions would have been needed for the 'legal horizon': the non-sick and non-dying.

Perhaps sobered by the prospect of having to formulate such instructions, the Government later decided to take a different approach. All cases of termination of life without an explicit request, as well as all cases of suffering deriving from a mental disorder and of somatic suffering if the patient's competence is in question, are to be dealt with directly by the Committee of Procurators-General. Each case is to be actually discussed by the PGs. This hardly seems realistic. As we have seen in chapter 5.3.5, the PGs discussed 120 cases in the 5 years 1991-1995. Termination of life without an explicit request by itself accounts for some 900 cases per year. The number of cases in which a somatic patient's competence is in question seems, from the experience of psychiatrists who are consulted by other doctors concerning a request for euthanasia, to be more than 30 per year.[40] In

---

40   A rough calculation on not entirely sufficient data (Van der Wal & Van der Maas 1996: 212-213) is as follows: Half of the members of the NVP were sent a questionnaire and 84% responded (N = 552). Thirty percent of the responding psychiatrists have been consulted in such a case. In three-quarters of the most recent cases of such consultation a somatic condition was the reason for the patient's request. In 38% of the most recent cases euthanasia or assistance with suicide took place. Of these 62 cases, the request was not well-considered in 5%, there was a treatable psychiatric condition in 11%, and there was some question of (counter) transference in 19%. If we assume these last categories (which were not exclusive) totalled about 20%, the number of cases in which there was some question of a well-considered request is 12, which extrapolated to all psychiatrists would be about 30 cases per year.

short, only a very small increase in the frequency of reporting will overwhelm the current capacity of the PGs. Of course, if reporting does not increase or even (for example, in the cases in which the patient's competence is in question) decreases, there will be no such problem, but then the goal of increased reporting will not have been reached either. Here, too, the Government seems to find itself securely speared on the horns of an enforcement dilemma.

6.2.6 Would 'legalizing' euthanasia help?

There are others who, although they agree with the Government that what most gives rise to concern in the present system of control over euthanasia is the low rate of reporting, disagree on what to do about it. The Medical Association, the Association for Voluntary Euthansia and others believe that it is the fact that euthanasia is still in some formal sense 'illegal' that is to blame.[41] They argue for the remedy of 'legalization' of euthanasia and assistance with suicide.[42] This puts them squarely in a tradition that goes back to the original reform bill of Wessel-Tuinstra in 1984, on whose theme practically all later proposals are variations. The common element of all these proposals is that a provision should be added to the Criminal Code to the effect that the prohibitions of euthanasia and assistance with suicide do not apply to a doctor who has conformed to certain 'requirements of careful practice' (which are included in the Criminal Code).

It does appeal to a lawyer's aesthetic sense that the exceptions to articles 293 and 294 worked out in legal practice at some point be included in the text of the Criminal Code itself,[43] and perhaps there are some practical reasons for doing so. However, the most important argument for legalization lies in the idea that it would increase the legal security of doctors, thereby (among other things) increasing their willingness to report. But putting the rules which have emerged in the case law into the Criminal Code does not change the conditions under which euthanasia can legally be performed. It is therefore not clear why such legalization would have the desired effect on the rate of reporting.

---

41   KNMG, 'Reactie op het evaluatieonderzoek naar de meldingsprocedure euthanasie [Reaction to the evaluation of the reporting procedure for euthanasia]' (27 November 1996); NVVE 1996. See also e.g. Leenen 1997.

42   With the exception of Kelk (1997), no one seems to think that legalization of termination of life without an explicit request is also possible. Leenen (1997) dismisses it as "not really possible," but he does not make clear why the justification that is already being worked out in the case law (see chapter 3.3; *Kadijk*, appendix II-3) could not be included in the amendments to the Criminal Code that the proponents of legalization have in mind. Whether this would be desirable is, for reasons set forth in the text, another question.

43   This would presumably be welcomed by those legal scholars, for example, who have argued that it is inappropriate to use article 40 – intended as an escape-valve for individual, exceptional cases – as the basis for a general legalization. See the introduction to appendix 2, note 3.

Quite the contrary. As we have seen, enforcement of the procedural requirements (for example, consultation) is currently in almost all cases a matter for non-criminal sanctions. But most legalization proposals incorporate these requirements in the Criminal Code, either as conditions for legal euthanasia or as distinct offences. If such a formal legal change has any effect at all, it will presumably be to make prosecutors and judges feel less free in applying the thus codified rules to the varying circumstances of individual cases. The risk taken by a doctor who reports a case in which, perhaps for good reasons, he did not meet all of the procedural requirements, is not decreased but increased. Such a doctor will therefore be less likely to report. The enforceability both of the substantive conditions and of the procedural requirements that have thus been incorporated in the Criminal Code will decline.[44]

Furthermore, legalization requires definitive formulation of the applicable requirements. When one thinks how much practical and moral insight have increased, and how much legal development has taken place, since the first legalization proposals were made in the early 1980s, one can only be thankful for the blockages in the Dutch political system that kept any of them from reaching the statute books. As far as the legal requirements governing euthanasia and assistance with suicide are concerned, with a few important exceptions, the process of legal change seems generally to have worked itself out. To the extent that that is the case legalization would not entail the risk of trying definitively to regulate matters we do not yet fully understand. Termination of life without an explicit request is, however, quite another matter, and codification would here run the risk of fixing matters long before political opinion and legal development are ripe for it.

In short, 'legalization' of euthanasia in the form of limited and qualified exceptions to the coverage of the existing provisions of the Criminal Code is an option that at first sight seems attractive but for which, on reflection, there is little to be said.

---

44   Increased fear of criminal enforcement will also mean that doctors are less willing than they now are to honor the legitimate euthanasia requests of patients. It is therefore ironic that the NVVE is a proponent of this sort of legalization.
The same objections apply, albeit perhaps with lesser force, to Kelk's (1997) proposal to include in the Criminal Code specific provisions in which not euthanasia itself but the failure to conform to the 'procedural' requirements is sanctioned.

6.2.7   A final verdict on criminal enforcement of legal requirements concerning MBSL

However one approaches the subject, it is criminal enforcement that remains the crux of the problem of effective control. A few improvements can undoubtedly be made in the current system,[45] but these will probably not have any profound impact on its effectiveness. If no better way of maintaining the legal norms that apply to euthanasia and other MBSL can be imagined, then Dutch society will have to live with a low level of reporting and with the fact that it is the problematic cases that are not reported and thus, in practice, largely escape control.

Of course, the argument in this section is far more damaging to the (implicit) claims of effectiveness of control over euthanasia and termination of life without an explicit request in other legal systems. Control in the Netherlands may not amount to as much as one would want, but it does amount to something more imaginative than a blanket prohibition that camouflages a situation of essentially no control at all.

6.3   Decriminalization and the prospects of non-criminal enforcement

There is a widespread assumption – not by any means limited to the euthanasia discussion – that the criminal law is the 'ultimate' remedy, not only in the sense of last resort, but also in the sense of 'really effective'. It is the criminal law that one must turn to if a value is 'too important' to leave to informal control or to civil or administrative forms of legal control. If a value is really important, nothing but a criminal prohibition gives

---

45   Two minor but not unimportant changes that have been proposed might improve the reporting rate somewhat and deserve to be mentioned. (1) Prosecutorial decisions in routine cases could be entrusted (as most other criminal cases) to the local prosecutorial offices; this would in any case substantially reduce the delays entailed by the present procedure (cf. Josephus Jitta 1997). (2) As the Government proposes, the role of the coroner could be strengthened, making general a practice of initial assessment by the coroner already in place in some judicial districts, so that the decision-making by the prosecutorial authorities would rest on sound medical advice (see the memorandum cited in note 37 above). See also the proposal of Josephus Jitta to increase the professionalism and expand the role of the coroner (note 28 above).

enough protection.[46] It is this unchallenged assumption that currently stands in the way of serious thought about the problem of regulating medical behavior that shortens life.

No proposal for reform that remains within the context of criminal enforcement seems to offer a real prospect of significantly improved control over euthanasia and termination of life without an explicit request. Most of them seem likely to have more or less dangerous side-effects. It is time to consider the alternative of decriminalization seriously. The strongest argument for decriminalization is that it is a prerequisite of effective control.

6.3.1 Legalization, decriminalization, and the 'medical exception'

The distinction between *legalization* and *decriminalization* is crucial to our argument. So far, the Dutch have gone a long way toward *legalizing* euthanasia in narrowly defined circumstances, but this has been done within the context of the criminal law. It is the criminal law that remains the guardian of the boundary between 'legal' and 'illegal' forms of MBSL. In current Dutch law and in essentially all proposals for legislative change, the procedural and substantive criteria for permissible euthanasia and termination of life without an explicit request are formulated as criminal prohibitions or as exceptions to criminal prohibitions; enforcement is entrusted to the normal criminal law apparatus.

Decriminalization, the alternative to be considered in this section, unlike legalization, does not primarily address the question what substantive and procedural standards should obtain. It addresses rather the question how legal standards, whatever they are, are to be maintained. Society as a whole must surely set limits on acceptable medical behavior and define the procedural requirements for acceptable medical decision-making on matters of life and death. It does not, however, follow from this uncontroversial proposition that the required societal control must be accomplished with criminal prohibitions and prosecutions.

Decriminalization amounts to the same thing as the 'medical exception', once promoted by Enschedé (see chapter 2.3.1) as the legal solution for the problem of regulating

---

46 Even so sophisticated an observer as Van der Wal (1992: 128) argues that because termination of life without an explicit request is intrinsically dangerous, which is assuredly true, it therefore must remain a criminal offence, subject to a possible defence of conflict of duties for extreme and exceptional cases. For euthanasia, on the other hand, he accepts that effective control requires decriminalization (1992: 121).

euthanasia.[47] Medical behavior that shortens life is considered to fall within an implicit exception to otherwise applicable sections of the Criminal Code defining various offences against the person. It is not controversial that such a medical exception applies to death due to abstinence and pain relief. What 'decriminalization' involves is simply that euthanasia and termination of life without an explicit request be handled in the

---

[47] Two opposing objections to this use of the idea of the 'medical exception' should be noted. On the one hand, in Leenen's (1994: 278-279) view only behavior that is subject to the 'medical standard' – norms of the medical profession itself, based on essentially medical criteria – can in the nature of things fall under the 'medical exception'. Behavior of doctors, such as abortion on non-medical grounds or euthanasia, for which no specifically medical criteria are available cannot be left to regulation by the profession itself. To this objection, our answer is that the norms applicable to euthanasia are, to be sure, norms imposed by society at large (specifically, by the courts or the legislature), but that this is in itself no reason not to leave their enforcement in the first instance to the professional group.

A second objection, by L.C.M. Meijers (letter of 4 June 1997), departs from quite the opposite perspective: the idea of an 'exception' wrongly suggests, Meijers argues, that the criminal law is 'privileged', that if they were not 'excepted' from it the criminal law would be applicable to the professional behavior of doctors. In his view it is the law regulating the medical profession that is 'privileged' as far as such behavior is concerned; medical practice falls entirely outside the scope of the criminal law and has no need for any 'exception'. "It does no justice to the specific character of medical-professional behavior when its acceptance by society is formulated as an exception to just one of the social control regimes that can be applicable to behavior." To the extent Meijers calls attention to the danger of assuming that the criminal law is the 'natural' way to regulate behavior, we agree entirely. The most important reason for nevertheless retaining the term 'medical exception' in our discussion is that whatever unfortunate connotation it may have, it has in fact played an important role in the political and legal discussion of the regulation of euthanasia in the Netherlands, a discussion to which our proposal is intended as a contribution. To the extent his argument goes farther and implies that there is something necessary or natural or intrinsically desirable in professional self-regulation, we would disagree. In our view what is involved is not a sort of 'group sovereignty' that the law is bound to respect but rather a delegation of societal control to a professional group; and this is not a matter of social philosophy (in effect, of 'corporatism' – see the *Prologue*) but a purely practical matter. On practical grounds there is, we would argue, much to be said for keeping regulatory activity as close as possible to the 'shop floor' where the behavior to be regulated takes place. And while the same state of affairs could also be analyzed in other terms (from the perspective of medical professional law, some behavior of doctors could be seen as subject to a 'criminal exception' to the normal requirements governing the behavior of doctors) there is nothing wrong with considering the behavior of doctors that (if they were not doctors) would amount to a criminal offence as, *from the perspective of the criminal law*, falling under an exception.

same way: deemed 'normal medical practice'[48] and subjected to the controls applicable to other behavior of doctors.[49]

As we have seen in chapter 2.3.1, early on in the process of legal change surrounding MBSL the Dutch Supreme Court rejected the 'medical exception' as a defence to a charge of euthanasia. This rejection was based on the Court's reading of the legislative history of article 293 and the views current at the time with regard to the concept of 'normal medical practice'. From the point of view of gradual, case-by-case legal development and the maintenance of public confidence in what was going on, the Court's preference for a casuistic approach was undoubtedly wise. Nothing stands in the way of the legislator more than a decade later taking another view. The Supreme Court itself may some day reconsider its view of the contours of 'normal medical practice' in the light of more recent societal developments and the opinion of the medical profession as that appears from subsequent position papers of the Medical Association and other professional associations (see chapter 3) and from the national research carried out in 1990 and 1995 (see chapter 5).

---

48 There are those who object to use of the term 'normal medical practice' in this connection, since some of the behavior involved in MBSL cannot, in their view, be regarded as 'normal'. This seems an essentially verbal matter and therefore not of much practical import. There are two ways in which the scope of the 'medical exception' (decriminalized control) can be described: (1) The scope of the exception is congruent with 'normal medical practice', but this is not limited to those MBSL currently regarded as unproblematic, including also euthanasia, assistance with suicide and termination of life without an explicit request. (2) The 'medical exception' covers *both* 'normal medical practice' (as currently understood) *and* 'exceptional medical practice', which includes euthanasia, assistance with suicide and termination of life without an explicit request (and perhaps a few other 'non-medical' activities of doctors, such as non-therapeutic abortion and circumcision).

49 The medical exception applies only to the doctor in his capacity as doctor (*lege artis*), not in his personal capacity. The border between a doctor's two capacities would be hard to define in the abstract, but it seems doubtful that this would present significant problems in criminal law practice (the expression 'in his medical capacity' would probably suffice to deal with the occasional murderer who happens to be a doctor).

In the context of MBSL the principle that the medical exception only applies to behavior in a medical capacity might well deserve being surrounded with some prophylactic requirements to guard the integrity of medical decision-making. The medical exception might therefore, for example, not apply to a doctor who has a close family or other relationship with the deceased, nor to the doctor who is provided for in a patient's will. In such cases (as for non-doctors in general), an appeal to the justification of necessity would remain for exceptional circumstances.

The 'medical exception' does not imply that society as a whole abdicates its control responsibility; it does not 'leave control over euthanasia and other MBSL to the medical profession' as is often rhetorically asserted by those who consider decriminalization inconceivable. The only thing the medical exception entails is that the necessary enforcement of societal norms take place with other instruments than the criminal law. There are existing enforcement mechanisms to ensure that 'normal medical practice' in the case of the far greater (and equally dangerous) categories of abstinence and pain relief takes place in a socially acceptable way. The question can be raised, as we shall do in section 6.3.3, whether these mechanisms require strengthening, but if so, this is probably more urgent for the other MBSL than it is for euthanasia.

A substantial number of the deaths due to negligent medical mistakes – roughly the same number per year as deaths due to euthanasia[50] – would, if analysed in terms of the concepts and categories of the criminal law, amount to serious crimes (e.g. negligent homicide – see Criminal Code article 307 in appendix I-A). Here a *de facto* 'medical exception' seems to obtain: the prosecutorial authorities steer well clear of the area, leaving control to civil law and to medical disciplinary law. Nor would a few more or less random prosecutions of doctors increase the level of control; on the contrary, they would deal a death-blow to efforts to bring the problem of medical mistakes out into the open.

The medical exception for euthanasia may have been rejected *de jure* by the Supreme Court and in the public and political discussion, but *de facto* it fairly well characterizes the current situation. Prosecutors, judges and lawyers are only really in a position to assess with much assurance whether the procedural 'requirements of careful practice' have been met. As far as the truly fundamental substantive requirements are concerned, they are in practice almost entirely dependent on the expertise of doctors, answering as expert witnesses the quintessential layman's question: 'How would you have done it, doctor?' Not only enforcement of existing legal norms, but legal development itself has been largely an affair of doctors: expert testimony and position papers produced by various organs of the medical profession have to a considerable extent determined its course. The trouble, however, with such a *de facto* medical exception is that the fiction of criminal enforcement continues to stand in the way of systematic attention to the question how non-criminal control can better be organized.

6.3.2 A system of decriminalized enforcement

What we present here is merely the general contours of a non-criminal enforcement system, for which, as we will argue, there is reason to think that it would be more effective than criminal enforcement in securing adherence to societal norms concerning medical

---

50   See Verkruisen 1997 for an estimate of about 3000 deaths per year due to medical negligence.

behavior that shortens life. If any of the concrete details turn out on further reflection to be infeasible or unwise, this does not really affect our argument, since they are intended only as illustrations of an underlying approach to the problem of decriminalized enforcement. No claim is made that any such system would be watertight. But since the current enforcement regime, as we have seen above, is as leaky as a sieve, it is not hard for an alternative to be significantly better.

The basic elements of a non-criminal enforcement regime would be roughly as follows:

- professional protocols
- open and transparent decision-making
- involvement of other persons than the responsible doctor in the decision-making concerning performance of a MBSL
- full record-keeping
- local, collegial assessment
- marginal control of this local assessment by a proactive agency
- backstop formal (non-criminal) sanctions in cases in which informal sanctions are inadequate or ineffective.

What might decriminalized enforcement look like? The best way to answer this question is to look at the ways in which societal norms are currently enforced within the context of the existing medical exception and the direction toward which legal developments in that regard seem to point. Initial responsibility for the maintenance of societal norms would be delegated to local groups within the medical profession itself. The local and professional character of such control enables it to remain flexible and casuistic. The fact that control is professional and not connected to any risk of criminal prosecution makes it embarassing for a doctor not to be cooperative and deprives him of the main incentive for not being open about his behavior.

The primary role of the law in a decriminalized regime is to ensure maximum openness of decision-making and practice, to provide the basic societal norms to be enforced, and to establish a procedure that structures and supports professional control. The law prescribes a number of simple procedural requirements – attached to objectively ascertainable situations – that the responsible doctor must fulfill in order to make professional control possible. And it provides external guarantees that the profession take its responsibility seriously.

What would reporting and professional control look like in such a system? After the death of the patient[51] the responsible doctor would submit a report of the case to a local professional committee (see below) using a legally prescribed form covering the basic substantive and procedural requirements and supported by appended documents (also in legally prescribed form).[52] The report would include, in addition to full information concerning the medical aspects of the case, the following elements set out in figure 6.1:

---

51   In addition to control after the fact, there have in the course of the public euthanasia discussion been a number of proposals for control in advance, for example by committees appointed for that purpose. With the exception of the consultation requirement, none of these has ever attracted much support, largely, it seems, because of the traditional opposition of the medical profession to collective responsibility for treatment decisions. Because of the dangers that bureaucratic regulation would pose to the casuistic nature of legal development in this area, the fact that such proposals have not gotten off the ground is probably not to be regretted. However that may be, we do not consider them further here.

52   As far as the procedure pursuant to the Law on the Disposal of Corpses for freeing the body for burial or cremation is concerned, the doctor would submit a declaration of death (possibly accompanied with the notation that the death in question was the result of a specified MBSL). It might be a good idea to have all death certificates subject to scrutiny by the coroner before they are forwarded to the authorities responsible for allowing burial or cremation of the body (see note 28 above for such a proposal).

Figure 6.1 Elements of the reporting requirement in a decriminalized control regime for termination of life

1   A full description of the life-shortening behavior including the drugs used (if any) with times and doses, treatment that was not initiated or that was terminated, etc.

2   A description of the competence of the patient and his or her ability to participate in the decision-making. In the case of a patient whose competence is in doubt, a statement of an independent doctor (psychiatrist?) should deal with the question of competence.

3   A full report of the discussions with the patient, preferably confirmed by a witness (whose written statement is included).

4   The request for or agreement to a medical procedure that shortens life, in writing and signed (or recorded on tape, or evidenced in some other unambiguous way).

5   A written statement by an independent doctor who was consulted with respect to the proposed life-shortening behavior.

6   Written statement(s) by the nurse(s) most immediately involved with the care of the patient concerning the patient's situation and request, and the decision-making process.

7   Written statement(s) by immediate family members and/or others in the immediate social surroundings of the patient concerning the patient's situation and request, and the decision-making process.

8   Written statements by the persons present at the time the termination of life was carried out.

If, in the circumstances of the case, any of the required procedural steps could not be taken, or the required statements secured, this would have to be fully explained.

Such requirements actually differ only in some rather minor respects from the existing practice of careful doctors as far as euthanasia is concerned. Most of them have been recommended by authoritative medical bodies, in roughly similar terms, for at least certain specific categories of MBSL (see chapter 3). It can be argued that many of them are already required, at least in some circumstances, by existing civil and medical disciplinary law. To the extent that all this is the case, the suggested regulatory regime would only clarify and make explicit requirements that already obtain and afford a structure for their enforcement.

Failure to report a case in this way would remain a specific criminal offence, the enforcement of which would be more vigorous than now seems usually to be the case.[53] The

---

53   Because euthanasia and termination of life without an explicit request have been decriminalized, the problem of self-incrimination involved in such a requirement is substantially mitigated.

chance of being caught would remain small, but since there would be much less advantage to the doctor in not reporting, even a very modest risk should be a substantial encouragement to do so. Furthermore, not reporting involves, in effect, lying to one's colleagues about what one has done. Once the reasons not to report connected with criminalization are removed, the situation should gradually arise in which it is simply 'not done' not to report. And once almost everyone does report, failure to do so is in itself highly suspicious, suggesting that there must be something really seriously wrong in the case, and for that reason alone something a normal person would rather avoid.

The whole report would be submitted to a local committee charged with reviewing such cases. In the case of larger hospitals, this committee could be an internal one of the hospital itself. In the case of smaller hospitals, nursing homes, etc., the committee could be of a regional group of such institutions. In the case of GPs, the local organizations of GPs (see the *Intermezzo*) could be made responsible for maintaining such committees.[54] The local committee would discuss the case in the presence of the reporting doctor and in complete confidence. Mistakes and differences of opinion would be fully aired. The committee would maintain in its archive a full record of every case and of the discussion in the committee.[55]

The local committees would report annually to the Medical Inspector concerning the numbers of cases of various sorts they have considered and the sorts of problems that became apparent in the discussions. Only cases of very serious or persistent violation of the applicable requirements would be reported individually to the Medical Inspector,

---

54   Mixed committees including non-doctors have been proposed, for example in the Government's most recent proposal for changes in the reporting procedure (see section 6.2.5), although not in the context of decriminalization. This may be an interesting idea, but it should be approached very carefully so as not to diminish the confidence of doctors in the committees and the absolute confidentiality of the procedure.

55   Bosma & Van der Wal (1997) have inventoried a number of control systems, with and without decriminalization. From their discussion it is apparent that the more a control system in which legalization but not decriminalization has taken place gives essentially binding advisory authority to local committees, the more the differences between legalization and decriminalization approach the vanishing point.

who could decide to issue a warning to the doctor concerned or to initiate disciplinary proceedings against him.[56] Of course, the risk of disciplinary proceedings will to some extent tend to deter reporting, in just the way the risk of criminal prosecution does under the present regime; it seems reasonable to expect, however, that the collegial character of the initial discussion in local committees, the reticence to be expected of the committees in reporting cases to the Inspector and of the Inspector in pursuing them, and the greater confidence that doctors apparently have in medical disciplinary law than in criminal law, will cause the balance to tilt far more often than is now the case in the direction of reporting.

The Inspector would make both random and directed audits of the functioning of the committees, having for that purpose access to their archives.[57] Apart from its accessibility to the Inspector in disciplinary cases and in his proactive audits, data from the committee's archive would only be available in quantitative and entirely anonymous form. The prosecutorial authorities would by law be denied any access whatever to the archive or to the information considered by or the discussions in the committee. In other words, the investigation and prosecution of possible crimes (that is, cases falling outside the 'medical exception') would remain possible, but no use whatever could be made of the reporting and control procedure.[58] Even if what a doctor reveals to the committee amounts to murder, the confidentiality of the procedure would be guaranteed. This aspect of the proposal seems shocking to some who encounter it for the first time. But it

---

56   A recent criminal prosecution (the *Schat* case – see chapter 3, note 57) affords a good example of a case that would seem to warrant such treatment: the facts found by the District Court, involving multiple and serious failures to conform to the requirements of careful practice, seem to call for a serious medical disciplinary measure, perhaps revocation of the license to practise medicine.

One objection occasionally heard to such an increased role for medical disciplinary law has to do with the limited protection of the defendant which has traditionally characterized it. Since article 6 of the EVRM is now regarded as applicable to disciplinary proceedings, this objection loses much of its force.

57   The Medical Inspectorate should be required to undertake more proactive control than it currently does. Analysis of the use of particular drugs as registered by the pharmacists who supply them (see chapter 3.1.3, 5.4.3) would be one possibility. Former Minister of Justice Hirsch Ballin once suggested that comparison of the number of reported cases of euthanasia in a particular hospital with the number normally to be expected could lead to a suspicion of underreporting that might call for further investigation. The same idea could apply, of course, to other MBSL that a doctor is supposed to report.

58   Thus reliance on information used in a medical disciplinary case resulting from the reporting procedure would also be excluded. It may also be necessary to exclude use of any of this information in civil cases.

is absolutely essential, since without such a privilege, doctors will not be open with the local committees concerning the most dubious situations, which are precisely those most in need of control. And a water-tight privilege involves no real loss to the prosecutorial authorities, since in the absence of absolute confidentiality cases suitable for prosecution would not be reported to the committees at all.

Reciprocal control by professional colleagues is not the only way in which such a regime would contribute to the maintenance of societal norms. The very act of reporting itself entails some control. Forms, despite their bad reputation, do influence the behavior of those who have to fill them in and are thus useful low-level instruments of control. At first sight one might think that the only thing really demanded of a doctor who fills in the required forms is that his paperwork meet certain requirements. Some reports will undoubtedly be twisted or falsified. But on the whole, especially when forced to commit things to paper, people prefer not to lie. This is even more so if the forms concerned are addressed to close associates such as colleagues. Outright fraud – also, of course, because it does carry some risk of discovery and criminal sanctions – will therefore probably not be a serious problem.

More serious is the risk that a lot of the 'declarations' of colleagues, nurses, family members and patients will be little more than standardized formulas, prepared in advance and pushed under their noses for signature by a hurried doctor. Sometimes the doctor will want them to sign statements that are not really quite true, and sometimes he will subject them to some kind of pressure to do so. We can be pretty certain that this sort of thing will occur. The important question is whether such corner-cutting is likely to be so prevalent that it seriously undermines the effectiveness of control. On that question it seems reasonable to be optimistic. People on the whole do not relish the idea that later on they will have to ask others to sign statements that are not quite true; it is embarrassing to have to do so and some of the persons asked will refuse, which is even more embarrassing. On the whole, most doctors most of the time will adjust their behavior so that it will be easy for them, after a patient has died, to ask for and to secure signatures on the necessary statements. If they have to get the family and the nurses to sign a statement to the effect that they were consulted – even if the statement is just a formula – then they will take the precaution of consulting them. And this is exactly the procedural guarantee that the proposed regime seeks to secure.

Accepting, then, the idea that the proposed regime to a significant degree consists of paperwork, is it *too much* paperwork? Some doctors will certainly complain about it. But in fact the paperwork aspect of the proposal is hardly more onerous than what is in principle already required for *all* medical decision-making on matters of importance and recommended by authoritative bodies within the medical profession itself.[59] Practice similar to what is suggested here is in fact common in at least some hospitals.[60] If we look

59   See e.g. Nederlandse Huisartsen Genootschap 1990.
60   See e.g. Blijham & Van Delden 1996.

around us at the accountability demanded of all kinds of other decision-makers, and the amount of record-keeping we consider reasonable and necessary in that regard, it does not seem too much to demand of someone who intentionally intervenes to shorten the life of another that he involve a certain number of other people in the decision-making and record the whole procedure in writing so that the rest of us can feel assured that what took place can bear the light of day.

Given such a context of formal reporting and collective professional responsibility for assessing what took place, actual enforcement of the applicable norms and informal sanctioning of deviations from them can in most cases be entrusted to the professionals themselves, who realize, after all, that they have the Inspectorate and (albeit not in individualized cases) the interested public looking over their shoulders.

We have said nothing so far about the *substantive* norms that might be applied in such a decriminalized regime. This is because our argument is not primarily concerned with the question whether these norms, in their current form, are in need of change. We would, however, like to note that a more casuistic approach to enforcement permits account to be taken of ethically relevant features of an individual case that the current legal rules – inevitably couched in rather black-or-white legal terms with an eye to their role in criminal enforcement – cannot encompass. As we have seen in chapter 3.1.3 and 3.5, for example, the idea that legal euthanasia should be confined to the 'terminal phase' has never been accepted in Dutch law. On the other hand, the problematic distinction between 'somatic' and 'non-somatic' suffering is the basis for different treatment of the patient's right to refuse treatment. What underlies both ideas – that the 'terminal phase' and that 'non-somatic suffering' are relevant – is the principle of proportionality: the greater the remaining life that is cut short, the more reservations we have about whether euthanasia should be allowed and the greater the care we want to see brought to the decision-making. A system of criminal enforcement has to treat the source of suffering or the medical situation of the patient in a more or less all-or-nothing way. Proportionality, however, is a matter of *degree* and of *circumstance*. A decriminalized, casuistic system could take account of gradual difference and of nuance, and it would therefore be possible to resurrect the idea of the terminal phase, but now as a factor whose weight in the doctor's decision-making should increase gradually with increased foreshortening of life. We would expect the doctor to insist more on treatment, and also to take increasing care in reaching a decision (for example in the form of multiple consultations) the greater the loss of life entailed by the patient's request.[61]

---

61   Compare chapter 5.2, note 18, for the sense among doctors that the less convincing the patient's claim that his suffering is 'unbearable', the stronger the preference should be for assistance with suicide.

6.3.3 A uniform regulatory regime for all MBSL?

So far the discussion has been limited to the question of control of euthanasia and termination of life without an explicit request in a decriminalized regime. It is now time to confront the question, raised at the end of chapter 5, whether a regime so limited can be effective or whether the structured professional control described above should apply to *all* MBSL: that is, including abstinence and pain relief.

At the end of the report of the 1990 research, Van der Maas and his colleagues made a pregnant observation.[62] The attention that has been devoted to the various sorts of MBSL – in the public discussion, in the literature, and especially in the contributions of the opponents of legalizing euthanasia – is in no proportion to their frequency and to the problems of effective societal control that they present. The public discussion in the Netherlands has addressed itself to a small and – from the point of view of control – relatively unproblematic category of MBSL: medical assistance to people who have explicitly requested that their life be ended. Since its existence became widely known as a result of the 1990 research, the small category of termination of life without an explicit request – much of which seems on close examination likewise rather unproblematic – has also received attention out of proportion to its magnitude.

On the other hand, almost no attention has been paid to the much larger group of deaths as a result of MBSL that are currently considered 'normal medical practice' and therefore receive little regulatory attention: abstinence[63] and pain relief. The differences between euthanasia and termination of life without an explicit request, on the one hand, and these other MBSL on the other, seem small when we recall the fact that the deaths in the latter case are frequently every bit as 'intentional' as in the former case, and that these MBSL often concern patients who were not asked what they themselves wanted or even informed about what the doctor proposed to do, and whose family and close friends were not included in the decision-making. If there is a real social problem surrounding MBSL it would seem in the first place to concern such cases.

Another reason for being concerned about the apparently problematic situation of legal control in the case of other MBSL is that this makes effective control of euthanasia and termination of life without an explicit request impossible. As we have seen in chapter 5.5, the boundaries of the different categories of MBSL are highly permeable, that is, a case to which the procedural guarantees surrounding euthanasia ought to be applicable can

---

62 1991: 164.

63 The contrast between the United States and the Netherlands is instructive in this regard. In the United States, where euthanasia is taboo, there has (therefore?) been far more attention paid to the regulation of abstinence. Compare Miller et al. 1994.

often be 'constructed' (consciously or unconsciously) as another sort of MBSL – as 'normal medical practice' – and thus escape the 'requirements of careful practice' and the reporting procedure altogether.

What seems to be needed, in short, is a single regulatory regime for all MBSL.[64] This will entail more explicit and legally structured control over the other medical procedures that shorten life. At the same time it will make effective legal control of euthanasia possible, since the applicable regulatory regime will no longer depend upon how a given death is constructed.

However important such an overall control regime for all MBSL may be, it is not clear that it would be wise to try to impose it on the medical profession in the near future. It seems doubtful whether a formalized system of control encompassing abstinence and pain relief, even if firmly in the hands of professionals themselves, could at present command the required support from doctors. That, in any event, is the tenor of the critical reactions of doctors and other 'insiders' to earlier versions of this argument.[65] In that case, our proposal is doomed to failure. It is probably a better idea to start with euthanasia and termination of life without an explicit request, where decriminalized control will be experienced by doctors as a substantial improvement over the present situation, and to consider expanding the regime only at a later date when organized professional control has become familiar and the growing realization in the profession that death due to abstinence and pain relief also require control has become general.

---

64 Quill (1996: 212-213) argues for similar reasons that legal safeguards are needed for all MBSL.

65 Doctors are alleged to experience 'intentional termination of life' as fundamentally different from death due to abstinence and pain relief. If this is so for most doctors (it certainly is not true for all of them – see e.g. Quill 1996), then despite the fact that from a legal point of view they are quite confused (since *all* MBSL are intentional), a legal regime that treats things they consider profoundly different as one undifferentiated whole will presumably not be capable of commanding their support.

The risk of 'defensive medicine' was a matter of concern for several readers of a previous version of this argument. A reporting regime for all MBSL might lead some doctors to continue treatment to the bitter end, to avoid life-threatening dosages of pain-killers, etc., simply to escape having to subject what they have done to scrutiny. If the risk of this is indeed great, the problem is certainly a serious one. It would have to receive careful attention before implementing anything like the proposed regulatory regime.

6.4   Conclusion

Earlier in this chapter we noted that the current system of criminal enforcement of the legal requirements governing euthanasia and termination of life is ineffective and that this is inherent in the tension between the fundamental concepts used for the analysis of criminal responsibility and the concepts familiar to the participants in medical practice, and in an enforcement system that of necessity must rely on infrequent and highly selective self-reporting. These problems are not really addressed by any of the current proposals for reform, which involve either a local committee as a buffer between the reporting doctor and the prosecutorial authorities or legalization of (some forms of) euthanasia (and perhaps also of termination of life without an explicit request) within the context of the criminal law.

An alternative has been suggested: decriminalization by extension of the so-called 'medical exception' to include not only abstinence and pain relief that shortens life, but also euthanasia and termination of life without an explicit request. Within the context of such decriminalization, a more effective enforcement regime could be created in which control is partly immanent in formal requirements and partly realized by reciprocal professional control by local medical committees whose work is audited by the Medical Inspectorate and followed with interest by the general public. Finally, we have argued that to be effective (and also to deal with comparable – but far more numerous – problems in the case of other MBSL), such a decriminalized control regime ought, at least at some time in the future, to cover abstinence and pain relief as well as euthanasia and termination of life without an explicit request.

As a matter of legal policy, the argument for decriminalization and primary reliance on professional control seems powerful. Opponents of legalization, defenders of the Dutch *status quo*, proponents of various sorts of adjustments to the current situation of criminal enforcement (including legalization), and most of all foreign observers who react with (hypocritical) horror to the partial legalization of euthanasia in the Netherlands need to be asked with increasing insistence what their answer is to this simple question: How do *you* propose to make criminal prohibition a credible response to the need for societal control over the life-shortening behavior of doctors? The spectacle of people who have profound objections to euthanasia putting all their faith in criminal prohibitions is tragically ironic. They seem quite oblivious to the fact that it is precisely the criminalization of euthanasia that makes effective control impossible. If there is a Devil, he is surely a fervent opponent of decriminalization.

7 Two Reflections on the Significance of the Dutch Experience

We would like to end this book with some brief reflections on the significance of the Dutch experience, in particular in connection with similar problems of legal policy elsewhere. We consider two questions: (1) How should the Dutch experience be interpreted if one is concerned about the danger of a 'slippery slope' which leads inexorably from legalization of euthanasia to social practices that are abhorrent? (2) Is the Dutch approach to euthanasia relevant in the circumstances of other countries, particularly a country so vastly different in many ways as the United States?

7.1   Whither leads the slippery slope?

The spectre of a 'slippery slope' from euthanasia in the Dutch sense to a general disrespect for human life and human autonomy, ending in the wholesale slaughter of the impaired, the sick and the otherwise expensive or undesireable, is the biggest gun that foreign critics of Dutch policy bring to bear. Inevitably (or at least probably) and 'logically' (or at least in fact) allowing euthanasia will lead to the legal acceptance (or to public acceptance, or at least to the actual practice) of forms of medical killing that are obviously wrong. What precisely the latter are and why they are so obviously wrong is – apart from ominous allusions to the Nazis or the like – not usually made clear and even more rarely actually argued.

As the foregoing makes clear, the 'slippery slope' is itself a slippery customer, hard to pin down, usually more a bit of suggestive rhetoric than a serious argument (see chapter 4.2.4 for further analysis of the idea of a 'slippery slope'). The way it generally is invoked in discussion makes it seem suspect, a last resort invoked by someone whose real concerns lie elsewhere but who fears his arguments against euthanasia itself may not be persuasive or who, for one reason or another, does not choose to make them. After all, someone who thinks euthanasia, in the Dutch sense, is morally wrong ought not to need the 'slippery slope'. The only position in the debate that honestly depends on the 'slippery slope' argument is that of the person who has no real objection to euthanasia in the Dutch sense but fears it will lead to practices to which he does object. But the weaker the suggested link to repellent practices in the future – and the link is usually pretty weak[1] – the less convincing it is to argue for the rejection of A when one's real objection is to B.

Nevertheless, the argument plays so prominent a role in the international discussion of the Dutch experience that despite the above general reservations we should give it some brief attention. When we considered the slippery-slope argument in chapter 1.4 as one of the forms that foreign criticism of the Dutch partial legalization of euthanasia often takes, we noted that the facts generally invoked as evidence of such a development are quite inadequate to the task. But we were not then in a position to offer evidence one way or the other of our own. We can now look back at the information on Dutch law and practice presented in the course of this book to see whether it supports the idea of a slippery slope.

Hendin characterizes the Dutch experience as "an increasing tendency to free the physician from legal control" and asserts that legalization of euthanasia has "encourage[d] involuntary euthanasia [sic]" in the Netherlands and will do so anywhere else where euthanasia is legalized.[2] Like so many others, he does not bother to offer significant support for the key elements of this powerful assertion:

1   Is there a tendency to free doctors from legal control?
2   What, precisely, is non-voluntary termination of life, and is there anything wrong with it in principle or in practice, and if so, what?
3   Is non-voluntary termination of life more frequent in the Netherlands than it was before partial legalization of euthanasia or than it is elsewhere where euthanasia is still prohibited?

We will return to the first question in a moment. As to the second question, we refer to chapter 3.3 and 4.3.4 for the complexity of the moral and legal issues and to chapter 5.3.2 and 5.3.3 for the complexity of the empirical picture. Non-voluntary termination of life covers a variety of different sorts of situations. Except for those who adhere to an absolutist interpretation of the 'right to life' (see chapter 4), Dutch legal developments in this area – although a reasonable person might certainly come to the conclusion that anoth-

---

1   On the whole, 'slippery-slope' arguments concerning euthanasia underrate the complexity of the moral judgments involved and the capacity of normal people to make distinctions along more than one moral dimension. Holsteyn and Trappenburg (1996) argue on the basis of evidence from public opinion research that the Dutch public is in fact more or less immune to 'slippery-slope' influences and quite capable of making moral distinctions between different sorts of MBSL (in which the principle of autonomy and the principle of beneficence are both relevant but considered of different weight in different circumstances).
2   Hendin 1994: 163, 165.

er approach would on balance be preferable – do not seem terribly shocking. There are certainly things in actual medical practice to be concerned about, particularly as far as effective legal control is concerned, but this area of medical practice is undergoing a process of normalization that, however one may judge it morally, does not present a social problem of great moment. In short, the direction the Dutch are moving does not seem so very horrible.

The third question: As to most of the various sorts of termination of life without an explicit request there is no reason to suppose that their frequency is increasing or that it is higher in the Netherlands than elsewhere. Between 1990 and 1995 the sum total seems to have declined slightly.[3] It is possible that the categories of severely defective newborn babies and long-term coma patients have shown short-term increases in the recent past, but if so this is probably due to advances in medical technology and over-enthusiastic application of the principle *in dubio fac;* disciplined application of the recommendations of the NVK and the CAL (see chapter 3.3) should be adequate to keep the number of such cases of termination of life to a minimum. One can speculate that the number of cases of termination of life in which there was some indication of the patient's wishes but it did not amount to an 'explicit request' may, as euthanasia gradually lost its taboo-character but had not yet become normalized and subjected to clear and generally-known norms, have undergone some temporary increase. As patients and doctors learn the rules, and in particular the importance of explicit communication well in advance, and of written requests, and the legal control system gradually increases its grip on the situation, any such increase – it there has been one – will wither away.

In the end, a reasonable observer would have to conclude, we think, that there is no significant evidence that the frequency of termination of life without an explicit request is higher in the Netherlands than it used to be; and if there has been any increase, it is almost certainly the result of things (medical technology; demographic changes) that have nothing to do with legalization of euthanasia. Nor is there any evidence at all that the frequency of termination of life without an explicit request is higher in the Netherlands than in other countries.[4] The only thing we know for sure is that there is more information available about it in the Netherlands. There is, in short, no empirical basis

---

3   The rate of death due to pain relief with a 'subsidiary purpose' to hasten death (the category of 'normal medical practice' most difficult to distinguish from termination of life), also declined slightly from 1990 to 1995 (see table 5.2).

4   From recent Australian research it appears that while the rate of euthanasia is quite similar to the Dutch rate, the rate of termination of life without an explicit request is significantly higher in Australia (3.5% of all deaths) than in the Netherlands. Abstinence and pain relief are also rather more frequent, often with the express purpose of ending the patient's life and usually without a request from the patient. (See Kuhse et al. 1997.)

for the assertion that the Dutch have already slid a bit down the slippery slope because there is no evidence that they have moved at all (let alone, of course, that legalization of euthanasia was responsible for the slide).

But it is the first question – whether there has been a relaxation of control – that is most interesting. And it is to this question that the most definite answer can be given. Those who claim that the Dutch experience is evidence of the dangers of a slippery slope tend to confuse *criminal prohibition* with *legal control*. As we have seen in chapter 6.3, even decriminalization would not entail lack of legal control – in fact, the main argument for it is that it is a prerequisite to a *more effective form* of legal control. And what the Dutch have so far done – partial legalization – does not even involve a relaxation of *criminal* control.

The slippery-slope argument, applied to the Dutch experience, seems in a paradoxical way to get the direction of legal development backwards. It assumes a tendency toward relaxing legal control over medical behavior, whereas what is really going on is a quite massive *increase* of control. Those who think Dutch legal developments amount to growing normlessness – a sort of medical Weimar Republic or 'last days of the Roman Empire', with the associated ominous associations – have simply not looked carefully enough at what is going on. In fact, a whole new array of norms is coming into being to regulate behavior that hitherto was entirely unregulated. Medical practice in connection with death is being legally domesticated.

As we have seen in chapters 2 and 3, since they brought euthanasia out of the taboo sphere, the Dutch have steadily worked on defining ever more precisely the circumstances in which it is permissible and specifying the procedural 'requirements of careful practice' that must be followed. They have recently gone beyond euthanasia to tackle the problem of termination of life without an explicit request and here, too, a body of substantive and procedural rules is emerging. The Dutch courts have produced an extensive case law dealing in ever more detail with the various problems that arise; there is national legislation and rules, and specific institutional facilities for their enforcement; a number of professional associations – in particular the Medical Association – have produced position papers, guidelines and protocols (much of which has a quasi-legal status); there is a growing tendency for hospitals, nursing homes and the like to have internal policies and regulations on the subject. Control over 'normal medical practice' (abstinence and pain relief) is less well developed but is beginning to be taken seriously, particularly by the medical profession itself. It is an impressive edifice of legal control, and there is nothing like it elsewhere in the world.

For reasons developed in chapter 6, the effectiveness of the control regime currently used to enforce this legal edifice leaves much to be desired (which of course does not mean that doctors do not on the whole conform, but that if they do, this is for reasons other than legal enforcement). Here, too, the Dutch are looking for practical ways to increase the effectiveness of legal control. We have argued that without decriminalization, none of these will be adequate to the task, but that is not the point here. The point is that however feeble legal control is in the Netherlands, it is vastly superior to that in countries which couple an absolute prohibition with an absolute lack of actual control. The Dutch are at least thinking seriously and debating vigorously about the effectiveness of their control regime, even if they have not yet solved the problems.

In short, if there is a slippery slope here at all, it is not one by which controls that formerly were in place and effective are being relaxed, but just the opposite. Those who invoke the hoary metaphor to criticise Dutch legal developments rely on local taboos in their own countries as if these described actual practice and contrast such a mythical situation with the actual empirical data that exist for the Netherlands. Meanwhile, the Dutch are busy trying to take practical steps to bring a number of socially dangerous medical practices that exist everywhere under a regime of effective control. They began with euthanasia and have moved on to medical practices that shorten life in the case of dying patients who cannot express their will: severely defective newborn babies, coma patients, etc. They have even addressed the problem of patients whose suffering is due to a mental disorder.

Hendin himself was especially exercised about assistance with suicide in the case of psychiatric patients. Looking specifically at these cases, where is the feared 'slippery slope'? In the first place, the numbers involved are negligible, and there is no indication of any increase (see chapter 5.3.4). More to the point: is a tiny number of highly-regulated cases of legal assistance with suicide really a serious social threat, or does the real threat lie in an unknown but probably larger number of totally unregulated cases? Anecdotal evidence suggests that psychiatrists have long engaged in practices that amount to assistance with suicide and there is no apparent reason to suppose they do so more often in the Netherlands than in the United States. There are psychiatrists who turn a blind eye to the fact their patients are storing up medicines for a suicide attempt; who allow the release of suicidal patients from institutions to enable them to commit suicide; who inform patients about the existence of organizations such as the Hemlock Society or call their attention to do-it-yourself books on suicide. How much of this goes on, we cannot say. The only thing we can safely say is that so long as it is underground, it is quite beyond any form of legal or other control.

The Dutch still have a long way to go. But triumphantly pointing to the shortcomings of Dutch control, as if these in themselves are a sufficient argument against the whole tendency of Dutch legal development, stands the problem of legal policy on its head. The appropriate Dutch response to this sort of criticism is not to deny the imperfections but to point out that conclusions concerning the ineffectiveness of current Dutch control apply *a fortiori* to the situation in countries where 'euthanasia' is entirely taboo, and that working step by step toward effective control is surely better than denial.

7.2   Is euthanasia law exportable?

There remains the question to what extent the arguments presented in chapter 6, addressed as they are to the situation in the Netherlands, are applicable in the different circumstances of other countries. Since this book has focussed exclusively on the Dutch situation, this is not the place to try to answer such a question, but it should at least be raised.

Two important features of Dutch society suggest themselves as possibly relevant. In the first place, it is characterized by a relatively high level of social solidarity, manifest among other things in the institutions of an advanced welfare state including a comprehensive health-care system. The fear often expressed in the American discussion, that poverty and the costs of medical care might drive dying people into requesting euthanasia when they do not really want it, or might induce doctors for economic reasons to engage in life-shortening practices such as abstention or pain relief, is rather far-fetched in the Netherlands.[5]

A second important characteristic of Dutch society concerns the level of confidence in public institutions and in professionals. It seems no accident that legalization of euthanasia is conceived in the United States, for example, in terms of the rights of *patients* (with doctors' organizations often prominent in opposition) whereas in the Netherlands the public discussion concerns the scope of the professional discretion of *doctors* (doctors having from the beginning been prominent in the movement for legalization). On the whole, the Dutch seem comfortable with the idea that doctors can be trusted with the discretion to perform euthanasia, so that the public debate largely concerns the boundaries of this professional discretion and the sorts of procedural controls to which it should be subjected. Where, as in the United States, poverty and racism are

---

5   This is not to suggest that 'economic' considerations play no role with respect to MBSL in the Netherlands. Official and medical circles do tend to react allergically to the mere suggestion. But there are occasional indications that such considerations affect decisions to grant or withhold treatment, as when the association of hospital directors announced several years ago that they would not make a life-prolonging but very expensive drug for ovarian cancer available in their institutions ('Protest van apothekers tegen verbod op middel Taxol in ziekenhuizen,' *NRC Handelsblad*, 27 December 1993). From the report of the 1995 research it appears that all the Medical Inspectors, some 12% of the doctors and 15% of the prosecuting officials interviewed expect that drastic budget-cutting in the health-care system could lead to increased pressure on doctors to engage in life-shortening practices (Van der Wal & Van der Maas 1996: 174-175). But economic considerations are in Dutch circumstances more likely to be institutional than personal. They are also certainly less relevant for euthanasia than for other MBSL.

endemic and access to health care is to a significant extent a function of ability to pay and is for a large part of the population not (adequately) assured, where the medical profession is said to be held in relatively low esteem and to feel itself on the defensive on many fronts at once, so that doctors have low professional self-confidence and are worried about being seen by their patients as potential killers: in such circumstances the conditions for legalization – let alone for decriminalization – may not obtain.

Nevertheless, before rejecting the Dutch experience as irrelevant to the situation in the United States, one should take account of the following considerations: (1) The key weaknesses we have identified in the Dutch system of control with criminal law (the 'constructibility' of any given case of 'physician-negotiated death'; the virtual impossibility of proactive control) apply with equal force to the situation elsewhere. (2) The unacceptable social consequences one might fear as a result of legalization therefore probably exist already. (3) If one seriously wants to keep such practices under control, there does not seem to be a real alternative to getting them out of the closet and into the light of day, even (or particularly) if one does not like what one is going to see; for this, some degree of legalization is probably a first prerequisite.

Perhaps the most important lesson to be drawn from the Dutch experience does not concern the virtues, defects, dangers and prospects of the way in which the Dutch have chosen to regulate medical practice that shortens life, nor the problems they have experienced in achieving effective control, but the quality of the Dutch public discussion itself. Perhaps it is not always as profound as one would wish. But nowhere else in the world are these questions being discussed so openly, so systematically, so calmly and thoughtfully, and with such a lack of ideological rigidity as in the Netherlands. Other countries may not choose to go the same way as the Netherlands, but they can hardly fail to learn from the Dutch experience, if only they approach it with modesty, open-mindedness and respect.

Appendix I: Some Relevant Legal Documents

A   Articles 40, 228(1), 255, 287, 289, 293, 294 and 307 of the Criminal Code[1]

Note on punishments: The maximum term of imprisonment in Dutch law is in effect 20 years (although a life sentence is in theory possible for a few offences) (Criminal Code article 10). The categories of fine referred to in the offences below are as follows (Criminal Code article 23):
– first: ƒ 500
– second: ƒ 5000
– third: ƒ 10,000
– fourth: ƒ 25,000
– fifth: ƒ 100,000
– sixth: ƒ 1 million.

Article 40
A person who commits an offense as a result[2] of a force he could not be expected to resist [*overmacht*[3]] is not criminally liable.

Article 228(1)
A physician or a midwife who intentionally issues a false certificate of birth, or of the cause of death or of the existence or non-existence, at that moment or in the past, of diseases, frailties or defects, is liable to a term of imprisonment of not more than three years or a fine of the fourth category.

Article 255
A person who intentionally places or keeps in a helpless condition a person he has, by virtue of law or contract, to support, nurse or care for, is liable to a term of imprisonment of not more than two years or a fine of the fourth category.

---

1   Reproduced with permission of the copyright holders (Universiteit Maastricht, Louise Rayar, Stafford Wadsworth) from L. Rayar and S. Wadsworth (transl.), *The Dutch Penal Code* (Littleton, CO: F.B. Rothman, 1997).
2   "[A]s a result of" is weaker than the Dutch '*gedwongen*', which means 'compelled', 'forced' or 'constrained'.
3   See chapter 3.1.3 and the decision of the Dutch Supreme Court in the *Schoonheim* case in appendix II for discussion of the concept of *overmacht*.

Article 287
A person who intentionally takes the life of another is guilty of manslaughter and liable to a term of imprisonment of not more than fifteen years or a fine of the fifth category.

Article 289
A person who intentionally and with premeditation takes the life of another person is guilty of murder and liable to life imprisonment or a term of imprisonment of not more than twenty years or a fine of the fifth category.

Article 293
A person who takes the life of another person at that other person's express and earnest request is liable to a term of imprisonment of not more than twelve years or a fine of the fifth category.

Article 294
A person who intentionally incites another to commit suicide, assists in the suicide of another, or procures for that other person the means to commit suicide, is liable to a term of imprisonment of not more than three years or a fine of the fourth category, where the suicide ensues.

Article 307
A person who by negligence or carelessness is responsible for the death of another is liable to a term of imprisonment or of detention of not more than nine months or a fine of the fourth category.[4]

B   The amendment to the Law on the Disposal of Corpses and the Order in Council pursuant to the law (1993)[5]

The amended Law

The substantive parts of the Law of 2 December 1993 (*Staatsblad* 1993: 643), effective 1 June 1994 (*Staatsblad* 1994: 321), amending Article 10 of the Law on the Disposal of Corpses, are as follows (added text indicated by underlining):

---

4   Article 309 permits, if the offence defined in article 307 is committed in an official or professional capacity, an increase in the punishment of up to a third and the judge may "order disqualification from practicing the profession in which the serious offence was committed, and he may order publication of the judgment".

5   The basic approach of this legislation, in which the criminal provisions concerning euthanasia and assistance with suicide are retained unchanged but 'requirements of careful practice' are formulated outside the Criminal Code and have no direct or necessary relevance for criminal liability, is similar to that of the Government's proposal of 1987 (see chapter 2.4).

Article 10

1 If the coroner [*gemeentelijke lijkschouwer*] is of the opinion that he cannot issue a death certificate, he shall without delay report to the prosecutor by means of a form prescribed by ~~Our Minister of Justice~~ Order in Council.[6] The Order in Council referred to in the previous sentence is to be submitted for approval by Our Minister of Justice and Our Minister of [Health].

2 The Order in Council referred to in section 1 does not become effective until at least three months [after publication in the Official Gazette]. Both chambers of Parliament shall be notified of such publication without delay.[7]

The Order in Council pursuant to the Law

On 17 December 1993 (*Staatsblad* 1993: 688) an Order in Council pursuant to article 10 was issued, effective 1 June 1994 (*Staatsblad* 1994: 321).[8] The relevant parts of Order in Council are as follows:

Article 1

The form for the report of the coroner to the prosecutor, provided for in article 10 of the Law on the Disposal of Corpses, concerning a death resulting from a doctor having terminated life upon request, having rendered assistance with suicide, or having actively terminated life without an explicit request, reads as follows:

   To the Prosecutor in the Judicial District …

   The undersigned, coroner of the municipality …

   –   declares that during the last two years he has given no [medical] advice or assistance to [name, date of birth and address of deceased], deceased on …;

---

6   The significance of this change is that an Order in Council [*algemene maatregel van bestuur*], while submitted by a Minister, must be formally approved by the Government (Queen and Council of Ministers) after advice has been received from the Council of State.

7   Such a requirement of formal notification of Parliament is somewhat unusual.

8   The Government recently submitted a proposed revision of the Order in Council to the Council of State for advice. The biggest change is the separation of the reporting procedure in two, one for euthanasia and assistance with suicide, reports of which are to be assessed in the first instance by regional committees; the other for termination of life without an explicit request and all cases in which there is "any reason for doubt that the patient at the time of the request was fully aware of the implications of his/her request and of his/her physical situation," which are all to be assessed by the Committee of Procurators-General. See chapter 6.2.5 for discussion of this proposed new procedure. The substantive changes (in the 'Points requiring attention') are fairly small: questions are added concerning discussion of the case with nursing personnel and concerning a written report by the consulted doctor, in both cases suggesting that this is in general desireable.

- declares that he personally examined the corpse;
- declares that the doctor responsible for the care of the deceased [*behandelend arts*] has informed him that the death was caused by his having terminated life upon request/rendered assistance with suicide/actively terminated life without an explicit request;
  [...;]
- declares that he has received a report from the responsible doctor, consisting of well-reasoned answers to all of the questions on the list of points requiring attention [*aandachtspunten*], set forth in the appendix which is a part of this Order in Council;
- declares that he has verified the facts included in that report and that his judgment with respect to the report is as follows ...;
- declares, in light of the report of the responsible doctor that he is not convinced that the death was the result of a natural cause;
- declares that he has/has not received a written request [for euthanasia or assistance with suicide]...

(date) (signature)

Appendix: Points requiring attention from the responsible doctor in connection with a report to the municipal coroner of a death resulting from termination of life upon request, assistance with suicide, or active termination of life without an explicit request, as referred to in article 1.[9]

In case of termination of life on request, assistance with suicide, or active termination of life without an explicit request from the patient, you are required to submit a well-reasoned and complete written report, based on the medical dossier, to the municipal coroner, covering the following points. This report does not affect the applicability of articles 287, 289, 293 and 294 of the Criminal Code.

I   MEDICAL ASPECTS

[1-4 Nature of the disease(s), treatment(s), doctors involved in treating the patient and their diagnoses and prognoses.]

5   a) Was the suffering so severe that the patient could and did experience it as unbearable?
      b) What was the nature of this suffering?
      c) In what respect was the suffering lasting and hopeless [without prospect of improvement]?

---

9   Also published in *Medisch Contact* (49: 697-699, 1994) and in KNMG 1995.

d) On what grounds was it assumed that the patient's situation, medically speaking, would lead to a further worsening of suffering already experienced as unbearable, with as a result such deterioration that the patient would no longer be able to die in a way consistent with human dignity?

e) How much longer did you expect the patient to live [...]?

6   a) Were there possibilities for making the patient's suffering more bearable and did you discuss these with the patient?

b) What was the patient's position in this regard?

II   THE REQUEST FOR TERMINATION OF LIFE

A   Termination of life on request and assistance with suicide in the case of patients with a somatic disorder

1   Was there a completely voluntary, explicit, well-considered and lasting request from the patient? (If not, answer the questions under part III, Active termination of life without an explicit request.)

2   When and to whom was the request first made? When and to whom was it repeated?

3   Is there a written request? If so, include it with this report. If not, what is the reason for this?

4   What basis is there for the judgment that when the request was made, the patient was fully conscious of its implications and of his/her physical condition?

5   Was the termination of life discussed with family and close friends [*naasten*]?
a) If so, with whom and what were their views?
b) If not, why not?

B   Termination of life on request and assistance with suicide in the case of patients with a psychiatric disorder

[1-3 Same as under A.]

4   Was in your medical judgment the patient capable of understanding the implications of his/her request and of insight into his/her situation, taking into consideration the nature of his/her disorder?

5   What basis is there for the judgment that when the request was made, the patient was fully conscious of its implications and of his/her situation?

6   a) Were there (medical, therapeutic or other) possibilities to make the patient's suffering more bearable or to cure it?
    b) If so, what basis is there for the judgment that the patient rejected these possibilities in a well-considered way?

[7 Same as under A (5).]

III   ACTIVE TERMINATION OF LIFE WITHOUT AN EXPLICIT REQUEST

1   What was the reason that there was no explicit request from the patient at the moment life was terminated?

2   Was there an earlier indication (written or oral) by the patient concerning termination of life?

    a) If so, what was its substance, when was it made, and to whom?
    b) If not, when did the question of termination of life arise and by whom was it raised?

3   What additional considerations influenced the medical decision-making and the time of termination?

4   Was the [proposed] termination of life discussed with family and close friends [naasten] and/or legal representative(s) [of the deceased]?
    a) If so, with whom and what were their views?
    b) If not, why not?

IV   CONSULTATION

(The following points are applicable both in the case of II Request for termination of life, and III Active termination of life without an explicit request.)

1   a) Which doctor(s) was/were consulted?
    b) What is his/their professional position?
    c) When did the consulted doctor(s) see the patient?
    d) Where can he/they be reached?
    e) Was/were he/they involved in the treatment of the patient?
    f) What is/are his/their relationship to you?

2   This point is only relevant if the patient was suffering from a psychiatric disorder (see II-B):

   a) Which psychiatrist(s) and/or other persons with knowledge of the psychological condition of the patient was/were consulted in addition to the doctor(s) mentioned under point 1?

   b) When did he/they see the patient and how did he/they form a judgment?

   c) Where can he/they be reached?

   d) What is/are his/their relationship to you?

3   What were the conclusions of the consulted doctor(s) with respect to:

   a) the patient's situation and remaining life-expectancy?

   b) possible alternatives?

   c) the voluntariness, well-consideredness and lastingness of the patient's request?

V   THE ADMINISTRATION OF LIFE-TERMINATING TREATMENT

1   When, where, by whom, and in what way and with what drugs did the termination of life take place?

2   Was information acquired with respect to the method to be used and if so, from whom?

3   a) Were you present at the time of administration?

   b) Who else was present and where can they be reached?

4   Was the administration of life-terminating treatment discussed with the head of the ward and/or with nursing personnel and/or with the visiting nurse?

   a) If so, with whom, when, and what were their views?

   b) If not, why not?

5   When and in what way was the director of the institution informed about the administration of life-terminating treatment?

C   Some Legislative Proposals

1   The proposal of the State Commission on Euthanasia (1985)[10]

Article 292b [new]

1   A person who intentionally terminates the life of another person, who is not able to express his will, because of severe physical or mental illness or disorder, is liable to a term of imprisonment of not more than six years or a fine of the fourth category.

2   The act described in the previous section is not punishable if the termination of life was performed by a doctor in the context of careful medical practice on a patient who, according to prevailing medical opinion, has permanently lost consciousness, and after treatment has been stopped because it was futile [*zinloos*].

3   Careful medical practice in the sense of the second section requires among other things that the doctor consult a doctor appointed by Our Minister of [Health].

Article 293 [in place of the existing provision]

1   A person who intentionally terminates the life of another person at that other person's express and earnest request is liable to a term of imprisonment of not more than four and a half years or a fine of the fourth category.

2   The act described in the previous section is not punishable if the termination of life is performed by a doctor in the context of careful medical practice [*zorgvuldig medisch handelen*] on a patient who is in a situation of hopeless necessity [*uitzicht-loze noodsituatie*].[11]

3   For the purposes of the second section, termination of life includes furnishing the means for suicide and assisting therein, in the context of careful medical practice.

4   Careful medical practice in the sense of the second and third sections includes among other things that:
   a) the patient is informed with respect to his situation;
   b) the doctor has convinced himself that the patient made his request for termination of life after careful consideration and has voluntarily adhered to it;

---

10   Staatscommissie Euthanasie 1985: 40-43.
11   Several members of the State Commission proposed to add the words: "and whose death is inevitable and imminent [*onafwendbaar aanstaande*]" (see chapter 2.3.2).

c) the doctor judges that on the basis of the facts known to him termination of life is responsible, because together with the patient he has reached the conclusion that there are no other solutions for the situation of necessity [*noodsituatie*] in which the patient finds himself;
d) the doctor has consulted a doctor appointed by Our Minister of [Health].

5   With respect to a patient who has made a written request for termination of life and who is no longer capable of expressing his will, careful medical practice in the sense of the second section includes among other things that:
a) the doctor has convinced himself that the patient's request for termination of life was made voluntarily and after careful consideration;
b) the doctor judges that on the basis of the facts known to him termination of life is responsible, because he has reached the conclusion that there are no other solutions for the situation of necessity in which the patient finds himself;
c) the doctor has consulted a doctor appointed by Our Minister of [Health].

Article 293b [new]

The doctor referred to in the second section of articles 292b and 293 who fails to consult a doctor appointed by Our Minister of [Health] before terminating the patient's life is liable to a term of imprisonment of not more than three years or a fine of the fourth category.

Article 293c [new]

Without prejudice to the provisions of article 228 [false death certificate], the doctor referred to in the second section of articles 292b and 293 who intentionally fails to comply with the duty imposed by or pursuant to law to report a death, or who does so untruthfully, is liable to a term of imprisonment of not more than three years or a fine of the fourth category.

Article 293d [new]

For the purposes of the provisions of this title [of the Criminal Code], the expressions taking life and termination of life do not include:
a)   not initiating or stopping a treatment at the express and earnest request of the patient;
b)   not initiating or stopping a treatment in a situation in which that treatment, according to current medical opinion, is futile [*zinloos*];

c) not treating a secondary illness or disorder in the case of a patient who according to current medical opinion has permanently lost consciousness;

d) hastening the moment of death as a subsidiary effect of treatment that is necessary in order to relieve the severe suffering of a patient and whose nature is directly appropriate to that end.

Article 294 [not substantively changed]

2   The proposal of Wessel-Tuinstra (1984-1986)[12]

Article 293 [in place of the existing provision]

1   A person who intentionally terminates the life of another person at that other person's express and earnest request is liable to a term of imprisonment of not more than four years or a fine of the fourth category.

2   The act described in the previous section is not punishable if the termination of life is performed by a doctor in the context of careful treatment [*zorgvuldige hulpverlening*] on a person who is in a situation of hopeless necessity [*uitzichtloze noodsituatie*].

3   Careful treatment requires:

a) that to the extent possible the person requesting help [*hulpvrager*] receives information concerning the situation he is in, in particular including treatments that could be effective in relieving his suffering;

b) that the person requesting help makes his request voluntarily and in a well-considered way and himself makes the request known;

c) that the doctor makes his decision after having convinced himself that the person requesting help is in the situation described in the second section and that the requirements of clause (b) have been fulfilled;

d) that the doctor has consulted an independent doctor with whom he does not have any intimate personal [*samenwonings*[13]] or family relationship.

---

12   The text presented here is that of the final version of 8 March 1986 (*Second Chamber of Parliament, 1986-1987*, 18 331 no. 38). Like the Government's tentative draft bill of 1986 (the so-called 'Proeve': see chapter 2.4), it adopts the basic structure of the proposal of the State Commission.

13   Literally: living together. Used in contemporary Dutch to refer to marriage-like relationships between people who do not choose, or are not able (e.g. homosexual couples), to marry.

4   If the patient is no longer able to express his will, but at some earlier time made a written request for termination of life should he be suffering unbearably, then this written request can be considered an expression of his will, on condition that the doctor is convinced that the written request was made after careful consideration and voluntarily.

5   If the person requesting help is not yet eighteen, his legal representatives must be included in the decision-making. If these persons or one of them cannot agree with the request for termination of life, no such decision shall be made.

6   The doctor shall keep a log for at least five years, and upon request shall make this available to the prosecutor, in which at least the following are covered:

    a) the facts and circumstances referred to in section 3;
    b) the attitude of the people in the immediate surroundings to the request and the treatment [*hulpverlening*[14]];
    c) the name and opinion of the consulted doctor;
    d) instructions to a nurse, as provided in article 293b.

7   The doctor shall without delay send a truthful statement concerning the death to the municipal coroner, pursuant to a form provided by Order in Council.[15]

Article 293b [new]

A nurse who acted on the instructions and under the responsibility of a doctor and who in good faith could believe that the doctor was not thereby guilty of a criminal offence, shall not be prosecuted for the offence described in section 293.

Article 294 [in place of the existing provision]

1   A person who intentionally incites another to commit suicide is liable, if the suicide ensues, to a term of imprisonment of not more than twelve years or a fine of the fifth category.

2   A person who intentionally assists in the suicide of another or procures for that other person the means to commit suicide is liable, if the suicide ensues, to a term of imprisonment of not more than four years or a fine of the fourth category.

---

14   From the text of the bill it is not clear whether the treatment referred to is that preceding and surrounding the request, or the administration of euthanasia itself.
15   See note 6 above on the character of such an Order in Council.

3   The act described in the previous section is not punishable if it took place in the context of careful treatment, as provided in article 293, sections 3, 6 and 7.

Article 294b [new]

The doctor who fails to comply with the requirements in article 293, sections 6 and 7, is liable to a term of imprisonment of not more than one year or a fine of the third category.

Article 294c [new]

1   No person is required to entertain a request for termination of life or assistance with suicide or to participate therein.

2   If a doctor has conscientious objections to termination of life on request or to assistance with suicide, he shall inform the person requesting such help of this fact immediately upon being approached with the request.

3   The first section does not relieve a doctor of the duty, if requested and if the person requesting help gives his consent, to provide other doctors with information concerning the situation of the person requesting help.

3   **The proposal of the Dutch Association for Voluntary Euthanasia (1996)[16]**

Article 293 [in place of the existing provision]

1   A person who terminates the life of another person at that other person's express and earnest request is liable to a term of imprisonment of not more than four years or a fine of the fourth category.

2   The act is not punishable if done by or in close consultation and cooperation with a doctor in the context of careful treatment [*zorgvuldige hulpverlening*], and the person concerned is suffering unbearably.

---

16   *Voorontwerp euthanasiewet* [Draft euthanasia law]: NVVE, 1996.

3   Careful treatment requires that the doctor:
    a) has convinced himself that the person concerned is unbearably suffering and that the request for termination of life is voluntary and well considered;
    b) has either consulted an independent doctor with regard to the seriousness and prospects of the suffering, or has consulted an independent expert with regard to the well-consideredness of the request for termination of life. If this well-consideredness might, reasonably speaking, have been influenced by a mental illness or disorder, then at least one psychiatrist must have been consulted with regard to the question whether that is the case and, if so, whether the influence is predominant;
    c) ensures that a good report is made of the decision-making and administration;
    d) immediately following the death of the person concerned makes that report available to the municipal coroner.

4   If the person concerned is no longer able to express his will, a voluntary and well-considered written request for termination of life can meet the requirement of an express and earnest request, as provided for in section 1.

Article 294 [in place of the existing provision]

1   A person who intentionally incites another to commit suicide is, if the suicide ensues, liable to a term of imprisonment of not more than twelve years or a fine of the fifth category.

2   A person who intentionally procures for another person the means to commit suicide is, if the suicide ensues, liable to a term of imprisonment of not more than three years or a fine of the fourth category.

3   The act referred to in the previous section is not punishable if done by a doctor in the context of careful treatment at the express and earnest request of a person who is suffering unbearably.

4   The provisions of the third section of the previous article are equally applicable in this case.

Article 294a [new]

1   The act referred to in the second section of the previous article is also not punishable if done by a doctor in the context of careful treatment at the express and earnest request of the person concerned.

2   In that case, careful treatment requires that the doctor:
a) has convinced himself that the request for the means to achieve a humane death [*zachte dood*] is voluntary and well-considered;
b) has consulted an independent doctor with regard to the well-consideredness of the request for termination of life, provided that if it might, reasonably speaking, have been influenced by a mental illness or disorder, at least one psychiatrist must have been consulted with regard to the question whether the well-consideredness has been so influenced and, if so, whether the influence is predominant;
c) ensures that a good report is made of the decision-making and if possible of the use of the means furnished;
d) immediately following the death of the person concerned makes that report available to the municipal coroner.

3   Fear of mental or physical deterioration that has become inescapable and imminent can suffice as the basis for a well-considered request to make the means for achieving a humane death available.

Appendix II: Three Leading Cases

Three leading decisions of Dutch courts in cases concerning the legality of medical behavior that shortens life are presented in this appendix. The statements of facts are based on those in the decisions of the Courts of Appeals.[1] The actual opinion of the court is indicated as such, and under this heading all but some purely formal passages have been translated directly and in full. All footnotes have been added. With this exception, all passages not directly quoted from the courts' opinions are placed between square brackets.

Contrary to the common assumption that the Common Law is characterized by flexibility, the Civil Law by rigid adherence to codes, the Dutch courts have exhibited considerable creativity in dealing with the problem of medical behavior that shortens life.[2] There are some Dutch criminal law scholars who regret the fact that the Dutch Supreme Court has given such an encompassing interpretation to the idea of necessity that a provision intended as an escape-valve for extraordinary situations has become the basis for the regulation of hundreds of cases per year.[3]

---

1   In Dutch criminal procedure, a Court of Appeals conducts a full trial of the case and makes its own findings of fact. The statements of facts presented below are, except where noted, limited to the facts as found by the Court of Appeals, which formed the basis of its judgment and, on appeal, that of the Supreme Court.

2   The contrast with the approach of the English courts is striking. Even under the extreme circumstances of the *Cox* case, in which the patient was so close to death that it was not even certain that the drug used (potassium chloride) had actually caused his death, the House of Lords considered itself not free to find an appropriate substantive solution. The problem of rendering justice to the accused was solved in sentencing: a suspended sentence and a mere 'admonishment' from the disciplinary authorities. See Goff 1993.

3   See e.g. Schalken, Note accompanying the decision of the Supreme Court in the *Chabot* case. *Nederlandse Jurisprudentie* 1994, no. 656: 14.

In fairness to the judges concerned, it should be noted that it is characteristic of Dutch opinion-writing style that rather little actual argument is given and the legal conclusions reached have a rather apodictic character.[4]

1   SCHOONHEIM[5]

Supreme Court of the Netherlands, Criminal Chamber, 27 November 1984, nr 77.091. Judges Moons, Bronkhorst, De Groot, De Waard, Haak [*Nederlandse Jurisprudentie* 1985, no. 106].

1   Procedure

The appeal[6] is from the Court of Appeals, Amsterdam (17 November 1983), which, setting aside the judgement of the District Court, Alkmaar (10 May 1983), found the defendant guilty of the offence charged: "taking the life of another person at that person's express and earnest request" as prohibited by article 293 of the Criminal Code. Applying article 9a of the Criminal Code, the Court of Appeals imposed no punishment or other

---

4   One reason for the absence of extensive argument may have to do with the absence of concurring and dissenting opinions in Dutch judicial practice. One consequence of this is that there can be pressure within a court to arrive at a compromise acceptable to all the judges (that the Supreme Court found this difficult in the *Chabot* case seems to be indicated by the fact that judgment was twice postponed: see Leenen, Note accompanying the decision of the Supreme Court in the *Chabot* case, *Tijdschrift voor Gezondheidsrecht* 1994 no.47: 355).

The explanation for the Supreme Court's oracular style is probably partly historical. Dutch cassation practice derives from French practice, in which the court consists both of judges and of an advocate-general, whose written advice to the judges includes fuller arguments and is to be read together with the rather bare conclusions of the court (cf. Remmelink 1981). To the extent they go further than or are of a different tenor from those of the Supreme Court, the arguments of the Advocate-General in the *Schoonheim* and *Chabot* cases have been indicated in footnotes at the appropriate places.

5   Translation by D. Griffiths.

6   Technically: request for cassation. The facts as found by the court below are taken as established and, when the prosecution appeals, only those issues specifically presented in the request for cassation are considered by the Supreme Court. In general, if the judgment below is found legally incorrect, the case is assigned to a different Court of Appeals for a new decision.

measure. The District Court had acquitted[7] on the ground of 'absence of substantial violation of the law'.[8]

The appeal is brought by the defendant, who is represented by G. Spong and E.Ph.R. Sutorius. The brief of the Advocate General of the Supreme Court, J. Remmelink, recommends rejecting the appeal.

2   Facts

The following facts were established by the Court of Appeals.

The defendant has been a general practitioner in Purmerend (province of North Holland) since 1974. Ms. B, born 27 November 1886, became his patient on 8 March 1976. From the beginning, she repeatedly made clear to the defendant and others that she was suffering seriously from the deterioration of her physical condition. She also repeatedly asked defendant to perform euthanasia.

Her wish to have her life terminated was especially manifest on two occasions. The first was in April of 1980, when Ms. B, at age 93, signed her living will. In this document she stated her wish that euthanasia be performed upon her in case her situation should develop into one in which no recovery to a tolerable and dignified condition of life was to be expected.[9] The second occasion was after she had broken her hip on 16 September 1981, and surgery was being considered.

---

7   Dutch criminal procedure distinguishes between two acquittal verdicts: *vrijspraak* is based on failure of the prosecution to prove the facts charged; if the facts charged are proved, *ontslag van rechtsvervolging* may nevertheless follow, either because the facts charged do not amount to an offence or because the defendant successfully pleads an excuse or a justification. The judgment of the Court of Appeals – as of the District Court – was an acquittal of the latter sort.

8   See below under 3.2.

9   The full text of this document is as follows:
"After thorough consideration, of my own free will, and in possession of my full faculties, I declare the following:
1. If at any time, whether due to illness, accident, or whatever other cause, I enter into a condition, physical, mental, or both, from which no recovery to a tolerable and dignified condition of life is to be expected, I wish:
    a. that no medicine or technology, intended to support or prolong vital processes, be applied;
    b. that no medicine or technology, intended to support or revive consciousness, be applied;
    c. that euthanasia be performed on me.
2. If my condition is as described under 1, and my state of consciousness permits, the responsible doctor is requested to ask me to confirm this declaration; if my mental condition is such that I am not able to participate in such deliberation, this declaration is to be taken as my explicit wish."

Ms. B suffered terribly from the steady decline of her health, which manifested itself in deterioration of her hearing, eyesight and power of speech, although the last showed temporary improvements. She had dizzy spells, she was permanently handicapped and bedridden due to the above-mentioned hip fracture, and there was no prospect of any substantial improvement of her condition.

In the weekend of the week preceding her death on Friday 16 July 1982, Ms. B was afflicted by a major deterioration in her condition. She was no longer able to eat or drink and lost consciousness. On Monday 12 July her condition had improved a little: she had regained the power of speech and was in full possession of her faculties. However, she had suffered severely under the collapse, mentally as well as physically, and she made clear that she did not want to have to go through something like this again. Once again she urgently requested the defendant to perform euthanasia upon her.

The defendant discussed the situation several times in depth with his assistant-physician, who had also spoken with Ms. B a number of times, and to whom she had also expressed her desire for euthanasia. After having spoken with Ms. B's son more than once as well, the defendant finally decided on Friday 16 July, with the approval of both his assistant and Ms. B's son, to comply with her request. In defendant's opinion, Ms. B experienced every day that she was still alive as a heavy burden under which she suffered unbearably. That same day, the defendant ended Ms. B's life, applying a medically accepted method.

A few hours later, the defendant reported the euthanasia to the local police.

3   The opinion of the Supreme Court

3.1   THE MEANING OF 'TAKING ANOTHER PERSON'S LIFE'

[The defendant's first argument was that he had not 'taken Ms. B's life' in the sense of article 293, since Ms. B had requested him to perform euthanasia. The argument is perhaps less far-fetched in Dutch than it seems in English because of the peculiar legal terminology of the offences against human life: these speak of 'een ander van het leven beroven', which means literally 'to rob another person of life'.

The explanatory statement accompanying article 293 of the Criminal Code [when submitted to Parliament][10] reads as follows:

---

10   More precisely, this is the explanatory statement accompanying article 317 of the first draft of what became the Criminal Code, offered to Parliament in 1879. In the final version of the Criminal Code (1886), article 317 was unchanged although it was renumbered article 293. It is important to realize that the legislative history that the Supreme Court uses to support this part of its decision is more than a hundred years old.

He who complies with another person's explicit and serious wish to take his life is to be subjected to a punishment considerably lighter than he who has been found guilty of plain murder. The consent cannot remove the punishability of taking another person's life, but it does completely alter the character of the act – the law, so to speak, no longer punishes the assault against a certain person's life, but the violation of the respect due to human life in general – no matter what the motive for the act may be. Crime against human life remains, crime against the person is absent.

Neither the legislative history – as the above shows – nor changes in public opinion provide ground for accepting the view, argued for in the first point on appeal, that article 293 of the Criminal Code should be interpreted restrictively in such a way that a physician who, in the course of conscientious medical treatment, ends a patient's life upon that patient's request, on the ground of long-lasting suffering, cannot be understood to be 'taking another person's life'. The phrasing as well as the tenor of article 293 – as the Court of Appeals rightly held – point towards an understanding of the words 'een ander van het leven beroven' as meaning simply: 'taking another person's life', and that is what the conduct that the defendant has been proved to have performed must be deemed to be.

[…]

3.2   ABSENCE OF SUBSTANTIAL VIOLATION OF THE LAW

[The second argument on appeal is that the defendant's conduct did not amount to a 'substantial violation of the law' and therefore is not punishable. The Court of Appeals had rejected this view.]

The defendant's counsel argued to the Court of Appeals, among other things:

–   that the right to self-determination concerning the end of one's own life should be included as a 'legal value' in the legal assessment of voluntary euthanasia;

–   that this individual freedom to make decisions about one's life and fate has gained in weight, to the point that it is now a norm of fundamental importance in determining the legal position of the patient;

–   that in some respects the right to self-determination is to be deemed more fundamental than the right to physical and mental inviolability or the respect for human life.

Considering – among other things – this argument provided by defendant's counsel, it must be assumed that the Court of Appeals intended to make clear that defendant's view that, under the circumstances, it was legitimate for him to comply with the two norms mentioned in the Court of Appeals' judgement – being (a) respect for the right to self-determination, and (b) assistance to a fellow human being in need, guarding his dignity, and relieving or ending his unbearable suffering – cannot be considered to be a view so generally accepted as correct throughout society that it can support the conclusion that euthanasia, performed in a fashion and under circumstances as in the present case, is as such legally permitted and therefore cannot be considered punishable conduct as described in article 293 of the Criminal Code.[11]

The Court of Appeals' opinion, so interpreted, is correct. Taking into account, among other things, what has been considered in the preceding paragraph, the grounds offered by the Court of Appeals for its opinion are neither unsound nor insufficient. Insofar as the Court of Appeals referred to the 'dangers evidently connected with euthanasia' it apparently – and correctly – assumed that those dangers are a matter of general knowledge.

This ground of appeal must, considering the foregoing, be rejected.

3.3   THE JUSTIFICATION OF NECESSITY

[Article 40 of the Criminal Code (see appendix I-1) provides that he who commits an offence due to a force he could not be expected to resist [*overmacht*] is not criminally liable. Beginning with a decision of the Supreme Court in 1923, this has come over the years to be interpreted so that two kinds of defence fall under the term *overmacht*. The first (comparable to the defence of duress in the Common Law) is construed as an excuse: the act as such is punishable, but the offender is not. The second type of *overmacht* is necessity (*noodtoestand*) in the sense of conflict of duties.]

Before both the District Court and the Court of Appeals, defendant's counsel argued, among other things, that the defendant acted due to *overmacht* in the sense that he was confronted with a "conflict of duties, in which he has, in a responsible way, made a correct choice". This appeal to a conflict of duties, which must be distinguished from the appeal, also made by defendant, to *overmacht* in the sense of a claim of conscience [*gewetensdrang*[12]], can hardly be interpreted otherwise than as an appeal to necessity, to the following effect: Defendant has carefully – more specifically: in accordance with

---

11   The brief of the Advocate-General extensively discussed the tendency toward greater acceptance of euthanasia when performed by a doctor, concluding, however, that no sufficiently definite social consensus had emerged to support a judicial decision that article 293 is no longer applicable to such behavior. Legalization, in his view, required legislation. The AG was of the opinion that prosecutorial discretion not to prosecute and judicial discretion in sentencing offer adequate ways of dealing with "honorable" doctors such as Schoonheim.

12   This term is sometimes used in Dutch to refer to *overmacht* in the sense of *inner* compulsion ('psychological *overmacht*'). It should not be confused with conscientious objection (to military service and the like).

norms of medical ethics, and with the expertise which as a professional he must be assumed to possess – balanced the duties and interests which, in the case at hand, were in conflict, and made a choice that – objectively considered, and taking into account the specific circumstances of this case – was justifiable.

By holding that "it has not been established with sufficient plausibility that defendant's views on which his conduct was based pressed him so forcefully to commit the established deed, that it was impossible for him to abstain from doing so," and offering arguments for this opinion, the Court of Appeals has rendered a sufficiently motivated decision on the appeal to a claim of conscience as an excusing condition, but it has not done so with regard to the defence of necessity in the above-mentioned sense.

Insofar as the Court of Appeals, by holding that it had not been established with sufficient plausibility that Ms. B's suffering, up to and including the time that the defendant actually ended her life, had to be deemed so unbearable that the defendant "reasonably speaking had no other choice" than to spare her this suffering by performing euthanasia, might have intended at the same time to reject the defence of necessity brought on behalf of defendant, the Court of Appeals has not provided sufficient motivation for that rejection, since the considerations which follow must be included in the assessment of such a defence.

The Court of Appeals found that among other things the following facts had been established:
–   that Ms. B was suffering terribly from the steady decline of her health and the absence of any prospect of substantial improvement;
–   that in the weekend preceding her death she experienced a major collapse as a result of which she could no longer eat or drink and lost consciousness;
–   that on Monday 12 July 1982 she was able to speak again and in possession of her faculties; but that she nevertheless had suffered greatly, both mentally and physically, from the collapse; that she stated that she did not want to experience something like that again and once more asked urgently for euthanasia;
–   that on Friday 16 July 1982 the defendant decided to comply with her wish "because, in his opinion, she experienced each day that she was still alive as a heavy burden under which she suffered unbearably".

The Court of Appeals can hardly have meant by the phrase "in his opinion" anything other than: "in his expert opinion as a doctor". Taking this and other things into account, further explanation is required as to why the Court, after having established the above-mentioned facts, nevertheless concluded that "it has not been established with sufficient plausibility" that Ms. B's suffering, at the moment that defendant ended her life – being, according to the facts established by the Court, on 16 July 1982, at which time she experienced each day she was still alive as a heavy burden under which she suffered unbearably – had to be considered so unbearable that defendant reasonably speaking had no other choice than to spare her this suffering by performing euthanasia, and as to why the Court in this connection speaks of a "not negligible level of doubt" concerning this pivotal issue.

Instead, one would have expected the Court of Appeals to have considered, after having established the above-mentioned facts and circumstances, and in light of the finding that Ms. B, on 16 July 1982, was still experiencing her suffering as unbearable, whether, according to responsible medical opinion, subject to the applicable norms of medical ethics, this was, as claimed by the defendant, a situation of necessity. In circumstances such as those in this case, the correct answer to the foregoing question is dependant upon several factors, which may vary from case to case. In this case the Court might, for example, in addition to the above-mentioned facts and circumstances, have deemed relevant –

1   whether, and if so to what extent, according to responsible medical opinion it was to be feared that the situation for Ms. B as an individual would involve increasing loss of personal dignity [*ontluistering*] and/or worsening of her already unbearable suffering;

2   whether, taking into account among other things the possibility of further serious collapses, it was to be anticipated that she might soon no longer be in a position to die in a dignified manner, something which, on 16 July 1982, was still possible; and

3   whether, and if so to what extent, there were any remaining ways of relieving her suffering.

The above is in no way affected by the Court of Appeals' judgement that the opinions of the defendant's assistant and Ms. B's son, who had both been consulted by defendant and had agreed with the euthanasia, "cannot be considered sufficiently objective and, in this connection, sufficiently independent". For the latter conclusion of the Court leaves open the possibility that the euthanasia performed by defendant, according to objective medical opinion, must be considered justified, as having been performed in a situation of necessity.

3.4   JUDGMENT

It follows from the above considerations that the decision of the Court of Appeals must be reversed, and the case be referred [to another Court of Appeals for further consideration[13]].

---

13   See note 6.

2   CHABOT[14]

Supreme Court of the Netherlands, Criminal Chamber, 21 June 1994, no. 96.972. Judges Haak (vice-president), Mout, Davids, Van Erp Taalman Kip-Nieuwenkamp, Schipper. [*Nederlandse Jurisprudentie* 1994, no. 656; *Tijdschrift voor Gezondheidsrecht* 1994, no. 47]

1   Procedure

The appeal[15] is from the Court of Appeals, Leeuwarden (30 September 1993), which (like the District Court, Assen, 21 April 1993) found the defendant not guilty[16] of the offence charged: "intentionally assisting another person to commit suicide" as prohibited by article 294 of the Criminal Code. The Court of Appeals found the defense of justification due to necessity well-founded and the question on appeal is whether the Court's interpretation of the scope of the defense was legally correct and whether the facts as found support the decision.

The appeal was brought by the Procurator-General of the Court of Appeals. E.Ph.R. Sutorius represents the accused. The brief of the Advocate-General of the Supreme Court, L.C.M. Meijers, recommends rejecting the appeal.

2   Facts

The following facts were established by the Court of Appeals.[17]

Defendant is a psychiatrist who on 28 September 1991 supplied to Ms. B, at her request, lethal drugs that she consumed in the presence of defendant, a GP,[18] and her friend Ms.

---

14   This translation by J. Griffiths of the *Chabot* case appeared earlier in the *Modern Law Review* (58: 232-248, 1995) with extensive critical comments on a number of aspects of the opinion, many of which appear elsewhere in this book.

15   See note 6.

16   See note 7.

17   More facts are known about this case than appear in the judgment of the Court of Appeals; these will be referred to in footnotes (some of which are based on correspondence with Dr. Chabot).

18   From the findings of the Court of Appeals one might assume that this was *her* GP. Chabot informs us that this was not the case: Ms. B did not want her GP to know when the suicide was to take place, because he was also her former husband's doctor and the latter was opposed to her plans. The GP present was a friend of Chabot's, asked by him to be present "to ensure that what I did was proper, in the technical medical sense" (letter BC to JG, 21 August 1994).

H. She died half an hour later. Defendant reported her death the same day to the local coroner as a suicide which he had assisted. He included what the Court of Appeals characterizes as an "extensive report" of the case, with "a very detailed account of the discussions with Ms. B (and her sister and brother-in-law), a report of the psychiatric investigation and defendant's diagnosis, his considerations concerning Ms. B's bereavement process and her refusal of treatment."

Ms. B was 50 years old. She had married at the age of 22 but the marriage was from the beginning not a happy one. She had two sons, Patrick and Rodney. In 1986 her older son, Patrick, committed suicide while in military service in Germany. From that time on her marital problems grew worse and the relationship more violent, and her wish to end her life began to manifest itself. According to her own statements, she only remained alive to care for her other son Rodney. These circumstances led to a brief admission to the psychiatric ward of a local hospital in October of 1986,[19] followed by polyclinical psychiatric treatment, neither of which had an effect on her situation: according to the psychiatrist at the time, she was not open to any suggestion of working toward an acceptance of Patrick's death.

In December 1988, shortly after the death of her father, Ms. B left her husband, taking Rodney with her; the divorce followed in February 1990. In November 1990 Rodney was admitted to hospital in connection with a traffic accident. In the hospital he was found to be suffering from cancer, from which he died on 3 May 1991. That evening Ms. B attempted suicide with drugs that she had received from her psychiatrist[20] in 1986 but had saved. The attempt was unsuccessful, and to her great disappointment she recovered consciousness a day and a half later. She immediately began to save drugs again with the intention of commiting suicide.

Finding a way to die came to dominate her thoughts. She discussed various methods with her sister; she gave an old friend a letter that was to be opened only after her death; she arranged for cemetery plots for herself, her two sons and her former husband and had her first son reburied so that there was space for her between the graves of her two sons. She attempted to get effective drugs for committing suicide and considered other methods as well, which she discussed with various people. However, she was afraid that a second failure might lead either to an involuntary committal to a mental institution or to

---

19   According to Chabot, the hospital chart shows an admission from Monday 6 (not 3, as stated in the decision of the Court of Appeals) through Monday 20 October, of which 2 weekends were spent at home, so that a total of 13 days were spent in the hospital (letter BC to JG, 12 October 1994).

20   Chabot informs us that the Court of Appeals was mistaken on this point: in fact, Ms. B got the drugs from her GP, not from the psychiatrist (letter BC to JG, 7 September 1994).

continued life with a serious disability. She made it known to others[21] that she wished to die, but in a humane way that would not involuntarily confront others with her suicide.

Ms. B approached the Dutch Association for Voluntary Euthanasia and in this way came in contact with defendant, who had indicated his willingness to give psychiatric support[22] to persons who might approach the Association for help. Between 2 August and 7 September 1991 defendant had four series of discussions with Ms. B, totalling some 24 hours.[23] He also spoke with Ms. B's sister and brother-in-law. Beginning on 11 August, after the second series of discussions with Ms. B, defendant approached 4 consultants. He furnished them with an extensive account of his findings and requested suggestions concerning matters that he might have overlooked in the psychiatric investigation of Ms. B or that required further clarification. He also asked whether they were in agreement with his diagnosis. Later, after the third series of discussions, he approached 3 more consultants.[24]

In considering the question "whether Ms. B was suffering from any illness" the Court of Appeals concluded that there was no indication of any somatic condition that might have been the source of Ms. B's wish to die. From the beginning of defendant's contacts with her it was clear that she was suffering from psychic traumas that in principle lent themselves to psychiatric treatment, so that defendant was justified in entering into a doctor-patient relationship with her even though that might ultimately expose him to a conflict of duties.

---

21 According to Chabot these included her GP, a psychiatric social worker and a clinical psychologist of the Association for Voluntary Euthanasia, all of whom declined to help or advised her to consult a psychiatrist. She also unsuccessfully sought help from close friends in obtaining lethal medications (letter BC to JG, 21 August 1994).

22 In Dutch: *zich bereid had verklaard tot opvang van mensen*. There is no suggestion in the Dutch word *opvang* (relief, care, support) that the support defendant was prepared to offer entailed assistance with suicide. Chabot himself states that he had informed the NVVE that he "was not in principle opposed to assistance with suicide, but that he assumed that in most cases it would be possible to redirect a wish for death into a desire to learn how to live in a different way, on the condition that one can win the confidence of the person concerned and that one takes the wish for death seriously" (letter BC to JG, 21 August 1994).

23 In other accounts of the case, the figure of 30 hours is often mentioned: the difference is due to the distinction between actual hours (24) and billable hours (30). Of the 24 hours, 20 were with Ms. B alone; 3 in the presence of her sister and brother-in-law; 1 in the presence of her friend Ms. H (letter BC to JG, 12 October 1994).

24 The 7 consultants included 4 psychiatrists, a clinical psychologist, a GP and a well-known professor of ethics (of Protestant persuasion) (letter BC to JG, 7 September 1994).

Defendant's professional judgment of Ms. B was that there was no question in her case of a psychiatric illness or major depressive episode, but that according to the classification system of the American Psychiatric Association (D.S.M.-III-R), she was suffering from an adjustment disorder consisting of a depressed mood, without psychotic signs, in the context of a complicated bereavement process.[25] In his opinion, she was experiencing intense, long-term psychic suffering that, for her, was unbearable and without prospect of improvement. Her request for assistance with suicide was well-considered: in letters and discussions with him she presented the reasons for her decision clearly and consistently and showed that she understood her situation and the consequences of her decision. In his judgment, her rejection of therapy was also well-considered.

The Court of Appeals found that defendant was an experienced psychiatrist who made his diagnosis in a very careful way. The experts consulted by him were agreed that Ms. B's decision was well-considered and her suffering long-term and unbearable, and that in the circumstances there was no "concrete treatment perspective"; the majority agreed without reservation with the way he had handled the case. Several of them observed that it was highly likely that, if not given expert assistance, Ms. B would have continued her efforts to commit suicide, using increasingly violent means. Although her condition was in principle treatable, treatment would probably have been long and the chance of success was small. None of the experts consulted considered that there was in fact any realistic treatment perspective, in light of her well-established refusal of treatment. Defendant had repeatedly tried to persuade Ms. B to accept some form of therapy and the Court of Appeals accepted defendant's testimony to the effect that if there had been an available treatment with a realistic chance of success within a reasonable period, he would have continued to pressure Ms. B to accept it and, if she continued to refuse, would not have given her the requested assistance.

Although two expert witnesses stated that in their opinion the doctors whom defendant had consulted ought to have examined Ms. B personally, neither was of the opinion that in this case that would have made any difference, nor that questions were thereby raised concerning defendant's carefulness. In the opinion of the Court of Appeals, defendant's conclusions could be adequately checked in this case against the information available from Ms. B's letters, from intimate acquaintances of hers, from her GP and from her pre-

---

25   The Court of Appeals observed in this connection that the absence of a somatic basis requires "great care in establishing that the wish to die is not a direct symptom or consequence of a psychiatric sickness or condition and that – in this connection – the request for assistance with suicide is well-considered and voluntary. Whether the diagnosis that emerges from investigation [of the person concerned] is labelled a psychiatric syndrome, a psychiatric condition or … a psychiatric disorder is in the opinion of the Court for these purposes not really relevant."

vious psychiatrist. Furthermore, defendant's very detailed and extensive reporting of the case was intended by him to make it possible for others to assess what he had done. The doctors consulted by defendant had been able on the basis of defendant's reports to reach firm conclusions.

The experts consulted in this case, a discussion paper of the Medical Association on the subject,[26] a discussion paper of the Inspectorate for Mental Health,[27] and a position paper of the Dutch Association for Psychiatry[28] all agree that from the point of view of medical ethics, there may be circumstances in which assistance with suicide is legitimate in the case of persons whose suffering does not have a somatic origin and who are not in the terminal phase of their disease.

3   The opinion of the Supreme Court

3.1   GENERAL CONSIDERATIONS

In particular over the past decade there has been a public debate concerning the prohibition of euthanasia and assistance with suicide, which has included the question whether article 294 of the Criminal Code should be revised. This debate has not, however, led to any revision. Legislative bills to that end have been rejected or withdrawn. This Court must therefore proceed on the basis that the prohibition has not been modified.

However, the circumstances of an individual case may be such that rendering assistance with suicide, like performing euthanasia, can be considered justifiable. This is the case when it is proved that the defendant acted in a situation of necessity, that is to say – speaking generally – that confronted with a choice between mutually conflicting duties, he chose to perform the one of greater weight. In particular, a doctor may be in a situation of necessity if he has to choose between the duty to preserve life and the duty as a doctor to do everything possible to relieve the unbearable and hopeless suffering [*ondraaglijk en uitzichtloos lijden*] of a patient committed to his care.[29]

When a doctor who has performed euthanasia or furnished the means for suicide claims that he acted in a situation of necessity, the trial court must investigate – this task is *par*

---

26   Reference is to CAL 4.
27   Geneeskundige Inspectie voor de Geestelijke Volksgezondheid 1993.
28   NVP 1992.
29   The exact formulation of the conflict of duties upon which the justification of necessity rests has taken different forms and the differences may be doctrinally important in connection with the balancing of values on which the defence rests (see chapter 3.1.3; chapter 4, note 41).

excellence that of the trial court – whether the doctor, especially in the light of scientifically responsible medical opinion and according to the norms recognized in medical
ethics, made a choice between mutually conflicting duties that, considered objectively
and in the context of the specific circumstances of the case, can be considered justifiable.
In this connection it should be observed that the procedure by which the doctor responsible for treatment [*behandelende arts*][30] is to report cases of euthanasia and assistance
with suicide, including thereby information on a number of specified items – a procedure that has been in effect in practice since 1 November 1990 and has recently received
a legislative foundation[31] ... – contains no substantive criteria which, if met by a doctor
who performs euthanasia or renders assistance with suicide, entail that his behavior is
justifiable. The reporting procedure offers a procedural structure within which the
responsible doctor can render account of his behavior and the prosecutorial authorities
or the trial court can assess it.

3.2   THE JUSTIFIABILITY OF ASSISTANCE WITH SUICIDE IN THE CASE OF NON-SOMATIC SUFFERING AND A PATIENT WHO IS NOT IN THE TERMINAL PHASE

The first ground of appeal depends on the view that assistance with suicide by a doctor,
in the case of a patient like Ms. B whose suffering is not somatic and who is not in the terminal phase,[32] cannot [as a matter of law] be justifiable.

This view cannot be considered correct. The specific nature of the defense of necessity,
which, depending upon the trial court's weighing and evaluation after the fact of the particular circumstances of the case can lead it to decide that the act was justified, does not
allow for any such general limitation.[33] A claim of necessity can therefore not be excluded simply on the ground that the patient's unbearable suffering, without prospect of
improvement, does not have a somatic cause and that the patient is not in the terminal
phase. The Court of Appeals found, and this is not challenged on appeal, that from the
point of view of medical ethics the legitimacy of euthanasia or assistance with suicide in
such circumstances is not categorically excluded. In answering the question whether in a
particular case a person's suffering must be regarded as so unbearable and hopeless that
an act that violates article 294 must be considered justified because performed in a situ-

---

30   That Chabot, in the circumstances, acted as Ms. B's doctor was not questioned.
31   See appendix I-B for the text of this legislation. See chapter 2.4 for the history of the reporting procedure and chapter 3.2 for its technical legal structure.
32   Dutch: *die niet in de stervensfase verkeert.*
33   The Court's fundamental point of departure – that there can be no general limitations on the defence of necessity – is made more explicit in the brief of the Advocate-General than in the Court's opinion.

ation of necessity, the suffering must be distinguished from its cause, in the sense that the cause of the suffering does not detract from the extent to which suffering is experienced. But the fact remains that when the suffering of a patient does not demonstrably follow from a somatic illness or condition, consisting simply of the experience of pain and loss of bodily functions, it is more difficult objectively to establish the fact of suffering and in particular its seriousness and lack of prospect of improvement. For this reason the trial court must in such cases approach the question whether there was a situation of necessity with exceptional care.[34]

3.3   THE VOLUNTARINESS OF THE REQUEST IN THE CASE OF A PSYCHIATRIC PATIENT

[The second ground of appeal challenges the Court of Appeals' holding that it is possible for a psychiatric patient voluntarily to request assistance with suicide; alternatively, it is argued that the judgment of the Court of Appeals that the request was voluntary is not based on sufficient evidence. The third ground of appeal challenges the Court of Appeals' holding that the fact that a second psychiatrist had not examined Ms. B is not an obstacle to accepting the defense of necessity. The Supreme Court deals with these various contentions together.

The Court holds that the prosecution's assertion that the request for assistance with suicide of a psychiatric patient cannot be voluntary "is as a general [legal] proposition incorrect." The Court of Appeals held "that the wish to die of a person whose suffering is psychic can be based on an autonomous judgment. That holding is in itself not incorrect."

The alternative challenge – to the sufficiency of the evidence – is, however, well founded, among other things in light of the fact that Ms. B had not been examined by a second psychiatrist.]

As stated above, in a case in which the suffering of a patient is not based on a somatic disease or condition, the trial court must approach the question whether under the circumstances of the case assistance with suicide can be justified as having occurred in a situation of necessity with exceptional care.

---

34   The brief of the Advocate-General (para. 11, 12) suggests some additional arguments for the Court's holding on this issue: the distinction between body and mind is artificial; the nature of the conflicting duties that give rise to the situation of necessity (respect for life; respect for the person of the patient) make the cause of suffering irrelevant; the decisions of lower courts and the literature support the view that the 'terminal phase' is not essential.

If a doctor who affords his patient assistance with suicide has neglected before acting to check his judgment concerning the situation with which he is confronted against that of an independent colleague, whether or not the latter conducts his own examination of the patient, this need not in general preclude the possibility that the trial court, based on its own investigation of the circumstances of the case, comes to the conclusion that the doctor acted in a situation of necessity and therefore must be considered not guilty. However, the situation is different in a case like the present one.

[When the case involves] a patient whose suffering is not based on a somatic disease or condition ... the trial court, in considering whether the claim of necessity is well-founded, must – considering the exceptional care with which it is to approach this matter – base its decision among other things on the judgment of an independent medical expert who has at least seen and examined the patient himself. Since the trial court must decide whether the defense of necessity is compatible with the requirement that the course of conduct chosen be proportional to the harm to be avoided and also the least harmful choice available,[35] the judgment of the independent colleague of the defendant, based partly on his own examination, should deal with the seriousness of the suffering and the lack of prospect for improvement, and in that connection also with other possibilities of providing help.[36] This is because in assessing whether suffering is so unbearable and hopeless that assistance with suicide can be deemed a choice justified by a situation of necessity, there can in principle be no question of hopelessness if there is a realistic alternative to relieve the suffering which the patient has in complete freedom

---

35   This requirement is called in Dutch the principle of *proportionaliteit en subsidiariteit.*

36   The usual association of the word *hulpverlening* in everyday Dutch is with more or less institutionalised forms of assistance. It is not clear precisely what the Supreme Court has in mind here. The brief of Advocate-General Meijers had suggested that the Court of Appeals – probably inspired by earlier decisions of the Supreme Court which seem to suggest a medical monopoly in euthanasia cases – had too narrowly interpreted the concept of 'hopelessness' as referring only to medical and psychotherapeutic treatment. He referred specifically to Ms. B's sister and brother-in-law, and to her good friend, as possible sources of help and noted that the evidence available to the Court of Appeals did not show whether this possibility had been explored. (Compare the brief of the Advocate-General, para. 25).

rejected.[37] The independent expert must also include in his examination the question, whether the patient has made a voluntary and well-considered request, without his competence being influenced by his sickness or condition.

Absent the judgment of an expert who saw and examined Ms. B, the Court of Appeals could not properly come to the conclusion that defendant as the responsible psychiatrist was confronted with an unavoidable conflict of duties and in that situation made a justifiable choice. In such a situation, the Court of Appeals should have rejected the defense.[38]

3.4   JUDGMENT

[The judgment below must be reversed. In general, this would lead to referral of the case to another Court of Appeals.[39] In the circumstances of this case such a referral – considering the absence of the essential report of an independent expert who himself examined Ms. B – could only lead to the conclusion that the defense of necessity must be rejected. In such a case it is more efficient for the Supreme Court to give final judgment itself.

The defense of necessity is rejected, and the defendant, not having made any other defense, is found guilty of the offence as charged.

---

37   This passage has proven particularly troubling to many commentators. It appears, with respect, to be *obiter dictum*, since the issue had not explicitly been raised on appeal and there is no suggestion that the stricture applied to the case of Ms. B (precisely this question having been extensively examined by the Court of Appeals). The Supreme Court does not use the reasonably well-defined term 'concrete treatment perspective' which the Court of Appeals had adopted from the Medical Association's discussion-paper on the subject (CAL 4), and it is not clear whether there is a reason behind the Court's use of a different and seemingly vague expression 'realistic alternative'. It is possible that the Court had non-medical alternatives in mind (see note 36). Nor is it clear what the idea of a rejection of treatment "in complete freedom" implies. The Court also does not explain why rejection of treatment stands in the way of necessity in the case of non-somatic suffering, whereas it is pretty well-established that this does not apply to somatic suffering. In short, the Court's observation in this regard exhibits the difficulties characteristic of *obiter dicta*. See further chapter 3.5.1, note 179, on the idea of rejection 'in complete freedom'.

38   The brief of the Advocate-General had argued (para. 19-21) that this ground of appeal was unfounded: a categorical requirement of independent examination was in his view inconsistent with the nature of the defence of necessity and not supported in existing case-law; the judgment of the Court of Appeals was, he argued, essentially a factual one and adequately supported by its findings.

39   See note 6.

However, "the person of the defendant and the circumstances in which the offence was committed ... have led the Supreme Court to apply article 9a of the Criminal Code and not to impose any punishment or other measure."][40]

4   The medical disciplinary proceedings against Chabot[41]

The prosecution in the criminal case had requested the responsible Medical Inspector, who was contemplating a medical disciplinary proceeding, not to go ahead with it while the criminal case was pending. When, with the decision of the Supreme Court on 21 June 1994, the criminal case was over, the disciplinary proceedings against Chabot got under way. The regional Medical Disciplinary Tribunal rendered a decision on 6 February 1995.[42] It concluded that Chabot had "undermined confidence in the medical pro-

---

40   In general, the Dutch response to the decision in the *Chabot* case – in legal, medical and political circles – was positive, and critical commentary was addressed not so much to the Supreme Court's decision as to what Chabot did. The most extreme criticisms are those of Hendin (1994) and Koerselman (1994), an American and a Dutch psychiatrist, respectively. Each of them takes Chabot to task for supposed oversights in his diagnostic examination of Ms. B and for his conclusion that her request was well-considered. Unfortunately, both Hendin and Koerselman base their criticisms on numerous and serious errors of fact in their accounts of Ms. B and of Chabot's interaction with her; neither of them makes use of the extensive psychiatric report of the case that Chabot furnished to the various consultants and that was later relied upon by the courts. Their position seems to be that a request for assistance with suicide *cannot* be well-considered and Chabot therefore *cannot* have done his work well. Their treatment of the facts is systematically slanted to conform to this ideological preconception and their conclusion – quite different from that of all the experts involved in the case itself – that Chabot's behavior was unprofessional seems essentially *a priori* rather than factual. See further for reactions to the *Chabot* case, NVVE 1995.

41   This account of the medical disciplinary proceedings appeared in *Modern Law Review* 58: 895-897 (1995).

42   *Gerritsen* v. *Chabot*, Medical Disciplinary Tribunal, Amsterdam, no. 93/185; *Medisch Contact* 50: 668-674 (1995). The statement of facts in the judgment of the Medical Disciplinary Tribunal is particularly careful and complete, and sheds additional light on some aspects of the case.

      A companion complaint by the Inspector against the GP present at the suicide at Chabot's request resulted in the holding that under the circumstances (in which he was only present as a witness to the proceedings and it was not "plainly apparent" that what Chabot proposed to do was inconsistent with the medical disciplinary norm) he was not responsible for what Chabot did. *Gerritsen* v. *Beukman*, Medical Disciplinary Tribunal, Amsterdam, no. 93/186; *Medisch Contact* 50: 675-676 (1995).

fession" (the basic disciplinary norm).[43] Chabot received a relatively severe sanction: 'reprimand'. On 19 April 1995 Chabot announced that he had had enough of legal proceedings and would not appeal this decision, so that the case was finally closed.

Chabot had wanted vindication on the merits from a tribunal of his peers (of the five members of a Medical Disciplinary Tribunal, all but the president – a lawyer – are doctors) so he instructed his lawyer not to raise the difficult issue of double jeopardy. The Tribunal was therefore not forced to confront the question whether, in the circumstances of this case, in which no issue was involved in the second proceeding that was not, or could not have been, raised in the first proceeding, it is not fundamentally unfair that the State should have two opportunities to make its case. Nor did the Tribunal address itself to the relationship between the substantive and procedural norms for euthanasia and assistance with suicide as worked out by the courts in criminal cases, on the one hand, and medical disciplinary norms on the other. The Tribunal seems to have accepted the contours of the defence of necessity to a criminal charge as delimiting acceptable professional conduct. This is not surprising since, although there is neither a doctrinal requirement nor an institutional guarantee of congruence between criminal and medical disciplinary law, the courts have in fact largely based their decisions on the scope of the defence of necessity in euthanasia cases on expert testimony concerning the norms of the medical profession. It would have been embarassing if the Medical Disciplinary Tribunal had taken quite a different view of the matter from that of the Supreme Court.

The Medical Disciplinary Tribunal held, as had the Supreme Court, that assistance with suicide can be legitimate in the case of a person whose suffering is of non-somatic origin and who is not in the terminal phase. The request must be the result of an "autonomous decision" and not of a treatable disorder. The consulted doctors must have personally examined the person concerned (the Tribunal is not entirely clear whether more than one doctor must be consulted nor whether this must be a psychiatrist).

The Tribunal considered that in the specific circumstances of the case Chabot had not adequately preserved his professional distance, particularly in light of the frequency and length of his sessions with Ms. B and the fact that these took place at Chabot's house in the countryside (where Ms. B, together with a couple who accompanied her, resided in a guest cottage on Chabot's property).

Finally, the Tribunal seems to have taken a more restrictive view than the Supreme Court on one crucial aspect of the case: the extent to which a doctor must insist on treatment as

---

43   For a discussion of Dutch medical disciplinary law see Verkruisen 1993.

an alternative to assistance with suicide.[44] The Supreme Court's opinion refers to a "realistic alternative," leaving room for the possibility that available treatment possibilities may not be considered 'realistic'. The Tribunal, on the other hand, takes the position that Chabot could not properly conclude that Ms. B's condition was untreatable until after treatment had in fact been tried. "The patient's refusal of treatment should have been a reason for [Chabot] to refuse the requested assistance with suicide, at least for the time being."

This difference between the two decisions reflects the fundamental difference of opinion between the experts whom Chabot had consulted and who testified in the criminal case, and one expert called by the Tribunal in the disciplinary proceeding. The Tribunal adopted the latter's view that treatment was possible in the circumstances of the case and that the patient's refusal of treatment ought not to have been honored.

There is something profoundly unsatisfying about this aspect of the Tribunal's decision. First, it seems unacceptable that the result on such an important matter should be so dependent upon the particular expert(s) who happen to testify. There is, more generally, an element of arbitrariness involved in the role of expert witnesses in these cases, a matter which the courts and tribunals involved have so far not adequately addressed. Second, if anything was indisputable after all the evidence in the two proceedings had been heard, it was that the psychiatric profession is deeply divided on the question whether in the circumstances of Ms. B – including her well-considered refusal of treatment – there was any realistic treatment perspective. It is hard to understand how the fact that Chabot acted on one of two apparently equally respectable medical opinions could be considered a breach of the medical disciplinary norm.[45]

---

44   In the Supreme Court's decision, the existence of a possibility of treatment is important in connection with the requirement that the patient's suffering be hopeless; in the Tribunal's decision, the importance of a treatment alternative is emphasized in connection with the question whether the request is an "autonomous" one.

45   Dutch periodicals were at the time full of statements of the opposing professional views. After the decision of the Medical Disciplinary Tribunal, four expert witnesses involved in the two proceedings protested publicly that the Tribunal had simply without argument rejected their professional opinion and preferred that of another expert witness (*Trouw* 29 April 1995).

3   KADIJK[46]

Court of Appeals, Leeuwarden, Second Full Criminal Chamber, 4 April 1996. Judges Boon, Dijkstra, Poelman [*Tijdschrift voor Gezondheidsrecht* 1996, no. 35].

1   *Procedure*

The appeal is from the judgment of the District Court, Groningen (13 November 1995), which found the defendant not guilty of the offence charged: "intentionally and with premeditation taking another person's life" (murder), as prohibited by article 289 of the Criminal Code.[47] The District Court found the defence of justification due to necessity well-founded.

The appeal was brought by both the prosecution and the defendant.[48] The defendant is represented by E.Ph.R. Sutorius.

---

46 Translation by D. Griffiths. In the *Prins* case, in which the facts were quite similar, the defendant was likewise acquitted (District Court, Alkmaar, 26 April 1995, *Nederlandse Jurisprudentie* 1995, no. 602; Court of Appeals Amsterdam, 7 November 1995, *Nederlandse Jurisprudentie* 1996, no. 113). For technical reasons, neither case was appealed to the Supreme Court.
  In *Prins* the doctor was a specialist (gynecologist) and the baby (which suffered from a number of very serious congenital defects) could probably have lived several years if it had undergone a series of operations. The decision to abstain was, even more so than in *Kadijk*, the crucial decision that the baby should die. The Court of Appeals held that that decision was, in light of the poor prospects for the baby and the suffering it would have had to undergo, justified. A decision which necessarily implied the child's death having been taken, the Court held that pain relief while awaiting death would not have been a medically sound treatment. In these circumstances, the doctor's decision actively to terminate the child's life was justifiable. The importance of the fact that the parents "expressly and in a well-considered way" agreed with the doctor's proposed course of action was particularly emphasized by the Court.

47 Defendant had also been charged with taking the baby's life "at the express and earnest request of the parents" in violation of article 293 (euthanasia). The District Court and the Court of Appeals both held that article 293 is not applicable to a case in which the request is not made by the person concerned.

48 Defendant appealed the acquittal because he sought *vrijspraak* rather than *ontslag van rechtsvervolging* as the ground for acquittal (see note 7 above and paragraph 3.5 of the Court of Appeals' opinion).

2   Facts

On 1 April 1994 a baby girl was born in the Delfzicht Hospital in Delfzijl (province of Groningen). It was immediately clear that she had various serious congenital defects, among which were a cleft palate and upper lip, defects of the nose, a protruding fore-head, and skin/skull defects on the top of her head. A chromosomal defect was suspect-ed. As a result of the defects, the baby was breathing poorly and in fits and starts. This caused her face frequently to turn blue. Every now and then artificial respiration had to be applied and if this had not been done the baby would have died at that time.

On 2 April the baby was admitted to the neonatology ward of the University Hospital in Groningen so that a precise diagnosis could be made. The conclusion was that, in all probability, this was a case of the chromosomal defect trisomy-13. The examination in Groningen had also shown that the baby's kidneys were functioning poorly.

The very unfavorable prognosis connected with the chromosomal defect was discussed with the parents. They agreed with the responsible doctors that, considering the very poor prognosis, artificial respiration and reanimation should no longer be applied. Since the parents preferred to have their baby nearby, the baby was returned to Delfzicht Hos-pital on 3 April.

Back in Delfzicht Hospital the responsible pediatrician, Dougle, noted that the baby was changing color less frequently and appeared to be feeling better. He was neverthless cer-tain that she would die soon: he assumed that she had from a week to a few months more to live. This was made clear to the parents. They understood that the baby would not live much longer and expressed the wish to take her home, so that they could be with her during the final days of her life.

On 7 April another pediatrician, Boersma, discussed with the parents the diagnosis of trisomy-13, which by now had been established definitively, and once again made clear to them that they should not expect the baby to live long. The parents stayed with the baby in the hospital for another week, to acquire experience in feeding her through a catheter and otherwise nursing her. On 12 April she was discharged from the hospital in a stable condition.

The parents took upon themselves the nursing care of the baby. Medical responsibility was assumed by the defendant, the family's GP. He had already come to the hospital on the day of the baby's birth, and again a few days later. The parents had requested him to maintain contact with the pediatricians of Delfzicht Hospital.

On about 19 April a complication arose. At the site of one of the skin/skull defects a swelling appeared, which then developed into a protruding bulge of tissue that turned out to be cerebral membrane. The bulge grew larger and the baby's condition deteriorated. After consulting with a pediatrician, it was decided to cover the wound with gauze and bandage. The pediatrician suggested contacting a dermatologist and surgeon, and the defendant discussed this possibility with the parents. But they were opposed to a surgical closing of the skin/skull defect because, on the one hand, of the pain and risks involved for the baby, and on the other hand her poor life-expectancy.

When the baby was picked up, when her diapers were changed, and when the wound on her head was being tended to, the baby was clearly in pain. The pain was treated by defendant with *paracetamol*. The baby started having light cramps, and a number of times she turned blue during feeding, a sign of breathing difficulty. It would be a few minutes before her breathing was back to normal. To suppress the cramps, she was given *stesolid*.

At this point the parents made clear to the defendant that they thought there were limits to the amount of suffering the baby should be made to go through. They asked defendant if he was prepared to end the baby's suffering if the pain and the bulging of cerebral membrane should get worse and the baby no longer responded to medication. The defendant told them that in principle he was willing to do this.

The next few days the bulge grew larger and there was repeated loss of blood and cerebral fluid. The baby grew paler and paler and her crying became more plaintive. She moaned when moved and, despite the continued medication, her cramps increased. The wound on her head began to smell, indicating a probable infection. In addition, there was a serious danger that the bulging cerebral membrane would tear, causing a lethal bleeding.

On Monday 25 April 1994 the parents concretely requested the defendant to investigate the possibility of ending the baby's life. He asked the parents to give the matter some more thought. In the meantime, he approached the local prosecutorial office for information. The next day, at defendant's request, GP De Bruijn studied the baby's medical file, examined her himself and discussed the situation with the parents. De Bruijn agreed with defendant's assessment of the situation and stated as his opinion that the baby's condition was hopeless, that her death was inevitable, and that further physical deterioration and increased suffering were to be expected. He advised positively with regard to the active termination of the baby's life. The defendant discussed the situation with pediatrician Dougle by telephone. He said that he could agree with a decision to terminate the baby's life. Defendant also discussed with him the manner in which and the means by which he intended to perform the termination. Dougle agreed.

During the course of 26 April 1994 the baby's health deteriorated further. She had by now ceased to urinate. At eight o'clock in the evening the defendant, by giving her a high dose of *stesolid*, brought her into a deep sleep. About an hour and a half later he injected her with *alloferin*. The baby died peacefully in her mother's arms. At ten o'clock the defendant recorded the baby's death.

3   The opinion of the Court of Appeals

3.1   DEFENDANT'S REQUEST TO DISMISS THE PROSECUTION[49]

3.1.1

The defendant's counsel argues that the prosecution should be dismissed, claiming that the 'reporting procedure in the case of termination of life' is a violation of the *nemo tenetur* principle,[50] which is implied (among other things) in the right to a fair trial, laid down in the first section of article 6 of the *European Convention for the Protection of Human Rights and Fundamental Freedoms*. The *nemo tenetur* principle provides that anyone 'charged with a criminal offence' has the right to remain silent, and does not have to contribute to his own conviction.

Article 7 of the Law on the Disposal of Corpses provides that the responsible doctor, if he is not convinced that a particular patient has died of a natural cause, may not issue a death certificate but must inform the coroner that it is not possible for him to do so. In certain cases, notably in a case such as the one at hand, this can lead to the suspicion that the doctor himself is guilty of an offence against the life of the deceased. This fact is a consequence of the professional responsibility of the doctor and does not in itself amount to a violation of the *nemo tenetur* principle, because the doctor, should it come to a prosecution with regard to that suspicion, is entirely free to decide what his position will be. Defendant's counsel has argued that the doctor who does not want to give account through the reporting procedure of a termination of life performed by him, has no other choice than falsely to issue a death certificate [thereby violating section 228 of the Criminal Code]. In the Court's opinion this is not the case.

The question whether the fact that there is a reporting procedure (whether based on the letter of the Minister of Justice of 1 November 1990[51], or on the Order in Council, in

---

49   The Dutch defence of '*niet-ontvankelijkheid*' is the functional equivalent of a motion to dismiss the indictment due to some formal obstacle to conviction (statute of limitations, violation of the right to a speedy trial, circumstances which make a fair trial impossible, etc.).

50   This is the same as the Common Law privilege against self-incrimination. See further chapter 3.2 on the self-incrimination aspect of the reporting procedure.

51   Reference is to a letter to local prosecutorial offices informing them of the reporting procedure agreed upon with the Medical Association (*Medisch Contact* 45: 1303-1304, 1990). See chapter 2.4.

effect since 1 June 1994, establishing the form [to be used for reporting euthanasia and termination of life] as provided for in article 10 of the Law on the Disposal of Corpses) for cases in which the doctor himself has actively caused the death, violates the *nemo tenetur* principle, is not at issue in the present criminal case. The question whether the prosecution must be dismissed and/or certain illegally acquired evidence be excluded, based on violation of the right to a fair trial, has to be considered in a concrete case. In the present case the defendant has made clear from the beginning and up to and including the hearing on appeal that he wished to account for his behavior. This procedural position, freely chosen by defendant, is not compatible with the defence asserted by his counsel to the effect that he 'was required, in violation of the law, to incriminate himself'.

3.1.2

Defendant's counsel has argued that, based on the telephone conversation defendant had with A.M. Koene [of the prosecutor's office] on 25 April 1994, he relied, and was was entitled to rely, on not being prosecuted.

However, neither from defendant's own statements … [at various points during the procedure], nor from Koene's statement, does it appear that defendant was promised or led to believe that he would not be prosecuted. The prosecution is therefore not responsible for defendant's anticipation or hope that he would not be prosecuted, in the sense that the prosecution must be dismissed. However, it does seem to the Court that the prosecutorial office might more carefully have advised this doctor about the legal implications of termination of life in the case of a non-competent person, implications as to which he apparently was not accurately informed. But this failure is not a sufficient reason to dismiss the prosecution.

3.1.3

Defendant's counsel has also argued that the decision to prosecute did not result from a reasonable and fair balancing of, on the one hand, the general interest in development of the law and, on the other hand, this doctor's interest in not being prosecuted, and that in this case the power to prosecute was employed for a different purpose from that for which it is intended. He argues that the prosecution was primarily brought in order to secure development of the law concerning termination of life in the case of seriously handicapped newborn babies, rather than to judge the blameworthiness of this doctor's behavior. Counsel argues that legal development in this field could be pursued in another way, with less serious consequences for the individual doctor. In the case at hand an additional factor is that in a similar case a criminal prosecution had already been brought against a different doctor.[52]

---

52   The *Prins* case, see note 46 above.

The Court rejects this defence. The prosecution was initiated in this case when the Minister of Justice, in a letter dated 2 December 1994, instructed the Procurator-General of the Court of Appeals in Leeuwarden to do so. The Committee of Procurators-General had earlier taken the position that – although one of the conditions listed in the reporting procedure, a written declaration of will, was obviously not satisfied – prosecution was nevertheless unwarranted, since the Committee did not expect the courts to convict the defendant. The Minister of Justice was sympathetic to this point of view, but she weighed the various interests differently and came to a different judgment. She wrote: "My opinion is that the question whether active termination by a doctor of the life of a seriously defective newborn baby can remain unpunished in a case like this, must be submitted to a court, since the case involves euthanasia [sic] on a non-competent person."

This standpoint is a consequence of the approach adopted by the legislator with regard to the whole question of euthanasia, assistance with suicide, and active medical intervention to shorten life without a request: namely, maintenance of the unqualified criminal prohibition of such behavior, subject to the recognition of the possibility that a doctor may, under certain circumstances and in the context of careful medical practice, be justified in violating the prohibition. The Minister's position is also consistent with the position formulated in the Government's Memorandum to the First Chamber concerning bill no. 22 572 on the amendment of the Law on the Disposal of Corpses (and confirmed in a further Memorandum), adopted by the (former) Government and supported by the Second Chamber, that every case of active medical intervention (not upon request) to shorten life should in principle be submitted to a court for judgment. In this light, the Court concludes that the authority to prosecute cannot be said to have been misused, nor can the balancing of interests that lead to the decision to prosecute be said to have been done without due care. This conclusion is not affected by the fact that both in the Minister's letters (the above-mentioned letter and one sent to the girl's parents, dated 24 May 1995) and in the position of the Committee of Procurators-General as described by the Procurator-General in his closing speech [to the Court in this case] very serious doubts, to say the least, are expressed as to the blameworthiness of defendant's conduct under the circumstances.

3.1.4

Neither considered separately nor taken together do the defences [discussed above] lead the Court to the conclusion that the prosecution must be dismissed.

3.2   THE MEANING OF 'TAKING ANOTHER PERSON'S LIFE'

[This defence is essentially the same as that considered by the Supreme Court in the first point on appeal in *Schoonheim*, except that here the applicability of the words 'taking another person's life' to the doctor's conduct is contested in the context of article 289 (murder), which uses the same expression, instead of in the context of article 293. The Court of Appeals concludes that "there is no reason at all to interpret the words '*van het leven beroven*' differently where the other articles in this title[53] are concerned than has already been done in the case of article 293 of the Criminal Code." The Court goes on to note that the medical behavior involved in this case is a subject of considerable debate, both publicly and within the medical profession, so that defendant's claim that such behavior can no longer be considered to amount to 'taking another person's life' is incorrect. The Court rejects the defence.]

3.3   APPEAL TO THE 'MEDICAL EXCEPTION'

Defendant has argued that he must be acquitted, because the 'medical exception' is applicable to his case, that is to say, that the provisions of Title XIX of the Second Book of the Criminal Code were not meant to apply to him, a doctor exercising his profession according to professional norms.[54]

The legislative history contains no grounds whatsoever for considering it equally obvious as in the case of a doctor acting according to professional norms who in a literal sense fulfills the elements of the crimes of intentionally causing pain and (severe) bodily injury, but who nevertheless does not fall under the provisions of the criminal law, that the Criminal Code is only applicable to a doctor's termination of a patient's life if the doctor in doing so has violated the norms of the medical profession.

Nor does the current state of affairs in the public debate about the permissibility of life-terminating conduct by doctors, referred to in the preceding section, give reason to suppose that, notwithstanding the original legislative intent, it has become generally accepted that intentional active termination of life by a doctor, provided that this has been done *lege artis*, falls outside the scope of the criminal law.

Especially during the past decade, the legislator has been occupied in depth with the issue of euthanasia (in a broad sense), and the position of the doctor under the criminal law. It has thereby explicitly maintained the position that termination of life by a doctor – whether or not upon request – remains within the scope of the criminal law. This fact, too, precludes a judge from holding the 'medical exception' applicable to life-terminating conduct by doctors, although the norms of the medical profession do play a very important role in assessing the justifiability of a doctor's conduct.

---

53   The Court here refers to Title XIX of the Second Book of the Criminal Code, which contains article 289, article 293, and the other offences against human life.

54   As we have seen in chapter 2.3.1, the Supreme Court in 1986 rejected the 'medical exception' for euthanasia.

The Court rejects the defence.

3.4   THE DEFENCE OF NECESSITY

[As his final defence, defendant argues that he acted in a situation of legal necessity in which he had to make a choice between two conflicting duties: on the one hand, the duty to preserve the baby's life; on the other hand, the duty to do everything possible to relieve her unbearable and hopeless suffering. Defendant chose actively to end the baby's life, and he argues that this choice was justified, because there were no alternatives.]

Regarding the punishability of the act, the Court regards the following facts as important:

(1) The diagnosis of trisomy-13 had been established with certainty, and the life-expectancy of a child with this defect is very limited. The expert opinion of H.A.A. Brouwers, pediatrician/neonatologist, describes trisomy-13 as a lethal disorder. Expert R. de Leeuw, pediatrician, writes that almost 90% of children with trisomy-13 die within their first year, as a result of the many anomalies that occur in connection with the syndrome. These children suffer from a serious growth-disorder. Respiration disturbances occur frequently due to brain defects and the cleft jaw. There is always serious mental retardation. There are also many neurological defects such as spasms and motoric retardation. All experts support the decision, in light of the unfavorable prognosis, not to apply artificial respiration or reanimation. In pediatrician Van Bruggen's words: "Treatment such as artificial respiration and reanimation would not have been proportionate in this case, because they prolong the process of dying. Having brought the child back to life, we would have nothing more to offer it than shortly thereafter to die once again." Surgical treatment of (some of the) symptoms is also characterized by all experts as disproportionate.

All experts consulted agree that the decision – after the situation had become reasonably stable – to hand over to the parents the nursing of their child, which they wished to do and of which they were capable, was correct. This made it possible for the child to die at home. The medical support of a GP in whom they had confidence, with support from the pediatricians in Delfzicht Hospital (see the letter dated 17 September 1995 sent by pediatrician Prof. Dr. E.R. Boersma, also on behalf of his colleague L.A. Dougle), made this decision justifiable.

The Court concludes that the circumstances which lead the defendant, in his capacity as GP, to be confronted with the choice whether or not to end the life of this seriously handicapped child by active intervention, were the result of decisions which were responsible by medical-technical standards and good as a matter of medical ethics.

It is clear that a situation later arose, in which the original intention of all those concerned, namely to let the parents take care of the child until its natural death, which was expected shortly, could not be realized, but in which the defendant, the responsible doctor, had to intervene. Because the parents – according to all experts, rightly – rejected surgery, as being pointless and too burdensome for the child, the defendant had two options: to treat the manifest pain and the discomfort of the baby as adequately as possible until she gave up the struggle, or actively to terminate the child's life in accordance with the parents' request.

(2) The Court finds that it has convincingly been shown that the parents' request was founded solely upon a deep-felt concern about the child's suffering and that the request was well-considered. Pediatrician Van Bruggen's position, that the parents could only have reached an independent decision if they had been given the opportunity to discuss their problems with an exponent of the view in medical ethics that only maximal palliative care and not active termination of life should be offered, has no basis in the reality of the situation. In the Court's opinion, there was no reason whatever for defendant to have checked the parents' consent to possible termination of life any more thoroughly than he did.

(3) With regard to the acceptability as a matter of medical ethics of the defendant's decision actively to terminate this girl's life, the Court regards the following as relevant. The report *To Act or to Abstain? The Limits of Medical Practice in Neonatology* [NVK 1992], issued by the Dutch Association for Paediatrics on 5 November 1992, states in chapter 6, section 2, that in the situation in which, after thorough consideration, the primary decision has been taken not to apply medical treatment in light of the poor prospects for the quality of future life, and the baby does not die within a short period, no consensus concerning intentional termination of life could be reached, but that almost all pediatricians respect the opinion of those who do choose that option, even if they cannot square such a decision with their own conscience. In its working paper 'Termination of life in the case of non-competent patients, Part I, seriously defective newborn babies' [CAL 1990], the Commission on the Acceptability of Termination of Life of the Royal Dutch Medical Association considers active termination of life acceptable in cases in which (further) treatment is not initiated or is discontinued because of the unfavorable prognosis, but contrary to expectation this does not have the intended result of the baby's death. "When a situation of needless continuation and/or worsening of suffering arises, it is the opinion of the commission that it can indeed be morally justifiable to resort to the administration of euthanatica."

Most of the experts consulted in this case are of the opinion that the defendant, as a matter of medical ethics, acted correctly. The above-mentioned expert Van Bruggen and H. Jochemsen, director of the G.A. Lindeboom Institute,[55] take a different view. Van Bruggen writes that in her judgment defendant did not act according to the centuries-old norm of medical ethics that it is the doctor's task to alleviate suffering and that it is forbidden for him wilfully to end his patient's life. Jochemsen states that life must be regarded as a given (in the double meaning of a gift and a fact that presents itself to us and with which we must reckon), as the basic value and point of departure for medical treatment, and that for that reason intentionally bringing about death falls outside of the task and authority of medicine. In their opinion, intentional life-terminating behavior always exceeds the limits of medical authority. However, both of them state that in their opinion the defendant acted according to medical-ethical opinion to which others adhere. In Van Bruggen's words: He acted with great care in a way that is currently regarded as responsible medical treatment in certain sections of the medical profession.

The Court concludes that, as in cases of termination of life on request and assistance with suicide, an act such as the one under consideration is, according to the norms of medical ethics, acceptable under certain circumstances.

3.5   JUDGMENT

The Court concludes that the defendant's choice to bring about the girl's death in violation of article 289 of the Criminal Code, in the circumstances of this case, in which the girl – whose death was inevitable and who had been taken home so she could die there – was visibly in great pain and for whom an inhumane death, in a fashion strongly contrary to her parent's feelings, was imminent, was justified.

Important for the Court's assessment of the decision-making and carrying out of the decision is

- the fact that there was no doubt at all about the diagnosis and the prognosis based on it, and that the parents as well as the defendant were familiar with these;
- the fact that there was no doubt at all as to the well-considered consent of the parents to the termination of life;
- the fact that the defendant secured the advice of an independent, experienced doctor (GP) and consulted one of the responsible pediatricians;
- the fact that he brought about the baby's death in a conscientious and careful manner, after having satisfied himself of the correctness of the chosen method;
- the fact that he has carefully given account of his conduct in this matter.

---

55   The Lindeboom Institute is a center for medical ethics that takes the Bible as its point of departure.

The Court comes to the conclusion that the situation in which the defendant found himself can, according to scientifically responsible medical opinion and the norms of medical ethics, be considered a situation of necessity in which the choice made by the defendant is to be considered justified, so that he must be acquitted.

3.6   ADDITIONAL CONSIDERATION

Defendant and his counsel have urged that he feels aggrieved by the characterization 'murder'. In this context counsel has argued that in cases such as this a 'generous acquittal' would be in order. [The idea of defendant's counsel was that a *vrijspraak* acquittal would be more appropriate than a 'stingy' *ontslag van rechtsvervolging* acquittal.[56]]

In this connection, the Court observes that the characterization of the offence ['murder'] in a case such as this is not consistent with the social sentiment generally attached to it. However, [murder] is a technical legal term which cannot be avoided, due to the way in which the legislator has wished the review of cases like these to take place. Ironically, this characterization (for which 'premeditation' is the essence) is convincingly established by the very carefulness exhibited in the decision-making process.

A *vrijspraak* in Dutch criminal procedure implies in principle nothing more than the judgement that it cannot be proved that the defendant did the things charged in the indictment, not the positive conclusion that he did not do them. Regarded from that point of view, only the reasons given for a *vrijspraak* could make such a verdict 'generous', as requested by defendant's counsel. Those reasons would not be different from those given above by the Court in connection with the punishability of the act, which in essence come down to this: Both the girl and her parents were in good hands with this doctor.

---

56   See note 7 above for the difference between the two acquittal verdicts.

Literature

Note: Most organizations are listed as authors only with the acronyms used throughout the book – see the Glossary for full names and explanations.

AARTSEN, J.G.M.
1989   Letter (signed by 25 persons prominent in the Dutch euthanasia discussion and associated with legal, medical, ethical and health-policy organizations). *Hastings Center Report*, special supplement, January/February 1989: 47-48.

ADMIRAAL, P.V.
1977   'Euthanasie in het ziekenhuis [Euthanasia in hospitals].' Pp. 188-209 in Muntendam 1977.
1980   *Verantwoorde euthanasie. Handleiding voor artsen* [Responsible Euthanasia. A Guide for Doctors]. Amsterdam: NVVE.
1983   'De verantwoorde uitvoering van euthanasie; kanttekening bij de discussie daarover [Responsible administration of euthanasia; comments on the discussion].' *Nederlands Tijdschrift voor Geneeskunde* 127: 964-966.

ALKEMA, E.A.
1978   *Studies over Europese grondrechten* [Essays on European Constitutional Rights]. Deventer: Kluwer.

AMUNDSEN, D.W.
1987   'Medicine and the birth of defective children: approaches of the ancient world.' Pp. 3-22 in R.C. McMillan, H.T. Engelhardt and S.F. Spicker, ed., *Euthanasia and the Newborn*. Dordrecht: D. Reidel Publishing Company.

ANDEWEG, R.B., and G.A. IRWIN
1993   *Dutch Government and Politics*. London: MacMillan.

ANJEWIERDEN, O.
1988   *Strafrecht en euthanasie* [Criminal Law and Euthanasia]. Nijmegen: Ars Aequi Libri.

ANSPACH, R.R.
1993   *Deciding Who Lives: Fateful Choices in the Intensive-Care Nursery*. Berkeley CA: University of California Press.

BATTIN, M.P.

1994 'A dozen caveats concerning the discussion of euthanasia in the Netherlands.' Pp. 130-144 in *The Least Worst Death. Essays in Bioethics on the End of Life*. Oxford: Oxford University Press. Reprinted pp. 88-109 in J.D. Moreno, ed., *Arguing Euthanasia. The Controversy over Mercy Killing, Assisted Suicide, and the 'Right to Die'*. New York: Simon & Schuster, 1995.

BEAUCHAMP, T.L., and J.F. CHILDRESS

1989 *Principles of Biomedical Ethics* (3d ed.). New York: Oxford University Press.

BEAUFORT, I. de

1987 'Op weg naar het einde [On the way to the end].' Pp. 10-32 in G.A. van der Wal et al., *Euthanasie. Knelpunten in een discussie* [Euthanasia. Points of Difficulty in a Discussion]. Baarn: Ambo.

BEAUFORT, I.D. de, and H.M. DUPUIS (ed.)

1988 *Handboek gezondheidsethiek* [Handbook of Health-Care Ethics]. Assen: Van Gorcum.

BENJAMINSEN, M.

1988 *Bij het einde. Een onderzoek naar terminale zorg en euthanasieproblematiek in Utrecht* [At the End. Research Concerning Care of Terminal Patients and Euthanasia in Utrecht]. Utrecht: Department of Policy Information, City of Utrecht.

BERG, J.H. van den

1978 *Medical Power and Medical Ethics* New York: W.W. Norton (translation of *Medische macht en medische ethiek,* Nijkerk: Uitgeverij G.F. Callenbach, 1969).

BLAD, J.R.

1990 *Tussen lots- en zelfbeschikking. De stand van het beleid ten aanzien van euthanasie in ziekenhuizen en verpleeghuizen in Nederland* [Between Fate and Self-Determination. Current Policy on Euthanasia in Dutch Hospitals and Nursing Homes]. Arnhem: Gouda Quint.

1996 *Abolitionisme als strafrechtstheorie* [Abolitionism as a Theoretical Approach to Criminal Law]. Arnhem: Gouda Quint.

BLANKENBURG, E., and F. BRUINSMA

1994 *Dutch Legal Culture* (2nd ed.). Deventer/Boston: Kluwer.

BLIJHAM, G.H., and J.J.M. van DELDEN

1996 'Richtlijnen voor het nemen van niet-reanimeerbesluiten [Guidelines for non-reanimation decisions]', *Medisch Contact* 51: 1066-1068.

BOOT, J.M., and M.H.J.M. KNAPEN

1988 *De Nederlandse gezondheidszorg* [The Health-Care System in the Netherlands] (revised ed.). Utrecht: Het Spectrum (Aula).

BOSMA, J.M., and G. van der WAL

1997 *Kwaliteitsborging en toetsing achteraf van euthanasie en hulp bij zelfdoding* [Maintaining Quality and Control after the Fact of Euthanasia and Assistance with Suicide]. Amsterdam: Free University.

BOSMA, J.M., G. van der WAL, and S.L. HOSMAN-BENJAMINSE

1996 'Late zwangerschapsafbreking in Noord-Holland. II. Zorgvuldigheid vooraf en toetsing achteraf [Late-term abortion in North-Holland. II. Careful procedure beforehand and control afterwards].' *Nederlands Tijdschrift voor Geneeskunde* 140: 605-609.

BRAUW, P.J.W. de, and L.E. KALKMAN-BOGERD

1988 *Rechtspraak medisch tuchtrecht 1976-1987* [Medical Disciplinary Cases 1976-1987]. Deventer: Kluwer.

BRENNAN, T.A.

1991 *Just Doctoring: Medical Ethics in the Liberal State.* Berkeley: University of California Press.

BRITISH MEDICAL ASSOCIATION

1988 *Euthanasia.* London: British Medical Association.

BRUIJN, J. de

1979 *Geschiedenis van de abortus in Nederland. Een analyse van opvattingen en discussies 1600-1979* [History of Abortion in the Netherlands. An Analysis of Views and Discussions 1600-1979]. Amsterdam: Van Gennep.

CAL

(Commissie Aanvaardbaarheid Levensbeeindigend Handelen) [Commission on the Acceptability of Termination of Life of the Royal Dutch Medical Association], Discussion papers on termination of life in the case of non-competent patients (for the final, integrated report see KNMG 1997):

CAL 1 *Zwaar-defecte pasgeborenen* [Severely Defective Newborn Babies], 1990.

CAL 2 *Landurig comateuze patiënten* [Long-Term Comatose Patients], 1991.

CAL 3 *Ernstig demente patiënten* [Seriously Demented Patients], 1993.

CAL 4 *Hulp bij zelfdoding bij psychiatrische patinten* [Assistance with Suicide in the Case of Psychiatric Patients], 1993.

CATSBURG, I., and C. de BOER

1986 'Meningen over euthanasie [Public opinion about euthanasia].' *De Psycholoog* 21: 237-253.

CBS

[Central Bureau of Statistics]

1987 *Overledenen naar doodsoorzaak, leeftijd en geslacht in het jaar 1987* [Deaths by Cause of Death, Age and Sex in the Year 1987]. The Hague: Centraal Bureau voor de Statistiek (serie B1).

1991 *Het levenseinde in de medische praktijk. Resultaten van een steekproef uit sterfgevallen juli-november 1990* [The End of Life in Medical Practice. Results of a Sample of Deaths in the Period July-November 1990]. The Hague: SDU.

1996 *Het levenseinde in de medische praktijk (1995, 1990). Resultaten sterfgevallenonderzoek 1995, deelonderzoek II van het evaluatieonderzoek meldingsprocedure euthanasie* [The End of Life in Medical Practice (1995, 1990). Results of a Study of Deaths in 1995, Part II of the Evaluation Study of the Reporting Procedure for Euthanasia]. Heerlen: Central Bureau of Statistics.

CHABOT, B.E.

1992 'Klaar met leven [Finished with life]'. *Medisch Contact* 47: 1536-1540.

1993 *Zelf beschikt* [Self-Determined]. Amsterdam: Balans.

1996 *Sterven op drift: over stervensverlangen en onmacht* [Death Adrift: Powerlessness and the Desire to Die]. Nijmegen: SUN.

CHORUS, J.M.J. et al. (ed.)

1993 *Introduction to Dutch Law for Foreign Lawyers* (2nd ed.). Deventer/Boston: Kluwer.

COMMISSIE REMMELINK

1991 *Medische beslissingen rond het levenseinde* [Medical Decisions Concerning the End of Life]. Report of the commission appointed to carry out research concerning medical practice in connection with euthanasia (Remmelink Commission). The Hague: SDU.

DAM, H. van

1996 'Ethisch beraad is broodnodig [Ethical reflection is urgently needed] (interview with E.Ph.R. Sutorius).' *Tijdschrift voor Verpleegkundigen* 1996: 582-585.

DAVIS, N.A.

1991 'Contemporary deontology.' Pp. 205-218 in P. Singer, ed., *A Companion to Ethics*. Oxford: Basil Blackwell.

DENT, N.

1988 'Rousseau and respect for others.' Pp. 115-135 in S. Mendus, ed., *Justifying Toleration. Conceptual and Historical Perspectives.* Cambridge: Cambridge University Press.

DESSAUR, C.I., and C.J.C. RUTENFRANS

1986 *Mag de dokter doden? Argumenten en documenten tegen het euthanasiasme* [May the Doctor Kill? Arguments and Documents against Euthanasiasm]. Amsterdam: Querido.

DEVLIN, P.

1965 *The Enforcement of Morals*. London: Oxford University Press.

DIJK, P. van, and G.J.H. van HOOF

1990   *De Europese Conventie in theorie en praktijk* [The European Convention in Theory and Practice] (3d ed.). Nijmegen: Ars Aequi Libri.

DILLMANN, R.J.M.

1996   'Euthanasia in the Netherlands: the role of the Dutch medical profession.' Pp. 65-74 in *Euthanasia and Assisted Suicide in the Netherlands and Europe.* Luxemburg: Office for Official Publications of the European Communities.

DILLMANN, R.J.M. et al.

1997   'Steun en consultatie bij euthanasie in Amsterdam [Support and consultation in euthanasia cases in Amsterdam].' *Medisch Contact* 52: 743-746.

DRION, H.

1992   *Het zelfgewilde einde van oude mensen* [The Choice for Ending Life by Elderly People]. Amsterdam: Balans.

DUPUIS, H.M.

1994   *Wel of niet behandelen? Baat het niet, dan schaadt het wél* [To Treat or Not to Treat. If It Does not Help, It Does Hurt]. Baarn: Ambo.

DWORKIN, R.

1977   'Liberty and moralism.' Pp. 240-258 in: *Taking Rights Seriously.* London: Gerald Duckworth & Co.

1985   *A Matter of Principle.* Cambridge: Harvard University Press

1993   *Life's Dominion: An Argument about Abortion and Euthanasia.* London: Harper Collins.

1997   'Assisted suicide: what the Court really said.' *New York Review of Books,* 25 September 1997, pp. 40-44.

DWORKIN, R. et al.

1997   'Assisted suicide: the philosophers' brief.' *New York Review of Books,* 27 March 1997, pp. 41-47

ENSCHEDÉ, C.

1966   'Abortus op medische indicatie en strafrecht [Abortion on medical indication and the criminal law].' *Nederlands Tijdschrift voor Geneeskunst* 110: 1349-1354.

1985   *De arts en de dood, sterven en recht.* [The Doctor and Death: Dying and the Law]. Deventer: Kluwer.

1986a 'Euthanasie, theorie en praktijk: andere wegen [Euthanasia in theory and practice: other approaches].' Lecture to the Royal Dutch Academy of Sciences, 12 May and 23 June 1986.

1986b 'Kanttekeningen bij het advies van de Staatscommissie Euthanasie [Comments on the Advice of the State Commission on Euthanasia].' *Nederlands Juristenblad* 61: 37-42.

ENTHOVEN, L.
1988 *Het recht op leven en dood* [The Right to Life and Death]. Deventer: Kluwer.

FAHNER, T.
1988 'De negatieve definities van euthanasie; levensberoving? [The negative definitions of euthanasia; homicide?]' *Medisch Contact* 1988: 817-820.

FEINBERG, J.
The Moral Limits of the Criminal Law, Parts I-IV:
1984 *Harm to Others.* New York: Oxford University Press.
1985 *Offense to Others.* New York: Oxford University Press.
1986 *Harm to Self.* New York: Oxford University Press.
1988 *Harmless Wrongdoing.* New York: Oxford University Press.

FENIGSEN, R.
1989 'A case against Dutch euthanasia.' *Hastings Center Report,* special supplement, 19/1: 22-30.

FERNGREN, G.B.
1987 'The *Imago Dei* and the sanctity of life: the origins of an idea.' Pp. 23-45 in R.C. McMillan, H.T. Engelhardt and S.F. Spicker, ed., *Euthanasia and the Newborn.* Dordrecht: D. Reidel Publishing Company.

FINNIS, J.
1995 'A philosophical case against euthanasia.' Pp. 23-35 in J. Keown, ed., *Euthanasia Examined. Ethical, Clinical and Legal Perspectives.* Cambridge: Cambridge University Press.

FISHER, A.
1995 'Theological aspects of euthanasia.' Pp. 315-332 in J. Keown, ed., *Euthanasia Examined. Ethical, Clinical and Legal Perspectives.* Cambridge: Cambridge University Press.

FRANCKE, A.L. et al.
1997 *Palliatieve zorg in Nederland. Een inventarisatiestudie naar palliatieve zorg, deskundigheidsbevordering en zorg voor zorgenden* [Palliative Care in the Netherlands. A Survey of Studies of Palliative Care, Promotion of Expertise, and Support for those Giving Care]. Utrecht: Nederlands Instituut voor Onderzoek van de Gezondheidszorg.

FREIDSON, E.
1975 *Doctoring Together: A Study of Professional Social Control.* New York: Elsevier.

GENEESKUNDIGE INSPECTIE VOOR DE GEESTELIJKE VOLKSGEZONDHEID
[Medical Inspectorate for Public Mental Health]
1993 *De meldingsprocedure euthanasie/hulp bij zelfdoding en psychiatrische patiënten* [The Reporting Procedure for Euthanasia/Assistance with Suicide and Psychiatric Patients]. Rijswijk: Geneeskundige Inspectie voor de Geestelijke Volksgezondheid.

GENERALE SYNODE DER NEDERLANDSE HERVORMDE KERK
1972 *Euthanasie. Zin en begrenzing van het medisch handelen* [Euthanasia. Meaning and Limits of Medical Treatment]. The Hague: Boekencentrum.

GERIATRIE INFORMATORIUM
[Information on Geriatrics]
1983+ Loose-leaf service. Houten: Bohn, Stafleu, Van Loghum.

GEVERS, J.K.M.
1991 *De rechter en het medisch handelen* [The Judge and Medical Behavior] (2nd ed.). Deventer: Kluwer.
1992 'Legislation on euthanasia: recent developments in the Netherlands.' *Journal of Medical Ethics* 18: 138-141.

GEZONDHEIDSRAAD
[Health Council]
1972 *Advies inzake euthanasie* [Advice Concerning Euthanasia]. Interim-advies uitgebracht door de Commissie Medische Ethiek van de Gezondheidsraad aan de Minister van Volksgezondheid en Milieuhygiëne. The Hague: Ministerie van Volksgezondheid en Milieuhygiëne.
1975 *Euthanasie bij pasgeborenen* [Euthanasia in the Case of Newborn Babies]. Tweede interim-advies uitgebracht door de Commissie Medische Ethiek aan de Minister van Volksgezondheid en Milieuhygiëne. The Hague: Ministerie van Volksgezondheid en Milieuhygiëne.
1982 *Euthanasie. Advies inzake euthanasie uitgebracht door de Gezondheidsraad aan de Minister en de Staatssecretarie van Volksgezondheid en Milieuhygiëne* [Euthanasia. Advice of the Health Council to the Minister and State Secretary of Public Health and Environmental Health]. The Hague: Staatsuitgeverij.
1986 *Advies inzake suïcide* [Advice Concerning Suicide]. The Hague: Gezondheidsraad.
1987 *Advies inzake zorgvuldigheidseisen euthanasie* [Advice Concerning the Requirements of Careful Practice for Euthanasia]. The Hague: Ministerie van Volksgezondheid en Milieuhygiëne.
1994 *Patiënten in een vegetatieve toestand* [Patients in a Vegetative State]. The Hague: Gezondheidsraad.

GINKEL, R. van
1997 *Notities over Nederlanders* [Notes about the Dutch]. Amsterdam: Boom.

GLOVER, J.
1977 *Causing Death and Saving Lives.* Harmondsworth: Penguin Books Ltd.

GOFF OF CHIEVELEY, LORD
1993 'A matter of life and death.' *Juridisk Tidskrift* 5: 1-17.

GOMEZ, C.F.
1991   *Regulating Death: Euthanasia and the Case of the Netherlands.* New York: The Free Press.

GRIFFITHS, J.
1987   'Een toeschouwersperspectief op de euthanasie-discussie [An observer's perspective on the euthanasia discussion].' *Nederlands Juristenblad* 62: 681-693.
1993   'Een Amerikaan over euthanasie in Nederland [An American looks at euthanasia in the Netherlands]' (review of Gomez 1991). *Medisch Contact* 48: 1208-1209.
1994   'The regulation of euthanasia and related medical procedures that shorten life in the Netherlands.' *Medical Law International* 1: 137-158.
1995a   'Recent developments in the Netherlands concerning euthanasia and other medical behavior that shortens life.' *Medical Law International* 1: 347-386.
1995b   'Assisted suicide in the Netherlands: the *Chabot* case.' *Modern Law Review* 58: 232-248.
1995c   'Assisted suicide in the Netherlands: postscript to *Chabot.*' *Modern Law Review* 58: 895-897.
1996   'De sociale werking van recht [The social working of law].' Pp. 469-513 in J. Griffiths, ed., *De Sociale werking van recht, een kennismaking met de rechtssociologie en rechtsantropologie* [The Social Working of Law, an Introduction to Sociology and Anthropology of Law] (version in English forthcoming).

GROENEWOUD, J.H. et al.
1997   'Physician-assisted death in psychiatric practice in the Netherlands.' *New England Journal of Medicine* 336: 1795-1801.

HAERSOLTE, R.A.V. van
1985   'Over het leven beschikken [Autonomy with respect to life].' *Rechtsfilosofie en Rechtstheorie* 14: 68-69.

HARRIS, J.
1985   *The Value of Life.* London: Routledge & Kegan Paul.

HART, H.L.A.
1963   *Law, Liberty and Morality.* Stanford: Standford University Press.
1967   'Social solidarity and the enforcement of morality.' *University of Chicago Law Review* 35: 2-29.
1968   *Punishment and Responsibility.* London: Oxford University Press.

HARTOGH, G. den
1996   'Recht op de dood? Zelfbeschikking en barmhartigheid als rechtvaardigingsgronden voor euthanasie [Right to die? Autonomy and beneficence as justifications for euthanasia].' *Recht en Kritiek* 22: 148-168.

HAVERKATE, M.A., and G. van der WAL
1996 'Policies on medical decisions concerning the end of life in Dutch health care institutions.' *Journal of the American Medical Association* 275: 435-439.

HAZEWINKEL-SURINGA, D., and J. REMMELINK
1996 *Inleiding tot de studie van het Nederlandse strafrecht* [Introduction to the Study of Dutch Criminal Law] (15th ed.). Alphen aan den Rijn: Samsom H.D. Tjeenk Willink.

HEEK, F. van
1975 *Actieve euthanasie als sociologisch probleem* [Active Euthanasia as a Sociological Problem]. Meppel: Boom.

HEIDE, A. van der, et al.
1997 'Frequentie van het afzien van (kunstmatige) toediening van voeding en vocht aan het levenseinde [Frequency of abstinence from (artificial) feeding and hydration at the end of life].' Nederlands Tijdschrift voor Geneeskunde 141: 1918-1924.

HENDIN, H.
1994 'Seduced by death: doctors, patients and the Dutch cure.' *Issues in Law and Medicine* 10: 123-168.
1996 *Seduced by Death. Doctors, Patients and the Dutch Cure.* New York: W.W. Norton.

HENDIN, H., C. RUTENFRANS, and Z. ZYLICZ
1997 'Physician-assisted suicide and euthanasia in the Netherlands.' *Journal of the American Medical Association* 277: 1720-1722.

HERBERGS, B.
1984 *Laat me sterven voor ik wakker word... Tien jaar strijd om het recht om een menswaardig levenseinde* [Let Me Die before I Wake... Ten Years of Struggle for the Right to a Dignified End of Life]. Amsterdam/Brussels: Elsevier.

HESSING, D.J., J.R. BLAD, and R. PIETERMAN
1996 'Practical reasons and reasonable practice: the case of euthanasia in the Netherlands.' *Journal of Social Issues* 52: 149-169.

HILHORST, H.W.A.
1983 *Euthanasie in het ziekenhuis, de 'zachte dood' bij ziekenhuispatienten* [Euthanasia in the Hospital: the 'Gentle Death' of Hospital Patients]. Lochem-Poperinge: De Tijdstroom.

HIRSCH BALLIN, E.M.H.
1984 'Over het leven beschikken [Autonomy with respect to life].' *Rechtsfilosofie en Rechtstheorie* 13: 182-187.

HOLSTEYN, J. van, and M. TRAPPENBURG
1996   *Het laatste oordeel. Meningen over nieuwe vormen van euthanasie* [The Last Judgment. Public Opinion Concerning New Forms of Euthanasia]. Baarn: Ambo.

HOOFDBESTUUR HUMANISTISCH VERBOND
1976   'Euthanasie [Euthanasia].' *Rekenschap* 1976: 43-45.

HORST, H. van der
1996   *The Low Sky. Understanding the Dutch.* The Hague: Nuffic.

ISRAEL, J.I.
1995   *The Dutch Republic – Its Rise, Greatness and Fall 1477-1806.* Oxford: Oxford University Press.

JACOBS, F.C.L.M.
1987   'De figuur van de veronderstelde will [The idea of a presumed will].' Pp. 83-109 in G.A. van der Wal et al., *Euthanasie. Knelpunten in een discussie* [Euthanasia. Points of Difficulty in a Discussion]. Baarn: Ambo.

JOSEPHUS JITTA, A.N.A.
1987   'Vervolgingsbeleid euthanasie [Prosecutorial policy in euthanasia cases].' in B.L. Berkemeier, B. Sluyters en J.D. Mulder Dzn, *Juridische praktijkproblemen voor de arts* Leiden: Rijksuniversiteit Leiden, Boerhaave commissie voor postacademisch onderwijs in de geneeskunde.
1997   'Nogmaals: de regionale toetsingscommissies [Once again: the regional assessment committees].' *Medisch Contact* 52: 253.

KASS, L.
1993   'Is there a right to die?' *Hastings Center Report*, January-February 1993.

KELK, C.
1990   'Aan de grens van het bestaan. Beschouwingen over euthanasie [At the edge of existence. Reflections on euthanasia].' Pp. 149-169 in J.K.M. Gevers and J.H. Hubben, ed., *Grenzen aan de zorg; zorgen aan de grens* [The Limits of Care; Care at the Limits]. Alphen aan den Rijn: Samsom H.D. Tjeenk Willink.

KENNEDY, J.C.
1995   *Nieuw Babylon in aanbouw. Nederland in de jaren zestig* [Building New Babylon. The Netherlands in the 1960s]. Amsterdam: Boom.

KENTER, E.G.H.
1983   'Euthanasie in een huisartspraktijk [Euthanasia in a GP's practice].' *Medisch Contact* 38: 1179-1182.

1989 'Euthanasie in een huisartspraktijk – vijf jaar later' [Euthanasia in a family doctor's practice – five years later].' *Medisch Contact* 44: 907-910.

KEOWN, J.

1992 'The law and practice of euthanasia in the Netherlands.' *Law Quarterly Review* 108: 51-78.

1995 'Euthanasia in the Netherlands: sliding down the slippery slope?' Pp. 261-296 in J. Keown, ed., *Euthanasia Examined. Ethical, Clinical and Legal Perspectives.* Cambridge: Cambridge University Press.

KERKHOF, A.J.F.M.

1996 'Suïcidepogers and suïcideplegers: gegevens en ervaringen [Persons who attempt and who commit suicide: data and experiences].' Pp. 3-15 in J. Broerse (ed.), *Suïcidaliteit in de geestelijke gezondheidszorg* [Suicide-proneness and Public Mental Health Care]. Utrecht: Nederlands Centrum Geestelijke Volksgezondheid.

KETTING, E.

1978 *Van misdrijf tot hulpverlening. Een analyse van de maatschappelijke betekenis van abortus provocatus in Nederland* [From Felony to Medical Treatment. An Analysis of the Social Meaning of Abortion in the Netherlands]. Alphen aan den Rijn/Brussels: Samson Uitgeverij.

KLIJN, W.C.M.

1985 'Euthanasie. Ethische analyse en waardering [Euthanasia. Ethical analysis and evaluation].' Pp. 17-68 in J. de Graaf et al., *Euthanasie. Recht, ethiek en medische praktijk* [Euthanasia. Law, Ethics and Medical Practice]. Deventer: Kluwer.

KLOOT MEIJBURG, H.H. van der

1989 Letter. *Hastings Center Report,* special supplement, January/February 1989: 48-49.

KNIGGE, G.

1997 'Hoezo, meldingsplicht? [Duty to report? what duty to report?]' *Rechtsgeleerd Magazijn Themis* 1997/3: 81-82.

KNMG

1971 'Richtlijnen ten behoeve van de uitvoering van abortus provocatus [Guidelines for carrying out abortion].' *Medisch Contact* 26: 1025-1028.

1973 'Voorlopig standpunt van het hoofdbestuur inzake het euthanasievraagstuk [Provisional position of the governing board with respect to the question of euthanasia].' *Medisch Contact* 19: 587 ff.; reprinted in *Medisch Contact* 31: 997-998 (1984).

1975 'Discussienota [Discussion paper of the working group on euthanasia].' *Medisch Contact* 30: 7-17.

1984 'Standpunt inzake euthanasie [Position on euthanasia].' *Medisch Contact* 31: 990-997.

1992 'Richtlijnen KNMG en Nieuwe Unie '91 [Guidelines of the KNMG and Nieuwe Unie '91].' *Medisch Contact* 47: 29-32.

1995 *Standpunt hoofdbestuur inzake euthanasie* [Position of the Governing Board on Euthana-
sia]. Utrecht: KNMG (also published as a supplement to *Medisch Contact* 50: nr 33/34,
1995).

1997 *Medisch handelen rond het levenseinde bij wilsonbekwame patiënten* [Medical Practice at the
End of Life in the Case of Non-Competent Patients]. Houten/Diegem: Bohn Stafleu Van
Loghum. This is an integrated final version of CAL 1-4. An English edition is planned.

KNMG-AFDELING ENSCHEDE
[Enschede branch of the KNMG]
1987 'Een euthanasie protocol [A euthanasia protocol].' *Medisch Contact* 42: 667-668.

KNMP
1994 *Toepassing en bereiding van euthanatica* [Application and preparation of euthanatica]. The
Hague: Koninklijke Nederlandse Maatschappij ter bevordering der Pharmacie.

KOERSELMAN, F.
1994 'Balanssuïcide als mythe [Rational suicide as a myth].' *Maandblad Geestelijke Volksgezondheid* 49: 515-527.

KOOIJ, J.
1996 'De normontwikkeling rond het levensbeëindigend handelen bij patiënten in een vegetatieve toestand in Nederland en de Verenigde Staten: een contextuele vergelijking [The
process of normative change in connection with termination of life in the case of patients in
a vegetative state in the Netherlands and the United States: a contextual comparison].' Grad-
uation thesis, University of Groningen, Faculty of Law, December 1996.

KROODE, H. ten
1982 'Stervensbegeleiding: een nieuw woord... een nieuw beroep? [Support in the dying process:
a new word ... a new profession?]' *Maandblad Geestelijke Volksgezondheid* 37: 1306-1322.

KUHSE, H.
1987 *The Sanctity-of-Life Doctrine in Medicine. A Critique.* Oxford: Clarendon Press.

KUHSE, H. et al.
1997 'End-of-life decisions in Australian medical practice.' *Medical Journal of Australia* 166: 191-
196.

LAU, H.S. et al.
1996 'Een landelijk onderzoek naar de frequentie van verzoeken om verstrekking van euthanasie
middelen in openbare en ziekenhuisapotheken en de afhandeling daarvan [A national survey of the frequency of requests for euthanatica in public and hospital pharmacies and the
response to them].' *Tijdschrift voor Sociale Gezondheidszorg* 74: 15-16.

n.d.   Letter to the editor, 'Physicial-assisted death and pharmacy practice in the Netherlands.'
       Forthcoming in *New England Journal of Medicine.*

LEENEN, H.J.J.

1977   'Euthanasie in het gezondheidsrecht [Euthanasia in health law].' Pp. 72-147 in Muntendam
       1997.

1987   'Euthanasia, assistance to suicide and the law: developments in the Netherlands.' *Health Pol-
       icy* 8: 197-206.

1994   *Handboek gezondheidsrecht. Deel I: Rechten van mensen in de gezondheidszorg* [Handbook of
       Health Law. Volume I: Individual Rights in the Context of Medical Care] (3d ed.). Alphen
       a/d Rijn: Samsom H.D. Tjeenk Willink.

1996   *Handboek gezondheidsrecht. Deel II: Gezondheidszorg en recht* [Handbook of Health Law.
       Volume II: Health Care System and Law] (3d ed.). Houten/Diegem: Bohn Stafleu Van
       Loghum.

1997   'Regulering van euthanasie, melding en commissies [Regulating euthanasia, reporting and
       assessment committees].' *Medisch Contact* 52: 45-48.

LEGEMAATE J.

1993   'Hulp bij zelfdoding in de psychiatrie: regels en opvattingen [Assistance with suicice in psy-
       chiatric practice: rules and opinions].' *Maandblad Geestelijke Volksgezondheid* 48: 750-769.

LIJPHART, A.

1968   *The Politics of Accommodation. Pluralism and Democracy in the Netherlands.* Berkeley: Uni-
       versity of California Press.

LOVEREN-HUYBEN, C.M.S. van

1995   *Ontwikkeling in verzorgingshuizen? Gegevens van longitudinaal onderzoek* [Progress in Resi-
       dential Homes? Data from Longitudinal Research]. Dissertation, Catholic University
       Nijmegen.

MAAS, P.J. van der, J.J.M. van DELDEN, and L. PIJNENBORG

1991   'Euthanasia and other medical decisions concerning the end of life.' *Lancet* 338: 669-674.

1992   *Euthanasia and other Medical Decisions Concerning the End of Life.* Amsterdam: Elsevier
       (also published as a special supplement of *Health Policy* 22 (1+2): 1-262). English transla-
       tion of *Medische beslissingen rond het levenseinde,* The Hague: SDU, 1991.

MAAS, P.J. van der, and J.P. MACKENBACH (eds.)

1995   *Volksgezondheid en gezondheidszorg* [Public Health and Health Care]. Utrecht: Wetenschap-
       pelijke uitgeverij Bunge.

MAAS, J. van der, L. PIJNENBORG, and J.J.M. van DELDEN

1995   'Changes in Dutch opinions on active euthanasia, 1966 through 1991.' *Journal of the Ameri-
       can Medical Association* 273: 1411-1414.

MAAS, J. van der, et al.

1996 'Euthanasia, physician-assisted suicide, and other medical practices involving the end of life in the Netherlands, 1990-1995.' *New England Journal of Medicine* 335: 1699-1705.

MARQUIS, D.B.

1991 'Four versions of double effect,' *The Journal of Medicine and Philosophy* 16: 515-544.

MELIEF, W.B.A.M.

1991 *De zorg voor terminale patiënten en de omgang met euthanasievragen door hulpverleners in de thuiszorg en de intramurale zorg* [Care of Terminal Patients and the Reaction of Medical and Social Work Professionals Involved in Home Care and Intramural Care to Requests for Euthanasia]. The Hague: Nederlands Instituut voor Maatschappelijk Werk Onderzoek.

MENDUS, S., (ed.)

1988 *Justifying Toleration. Conceptual and Historical Perspectives.* Cambridge: Cambridge University Press.

MILL, J.S.

1993 *Utilitarianism, On Liberty, and Essays on Bentham.* London: Dent.

MILLER, F.G. et al.

1994 'Regulating physician-assisted death.' *New England Journal of Medicine* 331: 119-123.

MULHALL, S., and A. SWIFT

1997 *Liberals and Communitarians.* Cambridge: Blackwell Publishers Ltd.

MULLER, M.

1996 *Death on Request: Aspects of Euthanasia and Physician-assisted Suicide, with Special Regard to Dutch Nursing Homes.* Amsterdam: Thesis Publishers [based in part on articles which appeared in *Journal of the American Geriatric Society* 42: 620-623, 624-629 (1994).

MUNNICHS, J.M.A.

1989 'Omgaan met de dood, vroeger en nu [Dealing with death, in the past and now].' Pp. 7-16 in L. Boon, ed., *Euthanasie en zorgvuldigheid. Dilemma's bij instellingsbeleid, richtlijnen, begeleiding zelfdoding, euthanasie jongeren en suïcide psychiatrische patiënten* [Euthanasia and careful practice. Dilemmas in connection with institutional policy, guidelines, support of suicide, euthanasia of children and suicide of psychiatric patients]. Amstelveen: Stichting SYMPOZ.

MUNTENDAM, P. (ed.)

1977 *Euthanasie* [Euthanasia]. Leiden: Stafleu's Wetenschappelijke Uitgeversmaatschappij.

MUSSCHENGA, A.W.

1987 'Kwaliteit van leven: grond voor levensbeëindiging? [Quality of life: a basis for termination of life?]' Pp. 110-141 in G.A. van der Wal et al., *Euthanasie. Knelpunten in een discussie* [Euthanasia. Points of Difficulty in a Discussion]. Baarn: Ambo.

MUSSCHENGA, A.W., B. VOORZANGER, and A. SOETEMAN (eds.)

1992 *Morality, Worldview, and Law. The Idea of a Universal Morality and its Critics.* Assen: Van Gorcum.

NEDERLANDSE HUISARTSEN GENOOTSCHAP
[Dutch Association of GPs]

1990 'Standaard 002: Medische verslaglegging [Guideline 002: medical record-keeping].' *Huisarts en Wetenschap* 33: 114-117.

NEDERLANDSE VERENIGING VAN VERPLEEGHUISARTSEN (NVV)
[Dutch Association of Nursing-Home Doctors]

1997 *Medische zorg met beleid. Handreiking voor de besluitvorming over verpleeghuisgeneeskundig handelen bij dementerende patiënten* [Responsible Medical Care. A Support Document for Decision-Making Concerning Medical Treatment of Demented Patients in Nursing-Homes]. Utrecht: NVV.

NEW YORK STATE TASK FORCE ON LIFE AND THE LAW

1994 *When Death is Sought. Assisted Suicide and Euthanasia in the Medical Context.*

NVK

1992 *Doen of laten? Grenzen van het medisch handelen in de neonatologie* [To Act or to Abstain? The Limits of Medical Practice in Neonatology]. Utrecht: NVK.

NVOG

1994 *Nota late zwangerschapsafbreking* [Policy paper on late abortion]. Utrecht: NVOG.

NVP

1992 'Mededelingen bestuur [Announcements of the governing board].' *Nieuws en Mededelingen* 86/2: 2-3.

1997 *Hulp bij zelfdoding door patiënten met een psychiatrische stoornis* [Assistance with Suicide in the Case of Patients with a Psychiatric Disorder]. Scheduled to be adopted by the NVP in the Fall of 1997; in this book the tentative draft of September 1996 has been used, supplemented by written information from the chairman of the drafting committee.

NVVE

1978 *Rapport van de Adviescommissie Wetgeving betreffende toelaatbare euthanasie uitgebracht aan de Nederlandse Vereniging voor Vrijwillige Euthanasie* [Report of the Advisory Committee on Legislation Concerning Acceptable Euthanasia to the Netherlands Association for Voluntary Euthanasia]. Amsterdam: NVVE.

1980   *Suicide en strafrecht* [Suicide and Criminal Law]. Amsterdam: NVVE.
1989   *Men moet ten slotte het recht hebben om als een heer te sterven* [After All, One Should Have the Right to Die Like a Gentleman]. Amsterdam: NVVE.
1995   *Knipselkrant (Chabot-special)* [Clipping service, special *Chabot* issue]. Amsterdam: NVVE (June 1995).
1996   *Voorontwerp euthanasiewet* [Draft Euthanasia Bill]. Amsterdam: NVVE.
1997   *Knipselkrant* [Clipping service]. Amsterdam: NVVE (July-August 1997).

OUTSHOORN, J.
1986   *De politieke strijd rondom de abortuswetgeving in Nederland 1964-1984* [The Political Struggle over Abortion Legislation in the Netherlands 1964-1984]. Amsterdam: Vrije Universiteit.

OVERBEEK, R. van
1996   *Tussen wens en werkelijkheid – een onderzoek naar het proces van omgaan met een verzoek om euthanasie of hulp bij zelfdoding* [Between Will and Reality – A Study of the Process of Reacting to a Request for Euthanasia or Assistance with Suicide]. Utrecht: Verwey-Jonker Instituut.

PHILIPSEN, B.D., G. van der WAL, and J.TH.M. van EIJK
1994   'Consultatie bij euthanasie en hulp bij zelfdoding door de huisarts [Consultation in the case of euthanasia or assistance with suicide by a GP].' *Huisarts en Wetenschap* 37: 478-481.

PIJNENBORG, L.
1993   'Life-terminating acts without explicit requests of patient.' *The Lancet* 341: 1196-1199.

POOL, R.
1996   *Vragen om te sterven. Euthanasie in een Nederlands ziekenhuis* [Asking to Die. Euthanasia in a Dutch Hospital]. Rotterdam: WYT Uitgeefgroep.

POSTEMA, G.J.
1992   'Public faces – private places: liberalism and the enforcement of morality.' Pp. 153-175 in A.W. Musschenga, B. Voorzanger and A. Soeteman, ed., *Morality, Worldview, and Law. The Idea of a Universal Morality and its Critics.* Assen: Van Gorcum.

PRESTON, T.A.
1994   'Killing pain, ending life.' *New York Times*, 1 November 1994.

QUILL, T.E.
1991   'Death and dignity. A case of individualized decision making.' *New England Journal of Medicine* 324: 691-695.
1996   *A Midwife through the Dying Process. Stories of Healing and Hard Choices at the End of Life.* Baltimore/London: Johns Hopkins University Press.

RACHELS, J.
1986   *The End of Life.* Oxford: Oxford University Press.

RANG, J.F.
1977   *Rechtspraak medisch tuchtrecht 1930-1976* [Medical Disciplinary Case Law 1930-1976]. Deventer: Kluwer.

RASKER, J.J. et al.
1987   'Een euthanasieprotocol [A euthanasia protocol].' *Medisch Contact* 42: 667-668.

RAWLS, J.
1972   *A Theory of Justice.* Oxford: Oxford University Press.
1993   *Political Liberalism.* New York: Columbia University Press.

RAYAR, L., and S. WADSWORTH
1997   *The Dutch Penal Code* (translation, with an introduction by G. van den Heuvel and H. Lensing). Littleton CO: Fred B. Rothman & Co.

RAZ, J.
1986   *The Morality of Freedom.* Oxford: Clarendon Press.

REMMELINK, J.
1981   'Plaats en taak van het Openbaar Ministerie bij de Hoge Raad in strafzaken [Position and role of the Procurator-General and Advocates-General of the Supreme Court in criminal cases].' Pp. 291-308 in A.J. Bins et al. (ed.), *Beginselen: opstellen over strafrecht aangeboden aan G.E. Mulder.* Arnhem: Gouda Quint.
1992   *Spanningen tussen recht en strafwet. Rede, gehouden door Prof. mr J. Remmelink ter gelegenheid van zijn afscheid als Procureur-Generaal bij de Hoge Raad der Nederlanden op de buitengewone zitting van het college op woensdag 29 april 1992* [Tension between Law and Criminal Code. Valedictory Lecture of Professor J. Remmelink as Procurator-General of the Supreme Court of the Netherlands, delivered at the extraordinary session of the Court on Wednesday, 29 April 1992]. The Hague: Ministry of Justice.

RIGTER, H.
1989   'Euthanasia in the Netherlands: distinguishing facts from fiction.' *Hastings Center Report,* special supplement, January/February 1989: 31-32.

RIGTER, H., E. BORST-EILERS, and H.J.J. LEENEN
1988   'Euthanasia across the North Sea.' *British Medical Journal* 297: 1593-1595.

RIJKSINSTITUUT VOOR VOLKSGEZONDHEID EN MILIEUHYGIENE (RIVM)
1993   *Volksgezondheid toekomst verkenning. De gezondheidstoestand van de Nederlandse bevolking in de periode 1950-2010* [Exploring the Future of Public Health. The Health of the Dutch Population in the Period 1950-2010]. The Hague: SDU.

ROSCAM ABBING, H.D.C.

1985 'Euthanasie en mensenrechten [Euthanasia and human rights].' Pp. 48-56 in: J. Elders et al.,
       Euthanasie, recht en ethiek [Euthanasia, Law and Ethics]. Assen: Van Gorcum.

ROZEMOND, K.

1995 'De waarde van het leven [The value of life].' *Recht en Kritiek* 21: 111-135.

SCHALKEN, T.

1984 'Euthanasie en de rechtspolitieke betekenis van het gewetensconflict [Euthanasia and the
       policy significance of a moral dilemma].' *Nederlands Juristenblad* 59: 38-50.

1991 'Euthanasie of de ontluistering van een mythe [Euthanasia or the degradation of a myth].'
       Delikt en Delinkwent 1991: 837-841.

1995 'Waar het recht capituleerde [Where the law capitulated].' Pp. 70-80 in H. Achterhuis et al.,
       Als de dood voor het leven. Over professionele hulp bij zelfmoord [Deathly Afraid of Life. Con-
       cerning Professional Assistance with Suicide]. Amsterdam: Van Oorschot.

SCHRIJVERS, A.J.P. (ed.)

1997 *Health and Health Care in the Netherlands. A Critical Self-Assessment by Dutch Experts in the
       Medical and Health Sciences.* Utrecht: De Tijdstroom.

SCHROTEN, E. et al.

1979 *Euthanasie. Rapport van een commissie van de wetenschappelijke instituten van KVP, ARP en
       CHU* [Euthanasia. Report of a Committee of the Research Institutes of the KVP, ARP and
       CHU]. The Hague: CDA.

SCHUIJT-LUCASSEN, N.Y. et al.

1991 'Euthanasie en hulp bij zelfdoding door verpleeghuisartsen [Euthanasia and assistance with
       suicide by doctors in nursing homes].' *Medisch Contact* 46: 1090-1092.

SCP

[Social and Cultural Planning Bureau)

1990 *Sociaal en cultureel rapport 1990* [Social and Cultural Report 1990]. Rijswijk: Sociaal en Cul-
       tureel Planbureau.

1992 *Sociaal en cultureel rapport 1992* [Social and Cultural Report 1992]. Rijswijk: Sociaal en Cul-
       tureel Planbureau.

1996 *Sociaal en cultureel rapport 1996* [Social and Cultural Report 1996]. Rijswijk: Sociaal en Cul-
       tureel Planbureau.

SINGER, P.

1985 *Practical Ethics.* Cambridge: Cambridge University Press.

1994 *Rethinking Life and Death. The Collapse of Our Traditional Ethics.* Oxford: Oxford Universi-
       ty Press.

SLUYTERS, B., and M.C.I.H. BIESAART
1995 *De geneeskundige behandelingsovereenkomst na invoering van de WGBO* [The Contract for Medical Treatment under the New Law]. Zwolle: W.E.J. Tjeenk Willink.

SMIDT, J.H.
1891 *Geschiedenis van het Wetboek van Strafrecht* [History of the Criminal Code] (vol. 2). Haarlem: H.D. Tjeenk Willink (2d ed.).

SOETEMAN, A.
1986 'Zelfbeschikking en uitzichtloze noodsituatie [Autonomy and the idea of a situation of irreversible necessity].' *Filosofie en Praktijk* 7: 57-74.
1992 'Liberal moralism in law.' Pp. 177-189 in A.W. Musschenga, B. Voorzanger and A. Soeteman, eds., *Morality, Worldview, and Law. The Idea of a Universal Morality and its Critics.* Assen: Van Gorcum.

SORGDRAGER, W., and E. BORST-EILERS
1995 'Euthanasie. De stand van zaken [Euthanasia. The current state of affairs].' *Medisch Contact* 50: 381-384.

SPORKEN, P.
1969 *Voorlopige diagnose. Inleiding tot een medische ethiek* [Provisional Diagnosis. Introduction to a Medical Ethics]. Utrecht: Ambo.

SPREEUWENBERG, C.
1981 *Huisarts en stervenshulp* [The General Practitioner and Assistance with Dying]. Deventer: Van Lochum Slaterus.
1982 'De huisarts en de vraag om beëindiging van het leven [The GP and requests for termination of life].' *Huisarts en wetenschap* 1982: 263-271.

STAATSCOMMISSIE EUTHANASIE
[State Commission on Euthanasia]
1985 *Rapport van de Staatscommissie Euthanasie* [Report of the State Commission on Euthanasia] (vol. 1). The Hague: Staatsuitgeverij.

STICHTING VRIJWILLIGE EUTHANASIE (SVE)
[Foundation for Voluntary Euthanasia]
1980 *Euthanasie en zelfdoding. Discussienota juni 1980* [Euthanasia and Suicide. Discussion Paper June 1980]. The Hague: SVE.

SUDNOW, D.
1976 *Passing On: The Social Organization of Dying.* Englewood Cliffs, NJ: Prentice-Hall.

TENO, J. et al.

1997a 'Advance directives for seriously ill hospitalized patients: effectiveness with the Patient Self-Determination Act and the SUPPORT intervention.' *Journal of the American Geriatrics Society* 45: 500-507.

1997b 'Do advance directives provide instructions that direct care?' *Journal of the American Geriatrics Society* 45: 508-512.

THE, A.-M.

1997 '*Vanavond om 8 uur...' Verpleegkundige dilemma's bij euthanasie en andere beslissingen rond het levenseinde* ['This Evening at 8 o'Clock...' Nursing Dilemmas in Connection with Euthanasia and Other Decisions Concerning the End of Life]. Houten/Diegem: Bohn Stafleu Van Loghum.

THIEL, G. van, A. HUIBERS, and K. de HAAN

1997 *Met zorg besluiten. Medische beslissingen rond het levenseinde in de zorg voor mensen met een verstandelijke handicap* [Deciding with Care. Medical Decisions in Connection with the End of Life in Institutions for Persons with a Mental Handicap]. Utrecht: Center for Bio-Ethics and Health Care Law.

THIEL, G. van, et al.

1997 'Retrospective study of doctors' "end of life decisions" in caring for mentally handicapped people in institutions in the Netherlands.' *British Medical Journal* 315: 88-91.

TILL d'AULNIS de BOUROUILL, H.A.H. van

1970 *Medisch-juridische aspecten van het einde van het menselijk leven* [Medico-legal Aspects of the End of Human Life]. Deventer: Kluwer.

TIMMERMANS, J. (ed.)

1997 *Rapportage ouderen 1996* [Report on the Situation of the Elderly 1996]. Rijswijk: Sociaal en Cultureel Planbureau.

TOL, D. van

1985 *De balanssuicide – medische en juridische problemen rond hulp bij zelfdoding* [Rational Suicide – Medical and Legal Problems in Connection with Assistance with Suicide]. Dissertation, University of Leiden.

TRAPPENBURG, M.J.

1991 'Euthanasie: recht en praktijk [Euthanasia: law and practice].' *Socialisme en Democratie* 1991: 530-532.

VEATCH, R.M.

1981 *A Theory of Medical Ethics.* New York: Basic Books.

VEEN, E.B. van

1995 'Schriftelijke wilsverklaringen [Advance directives].' *Tijdschrift voor Gezondheidsrecht* 5/1995: 276-287.

VEENHOVEN, R.

1996 *Leefbaarheid van landen* [Livability of Countries]. Utrecht: Research School for Labor, Welfare and Socio-economic Policy (AWSB).

VERKRUISEN, W.G.

1993 *Dissatisfied Patients: Their Experiences, Interpretations and Actions.* Dissertation, University of Groningen.

1997 'De medische aansprakelijkheidsexplosie in Nederland: de voorgeschiedenis en het te verwachten gevolg [The medical malpractice explosion in the Netherlands: its history and expected consequences].' *Nederlands Juristenblad* 72: 846-853.

VERHOEF, M.J., and H.W.A. HILHORST

1981 *De 'zachte dood' in de praktijk: Stervensbegeleiding en euthanasie in het verpleeghuis* [The 'Soft Death' in Practice: Assistance in Dying and Euthanasia in a Nursing Home]. Lochum: De Tijdstroom.

VERSLUIS, W.J.B.

1970 *Mia Versluis. Dossier van een medisch drama* [Mia Versluis. Dossier of a Medical Drama]. Epe: Het Medium.

VOLKSPARTIJ VOOR VRIJHEID EN DEMOCRATIE (VVD)

1981 *Rapport van de werkgroep Euthanasie* [Report of the Working Group on Euthanasia]. The Hague: VVD.

WACHTER, M.A.M. de

1989 'Active euthanasia in the Netherlands.' *Journal of the American Medical Association* 262: 3316-3320.

1992 'Euthanasia in the Netherlands.' *Hastings Center Report* 22: 23-31.

WAL, G. van der

1992 *Euthansie en hulp bij zelfdoding door huisartsen* [Euthanasia and Assistance with Suicide by Family Doctors]. Rotterdam: WYT Uitgeefgroep.

1993 'Euthanasie uit strafrecht, maar sterven niet bureaucratiseren [Take euthanasia out of the criminal law, but do not bureaucratize it].' *Nederlands Juristenblad* 68: 444-449.

WAL, G. van der, et al.

1992a 'Euthanasia and assisted suicide. I. How often is it practised by family doctors in the Netherlands?' *Family Practice* 9: 130-134.

1992b 'Euthanasia and assisted suicide. II. Do Dutch family doctors act prudently?' *Family Practice* 9: 135-140.

1996 'Evaluation of the notification procedure for physician-assisted death in the Netherlands.' *New England Journal of Medicine* 335: 1706-1711.

WAL, G. van der, J.M. BOSMA, and S.L. HOSMAN-BENJAMINSE

1996 'Late zwangerschapsafbreking in Noord-Holland. I. Incidentie en aandoeningen [Late-term abortion in North-Holland. I. Frequency and diagnosis].' *Nederlands Tijdschrift voor Geneeskunde* 140: 600-604.

WAL, G. van der, G.H.A. SIEMONS, and J. VERHOEFF

1994 'Weigeren van euthanasie. Zijn artsen verplicht om te verwijzen? [Refusal to perform euthanasia. Is a doctor required to refer the patient to another doctor?]' *Medisch Contact* 49: 1240-1242.

WAL, G. van der, and P.J. van der MAAS

1996 *Euthanasie en andere medische beslissingen rond het levenseinde* [Euthanasia and other Medical Decisions in Connection with the End of Life]. The Hague: SDU.

WEISZ, F.H.

1994 'Hulp bij zelfdoding. Verslag van een huisarts [Assistance with suicide. A GP's report].' *Medisch Contact* 49: 700-702.

WEYERS, H.

1997 'Weinig overtuigende verwoording van een bekend standpunt tegen liberalisering van euthanasie. Een commentaar [An unconvincing presentation of a well-known argument against liberalization of euthanasia. A comment].' Review of the Dutch translation of Hendin 1996. *Medisch Contact* 52: 173-175.

WIJMEN, F.C.B. van

1989 *Artsen en het zelfgekozen levenseinde. Verslag van een onderzoek onder artsen naar opvattingen en gedragingen ten aanzien van euthanasie en hulp bij zelfdoding* [Doctors and the choice for death. Report of research concerning the opinions and behavior of doctors with regard to euthanasia and assistance with suicide]. Maastricht: Department of Health Law, University of Limburg.

WILLEMS, J.H.P.J.

1987 'Euthanasie en noodtoestand [Euthanasia and the situation of necessity].' *Nederlands Juristenblad* 62: 694-698.

WILLIAMS, G.L.

1957 *The Sanctity of Life and the Criminal Law*. New York: Knopf.

WIT, J.J. de
1989 'De NVVE en de komende wetgeving [The NVVE and coming legislation].' *Euthanasievisie* 1989, no. 1: 1-3.

WÖRETSHOFER, J.
1992 *Volgens de regelen van de kunst* [According to the Rules of the Art]. Arnhem: Gouda Quint.
1996 'De meldingsprocedure levensbeëindiging: ongeoorloofd? [The reporting procedure for termination of life: invalid?'].' Pp. 41-56 in J.M. Reijntjes, ed., *Nemo tenetur* [Self-incrimination], Arnhem: Gouda Quint.

ZUSSMAN, R.
1992 *Intensive Care. Medical Ethics and the Medical Profession.* Chicago: University of Chicago Press.

ZWAVELING, J.H.
1994 'Euthanasie legt te zware last bij de arts [Euthanasia puts too heavy a burden on the doctor].' *NRC Handelsblad,* 25 November 1994, p. 9.

Index